To the Scaffold

TO THE SCAFFOLD

The Life of Marie Antoinette

CAROLLY ERICKSON

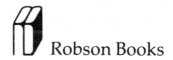

Robson Books

This edition published in 2000 by Robson Books,
10 Blenheim Court, Brewery Road, London N7 9NT

A member of the Chrysalis Group plc

First published in hardback in Great Britain in 1992

British Library Cataloguing in Publication Data
A catalogue record for this title is available from the
British Library

ISBN 1 86105 342 8

Printed and bound in Great Britain by
WBC Book Manufacturers Ltd., Mid Glamorgan

To the Scaffold

1

I N the birth chamber the cold November wind gusted through the open windows, lifting the rich cloth hangings and rustling the long skirts of the midwife and her assistants. Maria Theresa, Empress of Austria, sat patiently while the court dentist probed her tender gums, feeling for the decayed tooth that had been hurting her for the past several days.

Her labor pains had begun earlier that afternoon, and it had occurred to her that, as long as she was going to be in labor, she might as well undergo the agony of having the tooth extracted at the same time. So she sat in stoic silence as the dentist completed his examination, gripped the aching tooth with his cruel instruments and, with a practiced twist of his wrist, wrenched it out of her mouth.

Combining childbirth with dentistry was painful, but efficient—and Maria Theresa was a ruler of exemplary efficiency. Besides, as she had good reason to know, having given birth fourteen times before, nothing happened in the early hours of labor. She was not in the habit of wasting time. So, having recovered from the shock of the extraction, and with rolls of cloth in her mouth to absorb the bleeding, she called for her papers and sat for the next several hours reading and signing official documents, clutching her abdomen every now and again when the spasms became acute.

It had been the same the last time she gave birth, seventeen months earlier. Then too she had worked up until the last minute, making no concessions to her condition in the last month of her pregnancy except to attend the theater less often, and when she did attend, to leave early, "always having so much to do," as her Lord High Chamberlain Count Khevenhüller noted in his court diary. She did keep to her room more than usual in the last weeks, but not in order to rest; her secretaries brought her the usual piles of papers to read and sign, and she worked long hours at her desk. When her labor began, there was some trepidation among the courtiers, for the midwife who customarily delivered the imperial infants had died, and the new midwife appointed to replace her, though expert, had never attended the delivery of an empress before. Maria Theresa, however, had every confidence in her—and in herself. While her labor progressed she conferred with her ministers and with her husband Francis, and sat in on an important conference, before finally retiring to the birth chamber and bringing her fourth son, Ferdinand, into the world.[1]

This labor promised to go as smoothly as the last one had, and to be integrated with equal ease into the Empress's ongoing labors of governing. The chilly afternoon gave way to an even colder evening, and still she sat poring over her papers. As the birth did not seem to be imminent, her husband saw no reason to stay near at hand. He went to Mass, this being Sunday and the Day of the Dead, at the Augustinian convent adjacent to the palace. The courtiers, having been alerted to the fact that the Empress was closeted in the birth chamber, prepared themselves to offer their formal congratulations when the time came, and wondered aloud whether this time it might be another boy.

At thirty-seven, Maria Theresa had ruled Austria, Hungary, and a congeries of smaller principalities for fourteen years. She had inherited this checkerboard empire from her father, Emperor Charles VI, whose grave sorrow it was that he had no son to leave his kingdoms to. But he had failed to perceive his daughter's remarkable capacity. The young Empress had not ruled long before the other European sovereigns discovered her unique intelligence, ability and above all, her indomitable energy and strength of will. In the early years of her rule she withstood repeated invasions by the armies of Prussia, France and Bavaria, heartening her soldiers by riding at their head with vigor and panache, appealing at once to their chivalry and their manly pride. Her armies did not always win their battles—the forces of her implacable enemy Frederick, King of Prussia, often prevailed—but her determination never wavered even when they lost. Now in November of 1755, a decade and a half after her father's death, she ruled an empire at peace, its revenues greatly increased, its armies seasoned by warfare and ready to fight again, when called upon, for their Empress.

Maria Theresa was still, in the opinion of many, a beautiful woman. In her youth she had been exceptionally pretty, with lovely blue eyes, a clear porcelain complexion free of pockmarks, and a thick mane of reddish-gold curls. "Her gait is free, her bearing majestic," the Prussian ambassador had written, describing her as a young woman, "her figure large, her face round and full, and her voice clear and pleasant." "Her eyes are very large, lively and mild," he went on, "and their deep blue most striking. She has a regular nose, not hooked, and not blunt. She has very white teeth, and they are most charming when she laughs. Although her mouth is large, it is rather pretty; her neck and chest are well modeled, and her hands are exquisite." He was impressed by her stamina and emotional resilience. Though anguished and hard-pressed by constant warfare, the Empress was neither haggard nor irritable. "Her expression is fresh," the ambassador wrote, "and her skin very clear although she gives it but little attention. Her demeanor is sprightly and happy, and her greeting always warm and pleasant; there is no denying that Maria Theresa is a most charming and delightful woman."[2] The English ambassador was even more complimentary. "Her person was made to wear a crown," he remarked, "and her mind to give luster to it. Her countenance is filled with sense, spirit, and sweetness, and all her motions are accompanied with grace and dignity."[3]

Age and fourteen confinements had thickened her torso and added triple chins to her round face, yet at thirty-seven she was still handsome, her posture regally erect, her lovely blue eyes benign if watchful. She took pains with her appearance, devoting the first hours of her long day (she customarily rose at dawn) to dressing, grooming, and the elaborate curling and pinning and powdering of her hair. Cruel court observers said that she did this in a futile attempt to keep her husband faithful to her, yet this can only have been part of the reason. Her good looks were an asset, and she knew it; she used her femininity, as great queens of the past had done, to arouse her subjects' protective instincts and win their hearts as well as their respect. As for her husband's fidelity, on this delicate issue Maria Theresa was a realist. She knew that Francis had mistresses, she suffered in consequence—and she rose above her suffering. Her husband was not so much lecherous as indolent and pleasure-loving, she told herself. He was fond of her and of their children. God had blessed her with a good marriage, and she would not spoil it by her recriminations. As she once advised another woman whose husband had given her cause to complain, "Avoid reproaches, long explanations, and above all, disputes."

And at thirty-seven, the Empress was still extraordinarily robust. Her Lord High Chamberlain once noted that she could "withstand all fatigues, wherein she exceeds many men." She relied on her exceptional vitality to carry her through the demands and strains of her long work days, and to provide her with enough leftover energy to recreate herself strenuously and to bear and raise her growing brood of children. When she walked, she strode like a man. Her swift, purposeful gait was her trademark. It was said that she could never successfully disguise her identity at masked balls, for no matter how she dressed, she still walked like the Empress. And she exercised her walking muscles with vigorous four-hour hikes into the countryside, where the bracing fresh air invigorated her and eased her mind from its constant strain.

Riding was even better than walking for that, she found. She loved to ride, the faster and more recklessly the better, sitting astride her horse as men did and refusing to adopt the sidesaddle except when forced to in the later months of her pregnancies. She rode to country inns, or in the Prater, or in the huge enclosed riding school, where she and her ladies joined in the mock tournament called the carousel. Her chamois leather breeches and high-topped boots covered by a long skirt, the Empress was never happier than when galloping at breakneck speed. Sometimes, after dancing all evening, she would go to the riding school and join in a carousel that lasted all night. As she grew older she indulged in such feats of stamina less frequently, but even so she rode lustily and often. When not on horseback herself, she drove her carriage at a tremendous pace, and the soldiers of her Horse Guards who formed her escort had all they could to keep up with her.

In the birth chamber the candles guttered in the icy wind. The Empress, her face contorted with pain, pushed aside the papers she had been working on and beckoned to the midwife. In a moment of respite from the pains she was helped into the birthing chair. She gripped the arms firmly and began to push.

Emperor Francis was in the Augustinian chapel, singing a psalm, when he was informed that his wife was in the final stages of her labor. He returned to the palace immediately, his first concern being that his fourteen-year-old son Joseph, heir to the throne, should not "see or hear anything improper and unfitting for his age." Joseph was kept away, along with the eleven other children of the imperial family*, until the news from the birth chamber was announced. The announcement came swiftly, at a little before eight o'clock. The Empress had given birth to another girl. The baby was very small and delicate but apparently healthy, and she was to be called Maria Antonia Josephina Johanna.

Slumped in the birthing chair, her eyes closed and her breathing deep and regular, Maria Theresa rested while the midwife and her assistants attended to her and to the newborn infant. Her husband was handling the public ceremonies, the blessing of the child, the service of thanksgiving, the receiving of formal messages of congratulations from the courtiers. For the moment there was nothing that she had to do—except to say a prayer of thanks for her safe delivery, and for the divine gift of a living child. She rested, cooled by the night air coming in through the windows, sensing but not heeding the activity around her. Later, when the midwife had gone and little Maria Antonia had been taken to her wet-nurse in the children's wing of the palace, she got up heavily and moved to her desk, where she took up the stack of papers she had set aside and began to peruse them once again.

Though undersize, the new baby flourished. She looked like her father, with his broad brow and large, widely spaced eyes and bow-shaped lips. Her eyes, though, were the color of her mother's, of the particular shade called imperial blue, a pure light cerulean. Antonia—always called Antoinette at the French-speaking Austrian court—was a pretty enough baby, but only a girl, another Archduchess in a family that already had seven Archduchesses and only four Archdukes. The arrival of an eighth

*Three of Maria Theresa's children had not survived childhood.

Archduchess did not call for elaborate rejoicing. There was no large public banquet, as was customary at the birth of an imperial child. Instead, two days of official celebration were declared, with the court wearing full dress and the citizens of Vienna treated to special entertainments. After that the newest member of the family disappeared into the recesses of the nurseries, soon to be succeeded, the courtiers felt sure, by another baby.

Little Antoinette's siblings ranged in age from the seventeen-year-old Anna, the firstborn who suffered from ill health, to the seventeen-month-old Ferdinand. In between came Joseph, the singular, austerely detached heir to the throne, thirteen-year-old Christina, her parents' favorite daughter, twelve-year-old Elizabeth, ten-year-old Karl, the favorite son, nine-year-old Amalia and eight-year-old Leopold. Three years separated Leopold from the next-youngest child—a gap resulting from a pregnancy that produced a weak daughter who died shortly after her birth. Next in order came three girls aged five, four and three, Johanna, Josepha and Caroline, called Carlotta, who became Antoinette's playmate and friend. One more child, Maximilian, was to be born a year after Antoinette.

The stair-step sons and daughters of Maria Theresa and Francis of Lorraine were often to be seen at concerts, plays and other court events, sitting beside their parents, ranged in order of sex and age—boys nearest, then girls. The children were dressed as miniature adults, the boys in velvet coats and breeches and white silk stockings to the knee, the girls in square-necked silk gowns ballooning out from narrow-waisted bodices and supported by stiff whalebone hoops. Very frequently the children themselves were to be found on stage, exotically costumed, performing in ballets and operas and plays. Observers thought that they spent an inordinate amount of time preparing these entertainments, and wondered whether they were being adequately trained for the serious responsibilities of adult life. But their frequent performances delighted their parents, and Maria Theresa in particular encouraged them to prepare special evening entertainments for their father.

At one such evening in 1759 five-year-old Ferdinand played an overture on the kettledrums, followed by Maximilian, who though barely three years old was able to memorize some Italian verses composed by the court poet Metastasio in which he offered his "august Papa" his heartfelt homage. Next Antoinette, who was not quite four, sang a French song. Her sisters sang Italian arias and played the harpsichord, her older brother Karl performed on the violin and Joseph on the viol.[4]

None of the children rose above amateur ability either in singing or playing instruments, but they were at home with music; Vienna had become the musical capital of Europe, Gluck and Haydn composed for the court and the imperial aristocracy, the infant prodigy Mozart came to Schönbrunn and played for Maria Theresa and her family. The Empress herself had an extraordinarily beautiful singing voice and performed with finesse, though her musical taste lacked discrimination. In her choice of operas she invariably preferred the pleasant and conventional to the pathbreaking and profound. Still, she saw to it that her children's musical culture was extensive. Not only did they each play an instrument—Antoinette played the harp—but they joined together in trios and quartets and even formed a small orchestra on occasion.

Their musical education was much more thorough than their education in history, geography, mathematics and the classics. They were taught penmanship, reading, and French, with a scant hour or two a week devoted to studying maps and reading stories. Priests instructed them in morality and religion. The girls learned needlework and the boys fencing. But for the girls in particular, lessons were often perfunctory. When very young they were put into the care of Countess von Brandeiss, an overindulgent taskmistress at best from whom they learned little self-discipline or mental application. Besides, Maria Theresa was more concerned to have her children learn good manners and healthy eating habits, and to cultivate courage and self-confidence than she was about their formal lessons.

Her attitude is clear from a set of instructions she wrote for Countess Lerchenfeld, who was at the time in charge of supervising Johanna and Josepha, when Antoinette was an infant. "I insist on their eating everything, with no fault-finding and no picking and choosing," the Empress declared. "Further, they must not be allowed to criticize their food. On Fridays, Saturdays, and all other fast-days they will eat fish. Although Johanna in particular dislikes it, she must not be indulged. The sooner the habit is broken the better. All my children had the same aversion, and all had to overcome it." The girls were not to be allowed to neglect their appearance, but were to be "properly washed and combed" every day. "And never must they be allowed to be afraid," the Empress went on, "neither of thunderstorms, fire, ghosts, witches or any other nonsense. The servants must not talk about such things or tell horror stories." Even the most dreaded scourge of the court and countryside, smallpox, was to be discussed freely and openly in front of the children, so that they might become accustomed to hearing about illness and death and accept both as natural and inevitable parts of life.

The Empress insisted that the royal children learn to be polite toward everyone, even servants, and particularly toward strangers. They were to be neither haughty nor overly familiar, but to maintain a mean between these two extremes, a dignified and detached graciousness that did honor to their lineage without giving offense.

Maria Theresa was a conscientious and well-intentioned mother, but she was also an overburdened ruler. Of necessity she delegated the tasks of childrearing to others, relying on her court physician, Gerhard von Swieten, to look after their health, and on an array of imperial tutors to instruct them. During the winter months, when the court was at the Hofburg, she spent time with the children between meetings with her officials and sessions with her papers. But in the warm season, when the court moved to Schönbrunn, only the older children went with it; the youngest ones remained in Vienna, and saw their mother far less often. As an adult Antoinette recalled that her mother was so preoccupied with matters of state that she sometimes saw her children only every eight or ten days.

During Antoinette's earliest years her mother was more preoccupied than usual with the tasks of governing, for she was waging war.

In the mid-eighteenth century, two great colossi bestrode the European continent: Hapsburg Austria and Bourbon France. The Austrian lands embraced much of Central Europe, parts of Italy, and the Austrian Netherlands (modern Belgium). Through her husband Francis, who was Holy Roman Emperor, Maria Theresa held sway over the German principalities as well. The vast and wealthy territories under the governance of the Bourbon kings included not only an engorged France, its boundaries swollen to include Lorraine, but Spain, southern Italy and Sicily. France also had hopes of conquering Britain; several times King Louis XV had authorized the preparation of vast invasion fleets with the intention of launching them against the southern coast of England, only to have some last-minute accident of weather or shift in the diplomatic tide foil the plans.

Ever since the sixteenth century the two giants of the continent had been at odds. In battle after battle, through reign after reign the rivalry continued unabated, with now one side in the ascendant, now the other. By the mid-1750's, however, the time-honored enmity between Bourbon and Hapsburg was waning. England, not Austria, was becoming France's principal rival, for both the English and French possessed lucrative global empires which increasingly brought them into conflict. Austria, for her part, had come to fear and distrust the aggressive might of Prussia more than her traditional enemy France. Frederick of Prussia had already shown his teeth by conquering Silesia, Austria's richest province; clearly he would not be satisfied until he had seized even more Hapsburg land.

Maria Theresa wanted above all to recover Silesia, secure Austria's borders against the Prussians, and revenge herself against the man she called the "Monster," King Frederick. Thus when, to the surprise of the diplomatic world, Prussia and Britain signed a defensive alliance early in 1756, the stage was set for a rapprochement between the Austrians and French. Two diplomats, Count (later Prince) Kaunitz in Austria and the Duc de Choiseul in France, favored an Austro-French alliance and as a result of their efforts the Treaty of Versailles was drafted in the following May. Under its terms, each of the signatories promised to aid the other in the event of an attack by a third power, and each agreed not to interfere in the other's military ambitions.

War broke out when Prussian troops marched into Saxony in August of 1756. Confident of the support of her French ally, Maria Theresa was able to concentrate her energies on opposing the Monster, Frederick. Her primary concern was the well-being of her armies, a matter she considered far too important to be left to others. She took a personal interest in her soldiers' welfare, making certain that they were adequately provisioned, shod and clothed. No detail was too small to escape her attention, not the cut of a uniform, the thickness of a blanket, the strength of an axle for a gun-carriage. Tirelessly she sat hour after hour with her advisers, devising strategy and mapping out campaigns. Afterward, alone in her white-and-gold apartments at Schönbrunn, she pondered tactics and struggled with the exigencies of financing the army, ultimately deciding to pawn her jewels rather than send the men into battle under-equipped.

As the war went on she showed steely courage when the Prussians threatened Vienna. The city was all but undefended, for the Austrian army was concentrated in Bohemia where the Prussian attack was anticipated. Maria Theresa's ministers urged her to flee. She refused. "The court shall remain until the last extremity," she announced. To the Crown Princess of Saxony she wrote, "We will meet the Prussians as we can. And if we have no army here, we will arm ourselves with axes and bows and arrows, all women, as well as men, to force them out."[5]

Vienna was spared. An Austrian general attacked the Prussian supply wagons, forcing Frederick to order them destroyed lest their precious matériel fall into enemy hands. The loss forced the Prussian army to retreat, and the Austrian capital was no longer in danger. Yet the war dragged on, as year by year the Empress grew more hardened and more lined and her children grew older.

A stout, red-faced woman of Amazonian courage, a frown of resolute defiance on her face: such was Antoinette's earliest memory of her mother. When she was brought to see her mother, the Empress looked up from her papers to peer at her little daughter through a magnifying lens. Her features registered approval of what she saw. She asked a few probing questions of von Swieten and Countess von Brandeiss. Was Antoinette eating her fish? Had she developed any foolish fears? She looked small for her age. Was her health good? Satisfied with the answers, she returned to the pressing business of prosecuting the war. The quiet, pretty child, wide-eyed and agreeable, was ushered out of the room.

2

THE court of Maria Theresa was one of the most extensive in Europe. Some twenty-five hundred people waited on the Empress, carrying out her governmental orders and those of her ministers, sweeping, cleaning and furnishing the hundreds of rooms in her great palaces, buying and slaughtering the thousands of cows, pigs, sheep and chickens needed to supply the palace kitchens, repairing and painting and ornamenting the state apartments and those of the chief nobles who lived at court. Armies of servants were needed to tend the tall porcelain stoves that warmed the rooms, to wash the mountains of linen that accumulated, to haul off the wastes and turn the handles of the kitchen turnspits and perform in the elaborate nightly entertainments offered in the palace theater. The Empress's servants coped with the herculean tasks that went with the maintenance of a large household, yet they also were attentive to an infinity of detail. They saw to it that there was fresh snow, brought down from the mountains, for the imperial children's sleds to run on when the local snowdrifts melted. They kept filled with water the silver and gold pitchers and basins the great aristocrats used to wash themselves. And they never forgot to send to the Schönbrunn dairies for the few ounces of fresh milk the Empress required every day to fill her drinking cup.

The great court offices were hereditary, the duties passed down from father to son. Each generation had to learn anew the lore of each department of the household: the head steward mastered the protocol of the throne room, how and when to announce persons admitted to an audience with Maria Theresa; the horse master learned the workings of the stables, how to govern the dozens of trained grooms and stableboys that looked after the horses, what the needs of the imperial riding school were and how to fill them, how and where to buy coach horses, cart horses and the costly mounts favored by the Empress. The butler, the heads of the ewery and pantry, the chief falconer, the heads of the treasury and wardrobe—all took years to perfect themselves in the arcana of their offices. Maria Theresa employed hundreds of chamberlains who kept the budgets and paid the staff. These were the actual managers of palace affairs, responsible for the smooth day-to-day running of the court. Above them were the holders of ceremonial offices, members of the highest nobility who jealously guarded the prerogatives of their positions and partook of the Empress's glory. These luminaries each had his own court in miniature within the larger imperial court, complete with servants and under-servants, cooks and stableboys and hangers-on.

During the winter months the imperial household was in residence at the Hofburg, which was not a single building but a whole congregation of buildings, most of them cramped and very old, arranged around a series of courtyards. The Hofburg was more fortress than palace, its twenty-six hundred rooms more functional than grand. Schönbrunn, however, where the court moved in warmer weather, was dazzling in its white-and-gold splendor. Built by Maria Theresa on the site of a modest hunting lodge erected by her grandfather Leopold I, Schönbrunn took its name from a "beautiful fountain" in its gardens. Its long facade of nearly seven hundred feet gave way to a courtyard, and then to extensive gardens filled with statuary and more spectacular fountains. Hothouses, a menagerie, and botanical gardens were to be found in the vast grounds, along with a sumptuous marble summer house, the Gloriette, where the Empress liked to go to do her paperwork in fine weather.

"There is nothing in the world that appeals to me so much, not even diamonds, as that which comes from India," Maria Theresa once said, and at Schönbrunn she indulged her taste for things Indian to the full. Her private apartments on the ground floor near the orangery were painted in Indian style, the walls covered with date trees, birds, and festoons of flowers and fruit. The Blue Chinese Drawing Room, one of the palace's ornate state rooms, had handpainted wallpaper with exotic figures etched in gold and black on a background of deep greenish-blue—a color scheme whose Far Eastern flavor was thrown into relief by the preponderant rococo white and gilt of Schönbrunn. The Lacquer Room was paneled in black lacquer with chinoiserie decorations, the Porcelain Room displayed valuable Chinese vases and other objets d'art, their translucent surfaces illuminated by hundreds of candles set in rich chandeliers. For the adornment of the "Millions" Room, so called because its decor reputedly cost a million florins, the Empress ordered her ambassador at the court of the Sultan to buy antique Persian and Hindu miniatures; they were mounted around the walls, their scenes of elephants and horsemen, soldiers and temples rendered in brilliantly glowing colors.

The magnificence of Schönbrunn took many years to complete, and when the imperial household was in residence there the courtiers were forced to conduct their business and pursue their pleasures amid the chaos of ongoing construction. The enormous Great Gallery, scene of gala entertainments and solemn receptions, was filled with scaffolding throughout its hundred-and-fifty-foot length, and its vast ceiling took many workmen years to complete. Throughout the palace, painters and gilders labored, and in the acres of grounds, crews of gardeners and under-gardeners toiled year-round laying out walks and digging ponds and uprooting bushes and trees to replace them with neat clipped hedges.

The constant disorder at Schönbrunn was as nothing, however, compared to the turmoil and discomfiture of a court move. When the Empress traveled, her staff and servants had to travel with her, along with the personnel of her kitchens, table, wardrobe and secretariat. Even for short journeys her personal carriage—in which she customarily rode with her husband and the chief lady-in-waiting—was accompanied by at least two dozen more vehicles, plus postilions, trumpeters, couriers, pages and bodyguards on horseback. There were coaches for her ladies and maids, the master of her plate, her cellarer and numerous pastrycooks. Her apothecary rode in a chaise to himself, her master of table linen and gentlemen-at-arms in two carriages and her father confessor and chaplain in two more. Four special kitchen coaches carried provisions, utensils and implements (the cooks were already in residence at the final destination, having ridden on in advance), while huge baggage wagons, each drawn by twenty-four cart horses, were loaded with the courtiers' luggage and more provisions. Because the coaches and wagons frequently broke down en route the cortege had to include two coach masters and a blacksmith, and three reserve coaches and twenty reserve draft horses were kept on hand in case of need. Given the state of the narrow, unpaved country roads, pitted with deep ruts and holes, dusty in summer and muddy in winter, the Empress's traveling party did well to cover ninety miles in a good day, with three or four stops to change horses. When the weather was bad or the roads flooded, progress was much slower; when even the reserve coaches broke their axles and had to be repaired, there was no progress at all.

One contingent among the court population never moved: that which was in permanent residence in the capital.

The small, dark cramped city of Vienna sheltered within its bastioned medieval walls, three square miles of frenetic activity amid unspeakable filth. Everyone in the city, it seemed to visitors, was either employed by the imperial court or had continuing business there. The streets were filled with servants, officials and petitioners hurrying to and from the Hofburg, nobles in sedan chairs being carried to the palace, artisans bringing their wares to their noble and imperial customers. It was a polyglot crowd. Vienna's narrow alleyways were full of people of various nations, an English traveler wrote. "I constantly meet Hungarians, Greeks, Turks, and Poles, all habited in the peculiar dress of their respective countries. Nothing is more picturesque and amusing than such a diversity, which rarely occurs in London or Paris."[1]

Because of the enormous press of people requiring housing in the city, buildings were five and six stories high, with several families occupying each of the stories. "The builders seem," another visitor wrote, to have "clapped one town on the top of another." Aristocrats lived cheek-by-jowl with common folk and servants. "The apartments of the greatest ladies are divided but by a partition from that of a tailor or a shoemaker, and I know nobody who has above two floors in any house, one for their own use, and one higher for their servants."[2] By imperial command the lower floors of these apartment houses were reserved for court personnel. In the attics wig-makers, dressmakers, bootmakers and jewelers toiled at making the fine articles the courtiers demanded.

With so much of the city's space devoted to the imperial household and those dependent on it, there was no housing for ordinary citizens. Even tradesmen were for the most part forced to sleep in the sprawling suburbs, then to come to the city gates in the mornings and spend the day hawking their wares from door to door. The overcrowding bred dirt, smells and noise. It was all but impossible to clean the narrow streets, even if an effort had been made to do so. The stairways in the tall buildings belonged to no one and everyone; slops and garbage rotted on the marble landings, piles of refuse discolored the wide steps. From every street, corridor and alleyway rose a miasmic stench, leading the more fastidious of Vienna's citizens to hold scented handkerchiefs to their noses when they were carried abroad in their sedan chairs. The stink was matched by the din. Over the clatter of hooves and carriage wheels the street vendors tried to out-shout one another, their raucous cries clashing with the imprecations of carriage drivers and the indignant curses of foot travelers jammed together in spaces too small for half their number.

The babel in the streets of Vienna was matched—though in more subdued tones—by the babel at the palace. "Everybody here speaks three languages!" a French observer commented, and it was an understatement. The Hapsburg royal house spoke German, but the language of the court was French. Many of the courtiers were Hungarians, or Czech-speaking Bohemians, and on any given day one could hear Portuguese, Dutch, and Italian in the corridors of the Hofburg along with a variety of Slavic, German and Swiss dialects. A generation earlier, in the reign of Maria Theresa's father, the courtiers had been required to speak Latin, and to observe a stiff and punctilious etiquette; the current Empress had discarded much of the formality along with the Latin, though she had not substituted a prescribed new etiquette in place of the old. The Lord High Chamberlain Khevenhüller complained that "the etiquette is curiously confused and uneven at court nowadays," and noted that at one Schönbrunn banquet, "in order to avoid disputes about precedence, everybody sat down pell-mell."[3]

With the relaxation of formality went a loss of the austerity that had characterized the Hapsburg court in the days of Charles VI. Under Maria Theresa, the great nobles felt free to spend their extravagant riches extravagantly. And their wealth was indeed extraordinary. Feudalism still prevailed throughout most of the

Hapsburg lands. Twenty thousand serfs worked on the imperial manors alone; millions more toiled on the estates of the feudal magnates, their labor producing the wheat and timber and other crops that created riches. The Hungarian Esterhazys lived like royalty, ruling entire counties, numbering among their possessions dozens of castles and hundreds of villages. Nikolaus Esterhazy, called "Nikolaus the Magnificent," built a palace to rival Versailles, and some Bohemian landowners had incomes even higher than the Esterhazys.

Given such affluence, it was no wonder the nobles dressed with conspicuous brilliance at court, wearing rich stuffs embroidered in gold and silver threads, ruby buttons and diamond shoe-buckles, rings and watches sparkling with huge jewels. One aristocratic minister prided himself on possessing three hundred suits of clothes, no two alike, each suit complete with matching watch, snuffbox, Spanish cane and sword. His wardrobe was said to fill two entire large rooms in his palace—and in addition to the contents of these rooms he owned two hundred pairs of shoes, eight hundred dressing gowns and fifteen hundred wigs.

Entertainments too were extravagant. The lavish balls, fetes and masquerades held at Schönbrunn, where supper might be served to ten thousand people in three immense salons, were more than matched by the spectacular pleasure parties the nobles held for the Empress and her retinue. There were hunts and balls, feasts and theatrical performances. New buildings were often built for these occasions, new plays and operas commissioned, new gardens laid out.

When the Prince of Sachsen-Hildburghausen invited Maria Theresa to his palace, Schlosshof, in the fall of 1754, he spared no expense to make the three days of diversion memorable. On the first day the royal guests were treated to a concert and an outdoor play, staged in a beautifully illuminated garden. On the following day a spectacular hunt was held, with the Empress and her consort taking their places in a specially built shooting stand while beaters drove game out of the forest toward them. The day concluded with an opera and an abundant banquet. On the third and final day the Prince outdid himself, ordering his chamberlains to prepare an elaborate "water carousel," held in a large pond. At the center of the pond was an island where hundreds of wild animals were chained, setting up a cacophony of howls and roars. There were bears dressed in pantaloons, sows dressed as Columbines and two enormous bulls—plus dozens of ducks and geese and swans. In the midst of the noise and tumult a choir sang and musicians played, then at a signal game birds were loosed and foxes and hares released to swim across the pond to dry land. At the finale of the water carousel an immense sailing ship on wheels was dragged to the pond, its timbers groaning under the weight of the meats, breads and cheeses fastened to its sides.

Invariably seated alongside the Empress at these gala entertainments was her husband Francis of Lorraine, who in his mild-mannered, easygoing way was one of the chief adornments of her court.

"Don't mind me," Francis once said when a group of courtiers insisted upon showing him special honor, "I am only a husband; the queen and her children are the court." He was more than a husband, he was Holy Roman Emperor, Maria Theresa having secured for him the office her father had held. Yet he was, in demeanor at least, less than a monarch, with his pleasantly self-effacing manner, his atrocious German and his nervous cough.

Nine years Maria Theresa's senior, Francis had been brought up at her father's court, where he excelled at hunting and fencing and managed to avoid acquiring all but the rudiments of literacy. She adored him, and in due course they were married—though not without a considerable sacrifice on Francis's part. As a condition of the marriage, he resigned his hereditary rights to Lorraine, and thus became little more than Maria Theresa's consort. In time she saw to it that he was elected Holy Roman Emperor, but the title brought with it largely ceremonial duties and no real power. He tried soldiering, but proved to be a disappointing general (unlike his more rough-hewn brother Charles, who was an able commander and toward whom the Empress felt an enduring affection).

Yet if he was not a shining asset, Francis was hardly a liability at court, and certainly did not deserve his son Joseph's cruel description of him as "an idler surrounded by flatterers." He was clever with money, investing his own income profitably and advising on the handling of the imperial revenues. He contributed to the planning of Schönbrunn, he was something of an amateur chemist—though his experiments, which included many attempts to agglomerate a number of small diamonds into one very large one, bordered on alchemy—and he was always on hand when needed to be a gracious host and a handsome and personable escort for his wife. He diligently fathered sixteen children. And to Maria Theresa he was, quite simply, "the best husband in the world," whom she called *"mon vieux,"* and her "little mouse."

She loved him, and yet she knew full well that he was far from being the best husband in the world. He had a weakness for beautiful young women, and he indulged it all too publicly. In fact, hard as she tried to keep up an appearance of cozy domesticity, to maintain the appealing fiction that behind the facade of regality she, Francis and their children were in truth a conventional Austrian family, living a comfortable, decent life untainted by the corruptions attendant upon extravagance and sophistication, her husband's behavior shattered the illusion. And she, being the strong-willed, high-minded and powerful woman that she was, ultimately sought revenge.

Francis had strayed early and often, flirting with the charming young dancers and opera singers who appeared in the Vienna theaters, making a fool of himself over one young danseuse in particular, Eva Maria Violet, until she had to be hustled out of the country. The elegantly gowned, bejeweled women of the court he found alluring as well, and in 1755, the year the Empress gave birth to her fifteenth child, the eighth Archduchess Antoinette, he became enamored of one of them. She was Princess Auersperg, a seventeen-year-old beauty with masses of soft brown hair and a lovely face. Despite the difference in their ages—he was thirty years older than the Princess—Francis developed a deep and enduring attachment to her, relying on her as not only his mistress but his confidante and friend. Aside from her youth and beauty, she seems to have had qualities that the Empress lacked, and so he sought to be with her as often as possible, buying a house for her where they could meet and arranging rendezvous at his hunting lodges or in his theater box in Vienna.

Francis was not discreet about his liaison with Princess Auersperg. A visitor to the Austrian court wrote that "the Emperor makes no secret of his passion for her," and even the imperial children were well aware of what was going on. "The Emperor is a very good-hearted father," wrote Archduchess Christina, "one can always rely upon him as a friend, and we must do what we can to protect him from his weaknesses. I am referring to his conduct with Princess Auersperg." According to the Archduchess, her father was totally under the Princess's influence, and her mother was "very jealous of this devotion."[4]

In fact, in taking a mistress Francis was only doing what virtually all men of his class and station did. Vienna had always been "a city of free adultery," as one visitor remarked, with husbands and wives condoning each other's liaisons and showing courtesy to each other's lovers. "Men look upon their wives' galants as favorably as upon deputies that take the troublesome part of their business off their hands," Lady Mary Wortley Montagu had written during the reign of Maria Theresa's father, "though they have not the less to do, for they are generally deputies in another place themselves. In short, 'tis the established custom for every lady to have two husbands, one who bears the name, and another who performs the duties."[5] The extramarital liaisons were usually of long duration, and were sealed with agreements under whose terms the woman received a "pension" from her lover. Without such a pension, and a lover, no woman could be regarded as genteel, Lady Mary noted; securing the pension was considered an essential part of the bargain. So well established were these arrangements that hostesses regularly invited both a woman's husband and her lover to dinner, seating her equitably between them.

To be sure, the Church frowned on adultery. But this did not affect the habits of the Viennese. "They sin, pray and confess," a contemporary observed, "then begin all over again, never forgetting to attend Mass." Religion never interfered with pleasure, the old habits persisted even though it was becoming more and more obvious that the Empress was displeased.

Maria Theresa, who took both her religion and her marriage very seriously, was very displeased indeed, and was determined to use her authority to bring fidelity and decency to her subjects' private lives.

The chief agency in her campaign for morality was the Chastity Commission, a special department of the police whose five hundred officers were charged with suppressing vice. Aided by a huge cadre of spies and informers, the officers of the Commission infiltrated social gatherings, theaters, public banquets, even private houses, and seized everyone they suspected of departing from virtue. Men found in the company of "lowly women" were arrested, women found leaving their own doorsteps after dark without a respectable escort were accused of wantonness. Foreigners suspected of careless morals were expelled from the country, and companies of traveling entertainers, particularly Italians, were harried out of Vienna if the Empress had reason to think they were corrupting the local citizenry.

"I have heard," she wrote to the head of the Chastity Commission on one occasion, "that a man named Palm has taken advantage of a virtuous danseuse in the Deutschestheater, and by means of false promises, has brought her to serve him in the same capacity as his wife. You will investigate this case and find out the truth. It was very bad in Palm to be such a hypocrite, and also bad in the girl to injure him in this manner."[6]

Many hundreds of such cases were investigated, and many individuals found themselves at the mercy of the police. The long arm of the Chastity Commission reached across borders and into other realms. When the Empress heard that one of her subjects, a married nobleman, was living in Switzerland with his mistress, she instructed her commissioners to extradite both of them so that they could be properly punished. In due course they were brought back to Vienna, but Maria Theresa was dissuaded from placing the woman in a convent and having the man beheaded, as she at first insisted on doing. The usual punishment for immorality was harsh enough. The condemned were chained to stone pillars at the city gates, their ankles fastened to cannonballs. Often they were left there for weeks or months, dependent for their survival on the charity of passersby.

But if the chained wretches were meant to set a public example, the plan miscarried. Instead of seeing the offenders as miscreants to be scorned and reviled, the Viennese looked on them as martyrs to the Empress's wrongheaded obsession with purity. Instead of letting them starve, the citizens fed them, generously, and laughed at Maria Theresa while they did it. The campaign for chastity backfired, giving rise to jokes and jibes about the high-minded Empress with the profligate husband. People said that Maria Theresa herself had joined her secret police, disguising herself as a man and roaming the streets of Vienna, peering shortsightedly into dark corners in search of Francis. And the Empress, for her part, reacted to the public ridicule by becoming increasingly caustic and irritable, insulting her ministers, at times arrogant in flaunting her powers, her innate humanity and capacity for tenderness quite extinguished by her spite.

After less than a year she dissolved the Chastity Commission—though keeping its personnel intact, to continue their surveillance work and send in their reports—but she extended her campaign of moral improvement to other spheres, issuing an edict against dueling (which was largely ignored) and attempting to control the mania for gambling among her courtiers by forcing players for high stakes to pay a huge license fee for the right to gamble, and donating the proceeds from the sale of licenses to charity.

A less high-minded ruler than Maria Theresa might have foreseen the outcome of all her efforts. Vice became less visible ("I can imagine no city in Europe," wrote an English visitor to Vienna, "where a young gentleman would see fewer examples, or have fewer opportunities for deep gambling, open profligacy, or gross debauchery, than in Vienna"), but no less prevalent. Driven underground, it flourished more briskly than ever, and became more sordid. The police, bribed or compromised, looked the other way or joined in. There were stories of child prostitution, of an archbishop who profited from a brothel, of secret orgies involving prominent men and women at court, planned and even discussed, using a code language, in the very presence of the Empress. The order of Freemasons, which continued to exist in Austria even after it was banned by the Pope, was said to be implicated in the secret orgies. And Francis was a Freemason, though he always managed to avoid capture when the police raided his lodge.

Despite all her efforts, Maria Theresa had to admit that her subjects were worse, not better, at the midpoint of her reign. Every morning she heard the gunshots of the duelists who gathered at dawn just outside the city walls. In private her husband boasted to her that he had won twelve thousand ducats in a single night of gambling. And day after day she endured the humiliation of the Princess Auersperg's presence at court, the beautiful, knowing, increasingly hardened Princess Auersperg who counted not only Emperor Francis but a good many other men among her coterie of lovers.

It was no wonder the Empress was in low spirits. She was greathearted enough to face armies in battle, but the insidious stabs of ridicule and humiliation were too much for her. Her self-confidence was being slowly eroded. Her expression soured, she attacked her piles of papers with a vengeance. For comfort she turned to her prayer books and tried not to think of the corrupt clergy. "My depression never leaves me," she wrote to her confidante Countess Trautson. "Sad days are approaching."

3

THOUGH Maria Theresa felt that she was losing ground to the forces of immorality, she could at least protect her children from corruption. They were sheltered, guarded, kept as much as possible from contact with the sordid world. The girls in particular were kept innocent, encouraged in their religious devotions, their sexual curiosity discouraged. When they danced in court operas they were "not allowed to exhibit their chaste limbs." Unlike the generously rouged women and young girls who attended court functions they were forbidden to wear rouge, even on the most festive occasions, and the least tendency toward coquetry was frowned on.

They were taught to follow their mother's example in dressing simply when not on public view. Maria Theresa wore plainly cut, unadorned gowns and lace caps when alone with her family, and was economical and practical when it came to formal court dress. "For all court functions elaborate dresses are required," she once wrote, "but this does not necessitate a large wardrobe, as one can wear the same dress twenty days in succession."[1] Their mother set them an austere example where food and drink were concerned as well. Even at the most sumptuous banquets, where the long tables were piled high with meats and puddings and sweets and the guests prided themselves on the quantities of wine they could consume—the Saxon Minister of State Count Pflug boasted that he could drink ten bottles of wine at one sitting—the Empress ate and drank sparingly, nibbling at slices of orange and lemon and sipping lemonade from a golden goblet.

Her message to her children was clear: even though you are surrounded by luxury and excess, you must not let your exalted status corrode your character. Royalty means responsibility, duty, unceasing and exhausting obligation; there is no room for laxity or weakness, or the self-indulgence of vice. In everything she did, Maria Theresa presented an almost superhuman model of iron self-discipline.

This model impressed itself early on the youngest and smallest of the Empress's daughters. Antoinette learned to sit quietly and do as she was told, to cultivate her natural poise and dignity, to suppress her childish impulses. She was extremely attached to her mother, and eager to please her, and this, coupled with her amiable disposition, made her a model child. She had none of the truculence of her quarrelsome brother Leopold, none of her brother Joseph's obstinacy and hauteur. She was in many ways her mother's child, pretty, well made, feminine and with a winning spontaneity and charm. She lacked her mother's strong-willed self-direction, and her outstanding intelligence—qualities that her sister Caroline had—but Caroline was a large, raw-boned and bulky child with a pinched face and a severe expression, while Antoinette was dainty and slender, with delicate features and a smooth pink-tinted complexion. By the time she was five or six years old it was clear that Antoinette would be the beauty of the family, her doll-like prettiness surpassing that of her two most attractive sisters, headstrong Amalia and tragic Elizabeth, whose beauty was disastrously and permanently marred by the marks of smallpox when Antoinette was twelve. And as the beauty of the family, Antoinette could be expected to make the most advantageous marriage.

From her earliest childhood Antoinette was aware that she and her siblings were destined to be, as her mother once wrote, "sacrifices to politics." Their lives were not their own; they belonged to the state. In time the Empress would bestow each of them on spouses suitable to Hapsburg interests.

First to be sacrificed was the heir to the throne, the prickly, arrogant Joseph, whom his mother nicknamed *"Starrkopf,"* or Stubborn One. The celebrations attending his marriage to Isabella of Parma, granddaughter of King Louis XV of France, went on for days, balls and banquets and gaudy outdoor displays following one another in giddy succession. The immensely long wedding procession took many hours to wind its way through Vienna, the Archduke's magnificent silver and gilt coach escorted by scores of noblemen's coaches, each gilded and painted and upholstered, each with its team of matched horses and its complement of liveried postilions.

The event must have impressed itself on five-year-old Antoinette, and the presence at court of her brooding, melodramatic sister-in-law must have impressed her even more. Isabella was a tortured soul who, to her confusion, conceived a much stronger passion for her husband's sister Christina than she felt for him. A lesbian attachment was unthinkable at Maria Theresa's sternly moral court, and the unfortunate Isabella quickly retreated into mental illness. She began to hear voices. "Death speaks to me in a distinct secret voice that rouses in my soul a sweet satisfaction," she told her horrified in-laws. Death haunted her, and ultimately stalked her. Four years after marrying Joseph she died of smallpox, having been delivered of a dead child a few days earlier.

Joseph loved Isabella, disturbed though she was, and was piqued when his mother insisted that he marry again. He was far more piqued when he discovered that he had to choose between the repulsive Cunigunda of Saxony and the short, thickset and pimply Josepha of Bavaria. "I prefer not to marry either," the heir to the throne announced to his mother, "but since you are holding the knife at my throat, I will take Josepha, because, from what I hear, she at least has fine breasts."[2]

Fine or not, Josepha's breasts were ultimately judged to be as disappointing as the rest of her. After a funereally gloomy wedding, Joseph refused to have anything to do with his wretched bride, humiliating her by his public displays of indifference. He told whoever questioned him about his marriage that he found Josepha "insupportable," with horrible teeth and a shapeless and unappealing body. "They want me to have children," he snapped. "How can one have them? If I could put the tip of my finger on the tiniest part of her body which is not covered with pimples, I would try to have a child." Josepha, childless and sadly friendless, disappeared into her apartments and wept.

Maria Theresa's favorite son Karl having died in 1761, followed shortly afterward by his sister Johanna, the next child to be offered up on the altar of dynastic ambition was Leopold, whose wedding festivities—he married the Infanta Louise of Spain—

were marred by the sudden death of his father, Emperor Francis. Antoinette did not take part in the wedding ceremony, but most likely she associated it with her father's death, which plunged the court into prolonged mourning and effected a profound change in her mother.

The grieving widow had her rooms painted black, the windows draped with black velvet and her person veiled and swathed in somber widow's weeds. By nature energetic and affirmative, though plagued by periods of depression, the Empress now seemed to lose heart completely, sitting alone in her darkened apartments, her hair shorn, her thoughts increasingly morbid. She even spoke of entering a convent. For her nine-year-old daughter, herself grieving for her father, the transformation must have been disturbing, especially when Maria Theresa ordered her own coffin prepared and placed beside her husband's in the burial vault of the Capucin church. The Empress spent a large part of each afternoon in the vault, sitting beside Francis's coffin and the empty one waiting for her, praying and weeping. Once so efficient with her time, she now became prodigal with it, dragging out her days in visits to the Capucin church and in repeating the office of the dead. The only time that mattered to her was the time she had spent with her husband. "Emperor Francis I, my husband," she wrote in her prayer book, "died on the evening of the 18th of August at half past nine o'clock. He lived 680 months, 2,958 weeks, 20,778 days, or 496,992 hours. Our happy marriage lasted twenty-nine years, six months and six days, 1,540 weeks, 10,781 days, or 258,744 hours."[3] The calculations of time became a litany of her mourning, part of the several rituals of grieving that made up her days. And these rituals left her less time than ever to spend with her children.

Still, the business of marrying them off had to proceed. With Leopold gone, there were ten children left, but the eldest daughter, Anna, was unmarriageable because of her physical weakness and frequent illnesses, and Elizabeth too was a poor marriage prospect with her sadly pockmarked features. Both young women were given titular religious offices, Anna as Abbess of a convent in Prague and Elizabeth as Abbess of a convent in Innsbruck; they continued to live at their mother's court.

It must have been difficult for Maria Theresa to part with her favorite daughter Christina when she married Duke Albert of

Teschen, but by appointing the Duke Governor of Hungary she made certain Christina would remain reasonably nearby, in Pressburg. And she had the consolation of knowing that Christina and Albert were very much in love. Theirs was a happy marriage—a stark contrast to the sad misalliance between Joseph and Josepha. The miserable Josepha soon caught smallpox and died—indirectly causing another death in the imperial family when the Archduchess Josepha, her sister-in-law, became infected when visiting her sarcophagus in the family vault.

With Josepha's death, in 1767, there were five unmarried children left—Amalia, Caroline, Ferdinand, Antoinette and Maximilian. Ferdinand's betrothal had been arranged several years earlier, and Maximilian was still a very young boy. Amalia, high-spirited and headstrong, was determined to marry the man of her choice, who happened to be the Prince of Zweibrucken, but her mother forestalled this, saving her for a more advantageous match. Meanwhile the marriage contract that had been drawn up for Josepha, which arranged for her to wed Ferdinand of Naples, was still valid, and in the spring of 1768 the Empress determined that Caroline should fulfill it. (Caroline was in fact the third Hapsburg Archduchess to become betrothed to Ferdinand, her late sister Johanna having been the first.)

Caroline's marriage affected Antoinette far more than those of her other siblings. The two girls had been close companions from early childhood, forever laughing and gossiping together, making fun of their relatives, their servants, and Caroline's attendant gentlewomen. Three years older than her sister and far less tractable, Caroline was independent and self-confident, in her presence the compliant Antoinette could be boisterous and playful and unrestrained. The sisters were extremely fond of each other, Antoinette bringing out her older sister's protective instincts and Caroline offering Antoinette a liberating model of girlhood that departed widely from her stern mother's ideal.

Maria Theresa was not pleased with Caroline. "To my astonishment," she wrote her daughter when she set off on her wedding journey to Naples, "I have observed that you say your prayers without the proper piety. Reprimands mean nothing to you and only lead to harsh words and bad temper." In her mother's eyes, Caroline was thoughtless, irritable and rude; she was in fact outspoken and not overly eager to please, and besides, as a nervous fifteen-year-old leaving home for the first time to live among strangers, she was no doubt terrified. She had no idea what to expect in Naples, and wept when she and her Austrian escort reached the border, and the Austrians turned back. Things looked blackest when she met her husband-to-be for the first time, and found him ugly. Then came the wedding, and the wedding night, for which she was totally unprepared. The experience was so horrible that she wanted to die.

"One suffers real martyrdom," she was to recall later, in a letter to Countess Lerchenfeld, "which is all the greater because one must pretend outwardly to be happy. . . . I would rather die than endure again what I had to suffer. If religion had not said to me: 'Think about God,' I would have killed myself rather than live as I did live for eight days. It was like hell and I often wished to die." Having endured such anguish herself, Caroline dreaded what marriage would be like for Antoinette when her time came. "I pity Antoinette, who still has this to face," she told the Countess. "When my sister has to confront this situation, I shall shed many tears."[4]

Caroline's worries were none too premature. For the past two years Antoinette's future marriage had been discussed, hoped for and anticipated by the statesmen and diplomats at her mother's court. First proposed when she was only ten years old, the potential match came ever closer to becoming reality as she approached her thirteenth birthday. It was the brainchild of Prince Kaunitz and the Duc de Choiseul, architects of the Austro-French Treaty of Versailles and continuing advocates of strong ties between their two realms. Antoinette, Maria Theresa's prettiest and most personally agreeable daughter, they reasoned, would make the perfect bride for Louis XV's grandson, who would one day reign as Louis XVI.

For the obscure youngest Archduchess at the Hapsburg court, it would be a breathtaking match. If all went as planned, Antoinette would one day be Queen of France, mistress of Versailles and, with her husband, head of the most refined and exalted court in Europe.

She began to come out of obscurity. As if in acknowledgment of her forthcoming distinction, Joseph deigned to offer Antoinette a place in his theater box. It was a very public honor, as the elite of the Viennese court and society all attended the theater to see and be seen, and when Joseph entered his box the entire audience stood in respect. We can be certain that they took careful note of the delicate young beauty at his side, her lovely face framed in yards of creamy lace, a pastel satin ribbon tied in a coquettish bow at her throat, the pink tint of her complexion set off by a soft gray wig crowned with pearls.

Although there was as yet no formal betrothal between Antoinette and the fourteen-year-old dauphin Louis, she began to be called "the dauphine," and in the fall of 1768 her mother authorized her ambassador at Versailles, Prince Starhemberg, to spend the extravagant sum of four hundred thousand livres for her trousseau. All the clothes were to be made in Paris, commissioned from the dressmakers who regularly served the French court. It was customary for the dressmakers to send dolls—*poupées de la mode*—dressed in the current styles to clients in distant cities to enable them to make their selections. Scores of these dolls began arriving at the Hofburg as Antoinette turned thirteen, wearing miniature versions of the robes and gowns proposed for her.

That her trousseau would be extensive was a foregone conclusion. An Austrian Archduchess, soon to be dauphine of France and one day Queen—such a personage would require a wardrobe to rival any in Europe. The dresses, trimmings and accessories would have to be of surpassing excellence in their materials and workmanship, and they would have to conform to the rigid traditions of the Bourbon court, where each season had its prescribed fabrics and certain days their prescribed colors.

Styles were changing in the late 1760's. Voluminous petticoats were beginning to replace the stiff elliptical hoops that had been worn for a generation and more; the hoops were known as *paniers*, or "hen-baskets," because they resembled the poultry baskets peasant women carried to market. Hen-basket skirts, which spread out to a width of several feet on either side of the wearer's waist, took up the space of three or four people and made for enormous inconvenience in entering and leaving rooms, getting in and out of carriages, and walking up and down staircases. With the waning of the hen-basket skirt came an increase in the heel height of women's shoes and changes in the line of the torso, with more fullness in the bodice and at the hips. Such innovations were watched carefully by the style-conscious denizens of Versailles and other courts, but they were of interest to a wider public as well, for it was just at this time that fashion plates came into existence—and with them the beginnings of those broad shifts in public taste that we call fashion.

To be sure, formal court dress—as opposed to the informal clothes worn for ordinary occasions and in the privacy of the wearer's apartments—remained traditional. Court gowns had wide hoop skirts beneath heavily embroidered petticoats, with long trains fastened on at the waist and trailing along behind. Special stiff bodices, lined with whalebone, were worn above the petticoats, laced so tightly that they were ready to burst; the neck and chest were bare, the arms covered with rows of lace that fell to the elbow.[5]

The prevailing colors of the time—cream, pale green, China blue, silver, lavender-pink and pastel yellow—were flattering to Antoinette, and her trousseau must have included dozens of ball gowns, afternoon dresses, robes and petticoats in a score of delicate shades, the silks and brocades embroidered with floral designs or silk ribbon appliqué, the borders trimmed with serpentine garlands or silver and gold lace. French dressmakers outdid themselves in inventing ornaments, festooning their already overdecorated fabrics with fields of artificial flowers, feathers, tassels and silk ribbon bows, rosettes and ruffles, passementerie and beading and costly metallic fringe. The overall effect was one of deliciously playful sensuality, luxuriance and youthfulness—a perfect foil for the charms of a thirteen-year-old Queen-to-be.

Charming the future Queen certainly was, but charm alone would not be sufficient in one who was called to be mistress of Versailles. Her doll-like prettiness aside, Antoinette had flaws, and with her exalted marriage in prospect these flaws were magnified a hundredfold. Her longtime governess, Countess Brandeiss, had been accustomed to tie her abundant blond hair back with a woolen band, which pulled at her hair, thinning it and breaking it at the hairline. The new governess, Countess Lerchenfeld, knew better but the damage remained. An expert was called for. Starhemberg wrote to his colleague Count Mercy in Paris to request that a skilled Parisian *friseur* be sent to the Viennese court. The Empress, he wrote, "flatters herself that a man who is perfect at his trade will succeed in correcting, or at least in concealing this small defect either by cutting the hair, or by the employment of some innocent remedy calculated to increase the growth of the hair of which the forehead is denuded, or, in short, by the pains he will take to arrange the whole as it is to suit the face."[6] High foreheads, after all, might go out of fashion, and in fact coiffures were beginning to change shape in the late 1760's, becoming higher and more elaborate, putting women with high foreheads at a disadvantage.

A *friseur* was found, one Larsenneur, whose sole recommendation was that Starhemberg's wife had patronized him when in Paris. He was not a brilliant coiffeur, but he was adequate; he swept Antoinette's hair back off her forehead in a "simple and decent" style, softening it at the sides and lifting it at the crown. The Empress was pleased, and a visiting Frenchman remarked gallantly that the simpler style would no doubt be adopted by the young ladies of Versailles when their future Queen arrived among them. In truth, though the new style made Antoinette look older, it was not particularly becoming, as she herself realized. She was too kindhearted to complain to Larsenneur, but when his back was turned she tugged at her hair until she loosened it at the front, creating a more flattering line.

It was not only her hair that was less than ideal; her teeth too were flawed, and a French dentist had to be brought to Vienna to work on them over a period of three months. At the same time she had to learn, or rather relearn, how to walk, for the women of Versailles walked like no one else in Europe. They glided, taking very small, quick light steps in order to make their gowns float smoothly along the polished marble floors. Antoinette's dancing master, the celebrated choreographer Noverre, undertook to teach her the proper mincing steps and to teach her as well the intricate French court dances that she would be expected to execute.

Then too there was the much more complex matter of teaching her to play the role of royal hostess. At Versailles the Queen was expected to preside at receptions where a rather tedious game called cavagnole was played; these apparently modest gatherings were in fact governed by a rigorous etiquette, and as dauphine Antoinette would have to master its subtleties. She rehearsed for her cavagnole evenings several times a week, practicing on the Viennese courtiers and presiding with increasing graciousness and easy authority over the playing tables.

She was in fact slowly gaining that elusive nameless quality reserved to royalty, an emanation that made itself felt in small things—a gesture of the hand, the set of the head, a smile, a walk. The transformation did not go unheeded. "Her deportment, general tone, and her observations were universally applauded," wrote one observer. She was acquiring "an air of nobleness and majesty astonishing for her age."[7] She was ingenuous by nature; now she added to that ingenuousness graciousness and a degree of polish. She walked among her guests, a small yet regal figure, speaking obligingly to each and impressing each with her growing courtesy.

She impressed them even more at a ball held in October of 1769. Four thousand guests had been invited, and all of them were eager to glimpse the Empress's youngest daughter, the winning girl, not quite fourteen years old, who had been chosen to marry the dauphin. They surged forward when Maria Theresa walked through the crowded rooms, with Antoinette by her side. The Empress walked slowly and with some difficulty, encumbered by her increasing girth, her breathing evidently labored. An attack of smallpox two years earlier had left her with a weakened heart and unsteady nerves, and she looked aged and tired as she passed by.

"The day of her beauty and brilliancy was past," an eyewitness noted. "Her countenance, marked by smallpox, had lost its former charm and showed traces of the emotions produced by an illustrious but laborious reign, joined to an expression of weariness and lassitude."[8] She was tired, but triumphant. By arranging her daughter's marriage, she had saved Austria, for as long as Bourbon and Hapsburg were allied by marriage, the Monster Frederick of Prussia would remain at bay. But few in the crowd took notice of the Empress, except to remark on her evident ill health. Her day was past, while her daughter's was just dawning. It was the fresh-faced, lovely child with the striking coloring, the Archduchess Antoinette, who drew the attention of all eyes.

4

AT Versailles, the dauphin Louis Auguste was far from enthusiastic when he learned that he was to marry the Austrian Archduchess. He had no desire to be married, in fact he had no interest whatsoever in women and the subject of sex filled him with dread. At fifteen, he was a clumsy, loutish youth, pudgy and dirty, with appalling manners and a terror of public functions. His grandfather's mistress, Madame Du Barry, who was none too well-bred herself, called him a "fat, ill-bred boy" and the Neapolitan ambassador remarked wryly that he seemed to have been "born and raised in a forest." That this *enfant sauvage* should be the heir to the throne of his grandfather Louis XV was a disaster the King and his ministers would gladly have averted. The Duc de Choiseul, chief promoter of the Austrian marriage and a man of blunt pronouncements, prophesied glumly that if the dauphin grew into as embarrassing a man as he was a boy, he would one day be "the horror of the nation."

An unkind fate had thrust Louis into his role. The most unpromising of his father's four sons, bullied by his siblings, a piteously shy and sickly child, he had suddenly become dauphin at the age of eleven, when his father and older brother died. He wept from terror, and took refuge in his favorite haunt, the forest of Compiègne. There he could hunt, and bury himself in the forest depths far from the disapproving eyes of his grandfather's ministers. Louis was an eccentric child, poor at his lessons yet bookish and pedantic (he compiled a detailed, prosaic Description of the

Forest of Compiègne before he was twelve), ill at ease with other children and with the courtiers of Versailles, happiest in the company of ordinary laborers and servants. Maps were his passion, though in his early teens he developed an interest in history as well, particularly in the English Civil War with its sensational regicide. He also kept a diary, primarily to record his hunts and to keep a record of expenditures.

Overweight, uncouth, badly dressed and painfully self-conscious, the dauphin was not unaware of his shortcomings, yet he seemed incapable of rising above them, and still more incapable of coming to grips with the challenges of rule. "My greatest fault," he wrote candidly, "is a sluggishness of mind." Others were prepared to enlarge on this assessment. "This prince, by his face and his talk, shows only an extremely limited intelligence, much clumsiness," was the judgment of the Austrian envoy to Versailles, Count Mercy. "Nature seems to have refused everything to the dauphin."[1]

Nature had refused him everything—except a charming and pretty wife. In the summer of 1769, the French and Austrian diplomats began negotiating the betrothal contract, with an understanding that the wedding would take place in the following April. Antoinette's dowry was fixed at two hundred thousand silver florins in cash, with an equal amount in jewelry. With the pride of two great powers at stake, ceremonial details took on heightened significance. Who would sign the betrothal contract first, the French or the Austrians? Whose pageant would come first when the entertainment began? Who would escort the bride from Vienna to Paris, and what formalities would take place when she was handed over to her new family? What wedding presents would she receive? The imperial Chancellor Kaunitz, and his envoy Count Mercy, did battle with Choiseul and his deputy Durfort over these issues, with draft agreements going back and forth between the Austrian and French capitals throughout the summer and fall.

Mercy, a sophisticated Lorrainer and Kaunitz's close friend, played a key role in the negotiations, shrewdly able to assess the positions of both sides and to anticipate their demands. Knowing both courts well, Mercy could foresee difficulties, and not only with the legalities of the contract. And he foresaw that, unless

Antoinette received some proper education, she would be unfit to become the dauphin's wife.

Polite pretense aside, Antoinette was shockingly ignorant and all but illiterate. She hated to read, and no doubt read very badly, she wrote painfully slowly, and with great effort. Very likely she could not compose a simple letter without considerable help. She had been brought up to be idle, she had been overindulged by Countess von Brandeiss and Brandeiss's recent replacement, Countess Lerchenfeld, was not having much more success in educating her. Mercy found a French tutor for her, Abbé Mathurin Vermond, an inconspicuous, ingratiating man who undertook to remedy her deficiencies. It was an enormous task. The future dauphine's mind was a *tabula rasa* on which anything might be written. Vermond set about instructing his pupil in French history and customs, teaching her the names and histories of the leading families whose representatives she would encounter at Versailles, and going on to present French literature to her in as painless a manner as possible. All the instruction was conversational, though Vermond also sat beside Antoinette while she struggled with her writing exercises.[2]

To her credit, she did make progress under Vermond's tutelage. "She is cleverer than she was long thought to be," Vermond remarked. She was capable of learning, eager to please—if it didn't take too much effort—and possessed of sound judgment if she applied her mind to an issue. Vermond had difficulty "accustoming her to get at the root of a subject," as he put it, and he had to keep her amused in order to keep her attention. Still, he persisted.

"I began the history of France," he wrote in one of his periodic reports to Mercy, "but I only employed it as a background on which I could work up all the objects it is necessary to know in the ordinary course of life. Excepting the history of recent times, I only called her attention to important facts, especially to epoch-making occurrences in our habits or government. I profited by every opportunity of giving her ideas on the arts, on laws and customs; I rather tormented her by my questions on the reign of Henri IV." Since he was educating a future queen, Vermond paused frequently in his narrative of French history to pose questions about how this or that ruler ought to have reacted in a given situation. He was gratified to discover that his pupil "often took the right view." He spent a disproportionate amount of time covering the lives of the French Queens related to the house of Hapsburg, and found Antoinette particularly interested in them.

"We are now finishing the reign of Louis XIV," Vermond informed Mercy in October of 1769. "Her Royal Highness is already familiar with French names, she has some idea of genealogy, the journals of the reign of Louis XV will add to her knowledge, and assist me in giving her an idea of the important places about the court and in the kingdom while accustoming her to the names of those who fill them." The French army had special appeal for her, he discovered. "I am certain that shortly after her marriage she will know the colonels by name, and will distinguish each regiment by its number from the color of the uniforms."[3]

It remained only to improve her French, and this Vermond was finding it very difficult to do in the linguistic chaos of Vienna. Everyone was multilingual, but no one spoke any language purely and correctly, without corruption from other tongues. Bad French was rife at Maria Theresa's court, but good French was very rare. He did his best to weed the Germanisms out of Antoinette's French, but she still spoke very incorrectly. He could only hope that her linguistic faults would be overlooked for the sake of her liveliness and attractiveness.

She was becoming more attractive day by day. Concerns about her shortness of stature had receded, for she had grown considerably in the course of her fourteenth year. She was filling out as well, the tight bodices of her Parisian gowns displaying more than a hint of cleavage. The aged French Cardinal de Rohan, sent to Vienna to judge at first hand how she had grown, was quite awestruck. "The form of her face is a perfect oval," he wrote, "the eyebrows well furnished as a blond can have, and a shade darker than her hair, the eyelashes of a charming length. . . . She has a little mouth, scarlet as a cherry, the lips are thick, particularly the lower one, which is, one knows, the distinctive trace of the House of Burgundy [i.e., the Hapsburgs]." In common with all other observers, the Cardinal was impressed with Antoinette's unblemished porcelain skin and natural coloring. Setting aside her usual strictures governing the use of makeup by her daughters, the Empress had allowed Antoinette to rouge her cheeks, but the rouge only covered up her own blush, which was far more becoming. "Her natural dignity is softened by her sweetness," the Cardinal concluded, "also natural, and by the simplicity of her education."[4]

Antoinette was ripening into a woman. Only one thing was lacking: she had not yet begun to menstruate, and until she did, the French could not permit the wedding to take place. Then in February of 1770, two months before the scheduled date for the ceremony, her period arrived. Maria Theresa informed the French envoy Durfort, who sent a fast courier to Versailles with the happy news. The "little bride," as the Empress called Antoinette, was a woman at last.

If the bride-to-be had expressed any curiosity about the dauphin—and she was curious by nature—the surviving sources do not record it. Possibly such curiosity was thought to be unladylike, certainly it could have led to disillusionment. Louis XV had asked for portraits of Antoinette, but no portraits of his grandson had been sent to Vienna. Finally, as the wedding day approached, the Empress requested one. Two portraits arrived, neither of which was able to disguise the oafishness of the jowly, fleshy dauphin. Here too the sources are silent about Antoinette's reaction, save to note that she asked permission to hang one of the portraits in her sitting room.

Durfort believed that the likenesses had given satisfaction, but in truth the Empress was dismayed. Having known the deep contentment of a happy (if far from untroubled) marriage to a handsome man, she foresaw a misalliance of the most painful sort. She tried to prepare Antoinette for the ordeal of marriage to a clumsy boy, telling her that a wife must always be pleasing and submissive, that passionate love is only a fleeting pleasure and neither a sound nor necessary foundation for a marriage, that a man's personal appearance is far less important than what is in his heart. Antoinette listened, looking down at the dauphin's ring which she had worn since January, and looked up at her mother with her innocent, trusting blue eyes. Clearly she did not understand.

On April 15, Durfort entered Vienna at the head of an immense procession of coaches, with over a hundred liveried servants, pages and grooms in attendance. He and his entourage represented Louis XV, arriving to fetch his grandson's bride. Among the coaches were two very large traveling berlins, commissioned from a Parisian saddler, designed to carry Antoinette to

Versailles in comfort. Both were made of rare wood, lined with satin, upholstered in crimson and blue velvet. Their costly embroideries were works of art in themselves, thread-paintings of the four seasons and of bouquets of golden flowers. Durfort presented Antoinette with a letter from her future husband, and another portrait of him, this one mounted in diamonds and attached to a ribbon, to be worn as an ornament. Two days later Antoinette solemnly renounced all claims to her mother's lands, and, while Austrian officials and French diplomatic clerks looked impatiently on, scratched and blotted her way through her signature on the document of renunciation.

That evening a memorable supper was held for fifteen hundred carefully chosen guests, who consumed two thousand roast game birds, five hundred meat pies, ten thousand servings of delicious cakes and pastries washed down with hundreds of bottles of liqueurs and wines. A masked ball followed the supper, with a much larger guest list. Most of Vienna was lit with lanterns, and those citizens who were not lucky enough to attend the ball crowded into the streets to watch the favored guests arrive, and to see the fireworks that lit up the night sky as the dancing drew to an end.

Celebrating on this scale had not gone on for years, and the city was on holiday for the next several days with the streets illuminated every night and music, fireworks and spectacle available at every turn. On the eighteenth Durfort gave another banquet at the Lichtenstein palace, which served as the French embassy. A large Temple of Hymen had been built in the palace gardens, from which skyrockets rose and burst in a display even more dazzling than that of the night before.

On the following day, at six in the evening, the courtiers gathered in the Augustinian church for the wedding ceremony. In the dauphin's absence, his part was taken by Antoinette's brother Ferdinand, who knelt beside his smiling sister and placed the wedding ring on her finger. The papal nuncio, Visconti, celebrated the nuptial Mass, and when it was over the guns of the Hofburg were fired again and again, their thunder shaking the walls of the old church.

Antoinette was radiant, unperturbed by the long days and nights of ceremony and merrymaking, content to be the center of attention, her charm and poise at their best as she walked beside her mother in her luxurious wedding gown of cloth of silver. To judge from outward appearances, she did not dread her future, nor did she shrink from the obligations it would entail. Whether her composure came from true serenity, or whether she was largely oblivious to the real meaning of the events surrounding her, or whether, more likely, she was simply a young, naive and unaffected girl caught up happily in an exciting swirl of events, Antoinette took it all in stride. Her mother had instructed her in what she needed to know, and had promised to continue to give her advice once she left home. She trusted her mother, sad though she would be to leave her; that trust, and her own natural buoyancy, were all she needed. As always in the past, she would be amiable and do what was expected of her.

Already Maria Theresa was making her daughter's way easier by providing guidance in the form of rules to be read once a month. They enjoined Antoinette to attend to her spiritual observances faithfully, including private morning devotions, to do her best to conform to French customs, to avoid familiarity with underlings and avoid becoming involved in the requests or grievances of individual petitioners. "Do not be ashamed to ask everyone for advice and do nothing on your own," the Empress cautioned. Antoinette should show no initiative, grant no requests, and display no curiosity. "Read no book, even the most indifferent, until you have received your confessor's permission," Maria Theresa went on. "This is a particularly important point in France because books are published there which, although they are full of agreeable erudition, can nonetheless be pernicious to religion and morals."[5]

France was a dangerous place. The Empress did not say so, but she meant it. It would be very hard, she knew, for a naive and trusting young girl to keep her head and follow common sense at Versailles, even with the best guidance. There would be too much that was unfamiliar, and tempting, too many seductive voices calling her to follow hazardous paths, too few examples of innocence and decency. Her husband was not likely to protect her against any of these temptations, indeed he hardly seemed capable of protecting himself. Still, Antoinette was her mother's daughter, and she had a sweet nature. Perhaps her mettle would show in time.

Two days after the proxy wedding, on April 21, Antoinette got into one of the two huge berlins that had been fitted out for her comfort. She was allowed to take very few familiar things with her into her new life: some treasured personal belongings, enough clothes to last until she reached the border of France, and her little dog. Abbé Vermond went with her, but not Countess Lerchenfeld, who had died the previous year, or any of the servants she had known since childhood. One treasured possession she did take: her late father's "Instructions to my children both for their spiritual and temporal lives." This little tract exhorted Antoinette and her siblings to be sincere Catholics, to cultivate reserve and discretion, to be charitable toward the poor and not overly fond of luxury. "The world where you must pass your life is but transitory," Francis admonished her from beyond the grave. "There is nought save eternity that is without end." "We should enjoy the pleasures of this life innocently, for so soon as they lead us into evil, of whatever sort it may be, they cease to be pleasures."[6]

Some of Emperor Francis's advice he had been unable to follow himself, as when he told his children to "have no particular affection for any one thing," and "above all, to have no passion." His own particular passion for Princess Auersperg had been so intense that, after his death, his widow and his mistress had grieved equally. He had been a famous gambler, yet he instructed his children to have "a horror of high play."

"I recommend you to take two days in every year to prepare for death," he concluded, "as though you were sure that those two were the last days of your life; and thus you will accustom yourself to know what you ought to do under those circumstances, and when your last moment arrives, you will not be surprised, but will know what you have to do." Devotion, religion, virtue: these summed up Francis's ideals. "I herewith commend you to read these instructions twice yearly; they come from a father who loves you above everything, and who has thought it necessary to leave you this testimony of his tender affection, which you cannot better reciprocate than by loving one another with the same tenderness he bequeaths to all of you."[7]

The tender father was gone, the stern yet loving mother would soon be very far away. The berlin inched forward, then eased into its slow traveling speed. Many people lined the road to watch the dauphine pass by in her gorgeous coach, waving their hands and calling out to her. The more sharp-eyed of them noted that her cheeks were wet with tears. She lay back against the velvet cushions, "covering her eyes, sometimes with her handkerchief and sometimes with her hands, now and then putting her head out of the carriage to take another look at the palace of her ancestors which she was never more to enter." The long train of coaches escorting her berlin stretched out along the muddy road for several miles, the outriders covering their handsome blue and yellow liveries with drab cloaks as a cold spring rain began to fall. The crowds thinned out, Vienna receded into the far distance. Antoinette was on her way into a new life.

5

WITH tortoise-like slowness the dauphine's entourage crawled westward, traveling from eight to ten hours in a typical day, stopping for the night at convenient castles or monasteries or in towns whose inns could barely accommodate the hundreds of retainers and their horses. At the end of a week the traveling had become tedious; after two and a half weeks, when the party arrived at the Abbey of Schuttern, the last resting place before the Austro-French border, everyone, from the ladies-in-waiting to the secretaries to the lackeys and cooks, was exhausted. The dauphine herself bore up well under the strains of travel, her cheeks as usual pink with health and her spirits cheerful.

At Schuttern she was visited by the stiff, self-important Comte de Noailles, Louis XV's ambassador, who paid far less attention to her than he did to what he considered an insult in the wording of the documents under whose terms Antoinette was to be officially handed over to him. The document named Maria Theresa and her son Joseph, now reigning monarch of Austria, before naming the august King Louis. Such a slight could not be tolerated. The Count's Austrian counterpart, Starhemberg, pointed out politely but firmly that to put the French King's name first would be to insult their Austrian majesties. The two diplomats faced off, at an impasse, and not for the first time. Finally, to avoid conflict, the document was prepared in two versions, one for each court: in the Austrian version the Austrian monarchs were named first, and in the French version Louis XV received precedence.

The contretemps did not bode well for the next day's ceremony of *remise*, when Antoinette was to lay aside her Austrian
identity and become French. On neutral ground—an island in the
middle of the Rhine—she entered a building newly constructed
for the ceremony. Putting on a gown designated for this day (but
keeping her Austrian jewels and ornaments), she entered the *salle
de remise* and took her place in front of a table that symbolized the
boundary line between the two realms. On one side of the table
stood her Austrian escort, on the other the punctilious Noailles,
with two of his assistants. Noailles made a speech, then the act
was read under whose terms Antoinette became French.

As the room filled with official verbiage, Antoinette's attention
must have strayed to the large and brilliant tapestries that covered
the walls. They were of the finest workmanship, having come
from the palace of the Archbishop of Strasbourg who loaned them
specifically for this occasion, but their subject matter was, to say
the least, disturbing. They represented the horrific scene in which
Medea, goaded to fury by her husband Jason's desertion, murders
their children and then kills herself. A more suggestible girl than
Antoinette might have shuddered at the sight of them and taken
them as an ill omen. But most likely Antoinette, ever curious, was
more intrigued by them than alarmed—and it may have occurred
to her that whoever chose the tapestries was passing a sour judgment on the alliance between Bourbon and Hapsburg.[1]

The solemnities concluded, Antoinette's Austrian ladies filed
in to kiss her hand and take leave of her. She was delivered into
the keeping of Noailles, and of his flinty, officious sister-in-law
whose immediate response to Antoinette's childlike kiss of welcome was to draw back in indignation at the latter's impropriety.
The Comtesse de Noailles invariably stood on ceremony, and she
expected her new mistress to keep her effusions of sentiment to
herself. Her previous mistress, Louis XV's late wife Queen Marie
Leczinska, had been dull and retiring, and therefore easy to serve.
The Countess presented Antoinette with her ladies of honor, a
staid and matronly group, and then escorted her across the thresh-
old symbolizing her arrival in France.

A week later, on the evening of May 14, Antoinette finally met
the dauphin Louis, at the Pont de Berne on the outskirts of the
forest of Compiègne. It was a setting calculated to make Louis as
comfortable as possible, on the verge of the great forest near the

tall oaks and chestnuts that provided his favorite refuge. Nonetheless he was extremely ill at ease, uncomfortable in the ornate waistcoat and breeches, fine linen and lace that were so far from the rough clothes he customarily wore, nervous in the presence of his disdainful grandfather, uncomfortable at being the center of attention.

The sight that greeted him when Antoinette stepped down from her berlin must have made him blink his weak eyes in surprise: she was petite, blond, and every bit as pretty as his grandfather's ministers had said she would be. She was also gentle and amiable, with a wide-eyed, innocent friendliness that made him relax ever so slightly, though he maintained his outward reticence.

For her part, Antoinette gazed at the heavy and gawky youth whom she expected to marry and took pity on him. She saw at once how timid he was, and was not put off by his extreme detachment or by his brusque speech. He aroused her sympathy, the fear in his large eyes touched her. He was not really bad-looking, and would seem a good deal more presentable if he stood up straight and didn't shamble when he walked. He was untamed, but perhaps not untamable.

Any rapport she might have tried to establish with Louis was interrupted by the multitude of introductions and ceremonies the occasion called for. Antoinette abased herself before the King, who pulled his bow lips back in a smile and helped her up, muttering that she was charming. At fifty-nine Louis XV was still a very handsome man, with piercing black eyes, a Roman nose and a regal bearing. To Antoinette he must have seemed ancient, but others, visitors to the French court from England, found in him "the remains of a manly beautifulness" despite his advanced age and round shoulders. He was certainly a connoisseur of beautiful women, and though his taste did not run to ingenues, no doubt he saw at a glance that the young girl his chief minister Choiseul had chosen to be dauphine would grow into a very handsome woman indeed.

Louis had reigned for more than fifty years, but as a vapid figurehead. Choiseul, who knew him better than anyone, confided in his memoirs published after the King's death that he had heard his master refer to himself as "inconsequence personified," and add that he would not be surprised to discover that he was insane.[2] Overbred, overindulged, King since the age of five, this great-grandson of the Sun King Louis XIV had no real idea of who or what he was—beneath his carapace of regality—and had long since ceased to care. He knew, for his tutors had taught him, that being King, he was altogether different from ordinary men. He believed himself to be a "chosen vessel" of the Almighty, with the divine mission to protect the Catholic religion. And he believed (which belief did nothing to strengthen his character) that because he was a "direct emanation from providence," God would not punish him for his transgressions by sending him to hell, no matter how egregiously he sinned. Knowing that he could sin with impunity, he sinned—yet sin did not provide him with a sufficient means of defining himself.

"The King's character," Choiseul once wrote, "resembled soft wax, on which the most dissimilar objects can be temporarily traced."[3] His excessive malleability would have been unsettling in a private person; in a ruler it was disastrous. Vulnerable to becoming the prey of faction, the King fortunately had Choiseul to rely on—though Choiseul, naturally enough, headed a faction of his own. The chief minister did the King's work, sitting at a desk in a small room adjacent to his master's bedroom at Versailles. Whatever Choiseul recommended, King Louis acceded to, scarcely bothering to read documents before he signed them.

It was as if he ruled in absentia, but no alternative to this sorry state of affairs seemed possible, given the King's frequent lapses into vacuity. "When he is thoughtful," an English traveler wrote describing King Louis, "and not disposed to speak, he is apt to open his mouth, fix his eyes upon some one object, and let his chin drop; to such who only see him at such times, his looks are rather unfavorable."[4] He looked, in fact, as if he were drunk, and there were whispers at court that the King was growing much too fond of the bottle.[5]

Inconsequential and vacuous, King Louis was also virtually devoid of accomplishments, unless stag-hunting and making coffee could be considered accomplishments. Spectators who came to Versailles to watch the King eat noted the skill with which he knocked the top off a soft-boiled egg with his fork, and applauded the feat. Certainly the King was not a success as a husband, or as a father. He had ignored his late wife Queen Marie for a procession of mistresses, leaving her to fill her life with quilt-making, drawing, and long tedious evenings with her ladies of honor.

Toward his children the King was unpleasant at best. He had quarreled with his late son Louis, whose views on the monarchy diverged sharply from his own, and he looked on his four unmarried daughters with contempt, mocking and ridiculing them and treating them as nonentities. His grandson and heir he despised, not just because of his eccentricity but because there was nothing remotely virile about him, and Louis himself was nothing if not virile. The dauphin Louis was certainly not yet ready for marriage, if indeed he ever would be, and at the thought of this his grandfather was apt to fall into one of his glassy-eyed reveries.

Antoinette joined the King and the dauphin in the capacious royal carriage for the drive through the forest to the chateau of Compiègne. There she met the rest of her new relatives, a crowd of dukes and duchesses, princes and princesses whose names and titles must have gone by her in a blur, especially as there were so many of them and so many other courtiers for her to meet as well. Besides, there were only two days until the wedding, and many last-minute details required attention. After supper—and one wonders what sort of meal it was, with the pretty and amiable young newcomer seated amid a dozen or more highly judgmental strangers, her bridegroom so shy he barely looked at her, her own manners noticeably less formal than those of the French—she was shown to her room, where she received the King's Master of Ceremonies. He presented her with twelve wedding rings, which she tried on one after another until she found one that fit her perfectly. It was put away until the ceremony.

Two days later, at midmorning, Antoinette rode in her coach through the high ornate iron gates of the palace of Versailles. The sheer immensity of the sprawling stone edifice, with its enormous flanking wings and its three vast courtyards, must have made an impression on her, though she never mentioned her reactions to it or her opinions of it in letters to her mother. Far larger and grander than Schönbrunn, Versailles was also much older, and on the day Antoinette first glimpsed it, the palace looked shabby and unkempt. The fountains were broken, their basins dirty and full of debris. The canal too was dirty and mud-clogged. In the gardens, many statues had fallen over, and negligent servants and gardeners let them lie.

Dark and overcast though the morning was, no lanterns had been hung along the streets leading to the palace, and as Antoinette's carriage passed through the iron gates, there was no band waiting to serenade her with fife and drum, no welcoming escort of Swiss Guards or other soldiery. People milled about in the forecourt as always, and stared at the carriage as it rolled into the courtyard and stopped at the entrance to the Queen's staircase.

This being the dauphin and dauphine's wedding day, over five thousand people had been given invitations to the ceremony, and many thousands more, curious spectators who knew that this was to be a day of extraordinary pageantry, fought so persistently to get into the Hall of Mirrors that the guardsmen charged with keeping order were unable to prevent them from gaining entry. Tiers of seats had been erected in the long mirror-lined corridor especially for this day's events, but since early morning these had been filled by courtiers in their most resplendent dress, and the rest of the spectators were forced to find what space they could, flattening themselves against the temporary balustrades and pressing uncomfortably against the official guests. The press of people grew worse when thundershowers began; now everyone who had been outside in the courtyards came inside, their clothes dripping and their boots muddy.

At one o'clock the wedding procession began to wind its way from the State Apartments toward the chapel. The Grand Master of the Ceremonies led the way, with Louis and Antoinette, hand in hand, immediately behind him. Antoinette was smiling and poised. Her small figure glittered with diamonds. An English wedding guest, the Duchess of Northumberland, was surprised at how small she was, and thought that she looked no older than twelve. The Duchess was also critical of her wedding dress. "The corps of her robe was too small," she wrote in her diary, "and left quite a broad stripe of lacing and shift quite visible, which had a bad effect between two broader stripes of diamonds. She really had quite a load of jewels."[6] The dauphin, who was as usual terribly nervous, was dressed in a suit of dazzling cloth of gold covered with jewels and orders. According to the Duchess, Louis was timid and trembling, worn out with anxiety.

Behind the bride and groom came pages carrying Antoinette's long brocade train, then the Comtesse de Noailles, her titular guardian, then the royal princes—the corpulent Duc d'Orléans, the neurasthenic Duc de Penthièvre, the Princes of Condé and

Conti, the Ducs de Chartres and Bourbon, and Comte de la Marche—and the dauphin's two younger brothers, the Comtes de Provence and Artois. After them walked the King, looking bemused, then came his ten-year-old granddaughter Princess Clothilde and his three unmarried daughters Adelaide, Victoire and Sophie, the dauphin's aunts. A crowd of bejeweled court ladies brought up the rear of the procession, which paraded the entire two hundred and fifty foot length of the Hall of Mirrors, beneath the massive chandeliers, until it reached the entrance to the palace chapel. Here, amid the baroque magnificence of white marble and gilding, another audience of spectators awaited.

A drum and flute fanfare announced the entrance of the royals into the chapel, and all the assembled guests rose as Louis and Antoinette made their way to the altar and knelt on cushions to repeat their vows before the Archbishop of Rheims. The dauphin blushed beet-red when he placed the ring on Antoinette's finger, and fidgeted nervously throughout the nuptial Mass. Afterwards the couple signed the register, completing the formalities. Antoinette was now dauphine.

She was dauphine—and as such she was feared, hated and resented.

It was the paradox of Antoinette's position that, despite her extreme youth and inexperience, she was, in theory at least, the most powerful woman at court, and at a court where the men of the royal family were weak and apathetic, this made her doubly powerful. Her arrival upset the status quo—which had already been seriously upset the year before when the King had his buxom, exuberantly coarse mistress, Madame Du Barry, presented at court. Du Barry controlled the King, and was doing her best to gain control of the court through him. Antoinette, however, was capable of controlling the dauphin, who might become King at any time. Hers was the rising power, and the experienced courtiers, hardened by years of intrigue, presumed that she would lose no time in building and consolidating her faction. They were suspicious of her, and guarded in her presence; behind her back, many of them did all they could to work against her.

Under other circumstances the backstairs rivalries within the royal household would have had limited significance. But France in 1770 was a nation in disorder, with a vacuum at the center of power. According to the Austrian envoy in Paris, Count Mercy, who was extremely well informed, a "horrible confusion" reigned at Versailles, and the palace was "the abode of treachery, hatred and revenge." "Everything is worked by intrigues and inspired by personal ambitions," he wrote, "and it seems as if the world had renounced even the semblance of uprightness."[7] With no strong authority to provide moral ballast and give direction to affairs, the government became nothing but a sordid scramble for influence, with the rewards going to the greediest and most ruthless of the scramblers. And with the prospective ruler showing even less capability than the feeble Louis XV, seasoned observers such as Mercy shuddered to contemplate the future.

"This monarchy," Mercy had written a year before Antoinette came to France, "is so decadent that it would not be regenerated except by a successor of the present monarch who, by his qualities and talents, would repair the extreme disorder of the kingdom." But the dauphin lacked the requisite qualities and talents. "This prince, by his face and his talk," Mercy thought, "shows only an extremely limited intelligence, much clumsiness."[8]

It would be up to Antoinette, many thought, to shore up what rudimentary abilities her husband had, to civilize him, if possible, and in time to make a king of him. To do all this would have strained the capabilities of a mature, sophisticated woman. To expect it of a fourteen-year-old naïf was futility itself.

On the afternoon of her wedding day, Antoinette was installed in the apartments allotted to her, a smallish but exquisitely appointed suite of rooms with painted walls decorated with carved reliefs. Apart from her bedroom and bathroom, there were two sitting-rooms, a large library, two antechambers, and a private oratory. Here she received the officers of her household, each of whom in turn took an oath of fidelity to serve her. Her lady of honor, gentleman of honor, almoner, intendants, maître d'hôtel, first equerry and controllers-general all knelt to repeat their oaths, having themselves received the oaths of their dozens of underlings. There were nearly two hundred of these concerned with the preparation and serving of her food alone, from cooks to butlers to wine-bearers to the children of the scullery. A further hundred or so servants and officers looked after her every personal need, from the wig-maker who did double service as bath attendant to the two apothecaries to the nineteen valets de chambre. Antoinette had twelve aristocratic ladies to attend her and keep her company and fourteen waiting women to serve her, two preachers, five chaplains and an almoner (all of whom made Abbé Vermond superfluous), six equerries, nine ushers, two doctors and four surgeons, a clock-maker, a tapestry-maker, eighteen lackeys, a fencing master and two muleteers.

The afternoon was well advanced before the procession of servants and officials ended and the last of them bowed his way out of the dauphine's apartments. But the events of this exhausting day were far from over. The King, his grandson and granddaughter again presented themselves to public view, this time playing cavagnole at a table in the royal apartments while six thousand invited guests took advantage of the privilege of watching them. At the appropriate hour a wedding supper was held in the newly completed opera house, an exquisitely ornate theater whose balconies and wall moldings had been carved, painted and gilded by teams of fine artists. Here the royal family supped, while rain drummed down on the roof and thunder rolled outside. The guests, who had hoped to see a grand fireworks display later in the evening, were disappointed when the rain forced cancellation of the spectacle, and left feeling cheated. Still, they stayed long enough to watch the final event of the wedding day, the blessing of the nuptial bed by the Archbishop of Rheims. The King gave his grandson his nightshirt, and the Duchesse de Chartres helped Antoinette prepare for bed. There was no romance whatever and much embarrassment, at least for the pitifully gauche Louis, when the two young people climbed into bed and the courtiers took their leave.

Left alone with her new husband, half curious, half dreading what was to come, Antoinette waited. And waited. The bulky form beside her in the bed was still. Louis was asleep.

Night after night, over the following weeks, the same puzzling ritual was repeated. Antoinette retired, Louis came to her bed, lay down, and went to sleep without touching her. Though without experience, Antoinette was not naive about sex. Her mother had instructed her on what to expect as a wife, and she knew what her sister Caroline had been through on her anguished wedding night and in the first days of her nightmarish marriage. Something was very wrong, and it was soon a matter for common gossip. The pages and chamberwomen searched the dauphine's bedclothes for telltale signs that she was no longer a virgin; finding none, they passed this information along to whoever would pay for it—and many were eager to do so.

Among them was Mercy, Maria Theresa's worldly envoy who had promised the Empress that he would keep her informed of everything that went on at the court of Louis XV. Mercy was quick to report the odd state of affairs, sending his dispatch via a special courier who took the news to Vienna in the utmost secrecy. Mercy's private correspondence with the Empress, which began in the days following Antoinette's marriage, was a marvel in its time. A securely secret two-way exchange of information and instructions between a diplomat and his sovereign in a distant city was all but unheard-of in an era when spies were everywhere and all posted letters were routinely intercepted and opened. Louis XV and his ministers had an army of informers scattered throughout Europe whose sole purpose was to subvert clandestine communication. Yet the young Austrian and Hungarian couriers recruited to carry Mercy's lengthy despatches to Maria Theresa and hers back to him managed to outwit and elude these informers for years, making it possible for the Count to commit to paper candid observations he would never have dared advance otherwise, and allowing Maria Theresa to feel that, through her representative at Versailles, she was at her daughter's side.[9]

Mercy's earliest reports were grim. The dauphin, he wrote, had "relapsed into the disagreeable state to which he is inclined by nature. Since their first interview he has not shown the slightest sign of predilection for the dauphine, or anxiety to please her—in public or private." Maria Theresa read between the lines. Her awkward, eccentric son-in-law, whom people said was "very much like a eunuch in his figure," was possibly a eunuch in fact. Her daughter might never produce an heir to the French throne.

The Empress, her envoy, King Louis and his ministers—all were urgently concerned about the situation. The royal doctors were consulted. Nothing was wrong, they said. The dauphin was not yet quite sixteen years old. He was not yet mature. In time, with the right food and sufficient exercise, he would be able to perform perfectly well as a husband.

In fact, the unfortunate Louis had phimosis, a deformation of the foreskin that made it painful to retract and therefore prevented erection. He was not impotent; it was merely that the attempt to make love cost him excruciating agony. Even mild sexual arousal caused him pain, and triggered fear of more pain. The thought of submitting his tender flesh to the cruel knives of the court doctors caused Louis the most pain of all. He may or may not have had an adolescent boy's gargantuan sexual appetite—though one could argue that he did, and that he sublimated it by stuffing himself with food, so often and so voraciously that he frequently made himself ill—but it is clear that in order to avoid pain he chose to deny himself gratification. And given his blushing timidity, it is easy to understand his running away from the problem entirely rather than confronting it and seeking a cure.

Louis continued to stay away, and to ignore Antoinette on those occasions when court etiquette forced them together. They were rarely alone together, however. They were always surrounded by servitors, courtiers, officials, and the everpresent onlookers who thronged the corridors of the palace, eager for the spectacle of royalty, eager to observe the latest nuance in the dauphin's behavior toward the dauphine. The unconsummated royal marriage was the universal subject of conversation. Was Louis impotent? Did he find Antoinette distasteful? Without her silks and diamonds, shorn of her petticoats and her high-piled hair, was she much less enticing than she appeared to be?

Both young people must have been made uneasy by all the gossip, the staring and whispered comments and sly smiles—not to mention the spying and talebearing. Antoinette maintained her outward poise and self-confidence, but in unguarded moments she appeared grave and thoughtful. "Under her assurance I see moments of sadness," her confessor, Abbé Vermond, wrote to Kaunitz, adding, "My heart is wrung by all this."[10]

But by July there were signs of change. Antoinette's warmth and good-humored acceptance of her awkward young husband had begun to win his trust. He was beginning to speak to her, to seek her out, even to confide in her. He beckoned to her as she passed through his apartments and indicated that he wanted to talk, then drew her away to her own rooms where he could be free of his importunate gentlemen-in-waiting and his tutor, the Duc de la Vauguyon, who made it his business to overhear everything the dauphin said. (On one occasion Louis and Antoinette discovered the eavesdropping Duke, hiding behind a door, "stuck like a piling on a fence, unable to back away" when the door was opened.[11])

One Sunday Louis broached the subject everyone else had been talking about since their wedding night. According to Mercy, who wrote to Maria Theresa a week later, Louis told Antoinette that he was perfectly acquainted with the sexual side of marriage, but had decided to postpone intimacy until an appropriate time—presumably his sixteenth birthday, which would be on August 23. On that day the court would be at Compiègne, and there, he assured his wife, he would live with her "with all the intimacy required by their union."[12]

Delighted, Antoinette wrote her mother that her "dear husband" had "changed much and all for the best." "The dauphine is winning her way to the dauphin," Mercy told the Empress, "and is so gay and so graceful that the somber, reserved young prince, impenetrable to all, has yielded to her charm."[13] Louis liked being with her, she brought out his softer side. When they were together he "showed her a kind of good will and sweetness which he was not thought to possess." He was even submissive. According to Mercy, Antoinette "ruled him for all the little things and he never contradicted her."[14]

The savage, it seemed, had been tamed. But he was not yet ready to be a husband. August 23 came and went, and Antoinette was still a virgin. If Louis had hoped to overcome his phimosis, he lost his nerve. Once again the gossipmongers made their rounds, and the dauphin, mortified, rode violently off to hunt in the forest and returned hours later, reeling and staggering, so exhausted that he could barely stand.

6

Antoinette had been in France only three months, and already she sensed that the court had turned against her. She was wife in name only to the dauphin, her governess, the Comtesse de Noailles, disapproved of her and the King, though undeniably charmed with her, was too preoccupied with his favorite Madame Du Barry to pay her much attention.

She had not been prepared for Madame Du Barry. Her mother had not warned her about Louis XV's buxom, blue-eyed mistress or her increasing dominance over the King.

Born illegitimate, the daughter of a poor dressmaker who turned to prostitution to supplement her meager earnings, Jeanne Bécu followed her mother's example and eventually came to the King's notice as the mistress of one Jean Du Barry. Pretty without being a great beauty or even particularly striking, she was nonetheless appealingly sensual, with a look of frank invitation in her widely spaced blue eyes. King Louis was so utterly captivated that he envisioned bringing Jeanne to court—not as just another girl in his private brothel, the Parc-aux-Cerfs, but as his official mistress. To this end he arranged for her to marry Jean Du Barry's brother Guillaume, who was Comte Du Barry. In her new status as Comtesse Du Barry Jeanne was formally presented at court in April of 1769, dazzling even the jaded courtiers of Versailles in robes garlanded with bouquets of diamonds. The King had showered her with glittering gems, and she wore them everywhere, even on the heels of her shoes.

On the day of her presentation her beauty too was dazzling, though her enemies did their best to disparage it. "Her bloom is entirely gone off," wrote an English duchess visiting Versailles, and "she has a kind of artificial smirk which also savors strongly of her old trade." The wanton look in her eyes, her loud voice and vulgar manner marked her as a former woman of the streets.

"Her behavior [is] extremely free and cheerful," the Duchess wrote, "her disposition benevolent, good natured, generous and charitable, but her temper I imagine [is] as warm as her constitution, her language very rough and indelicate when she is angry."[1] Not all the diamonds in the world could make a common prostitute into a lady of refinement. Still, the King was captivated, and that was what mattered. Others might sneer at Madame Du Barry's affected lisp, or raise their eyebrows when she swore at her chamberwomen, or criticize her for failing to powder her hair and for preferring simple gowns to the *grande toilette* always worn in the royal presence, but King Louis would not hear a word against her. "She has given me delights I did not know existed," he confided to the Maréchal de Richelieu, like himself an aging libertine, and Richelieu had no doubt what his master meant.

Comtesse Du Barry's rise to wealth had been swift and spectacular. The King lost no time in giving her her own small chateau at Louveciennes, an exquisite miniature palace with marble walls, painted ceilings and a large white-and-gold dining room where crystal chandeliers sparkled in the firelight. The luxurious decorations were extravagantly expensive, rich tapestries, fine china and glass, bronzes, furniture upholstered in embroidered satin. Visitors to Louveciennes marveled at how everything, even the handles of the doors, was made of the finest materials the King's treasury could buy. And they did not fail to remark on the large staff of servants, each dressed in a costly livery of crimson or pale yellow, that waited on the royal mistress. At Versailles too the Countess had a large establishment, its most conspicuous member her exotic Bengali page Zamor, who strutted along behind her in his pink velvet jacket and trousers, a white turban wound around his head, a small sword at his side.

By the time Antoinette arrived at Versailles, Madame Du Barry was a power to be reckoned with, and she did not welcome her young Hapsburg rival. When told of Antoinette's good looks she was spiteful. "I see nothing attractive in red hair, thick lips, sandy complexion, and eyes without eyelashes," she said. "Had she who is thus beautiful not sprung from the House of Austria, such attractions would never have been the subject of admiration." Antoinette returned the insult with good measure. She resented having to sit at the same table with her grandfather's vulgar mistress at his private suppers, and being forced to spend time with her at the gaming tables. "She is the most stupid and impertinent creature imaginable," Antoinette wrote to her mother. "She played cards every night with us at Marly; twice she sat next to me, but she did not speak to me and I did not try to open a conversation with her. But, when it was necessary, I did speak to her."[2]

The rivalry between the two women was played out through their subordinates. A member of Antoinette's entourage, the Comtesse de Grammont, insulted the Comtesse Du Barry one evening by refusing to make room for her at a theatrical performance. Madame Du Barry went to the King and had the Countess sent away from court. Antoinette, on the advice of Mercy, went to her grandfather and gently asserted her prerogative. The Countess ought not to have been sent away until she, Antoinette, had been informed of his displeasure. The King, embarrassed by the contretemps and caught between his doting affection for his mistress and his fondness for his granddaughter, blamed the minister of his household, the Duc de la Vrillière, and eventually permitted the Countess to return.[3]

On the surface a petty exchange of affronts involving a minor personage, in reality the incident had a deeper political dimension. Through her sister-in-law, Madame de Grammont was a relative of the King's chief minister Choiseul, and Choiseul was the sworn enemy of Madame Du Barry. He was also the principal architect of the dauphin's Hapsburg marriage—a marriage that had so far been fruitless and that many said was no marriage at all. Antoinette's failure as a wife was Choiseul's failure, just as his enmity with the King's mistress was hers.

Choiseul had urged the alliance of France with Austria, in order to prevent Maria Theresa from joining forces with Russia and her old nemesis Frederick the Great in Prussia. Such an alliance would threaten the diplomatic stability of the continent and might well lead to war. Yet despite Choiseul's efforts, Austria and Prussia were moving closer together (Maria Theresa's eldest son Joseph, who had perversely taken Frederick as his hero, had begun meeting with him in person to plot the eventual partition of Poland), and Austrian-Russian ties were also becoming strengthened. Choiseul's policies had not been successful, and Madame Du Barry had become the focus of a faction working to undermine him—and to turn the King against the dauphine he had brought to France.

But Choiseul had his supporters, and these, naturally enough, attached themselves to Antoinette. Here domestic politics had a role to play, for within the royal family itself there were factions, rivalries and grievances. Beyond the rivalry between the dauphin and his younger brothers, particularly the precocious fifteen-year-old Stanislaus Xavier, Count of Provence who was as arrogant, witty and sophisticated as the dauphin was shy, gauche and untutored, there was a formidable rift between King Louis and his three unmarried daughters who lived at court. (His fourth unmarried daughter, Louise, had recently become a nun at Saint-Denis—some said in order to pray for her father's sins.) All three women were in their late thirties, but they impressed visitors as much older, and the novelist Horace Walpole's contemporary description of them made them into figures of farce.

"The four Mesdames," Walpole wrote, "who are clumsy, plump old wenches with a bad likeness to their father, stand in a row with black cloaks and knitting bags, looking good humored, not knowing what to say and wriggling as if they wanted to make water." Walpole had a tendency to turn people into grotesques; another observer thought the King's daughters were "kindly old women." But in his malice King Louis referred to his daughters Adelaide, Victoire and Sophie as "Rag," "Piggy" and "Snip," and mocked them without mercy. Antoinette, isolated and homesick, gravitated toward her aunts and they in turn, seeing in her an avenue of influence that could be used against their father and his upstart mistress, drew her into their circle.

Of the three, stout Victoire was the most agreeable, though she suffered terribly from fits of nerves, brought on by childhood terrors; as a little girl she had been shut up in the dark vault of the Abbey of Fontévrault, where the nuns were buried, and forced to do penance. A madman was shut up nearby, and his shriekings and ravings, added to the imagined horrors of the tomb, must have left the poor child marked for life.[4] Victoire was nonetheless "good, sweet-tempered and affable," according to Madame Campan, the lively chronicler of the French court whose first position was as reader to the King's daughters. Benevolent and smiling, Victoire loved good food and the comfort of a soft couch by the fireside. She was particularly welcoming to Antoinette.

Sophie was more hard-bitten, a repellently ugly woman whose air of hauteur masked a deep diffidence. She read a good deal, but always alone; according to Madame Campan, "the presence of a reader would have disconcerted her very much." People invariably disconcerted Sophie, and she always walked quickly through the crowded corridors of the palace in order to avoid contact with them. When there was a storm, however, her fear got the better of her shyness, and she ran to embrace anyone within reach, so great was her dread of thunder and lightning.

The third sister, Adelaide, was made of sterner stuff. She was, in fact, the most forceful personality of the three and the most aggressive. Even as a child she had dominated her masters, stamping her foot and insisting on her way with a stubbornness that became more pronounced as she got older. She had been outspokenly opposed to the Austrian marriage, and her opposition did not end when she met the charming Antoinette. According to Madame Campan, Adelaide was "wearied with the somewhat obtrusive gaiety of the dauphine." But, wearied or not, Adelaide was a politician, and as a politician she saw that Antoinette would be useful to her. She swallowed her distaste and cultivated the dauphine— though in small ways she maintained a tacit rivalry with her. After Queen Marie Leczinska's death, the evening card parties were moved to Adelaide's apartments, and when Antoinette took over as hostess of these gatherings, Adelaide refused to attend them, continuing to entertain a few stalwarts in her own rooms, in private.

With Adelaide taking the lead, the dauphin's aunts saw to it that Antoinette came under their influence. Mercy saw the danger of this, and warned the Empress. "Mesdames love to mix themselves up in little intrigues," he wrote, "and it will be dangerous if they drag in the dauphine." They hated Madame Du Barry, and were constantly criticizing her and watching for opportunities to slight her and diminish her influence. In this they worked through Antoinette, playing on her inbred aversion to the very idea of a royal mistress (and her distasteful memories of her father's mistress Princess Auersperg), knowing that, given her free and critical tongue, everything they told her about Madame Du Barry would be repeated.

Antoinette, for her part, needed no prompting. She disliked her grandfather's mistress personally. Though capable of boundless kindness and generosity to menial servants and other commoners—kindness she showed repeatedly during her early months at the French court—she did not look kindly on people of low birth and no breeding who attempted to lord it over their betters. She, Archduchess Antoinette, was the daughter of an Empress, Jeanne Bécu was the daughter of a prostitute from Vaucouleurs. One day she would be Queen of France, and when that day came, if not before, the Comtesse Du Barry would suddenly find herself bereft of friends, influence and income.

Antoinette spent a good portion of her time each day in the company of her aunts. She got up at nine-thirty or ten every morning, and having dressed and said her prayers, and had her breakfast, went to her aunts' apartments where the King also was often to be found. She stayed there until eleven, when she had a daily appointment with her hairdresser. With her hair suitably arranged she carried out the public ceremony of washing her hands and applying her rouge, while interested spectators looked on, and after that her women dressed her. At noon it was time for Mass, which she attended in company with the King, the dauphin and her aunts. After Mass Antoinette and Louis dined together—once again in public, but very quickly, and then they went to his apartments; if he was occupied (and he nearly always was occupied, usually with the hunt) then she went to her own rooms where, truth to tell, she had all too little to do, though she made fitful efforts to read or to work at her embroidery.

"I am making a vest for the King," she told her mother. "It is going badly, but I hope that by the grace of God it will be finished in a few years' time." Nothing more was ever heard of the vest.

At three o'clock she went to her aunts' apartments again, where the King usually joined them, then at four she returned to her own rooms where her confessor, Abbé Vermond, came to her. At five she had a lesson with the music master or the singing teacher. At six-thirty it was back to Adelaide, Victoire and Sophie, with the dauphin in tow. From seven to nine she presided over the card tables, unless the weather was fine, in which case she went for a walk. Supper was at nine, and when the King was not present (he often took his supper with Madame Du Barry and a small informal company) the aunts ate with Antoinette and the dauphin. When he was present Antoinette and Louis ate in the aunts' apartments, where the King joined them a little before eleven. Antoinette got sleepy waiting for him, and took a nap on a large sofa.[5]

It was a long day, made longer by the tedious public rituals and the lack of variety or stimulation. For company Antoinette had her self-conscious husband, who was particularly uncomfortable in his grandfather's presence, the King, who indulged her but teased and tormented the aunts and the dauphin when he was not staring vacantly into the distance, and Adelaide, Victoire, and Sophie, who gossiped about Madame Du Barry and goaded Antoinette to insult her. They also probed for information of a very personal kind. Had the dauphin come to her bedroom the previous night? Adelaide had had a talk with him, exhorting him to be courageous and play the part of a man. Had this talk made any difference? Upset and anxious, Antoinette had to admit that he had not come to her bed, despite repeated promises to do so. Not even King Louis's intervention had had an impact.

"I find my wife charming," the dauphin had informed his grandfather with newfound dignity. "I love her, but I still need a little time to overcome my timidity."

The months passed, the year was ending. Was it possible the marriage would never be consummated? There were whispers about a divorce—or rather, an annulment, easy enough to arrange under church law when the married pair were still virgins. The courtiers were giving up on the impossible dauphin and looking to his brother Provence to fulfill the hopes of the dynasty.

Provence was betrothed, his wedding would take place in May of 1771. The bride-to-be, Marie-Josephine of Savoy, might produce an heir to the throne if Antoinette could not. And Provence would in any case make a much more presentable king than the dauphin ever would.

Then just before Christmas Antoinette lost her most powerful political ally. Choiseul was sent away from court, deprived of his ministerial responsibilities and exiled to his estate. Madame Du Barry and her party had triumphed, her ally the Duc d'Aiguillon replaced Choiseul as Minister of Foreign Affairs. Equally significant was the fact that the Comtesse Du Barry now moved into new quarters at the palace—a sumptuously decorated suite of rooms linked by a staircase to the King's. These rooms became the informal center of government, the place where the King met with his ministers and ambassadors and where much of the behind-the-scenes work of the court was done. Here Madame Du Barry presided, dressed like a queen and surrounded by regal splendor. And the King, it seemed, was rarely out of her sight, wanting her beside him, sitting on the arm of his chair, while he read letters or discussed business. He even permitted her to sit in on meetings of the royal council, where, Madame Campan wrote, she behaved like a bored child and distracted him with her silliness.[6]

It was a dangerous situation, one designed to test Antoinette's astuteness. Distasteful though it was, she would have to come to terms with Madame Du Barry's ambiguous but powerful position. The King wished it; she was the King's subject as well as his daughter-in-law.

King Louis summoned Mercy to his mistress's drawing room to make his will known.

"Until now you have been the Empress's ambassador," Louis said with unctuous politeness. "I beg you to be mine, at least for a short time. I love Madame la dauphine dearly. I think she is charming, but as she is lively and has a husband who is not in a position to guide her she cannot possibly avoid the traps set for her by intrigue."

He did not mention Adelaide, but the implication was clear. Antoinette, he insisted, must treat every person presented at court with courtesy. Madame Du Barry was among those who had been presented. Therefore Antoinette owed her some degree of acknowledgment, however slight. If she would speak to her once, that would be sufficient. But speak to her she must.

Far more was at stake than Antoinette's pride or Madame Du Barry's ego. The fall of Choiseul, coupled with Austria's designs on Poland—France's sometime ally—were bound to affect French foreign policy. Antoinette too was headed for a fall, unless she moved adroitly. Vermond cautioned her to affect grief for Choiseul while not showing anger or mortification at Madame Du Barry's triumph. But Vermond's position too was imperiled by the shifting of power at court; Maria Theresa was certain he would be dismissed, and without him Mercy would have no direct conduit to Antoinette. She would be more isolated than ever, vulnerable to the clever intriguers who surrounded her.

And it was clear, at least to Mercy, that she could not trust her aunts. Once a vehement supporter of Choiseul, Adelaide became one of the first to turn against him the moment he was out of favor. And Mercy noticed that as the new year began, all three of the King's daughters were trimming their sails to the prevailing winds, doing small favors for Madame Du Barry, holding back their caustic comments about her, all the while urging Antoinette to snub her and judge her harshly. They were using Antoinette, Mercy thought, "as an instrument of a hatred they dared not avow."[7]

Caught in a web of intrigue, yoked to a boorish, pathetically incapable husband, still a child yet burdened with intractable adult problems, Antoinette struggled to maintain her equilibrium. The "somewhat obtrusive gaiety" that wearied Adelaide was partly a pose, a smokescreen designed to obscure anxiety. But the anxiety was at times all too evident. Antoinette fretted when her mother's letters were delayed, and when they finally arrived she dropped whatever she was doing and jumped out of her chair, exclaiming *"Gott sei dank!"*—"Thank God!"—as if her survival depended on the packet from Vienna.

"I swear to you," she wrote to the Empress in July of 1770, "that I have not received one of your dear letters without having the tears come to my eyes. . . . I ardently wish I could see my dear and very dear family for an instant at least."[8] The warm family life of Vienna was gone forever, to be replaced by the chill of constant suspicion and scheming. There were no safe havens at Versailles, no places where she could go to be free from prying eyes and whispers. The King, Madame Du Barry, Mercy had spies in every dark corner, watching and listening; every keyhole seemed to invite surveillance.

Antoinette became particularly anxious about locks and keys during her early months at Versailles. She didn't feel safe in her own apartments, and worried that her enemies had skeleton keys that they used to enter and leave at will, and also to open her desk and read her letters. She confessed to Vermond that she imagined her own keys were taken from her pockets at night—and without them, especially the one Adelaide had given her so that she could come and go at will to Adelaide's own rooms, she would be a prisoner of her entourage. Indeed even with her keys she had no true freedom, bound as she was by etiquette, routine and the confines of the great labyrinthine palace, whose corridors, never truly bright with welcome, now began to seem forbiddingly dim.

7

I N Antoinette's large, chilly rooms at Versailles, disorder
reigned. The huge guardroom at the top of the wide marble staircase was cluttered with weaponry and the accoutrements of the guards, who whiled away their idleness
gambling and telling stories while all around them tradesmen
waited for a chance to show the dauphine their wares and messengers and visitors to court milled expectantly. In the antechamber,
where her attendants waited for their turn to serve her and where
the "Great Table" was laid for the midday dinner, there were
holes in the tapestries where Antoinette's two curly-tailed pug
dogs had scratched at them, and the parquet floor was muddy
with paw prints. "Madame la dauphine loves dogs very much,"
Mercy told Maria Theresa, adding that she had requested that
another dog be sent from Vienna, a tawny pug with a black nose.
Mercy was willing to endorse the request, though he noted that
the two dogs she already had were "extremely unclean."[1]

The state chamber too, with its huge bed, bore the marks of
the dogs, but their depredations were greatest in the private
rooms, where Antoinette let them romp freely on the damask-
upholstered furniture and chew at the gilded chair legs. They
relieved themselves wherever and whenever they liked, as Antoinette did not bother to prevent them and none of the servants
was assigned the specific duty of looking after the royal pets.
Adding to the chaos were two little children, one four years old
and the other five. One was the son of the dauphin's chief valet,
Thierry, and the other belonged to Antoinette's first bedchamber

woman. The children were always underfoot, running and chasing each other, playing with the dogs and creating a cheerful mayhem, especially when Antoinette was supposed to be receiving instruction from Vermond or having a singing lesson or embroidering the King's vest.

Madame de Noailles, "Madame Etiquette" as Antoinette called her, was dismayed at the chaos. She had been deeply offended when her mistress, in an attempt to cut through the time-consuming procedures required to make an appointment to her household, sent Madame Thierry to her to say that the dauphine wanted her in her service. Injured and furious, Madame de Noailles had gone to Antoinette in a huff and announced that she had no intention of taking orders from a chambermaid—especially one who had not yet been formally appointed to her position. It had taken all of Mercy's diplomacy to soothe the injured pride of Madame de Noailles—who was on the point of resigning—and restore some semblance of harmony. Mercy discovered that, as usual, Adelaide was the chief troublemaker; she had told Antoinette to circumvent protocol by sending Madame Thierry directly to Madame de Noailles—knowing full well what the issue would be. Mercy could not reprimand Adelaide, he could only try to warn Antoinette about the perils of listening to her advice.[2]

Madame Etiquette was dismayed by Antoinette's dirty apartments, and by the "very noisy, dirty and plaguy" children who "spoiled her clothes, tore and broke the furniture, and put the whole of her apartments into the utmost disorder." The dauphine, it appeared, could not manage to keep clean or tidy. She was forever coming in wet and bedraggled from following the hunt in her coach, she neglected her coiffure, she paid so little attention to her grooming and her clothes that a visiting Austrian noblewoman was shocked, and made a severe report to Maria Theresa. "She told me," the Empress complained to Antoinette afterwards, "that you take poor care of yourself, even when it comes to cleaning your teeth; this is a key point, as is your figure, which she found worsened. . . . she added that you were badly dressed and that she dared tell your ladies so."[3]

The rigid whalebone corset then in fashion was a particular cause of grief to Madame de Noailles. Antoinette refused point blank to wear it; Madame de Noailles complained; Mercy heard of the problem and informed Maria Theresa, who wrote at once to her daughter offering to have some corsets made for her in Vienna, adding tactfully that "the ones they make in Paris are too stiff."[4] In truth any corset would have been too stiff for the sort of free-wheeling, rough-and-tumble life Antoinette preferred to lead, but after a few months of resistance she gave up and let her ladies strap her into the whalebone once again.

With her cheerful disregard for the exacting usages of the court Antoinette was bound to clash with her punctilious, scrupulous *dame d'honneur*. Of the Comtesse de Noailles Madame Campan wrote, "She had no outward attraction. Her deportment was stiff, her look severe; she knew her etiquette backwards." Madame Campan had occasion to evoke that severity one day when she was in Antoinette's apartments and a visitor newly presented at court was being received. "Everything was in order, or so, at least, I supposed," she recalled. "Suddenly I noticed the eyes of the Comtesse de Noailles fixed upon mine. She made a little sign with her head. Her eyebrows were raised, lowered and raised again. Then she began to make little gestures with her hand. I had no doubt from this dumb show that something was not *comme il faut*."

Puzzled, Madame Campan looked around to see if she could tell what was wrong. Meanwhile the *dame d'honneur* was gesturing more pointedly. Then Antoinette noticed what was going on and smiled at Madame Campan, who worked her way to her side. It seems the latter had neglected to loosen the hanging flaps, or pinners, of her headdress. "Undo your pinners," Antoinette whispered, "or the Countess will die of it!" The flaps were loosened, and the Countess's agitation subsided.[5]

In this instance Antoinette handled Madame de Noailles's irritating scrupulosity with grace and good humor, but at times the exigencies of the Countess must have been very hard to bear. The dauphine was "perpetually tormented" by her *dame d'honneur*, who dogged her steps and corrected her a thousand times a day, telling her how she ought to have greeted one person one way, and another in another way, criticizing her speech, giving her disapproving looks and shaking her head in despair.[6]

It was no wonder Antoinette broke the tension by making fun of the sober, unsmiling people around her. Even when dining with the dauphin, in a room full of courtiers and spectators, she burst out laughing, disconcerting those who were watching her.

Mercy often saw her "whispering in the ears of the young ladies" and then "laughing with them." "She sometimes jokes about the people who appear to her ridiculous," he wrote, adding, "she knows how to use wit and sarcasm so as to make her comments very biting." It made no difference that she was "of a cheerful nature and without any bad intention"; the remarks stung just the same.[7] And when she made "satirical and hateful" remarks about Madame Du Barry, the King was annoyed—though he never told her so directly, always through intermediaries.[8]

The King was preoccupied just then by far weightier matters than the dauphine's satirical tongue. The country faced a fiscal crisis. The treasury was bankrupt, more revenues needed to be raised. In fact the entire system of taxation cried out for reform. Yet reform was impossible as long as the King's authority was blocked by the local parlements, law courts where the nobility claimed to have, in effect, a veto power over royal edicts. In the political turmoil of December 1770, Choiseul had lost his offices because he supported the parlements, while the Controller-General, the Abbé Terray, opposed them.

The French parlements were not, like the English Parliament, representative bodies with weighty political power; they were archaic institutions where the nobility asserted its claims to be independent of royal authority. Not every French province had a parlement. There were thirteen parlements, of which the parlement of Paris was the largest and most dominant. But every parlement claimed to be the supreme court of appeal for its own region, with the power to resist the imposition of royal law. In the area of taxation the parlements were stubborn and intransigent: whenever the King's ministers attempted to remove the nobles' tax exemptions the parlements refused to function. Legal proceedings came to a halt, and the King, though he took punitive measures, could not enforce his edicts.

The ambiguous role of the parlements in the French political system was a measure of its inherent internal strains. On the one hand, the parlements were self-serving bodies, jealously guarding the prerogatives of their noble members. On the other hand, in the rising climate of eighteenth-century liberal thought, the noble opposition to the King could and did take on the character of opposition to despotism, opposition rooted in a tradition of liberty which, its proponents insisted, stretched back to the time of

Charlemagne and beyond. Thus the struggle of the parlements and the crown was often presented as the struggle of the French people against their tyrannical ruler, with the nobles as the people's champions. Without such bodies as the parlements to check him, Montesquieu wrote, the King would be an autocrat; the parlements were a bastion of popular rights.

Ideology aside, the monarchy and the nobility, through the parlements, were simply engaged in a power struggle, with the nobles seeking an ever greater share of royal authority. The parlements were indeed a bastion—but a bastion of noble privilege, and one that, in the circumstances of the early 1770's, stood in the way of greatly needed financial reform.

With Choiseul gone, the Abbé Terray and the Chancellor Maupeou, a ruthless and able lawyer, persuaded the King that the parlements had to be suppressed if reform was to proceed. At a stroke the old legal system was swept away and new law courts were set up. Terray began to attack the problem of debt and arranged forced loans. Slowly there was improvement—but at the cost of an enormous outcry from the noble establishment, men of letters and the Parisian middle class.

The appointment of D'Aiguillon to replace Choiseul was an added insult to the parlementaries, for he had fallen afoul of the parlements of Brittany and Paris and in the resultant political clash had become a symbol of the monarchy's determination to crush the independence of the nobles. There were repercussions within the royal family itself, where the Princes of Condé and Conti and the Duc d'Orléans went into exile from court over the suppression of the parlement of Paris. (King Louis referred to the Prince de Conti as "my cousin, the wrangling attorney.")

But if the King roused himself to take vigorous action against the nobles who opposed him, his general health was visibly weakening, and the question of the succession loomed.

Provence was married in May of 1771, and he boasted pointedly to the dauphin that he was "four times happy" on his wedding night. His bride, Marie Josephine of Savoy, also enjoyed herself "marvelously," Provence said, and the courtiers settled back to watch for signs that she was pregnant. The new Comtesse de Provence could not have attracted attention for any other reason; she was squat and swarthy, with heavy black eyebrows and an unfeminine thicket of hair on her upper lip that unkind people called a mustache. Her coarse red complexion was not admired, and she very often neglected to bathe. King Louis, disgusted with his new granddaughter's personal habits, wrote to her parents asking them to tell their daughter to wash her neck.

Josephine was no more pleasant in personality than she was in appearance. "Her countenance is cold and embarrassed," Mercy thought. "She speaks little and awkwardly." She may have been abashed by the grandeur of Versailles and its formidable inhabitants; once Antoinette befriended her, she found Josephine to be "very sweet, very agreeable and very cheerful in private, though she does not appear so in public." "She likes me very much," Antoinette told her mother, "and has much confidence in me. She is not at all on the side of Madame Du Barry."9 This was to change, but in the summer of 1771 at least Antoinette had a companion of her own age.

There was another companion too—the Princesse de Lamballe, a rather melancholy young widow who was the daughter-in-law of the Duc de Penthièvre. The Princess had been married briefly to the dissolute Prince de Lamballe, who had expired very young, the victim of his excesses; she was six years older than Antoinette, but paler in personality, her obliging gentleness and good nature a flattering foil for the dauphine's vivacity. The Princess was delicate, her features irregular but not unpleasing. Her hands were her worst liability, a court memoirist thought, her candor and lack of intrigue her greatest asset.10 In the winter of 1770–71 she and Antoinette became friends. Her "infantine air" endeared her to the dauphine who loved children, and the fact that she too was a foreigner, a Piedmontese, bound her to the Austrian Princess.

Antoinette was beginning to make a life of her own, by choosing her own friends, setting her disorderly stamp on her apartments, expressing her will, within limits, on matters great and small. She was even beginning, in little ways, to dare to defy her mother's orders, though she confided to Mercy that she was very much afraid of Maria Theresa.11

The Empress's long, forceful letters arrived every month, written with the concision and immediacy that were second nature to her but that were intimidating to her sensitive young daughter. The letters were full of criticisms and corrections, a written counterpart to Madame de Noailles's verbal chidings. An-

toinette's handwriting was bad, the Empress complained. Her
"look of youth" was gone—it was clear from her portraits. She
ought to pay more attention to the Austrians at court. She mustn't
ride horses. She ought to read more. She ought not to be so intimate with Adelaide, Victoire and Sophie. She must speak to
Madame Du Barry, no matter how disagreeable it might be. She
must watch herself carefully and protect herself from attack.
Above all, she must make people like her.

"Making people like us," the Empress wrote, "is the only
amusement and happiness of our [royal] condition. It is a talent
which you have mastered so perfectly! Do not lose it by neglect-
ing that which gave it to you: you owe it neither to your beauty
(which in fact is not so great), nor to your talents or culture (you
know very well you have neither); it is your kind heart, your
frankness, your amiability, all exerted with your good judgment."[12]

There were injunctions about food, exercise, dress and deportment—and marriage. Maria Theresa was very opinionated on
how to coax a shy husband into boldness. (Always assuming that
shyness, and not incurable impotence, was the dauphin's problem.) "Be prodigal with your caresses," she told Antoinette. The
letters were full of chastisements, and even expressions of despair
("I see you striding with a nonchalant calm toward ruin," the Empress wrote in October of 1771), but as the months passed they
were gradually becoming softer and on occasion even plangent.
For Maria Theresa was aging, and was feeling her age.

"I have been so full of hindrances," she confessed in August of
1771, "and I am starting to age at a furious pace; even when I
work it takes me twice as long as it did."[13] She was only fifty-four
when she wrote this, but she felt closer to seventy. Two years
later she admitted, this time to her son and co-regent Joseph, that
her deterioration was rapidly advancing. "My capabilities, my
looks, my hearing, my skill are swiftly declining." Her faculties
were dimming, and she no longer felt at home in a changing
world. "The irreligion, the deterioration of morals, the jargon
which everybody uses and which I do not understand, all these
are enough to overwhelm me," she complained. She was lonely
for her children, most of whom lived far from her, and for the
husband whose loss she never ceased to mourn.[14]

Joseph was a constant source of aggravation, rude and

brusque, "an intellectual cocotte," as she called him, as radical as she was conservative. He irked her, and when she was feeling her age, he wearied her with his demands and his constant threats to resign from the co-regency. Joseph was a present worry, Amalia a more distant one. Her marriage to the spineless Don Ferdinand of Parma had turned into a nightmare. Amalia ran the court, or tried to run it. Maria Theresa all but disowned her wayward daughter, and caused a family rift.

Of all her daughters, Caroline and Antoinette pleased the Empress most, but Antoinette did not realize this. Indeed she confided to Mercy that she "always imagined she was not loved, and that she would always be treated sharply."[15] She was constantly apprehensive, constantly on guard lest she offend her fearsome mother. "I love the Empress, but I fear her," she told the ambassador, "even from far away; even in writing I am not at my ease with her." It was worse when she had to write bad news. With tears in her eyes Antoinette confided to Mercy that she was afraid to tell her mother "things that go wrong." "My heart is always with my family [in Austria]," she told Mercy on another occasion, "and, if I quarrel with them I feel that my duties here would be too heavy for me to bear."[16]

Antoinette was bonded to Maria Theresa by strong ties of fear and love. Much as she dreaded the letters from Vienna, she dreaded even more the thought that one day they would cease forever. In late February of 1772 word came that the Empress had been very ill, and that her doctors had bled her twice. Antoinette burst into tears and shut herself in the inner recesses of her apartments, canceling a previously arranged audience. Taking up the chaplet of beads Maria Theresa had given her, she knelt to pray, as fervent in her distress as she was ebullient in her lighter moods. The dauphin prayed at her side, sympathetic and loyal to his wife despite his dislike of Austria and Austrians and his indifference to the mother-in-law he had never met.[17]

Louis and Antoinette were on the best of terms—as friends. To please her he ordered that a ball be held in her apartments once a week, and escorted her to receptions given by various courtiers. Everyone remarked on the change in him; he was trying, in his awkward way, to be sociable, though he still preferred his solitary pursuits and was evidently making the effort solely to gratify his wife. Antoinette professed to be happy with him, and insisted that "the wicked rumors people whisper about his impotence are just so much nonsense." He slept beside her most nights, and treated her "in the most friendly way." But they were not yet husband and wife, and Antoinette, watching the pregnancies of the other women at court, and then seeing them with their newborn babies in their arms, was at times in despair. Even when their pregnancies ended in tragedy, she envied them. In October of 1771 the Duchesse de Chartres was delivered of a stillborn child. "Even though it is terrible," Antoinette wrote in a letter to Vienna, "I still wish it had been me in her place, but there is still no hope of it."[18]

"General Krottendorf" was the name Antoinette and Maria Theresa had agreed to use in their correspondence to refer to menstruation. In 1771 the "General" made his appearance with melancholy regularity, though during the previous year his visits had been quite erratic.[19] Antoinette was still very young, not too young to bear a child but perhaps too young to be consistently fertile. She was still growing, her height increased considerably during her first several years at the French court. She was filling out as well, especially after she began drinking fresh milk every morning at her mother's request. The Empress had always believed in the health-giving qualities of fresh milk, brought straight from the dairy.

She was growing mentally too, learning to find pleasure in the reading of instructive books, having the Abbé Vermond (who was not dismissed after all) read to her for hours at a time from works on the history of France or from the memoirs of courtiers in earlier reigns. She sat patiently, her needlework in her lap, listening to the Abbé or discussing with him the biblical commentary that her confessor had given her to read or Hume's History of Europe, which she had been reading on her own. ("It seems full of interest," she remarked to the Empress about Hume's History, "but one must remember that it was written by a Protestant."[20])

By the second anniversary of her arrival in France Antoinette had become a different girl. She retained her charm, but added to it intelligence, acumen and perspicacity. Though she disliked and even feared politics, she understood it, up to a point, and grasped with alacrity the political explanations made to her. She was learning to make her way past the shoals of court politics, steering between the King and the Du Barry faction and those who would use her as their stalking-horse. She eventually gratified the King by breaking her long silence toward his mistress, yet she did it in such a way that her own dignity remained intact.

On New Year's Day, 1772, in the midst of the elaborate ceremonies customary on the first day of the year, Antoinette decided to say the few words that made all the difference. Speaking briefly to each of the women who bowed before her in turn, she did not neglect Madame Du Barry. "There are a great many people at Versailles today," she said as the Countess knelt at her feet, keeping her tone so nonchalant that it belied the enormity of the communication.

The difference in the dauphine was apparent in how she spent her time. Once in a while she sought out her aunts, but more often she was to be found improving her mind, or giving audiences to ambassadors' wives, or practicing the harp music her mother sent her, slowly learning first one hand's part, then the other. The children of her bedchamber women were rarely in evidence in her apartments now, though the dogs were still there. Yet many afternoons found the dogs napping on the couches, or pawing at the doors, restless in their loneliness. Their mistress was at the hunt, riding one of the fine horses her grandfather had bought for her, looking her best in the hunt uniform of royal blue velvet with a white-plumed hat.

She rode nearly as boldly as Adelaide, her plumes flying, her cheeks pink with excitement, her blue eyes large and bright. The "sweet and gentle" donkeys she had ridden in her earliest months in France no longer satisfied her. They were too slow, they frustrated her, especially when she had to ride along with all the ladies of her suite following behind her in a huge procession sixty or eighty donkeys long. On her splendid Suffolk hunters she could gallop to her heart's content, free of her mother, free of Madame de Noailles, free, for the moment, of the cares of her situation and of fretful thoughts about her future.

8

THE King was aging rapidly. His health was declining, he walked with an old man's gait. His sight was dimming, though his lips still curved upward in a cadaverous grin when he saw Madame Du Barry. He repeated himself constantly, and his vacuity was swiftly turning into senility. "The King is not old in actual years," an observer wrote in 1773, "but very much so in fact, in consequence of the life he has led." He was dying of dissipation, and the courtiers, seeing that he was dying, were deserting him in droves.

Mercy, who had no love for King Louis, nonetheless had a sharp eye for his pitiful state. "He is isolated," the ambassador noted, "without comfort from his children, without resources, zeal, attachment or fidelity on the part of the bizarre assemblage that comprises his surroundings."[1] Madame Du Barry was his constant companion, hanging over his shoulder when he was seated, walking beside him on his ever slower promenades, presuming to read his letters and generally claiming precedence over every other member of the court save the royal family.

She acted as though she expected him to live forever, continuing to spend lavishly, drawing funds from the bankrupt treasury to buy gold dinner services and golden mirrors crowned with cupids. She continued to receive costly gifts from kings and ambassadors. (King Gustavus of Sweden made her a present of a collar and chain for her dog Dorine, a Blenheim spaniel, composed entirely of diamonds and rubies.) Yet the reality could not be denied: before long her protector would vanish from the scene, and then her enormous revenues—far in excess of 1,500,000 livres a year—would cease, her jewels and gowns and plate and furnishings would all have to be returned.

A year earlier, in 1772, King Louis had made an attempt to arrange a divorce for Madame Du Barry so that he could marry her. Her fortunes had then been at their height, the King's bounty endless and the luxuries to be enjoyed in her white brocade boudoir without limit. But the divorce attempt had come to nothing, and the courtiers, who for a time had begun to consider the astounding possibility that Jeanne Bécu might become Queen, and might even bear a new dauphin, had come to realize that before long she would not have any further influence whatever. They no longer flattered and served her as they once had, and even balked at attending her soirées.

In March 1773 the Countess gave a fete to inaugurate the pavilion the King had built for her in the gardens of Versailles. He had spared no expense, the building was sumptuous "to the point of indecency." To show it off Madame Du Barry planned a spectacular entertainment, with a hundred singers and dancers, scenic devices worthy of the best Paris theaters, and a dramatic finale in which a huge egg opened to reveal an armed cupid. All the important courtiers were invited, including the chief ladies. But when all was in readiness, and the hour for the fete arrived, the pavilion was all but empty. The King did not attend, and out of the hundreds of guests invited only thirty made their appearance.[2]

It was a clear sign that Madame Du Barry's power was on the wane—and that the dauphin's faction was growing. Another clear sign was the increasing number of songs and epigrams written about the Countess, ridiculing her origins and satirizing her pretentions. "The streetwalker" had had her day, the songs implied, but her sun was setting and her attractions were losing their power to charm. An Englishman who saw Madame Du Barry at about this time exclaimed that her face was "rather upon the yellow leaf," the Indian summer of her beauty at its end.

As the King declined, and the day drew nearer when Louis and Antoinette would reign, power shifted their way. The cabals that schemed to make Provence King instead of Louis were silent, for Provence, despite his vaunted prowess on his wedding night, had not yet fathered a child and displayed an indifference toward his wife that verged on disgust. Provence had also been ill, with a skin disease on his hands and "humors in the blood," while the dauphin was growing taller and stouter and more healthy every day.[3]

Interest was now focused on the younger royal brother, Artois. Adelaide had attached her hopes to him, had taken over the supervising of his education and was attempting—over the squabbling objections of Madame Du Barry—to play the dominant role in the selection of his household staff. His betrothal had been arranged. He was to marry Marie Theresa of Savoy, the sister of Provence's wife Josephine, and though Theresa was reputed to be even less attractive than her red-faced, mustachioed sister it was hoped that the couple would prove fertile.

Antoinette, who was not yet seventeen, had learned to take a somewhat stoic view of her childlessness, and even to make light of it. Writing to her mother about the very fertile Madame de Schwartzenberg, who had thirteen children, she remarked, "I wish she would lend me a little of her fecundity." And in another letter she was optimistic. "Perhaps they [her future children] will be all the healthier for coming late."[4]

She was maturing mentally, learning to take the wider and longer view of things. Mercy's astute guidance, Abbé Vermond's gentle promptings, the Empress's scoldings and caveats had taken root. Antoinette had begun to find her own way through the maelstrom of intrigues and tiresome etiquette, she was making an identity of her own. "When I first came to this country," she told Mercy, "I was too young and thoughtless. I believed everything I was told, but now—" She did not need to finish the thought. The difference was clear. She had begun to take her own education in hand.

To this end she drew up a new regimen for herself, filling her time as usefully as possible after allowing for the unavoidable demands of ritual. On arising in the morning she said her prayers, then had a music lesson and practiced her dancing, then devoted herself to an hour of what she termed "reasonable reading." Her public toilette came next, then a visit to the King with whom she went to Mass. After dinner she devoted herself to more "reasonable reading" for an hour and a half, then went out walking or joined the hunt. Conversations with her husband and other relatives closed out the day. "I do not know if I shall fulfill all that quite exactly," Antoinette said as she showed Mercy her new schedule, "but I mean to try my best."[5]

She was showing signs of improving, of taking herself and her responsibilities seriously. And it was just as well, Mercy thought, for he was convinced that the dauphin would never have the fortitude to be King. Antoinette would have to rule for him, to direct his actions and decisions and so, in effect, rule France. He often spoke of her in the spring of 1773 as a stateswoman "who will one day govern this kingdom." "The dauphine," he told Maria Theresa, "has such great powers of mind and character that there cannot be the least doubt that we may rely upon their effects."[6]

Antoinette was making occasional efforts to prepare herself for her future role. Her husband, however, was not. He shuffled through his days, wearing old clothes unless his valets insisted on more elegant attire, squinting nearsightedly at the courtiers and doing his best to learn to dance. Alone in his apartments, the doors locked against intruders, he stumbled through the steps of the intricate court dances, "sweating great drops," while a lone fiddler scratched out the tune. Exhausted by his efforts, he joined his brothers in their private game of tormenting their grandfather's servants, "running with great glee" to tickle the King's valets de chambre as they entered and left the royal apartments laden with trays and baskets. When this palled, the dauphin escaped to the hunt, or to a construction site where he happily joined the laborers at their work.

"Despite her efforts," a visitor to Versailles reported, "the dauphine is unable to make her husband control his unusual taste for all that concerns construction, such as masonry, carpentry and other such things." Louis was forever discovering something that needed fixing, then calling in workmen to repair it and pitching in alongside them. "He works himself with the laborers in moving materials, girders, paving-blocks, and devotes whole hours to this toilsome exercise. Sometimes he comes home more tired than any laborer who is obliged to do such work for a living." It was embarrassing how avid the future King was for humble manual labor. Always self-conscious and stiff in the palace, he became relaxed and at peace in the mud and grime of the workplace, lost in the pleasures of exertion and the satisfactions of physical labor. Nothing delighted him more than to toil beside the carpenters and masons for hours on end, then to return to his apartments sweaty and filthy, a look of utter satisfaction on his chubby face.

It was hard to imagine this royal misfit as King. "The dauphin shows certain savage virtues," wrote the Comtesse de la Marck, "but he is without wits, without knowledge, without education, without even taste." He was afraid of women, the Countess added, "and as even his own wife has not cured him we can believe that none will."[7] The dauphin's fear of women worked in Antoinette's favor. She gentled him, he wanted very much to please her and this made him adaptable. Oddly, with her kind and uncritical nature, her warmth and sympathy, she was more mother than wife to her husband. She sometimes scolded him until he cried (though his tears often led her to cry as well, from empathy), and let him feel the sting of her acid tongue. She often intervened to stop fights when he warred with his two brothers. Louis had never ceased to feel defensive around his siblings, vulnerable to Provence's quick wit and Artois's teasing. He lashed out at them physically, kicking them and hitting them and sometimes taking revenge by destroying their possessions.

Provence had a beautiful piece of porcelain that stood on his mantel. Louis liked to torment his brother by lifting the fragile thing and toying with it. One day he broke it, and Provence, infuriated, threw himself on his taller and older brother, slapping and scratching him with all the intensity pent up in a jealous younger sibling. The dauphin struck back with a vengeance; the two looked murderous and Antoinette, accustomed since birth to the inevitable scrapping in a large family, stepped in and separated them. She came away with a scratched hand, but was otherwise unhurt.[8]

Another time Antoinette was having a game of piquet with Provence, who had developed an uneasy rapport with her (they laughed together over the songs and jokes about Madame Du Barry). Louis stood nearby with a small whip in his hand, watching the game. Out of jealousy or irritation he struck his brother's arm with the whip again and again, ignoring Provence's complaints. Tensions rose, and eventually the whip struck once too often. Provence grabbed for the whip and tried to yank it out of the dauphin's hand; a struggle ensued, they were about to come to blows. Again Antoinette stepped in, snatched the whip, broke it in two and so prevented violence. No doubt Louis received a lecture later on, when they were alone.[9]

Antoinette was old enough to perceive how her husband's deficiencies were bound to hamper him as King. She knew, thanks in part to Mercy's tutelage, that much would be expected of her as Queen—that in fact, after she became Queen she would be even more under siege from intriguers and the ambitious, even more the target of faction and gossip and importunate schemers. Her sense of duty prompted her to bow to the inevitable—yet another instinct was becoming stronger. Mercy noted it with alarm.

"She never allows herself to suppose that she may one day possess both authority and power," he wrote to Vienna, "from which it results that her character acquires daily a dependent and passive trend: hence ensue habits of timidity and fear on the least occasion." She sensed the onset of an overwhelming burden, and she backed away from it, possibly because she knew that she would never become strong enough to face it squarely, possibly because she had grown up under the shadow of a mother impossibly overburdened with the grinding labor of government, whose entire life had been a paean to duty, and partly, too, because of the shallow, frivolous streak in her nature, which led her to shut her eyes to duty and simply enjoy herself.

Mercy was exasperated with her. "It is important that the Archduchess should learn better to know and appreciate her own strength," he said, for she had all the intelligence, character and good judgment to be her husband's badly needed partner in affairs. But her willfulness, her fondness for "dissipation and amusement" were a handicap, and one she did not want to overcome. She was troubled by thoughts "upon which she could not express herself." Moreover, she was, in 1773, old enough to be beyond the reach of his instruction. Her basic character was formed, it would not change very much. [10]

The King was aging rapidly, and before he died his heir needed to present himself, with his wife, to the people of Paris in the Joyeuse Entrée.

On the morning of June 8, 1773 the throngs of people pouring into the narrow streets of the capital made the work of the street cleaners nearly impossible. The black, sulfurous mud that collected on the cobblestones and in the gutters, reeking of ordure and rotting garbage, had to be shoveled into carts and hauled away to the countryside, where it could not offend the noses of the next King and Queen. But the crowds of spectators interfered with the labor, shouldering aside the workmen with their carts and shovels, bringing new mud in on their boots, littering the thoroughfares and alleyways as they tramped enthusiastically toward the Porte de la Conference where the dauphin and dauphine were to make their entry. Many went on beyond the gate toward Versailles, hoping to meet the royal entourage on its passage from the palace to the city.

The usual morning activities had been suspended. There were no markets, no flocks of sheep or herds of cattle were permitted in the streets, no grain changed hands, even the peddlers were shooed away from the route the procession was to take. Women carrying café au lait—the Parisians' usual breakfast—in tin vessels mingled with the gathering throng, doing a brisk business at two sous the cup. The nuns of the Foundling Hospital took inside the dozen or so abandoned babies left at their gate during the previous night and received others from the police; it would not do to let the wailing of infants dampen the day's celebrations, even the weak wailing of newborns. Similarly, the most unsightly of Paris's thousands of beggars were driven off or locked away, lest the royals be displeased by the sight of their crippled and palsied limbs. The hordes of prostitutes that normally earned their day's livelihood from the farmers in the grain market or the pleasure-seeking roués in the Palais Royale were forced to look for new clients, and they roved through the crush of spectators eyeing likely men and calling out boldly to them.

It was a noisy crowd, Parisians were notoriously loud and talkative. They were a heterogeneous lot, affluent bourgeois in their best velvet waistcoats and lace-trimmed cuffs, tradesmen in coats and breeches of plain tailored cloth, here and there a gentleman in buckled shoes, silk stockings and beribboned periwig, his sword in its low-slung scabbard swinging perilously along behind him. There were vintners and grocers, tanners and dentists, bankers and lawyers—but many more casual laborers, apprentices freed from their workshops for the day, water carriers and street porters, bargemen and peasants from the villages nearest to the capital who had walked through the night in order to be able to witness the spectacle of the Joyous Entry. They rushed to find places along the route the royal carriages would take, and in the gardens of the Tuileries, embroidresses and grimy chimney sweeps vying for space with students, fishermen up from the river and renegade monks.

Paris hid a multitude of sins, and of crimes; along the southern perimeter of the city there was constant apprehension because it was to nearby Bicêtre that convicts from many northern French cities were sent to prepare for deportation. From Bicêtre they were transported to Brest and Rochefort and Toulon, but many escaped en route, and lost themselves in the dim, crooked alleyways of the capital from which they emerged to terrorize honest citizens.

A bare two weeks had passed since the last gathering at Bicêtre, and the city was full of tales and rumors, stories of escape and recapture, of multiple murders and grisly discoveries. Police spies were everywhere, keeping watch on the Seine bridges for escapees, haunting taverns and tollgates, waiting to overhear the indiscreet conversation that could lead them to their quarry. They were especially vigilant this day, for pickpockets and cutpurses loved crowds and burglaries invariably increased on holidays.

By midmorning the city officials were in their places and the orchestra was tuning up. Ten carriages were drawn up by the Porte de la Conference, occupied by soldiers, councillors and their retinues; the chief carriage contained the governor of Paris, the aged Maréchal de Brissac, the provost Michodière, and Sartines, lieutenant of police in charge of keeping order. Squadrons of town guards and horsemen of the watch formed up at the gate, ready to escort the dauphin and dauphine and to prevent the hordes of onlookers from engulfing the objects of their curiosity.

At eleven-thirty the first of the royal carriages was sighted, and the signal was passed to the trumpeters who blew a fanfare. At almost the same moment the cannon of the Invalides boomed out a salute, followed by the guns of the Hôtel de Ville and the Bastille. Thick black smoke rose into the clear summer skies and then settled over the city as the thunderous cannonade proceeded. The crowd cheered, people surged forward until beaten back by the police. At last the four royal coaches rattled through the gateway and came to a halt, and Maréchal de Brissac came forward to kneel before the future sovereigns and extend greetings, handing the dauphin the symbolic key to the city. The provost made a speech, but the noise of the crowd drowned it out. They cheered, they whistled, they sang songs written specially for the Joyous Entry and sold on printed sheets. They kept on singing and shouting as the speechifying continued, their roaring covering the decorous playing of the orchestra.

To Antoinette the deafening noise of the crowd was both exciting and gratifying. She had had little opportunity to come face to face with the French people, having been entombed at Versailles for three long years. But now here they were in their thousands, rich and poor together, clamoring for a closer view of her and of her husband, coming as near as they dared to the carriage in which she rode, wide grins on their pockmarked faces. She watched them in smiling fascination as the procession of coaches made its way along the quays to Notre Dame, stopping at the Conti quay where the prefect of the Mint made a speech. The Archbishop of Paris celebrated Mass at Notre Dame, after which the dignitaries returned to their carriages and made the brief journey to the Collège of Louis le Grand where the rector of the university made an address.

The official ceremonies were tedious, but to Antoinette's eager, curious eyes the city and its inhabitants were endlessly engrossing. The tumult, the incessant cries of "*Vive le dauphin!*" and "*Vive la dauphine!*," the flowers strewn in their path, the quaint medieval buildings in the oldest part of the city, even the pungent odors that lingered near the river were a panorama of delight. After three years she was finally meeting those who would soon be her people, and seeing her famed capital. It was almost too much for her.

"I shall never forget it as long as I live," she wrote to her mother some days later. "As for honors, we received every honor one could imagine—but all that, though very well in its way, was not what moved me most: it was the fondness and eagerness of the poor people who, despite the taxes which burden them, were carried away by joy at the sight of us."[11]

The dauphin and dauphine drew the largest crowds Paris had known since the arrival of a celebrated faith healer, whose fame attracted thirty thousand people to the city. Then the people had filled the rue des Ciseaux and spilled out into the surrounding streets, the crush made worse by the crutches of the many invalids seeking the man's healing touch and the dogs that accompanied the many blind men. The crowd had kept its hopeful vigil outside the healer's lodgings until word spread that the police had driven him out of town; even then the people kept their composure, and murmured blessings on him wherever he had gone.[12]

Now there was an even more compelling sight to attract the Parisians, and they clamored for Louis and Antoinette from rooftops and attic windows, and from the packed gardens of the Tuileries, where the dauphin and dauphine went to dine. After the public dinner the two young royals went out into the gardens, where the acclamation was deafening and the crowd pressed in on them so tightly from all sides that they couldn't move. "We remained for three-quarters of an hour without being able to go forward or back," Antoinette wrote. The guards, accustomed to lashing at crowds with whips or with the flat of their swords, heeded the dauphin's orders to do nothing, to let the people swarm close to him. This unheard-of lenity "created a very good impression," and fortunately did not result in any injuries. (Such mob scenes were rarely so innocuous. Three years earlier, when all Paris rushed into the rue Royale to watch the fireworks celebrating the dauphin's marriage, there was a stampede and in the resultant panic more than a hundred people were suffocated or trampled to death.) Later Louis and Antoinette went up onto a terrace overlooking the garden, and stayed there for half an hour acknowledging the continuing acclamations of the crowd.

"I cannot tell you, dear mama, what rapture, what enormous fondness were shown to us during that time." From her vantage point on the balcony Antoinette could now gauge the true size of the enormous mass of humanity that had come to pay her homage.

"My God!" she cried out, "what a crowd!"

"Madame," said Maréchal de Brissac, at her elbow, "without prejudice to Monsieur le Dauphin, here you have two hundred thousand lovers."

As ardent as lovers in their passionate cheers and shouts, the Parisians cried themselves hoarse, tears mingling with smiles. They were delighted with the dauphin, who looked to them strapping and stalwart, a man's man, and who on that day surpassed himself in responding with dignity to the speeches and the acclaim. They were even more delighted with his Austrian wife, whose doll-like delicacy, enchanting coloring and vibrant grace captivated them. She was then seventeen; at about this time Edmund Burke saw Antoinette at Versailles, and wrote an ecstatic reminiscence of her. "Surely never lighted on this orb, which she hardly seemed to touch," Burke wrote, "a more delightful vision. I saw her just above the horizon, decorating and cheering the elevated sphere she had just begun to move in—glittering like the morning star, full of life, and splendor, and joy."

Ten months later, in April of 1774, the young couple shut themselves in Antoinette's apartments at Versailles and prayed that the old King's life would be spared. He was very ill, he had been bled twice by the five surgeons who attended him and purged at the order of his three apothecaries. Adelaide, Victoire and Sophie kept watch by his bedside during the day, Madame Du Barry watched over him at night. Privately, one of the doctors who diagnosed "catarrhal fever" confided to a courtier that he did not think the King would live. In Paris, the lieutenant of police began to make plans for controlling the outbreak of violence that was sure to come when the news of the King's death spread through the capital.

The dauphin, supported by his frightened but loyal wife, waited in anguish for the medical bulletins that came from the sickroom, aware of a subtle change in the way he was being treated by the servants and courtiers. If the King was bled a third time, the Archbishop of Paris would be summoned to give him extreme unction. The third bleeding was a sentence of death. Pale and restless, his nerves in shreds, the dauphin knelt and begged to be spared awhile longer the awful responsibility of ruling the kingdom of France.

9

I N the dimly lit sickroom at Versailles, where Louis XV lay in torpor, his three daughters were alarmed. The King did not acknowledge them or speak to them. The surgeons and physicians filed past his narrow bed, each in turn bending over him. The servants, instructed to keep the room dark as the light hurt the King's weak eyes, stood in the gloom, waiting for instructions. Suddenly a torch flared, and in the instant of brightness the cadaverous royal head was illuminated. The face was covered with dark red spots. The King's illness was not catarrhal fever, but smallpox.

In France, inoculation against smallpox was still an exotic practice, widely distrusted. The King had not been inoculated, nor had any of the other members of the royal family. (And in fact, several of the courtiers who had been inoculated had died soon afterwards—including the Comtesse de Noailles's son— which argued against the procedure.) But smallpox was dreaded, and there was a general shudder when the King's spotted face was disclosed. He had had smallpox once before, in the long-ago year of 1728, but that was no protection against a fatal recurrence of the disease, and he himself seemed to sense that he would not recover. He had become ill on April 27; on May 4 he sent Madame Du Barry away, so that he could give at least the appearance of repentance and die an edifying death.

He was in considerable pain. The powdered elm bark the apothecaries administered to him did not ease his agony. After eight days of illness he stank horribly, as if his wasted body already gave forth the stench of death. The dauphin was kept strictly away, but Adelaide, Victoire and Sophie were in daily attendance, risking their lives out of filial duty. And the royal ministers too came and went from the sickroom at intervals, alternating with the doctors who were well aware that, having failed to cure their master, their own positions were precarious. Antoinette was allowed to see the dying King on the morning of May 7, and was informed that he had summoned his confessor and desired to receive the eucharist. As Louis XV had not made his confession in nearly four decades, the courtiers took this to be an unmistakable sign that his end was near.

The courtyards of the great palace were filling with people, some in tears, many mumbling prayers, others eager to be rid of the hateful old roué who had ruled them since his boyhood. However mild his actual attitude toward his subjects was, however useful his recent belated attempts at governmental reform, he was widely regarded as cruelly indifferent to the needs of the people. In her memoirs Madame Campan recorded a chilling encounter between Louis and a peasant in the forest of Senart. The King was hunting when he came across a man on horseback carrying a coffin.

"Where are you taking that coffin?" Louis asked.

"To the village of————," answered the peasant.

"Is it for a man or a woman?"

"For a man."

"What did he die of?"

"Of hunger," was the blunt response.

The King spurred his horse and rode on.[1]

Now death had come for the man who had shown so little concern for the starving. By May 9 he was delirious at times, too weak to do more than whisper. He was unable to pronounce the words of the public repentance his confessor had enjoined on him, so Monsignor de la Roche-Aymon, grand almoner, read it for him. "Gentlemen," the Cardinal said solemnly to the assembled courtiers, "the King has charged me to tell you that he asks pardon of God for having offended him and for the scandal he has caused his people."

The courtiers, fearing the contagion that lurked in the King's apartments and knowing that, once he died, the court would immediately move to another palace, rushed to gather their possessions and make arrangements to leave. The soldiers of the guard were ready to march, there were hundreds of saddled horses in the crowded courtyards and the royal coach waited to carry the new King and his brothers to safety.

The old King lingered until May 10, groaning in agony, his swollen face black with corruption. Finally in midafternoon he died, and the Grand Chamberlain, the Duc de Bouillon, emerged from the dim sickroom to make the solemn announcement.

"Gentlemen, the King is dead. Long live the King!"

The news was passed down the staircases, along the corridors, into the farthest reaches of the vast palace. In the courtyards, horses pawed the pavingstones and grooms shouted to one another to prepare to leave. With a thunderous noise, the courtiers rushed to Louis's apartments, paid their respects to their white-faced new young King, and then sped to their waiting vehicles. Within an hour Versailles was deserted. Only the corpse was left, and the few officials entrusted to escort it to St.-Denis for burial.

Louis and Antoinette joined the departing cavalcade, bound for Choisy, just outside Paris. They soon moved on to La Muette, in the Bois de Boulogne. Louis was now in command, his word was law, his person sacred. Having had no preparation whatever for this, his first day as King, he trembled—yet he was not entirely without resources. He brought with him to Choisy a document written by his late father, a "List of various persons recommended by the Dauphin to that one of his children who shall succeed Louis XV." The list was not long, nor were its recommendations prolix. M. de Nivernois, it said, had "spirit and grace," M. de Castries was "good for the army," M. de Muy was "virtue personified." Louis chose M. de Machault ("a man of unbending temper and some errors of judgment, but a man of worth"). But Adelaide, debilitated and poxy as she was from her weeks of vigil by her dying father's bedside, intervened: Louis, she said, must send for the aged Comte de Maurepas ("has retained the true principles of politics") and none other.[2] Louis allowed himself to be persuaded. Maurepas it was.

Meanwhile the courtiers, anxious above all to align themselves with the real power at court, flocked to Antoinette and made their approaches to her with all the subtlety of leeches attaching themselves to a swimmer. She received them, clad in black mourning and devoid of rouge—though quite as enchanting without it—and showed the younger of them her usual warmth and sparkle. The older women, however, felt the sting of her acerb tongue when they came to pay their formal "mourning respects." Hating all ceremonies as she did, and determined, now that she was Queen, to pare them down or do away with them, Antoinette smiled at the sight of these "centenarians" and "prigs," as she called them, and "most improperly burst out laughing" in their wrinkled faces. It was an ill-advised debut; the elderly Duchesses and Princesses were enraged, especially when they heard that the Queen, who was not yet nineteen, had remarked flippantly, "When one has passed thirty, I cannot understand how one dares appear at court." Such cruel impudence would not be tolerated even in a French Queen, but in a brazen Austrian! The women gossiped, censured, slandered. Antoinette became the victim of a new song, of the kind she and Provence had once sung about Madame Du Barry:

> Little Queen barely twenty
> You who mistreat people so badly
> You'll be sent back home.

New cliques were forming among the courtiers, new battle lines being drawn in the constant struggle for place and prestige. It had been assumed that the new King would be shy, feeble and ineffectual, that he would be governed by his wife. But Louis was showing himself remarkably forceful. When approached by his grandfather's ministers and asked for his commands, he was decisive, regally curt. Among his first acts was to disgrace the doctors who had failed to cure the old King. With the help of Maurepas, his chosen mentor and guide, he began to study foreign policy, taxation, above all finance. Setting aside his passion for locks, hunting and construction, he spent all day at his desk, writing letters, reading dispatches and recommendations, learning the intricacies of Abbé Terray's accounts. Lest the tax burden on his subjects be increased, he announced that he would not ask for the tax of forty million livres traditionally assessed on the accession of a new monarch. The people, overjoyed, stood in their hundreds outside the gates of La Muette and shouted "*Vive le Roi!*"

Louis was at first possessive about his newfound power. He

confided in Maurepas and Terray, and not in Antoinette. When she approached his desk he covered up his papers and struck a pose of irritability. "Madame," he said, "I have business to attend to." Others heard him say pointedly that "what has always ruined this country has been women, whether legitimate wives or mistresses."[3] The British ambassador Lord Stormont reported to his superiors in London that Louis did not appear to consult his wife at all, and that he firmly believed that women ought not to involve themselves in politics.

Common sense told Louis in his first few weeks as King that the expenses of his swollen and extravagant court were worsening the country's fiscal crisis. "He is eternally repeating the words economy, economy," Lord Stormont wrote. Yet economy was impossible in a season of royal mourning. The hundreds of palace servants had to have new black liveries—the stable staff alone required nearly fourteen hundred new suits—plus shoulder knots of blue. Thousands of ells of dark cloth had to be ordered to drape the beds and furnishings of the royal palaces, and more cloth of violet for the King's carriages. Mourning wardrobes for the royal family and courtiers were costly, for it was not sufficient to order black clothing alone—there had to be new black coifs, stockings, gloves and even fans to match it.

Ordering new clothing was in fact one of the few permitted amusements during the drawn-out months of mourning. No balls were held, visits to the theater were not permitted. Antoinette filled in the hours by taking a harp lesson daily and giving an informal concert in the afternoon, walking or riding on fine days, and submitting to pose for the painters who, she complained, "worried her to death" demanding royal portraits. Twice a week she looked forward to the visit of her dressmaker and milliner Rose Bertin, proprietress of the fashionable shop called the Grand Mogul in the rue St. Honoré. Madame Bertin was no stranger to the court, having enjoyed the patronage of the Duchesse de Chartres. But the Queen's patronage was precious, and with the aid of her skillful dressmaker she rapidly became the leader of fashion. What Antoinette wore, every woman coveted.

This was true of gowns, but even more of hats—and of the high-piled coiffures that went with them.

In the summer and fall of 1774, the women of the court succumbed to a sort of millinery madness. To begin with, there were

hats *à l'Iphigénie*, which celebrated the recent performance in Paris
of Gluck's *Iphigenia*—an opera that Antoinette championed (Gluck
had been her clavichord teacher in Vienna) and which had a great
vogue just before Louis XV's death. The Iphigenia hats, circlets
of black flowers with short veils and a crescent moon, were relatively modest in size, but the *poufs à la circonstance* that appeared
the following month were much more elaborate. These featured a
cypress and black marigolds, a wheat sheaf, and a cornucopia
filled with every sort of fruit and white feathers. The allegorical
meaning of the Circumstance Pouf was that while mourning Louis
XV, France welcomed the bounty certain to be enjoyed under the
new King. A medical coiffure came next, the *pouf à l'inoculation*.
Louis had submitted to being inoculated against smallpox about a
month after becoming King, and the new hairstyle commemo-
rated this with a rising sun, an olive tree and a serpent entwined
around the trunk, a flowery club near him.

Hair and its adornment had been receiving more and more
attention in the last years of the old reign. Bonnets named for the
Turkish Sultan, for the royal treasury, for the Carmelite nuns
brought notoriety to Rose Bertin, and women were accustomed to
sitting patiently while their hair was wrapped in curling papers
and frizzed with hot irons, combed out with nettle-juice and powdered with a nourishing mixture of rose roots, aloes wood, red
coral, amber, bean flour and musk. For several years the hair had
been elevated, with false hair added to the natural locks to provide
height and fullness. But these trends were greatly accelerated once
Antoinette became Queen. Now the coiffures called for large
horsehair cushions to be placed on top of the scalp, with false and
natural hair combed over them and long steel pins driven through
the hair and cushion to anchor the latter in place. Into this high
tower of hair were placed the flowers, jewels, fruit, feathers and
figurines that made up the current modes.

Hours in the construction, these creations were naturally pre-
served as long as possible, which meant that the scalp, itching and
perspiring under its heavy load, had to be protected with pomade.
But the pomade, being organic, turned rancid within a few days,
and to its stink was added the torment of the sharp pins. Critics of
the high-piled hair pointed out that it made women's blood rush
to their heads, and caused eyestrain, headaches and erisypelas.
Hair fell out, teeth ached, fleas and lice bred in the nests of curls;

genteel women carried long thin sticks with small ivory claws at the end to reach into their headdresses and scratch their heads.

But the effects produced by the magnificent—if ridiculous—edifices were worth any amount of inconvenience and pain. To be in fashion was the thing, even if a coiffure two or three feet high prevented one from sitting in a coach seat (the women knelt on the floor) or entering a ballroom (one of Antoinette's most fantasticated piles had to be dismantled, then rebuilt so that she could attend a soirée). Sacrifices were expected. Sleep was made uncomfortable, if not impossible. "At night," wrote the contemporary social critic Mercier, "the whole erection is compressed by means of a sort of triple bandage which everything goes under, false hair, pins, dye, grease, until at last the head, thrice its right size, and throbbing, lies on the pillow done up like a parcel, so that even in sleep the coiffeur's handiwork is respected."[4]

The fantastic coiffures were, for Antoinette, an engaging distraction, and one she needed only too badly, for now that she was Queen she found herself caught in a steel web of etiquette and obligation.

Private life, private action were a thing of the past. She could not make a gesture, take a step, utter a word without triggering a reaction in the attendants who never left her. Her first morning yawns brought a wardrobe woman into her bedroom with a basket of underclothes, handkerchiefs and towels. A waiting woman presented her with the day's first task—the choice of her dresses: a formal court gown, an informal afternoon dress, and a gown for the evening entertainment and supper. The choices were made from a picture book with drawings of all the various available toilettes. Antoinette marked those she wanted with a pin, and the waiting woman left to fetch them. A tub was rolled into the bedroom for the Queen's morning bath, and with it came the bathing corps with all things necessary—including the long flannel gown, lined with linen and buttoned up to the neck, in which the modest Antoinette bathed. She emerged from the tub screened from the servants' eyes by a sheet held in front of her; then she put on a wrapper of white taffeta and dimity slippers trimmed with lace and went back to bed until it was time for her sparse breakfast of hot chocolate or coffee.

The rest of the morning was taken up by visits from Abbé Vermond, Provence or Artois, the Princesse de Lamballe or others of the Queen's young friends. A few minutes with Louis were squeezed in, but family and friends and those possessing the coveted privilege of the *petites entrées* (the chief physician, chief surgeon, physician in ordinary, reader, closet secretary, the King's four first valets de chambre and the King's chief physicians and surgeons) took up most of the morning. Then came the time to begin the Queen's grand toilette, the chief ceremony of the day attended by the Princes of the blood, high court officials and all others possessing the *grande entrée*.

At noon the huge, ornate toilet table was brought into the middle of the room and folding chairs and sofas placed in a circle around it. The dignitaries entered, and each received an acknowledgment from Antoinette appropriate to his rank, from the slight nod due to a captain of the guard to the larger gesture (the Queen leaned upon the toilet table as if about to get up) required by the Princes. Also present were the ladies of honor and tirewomen. (The bedchamber ladies, whose duties did not include dressing the Queen, waited in the nearby "great closet" until the grand toilet was complete, then entered to accompany Antoinette to Mass.) After the coiffure ·was complete, the dressing began: the lady of honor put on the chemise, and poured water into the basin in which the Queen washed her hands, then the tirewoman attached the wide hooped skirt of the gown, adjusted the neckerchief, and tied on the necklace. The long court train was put on last of all.

While all this was going on, the serious business of the grand toilet took place. Petitions were presented for the Queen to sign. Departing military officers made their formal leavetakings. Ladies were presented, ambassadors introduced, foreigners brought in to meet Her Majesty. An usher stood at the entrance chamber, guarding the high folding doors to ensure against unauthorized entry, and to announce the names of the important visitors. (In keeping with etiquette, he announced them to the lady of honor, who in turn announced them to the Queen.) Finally, when the last presentation had been made and the last ornament added to the royal toilette, the Queen returned to her bedchamber and stood in the center of the room while her entire entourage assembled—the Princesse de Lamballe, superintendent of her household, the ladies of honor and tirewomen, the bedchamber ladies, the first gentleman usher, the chief equerry, the clergy whose duty it was to attend her to Mass that day, and the Princesses of the royal family (with all *their* ladies, tirewomen and attendants). The entire group then went together to the chapel for Mass.

An English visitor, Sir Samuel Romilly, wrote his impressions of a Mass he attended at Versailles where Louis and Antoinette were present in all their splendor. "The moment his majesty appeared," Romilly recalled, "the drums beat and shook the temple, as if it had been intended to announce the approach of a conqueror. During the whole time of saying Mass, the choristers sang, sometimes single parts, sometimes in chorus. In the front seats of the galleries were ranged the ladies of the court, glowing with rouge, and gorgeously apparelled, to enjoy and form a part of the showy spectacle. The King laughed and spied at the ladies; every eye was fixed on the personages of the court, every ear was attentive to the notes of the singers, while the priest, who in the mean time went on in the exercise of his office, was unheeded by all present." Even at the elevation of the host, Romilly noted, the most solemn moment of the Mass, the crowd in the chapel paid attention to nothing but the King, everyone "endeavoring to get a glimpse" of him.

Following Mass came the ritual of the midday dinner, which was at its most splendid on Sundays. Louis and Antoinette dined together, with Antoinette's ladies in attendance, some sitting on sofas and some standing around the table. The table was laid with a damask cloth, the dishes were silver, the cutlery gilt. Behind the King's chair the Captain of the Guards and the first gentleman of the chamber stood guard; behind the Queen were her first maître d'hôtel, her first gentleman usher and the chief equerry. When the maître d'hôtel entered the room, holding his seven-foot staff surmounted by a fleur-de-lis crown, the dishes were brought in and the meal began. The Queen was presented with a menu card, and the servants laid the platters of meat and fowl and pudding in front of their majesties. It was a very ceremonious meal, but not necessarily a somber one. An Englishman who watched the King and Queen dine at Versailles in 1775 wrote that "their Majesties talked and laughed much at dinner. The Queen is young and very handsome. She appears to be extremely lively and gay, without the forms and attentions that might be expected from her high rank." (By contrast, the same visitor was struck by the "mighty silence" at the dinner table of Provence and his wife, who "sat like two people stuffed with straw.")

When they had dined, the King and Queen went their separate ways. Antoinette, still surrounded by her entourage, returned to her apartments, where she was divested of the bulky formal court gown, with its hoop and train, and put on a simpler afternoon dress. Conversation with her relatives filled the earlier part of the afternoon, and harp music, audiences with visitors, walks and drives the latter part. Gambling, supper, and a return to the family circle occupied the evening, but shortly after eleven every night, when Louis went to bed, Antoinette went to join her young friends in the apartments of the Princesse de Lamballe or the Princesse de Guéménée—rendezvous that gave rise to gossip and criticism. There, in the relative privacy and informality of her confidantes' rooms, Antoinette could let herself go, forget the constant alertness that the day's rituals called for, unbend and laugh to her heart's content. In those apartments, and in her own retreat of the Petit Trianon, the small pavilion Louis had given her in the gardens of Versailles, she could be herself.

The Petit Trianon, though only a mile from the palace of Versailles, was infinitely more distant in atmosphere. A delicate neoclassical structure, simple and perfectly proportioned, it seemed as if sculpted from honey-colored stone. Inside there were only seven rooms—albeit exquisite rooms, which Antoinette made warmly elegant with flowery silk and velvet curtains and wall coverings and small, spindly-legged writing desks and tables and cabinets, many of them unique works of art in rare woods with ornamental inlaid porcelain. There were flowers everywhere, fresh flowers from the gardens, woven flowers in soft pastel shades in the counterpanes and hangings, lilies and roses in the carved plasterwork of the wall panels and in the marbles of the fireplace. Though she had never seen it, Maria Theresa called the Petit Trianon "the most adorable of houses," and it was to be Antoinette's adored obsession. She acquired it from her indulgent husband in the first month of their reign, and began at once to order alterations to its gardens.

In keeping with the current vogue for things English—English hats, boots, gowns, horse races—she ordered the creation of an English garden, and before long the small plot of land surrounding the house had been transformed. A lake was dug, small hills created, a grotto formed. Groves of trees, many of them exotic species brought from all over the world, adorned the smooth lawns, and a small river wound through the groves. On an island fragrant with lilac and laburnum was a Temple of Love, with a statue of Cupid inside. When complete, the gardens were a perfect miniature utopia, a magical place of great beauty, tranquillity and repose where nightingales sang and the strident voices of grasping courtiers could not be heard. "One could fancy oneself three hundred miles from court," wrote the Prince de Ligne, a favored guest of the Queen at Trianon.

Antoinette's private, fanciful enclave, her own small palace, represented to her the simpler existence she had known as a girl, and which she longed to know again. Her mother had created a similar oasis of privacy at Schönbrunn, and had taken pains to insulate her family from the stiff formalities of court ceremony. Now Antoinette had a place to which she could withdraw, where she could be herself, free of the attendants and guardsmen who dogged her steps at the larger palace. She liked to picnic on strawberries from the Trianon gardens—the strawberries, in all known varieties, which Louis XV's distinguished gardeners had cultivated there at his request—sitting on a simple bench and "behaving in the most informal way imaginable." It delighted her to be able to admire the flowers, listen to the nightingales, smell the laburnum and feel, through her thin slippers, the dew on the lawns. After all, there were plenty of servants to look after the little house and its elaborate grounds, plenty more amusements to turn to when these palled, plenty more pairs of slippers to replace those she ruined on her afternoon walks. Louis, thinking that Antoinette's taste for the simple life meant that she wanted to learn the humbler pursuits of country folk, made her a spinning wheel in his workshop and presented it to her proudly. She was charmed, she thanked him warmly—and as soon as he had gone, gave the spinning wheel away.

10

LONG before dawn the tiny closets and dim corridors of Versailles were bustling with life. Pages, footmen, kitchen servants and grooms washed and dressed hurriedly in their liveries, standing before the low hearth fires that barely warmed their cold, drafty rooms and gulping down a few bites of bread in their haste before dashing off to take their appointed places and begin their morning duties. Noble men and women too rose early and dressed quickly, though they had servants of their own to assist them at their more elaborate toilettes; for exalted though the nobles were, at court their duties were those of menials—the opening of a door, the holding of a wig or cane, the arranging of flowers in porcelain vases. And they had to be ready to perform these tasks as soon as their masters and mistresses arose.

There were nearly nine hundred officials and servants at the court of Louis XVI. The *Almanach de Versailles* listed them all, and the list alone covered one hundred and sixty-five pages. Each had his or her particular obligations and privileges, precisely defined and jealously defended. The captain of the King's mule carriage would not have dreamed of driving horses, the gentlemen who brought the King his *chaise percée* and removed it when he was finished with it would never have presumed to comb his hair, the valets who rubbed him each morning with hard-bristled brushes soaked in perfumed spirit would have balked at folding and knotting his cravat. The honor of the servant depended on the nature of his service; what he did was who he was. Life at court was an intricate choreography of special acts and functions carried out by designated personages, each of whom derived his dignity and identity from his part in the great royal dance.

For if the King and Queen were captives of etiquette, their hundreds of servants were obliged to be masters of it. Antoinette's lady of honor, Madame de Noailles, with her nagging reminders of proper form and her punctilious attention to detail, was only doing her job, albeit officiously; good service called for correctness in every particular. Officers and servants new to court had to master hundreds of rules and observances: what kind of bow to tie in the ribbon that bound the Queen's paniers, which liveries were to be worn at Choisy (blue) and which at Compiègne (green), which doors could be knocked on and which had to be scratched with the fingernails instead. In some rooms servants were permitted to sit, but in others, such as the King's bedroom, they had to stand, even if the King was not present. Only the King's family and those on intimate terms with him could speak to him directly; others had to use polite indirection and speak to him in the third person. ("Did the King enjoy a good hunt?" "Does the King still have a cold?") Even inanimate objects had to be approached in different ways at different times. Thus the Queen's bed was considered furniture, to be tended by the first upholsterer of the bedchamber, only when the Queen was not lying in it; when she was in bed the upholsterer had no jurisdiction over it and had to yield to the bedchamber servants.

"I should never finish," Louis XVI's page, the Comte d'Hézècques, wrote in his memoirs of service at Versailles, "if I recounted all the little things that one must know, not only to be a perfect courtier, but in order not to make mistakes." Mistakes could be costly. Servants who forgot the rules or who transgressed in other ways could be suspended from their positions for two weeks, a month, or even longer. Dismissal was a more common punishment than suspension. Absolute obedience to their superiors was required of all servants, and disobedience was harshly punished, sometimes with extra duties, sometimes with beatings or worse cruelty—the page Hézècques was shown a livid scar borne by one of his colleagues, the mark burned into the man's flesh by a red-hot spur.

One of the things a court officer had to learn was how to stay out of his colleagues' way. The office of train-bearer to the Queen, a minor post but one involving "daily and assiduous duties," could only be held by a nobleman, one whose lineage was distinguished enough to match that of the first gentleman usher. (The train-bearer and first gentleman usher had to share a carriage when the royal household moved; the latter dignitary could not be expected to ride with a social inferior.) Yet the train-bearer could only exercise his office within a very limited sphere, for as soon as the Queen left her own apartments and passed through the Galerie des Glaces, he had to yield the train to another servant, either a page of the King's bedchamber or a chapel servant. To console him for the frustrations of his severely curtailed responsibilities, the train-bearer was allowed to hold the Queen's pelisse or mantle—but never to hand them to her directly, only to hand them to the first gentleman usher or first equerry.[1]

The memoirs of the Comte d'Hézècques provide an intriguing view of what it was to be a page at the court of Louis and Antoinette.[2] He came to Versailles as a boy of twelve, owing his appointment as page of the King's chamber to the influence of a relative who was one of the chamber gentlemen. When he arrived there were fifty-eight pages in all, not counting those who served the Princes of the blood. Eight of these were assigned to the King's chamber, where their duties consisted of attending the grand *lever*, escorting the King to Mass, lighting his way with torches when he returned after dark from the hunt, and handing him his slippers at his nightly *coucher*. The duties were not strenuous, but the initiation was, as Hézècques found to his dismay. As a novice page he was at the mercy of the *anciens*—pages who had held their posts for two years and more and who were despotic in the extreme. The *anciens* punished every fault of the novices mercilessly, and the novices were expected, not only to perform their duties flawlessly, but to guess the wishes of their superiors or else face a beating with a cane.

To be a royal page was a coveted honor open only to boys who could prove noble ancestry stretching back two hundred years or more. Each page was required to have a pension from his family of six hundred livres per year. But this was for incidental expenses only, for everything else was provided: abundant food, liveries and other clothing, medical care, and education. Hézècques felt that he was looked after with "a truly royal magnificence." The eight chamber pages had two governors and a preceptor, or teacher, to supervise them in their lodgings in the rue de l'Orangerie. They spent their mornings (before the King's *lever*, which was usually not until eleven or eleven-thirty) learning horsemanship; later in the day, when not attending the King, they were tutored in mathematics, German, drawing, dancing, fencing and firearms, tumbling, and athletic exercises.

Boys such as the future Comte Hézècques were proud little lordlings, conceited and disdainful. Such conceit naturally bred quarrels, and the pages often fought duels among themselves which their governors were not vigilant enough to prevent. Duels between the King's pages and those of the Prince de Condé or the Prince de Conti were also common, though rarely fatal. The wounded were taken to surgeons in the town of Versailles or to one of the Queen's "common surgeons" who normally attended the inferior servants of her household but who could be pressed into service for emergencies. Dueling was officially disapproved, yet it was a recognized part of the life of an army officer, and all the royal pages were being groomed for careers in the army. At the end of their terms, when they were seventeen or eighteen, they expected to be given commissions in the guards, as Hézècques was.

After four years as a page of the King's chamber, the sixteen-year-old Hézècques, now an *ancien* ruling the lives of other novice pages, was transferred to the great stable, where the regimen was much more lax and the pages were free to roam about the town for five or six hours every day. The fifty boys assigned here were quartered in one wing of the vast stable, in small rooms, each painted yellow, each with identical furnishings, that were scarcely larger than horse stalls. Four huge stoves kept them warm, and they shared a large study room and dining room. Though the formal education of the stable pages was neglected, their training in horsemanship was superb, under the tutelage of the "strict, but never ferocious" Prince de Lambesc, scion of the heretofore royal house of Lorraine (and thus a distant kinsman of the Queen). The Prince rose before dawn every morning, even in winter, and began his tutelage of the pages by five o'clock, teaching them not only how to handle the superb horses kept for the King (there were some three thousand horses in the royal stables) but how to groom them and care for them.

The duties of the stable pages were relatively light. An elite group chosen from among them accompanied the King on his hunts, wearing special hunting livery with gold braid trim (the trim was worn in a variety of ways depending on which animal was being hunted). They carried his loaded guns, handing them to him and taking them back from him when he had fired, then taking the empty guns to the *arquebusier* who loaded them again. At the end of the hunt, after the game was distributed, the pages feasted on what was left—and were often given a dozen bottles of champagne to wash it down with.

The Queen's household was smaller than the King's, but it was still very large—perhaps a total of five hundred officers and servants—and very complex. Antoinette revived the office of superintendent of the Queen's household and gave it to the Princesse de Lamballe, her friend and confidante, soon after she became Queen. (The elevation of the Princess put Madame de Noailles in the shade, and she soon resigned, as no doubt Antoinette meant her to.) As superintendent the Princess had vast authority, and given her mild and benign nature she did not abuse it. Beneath her was the chief lady-in-waiting, the Duchesse de Cossé, succeeded by the Princesse de Chimay and then by Madame de Mailly, who held the post until 1781. Madame Campan, Antoinette's loyal servant and biographer, was one of the two chief bedchamber women, in charge of all the bedchamber servants, responsible for the Queen's private funds and entrusted with her jewels. The Abbé Vermond held the position of reader to the Queen.[3]

The running of Antoinette's household involved a wide variety of activities, from the checking and paying of bills to the answering of letters from foreign sovereigns announcing births, deaths, and other events in their families. Two secretaries were kept busy with this correspondence alone. The repair and maintenance of the Queen's vehicles, including the gilded sledges she went riding in when especially harsh winters provided enough snow, was another time-consuming task. Each time the court moved to Marly, Choisy or Fontainebleau, invitations had to be sent out for balls, suppers, and hunting parties—thousands of invitations in all. Then too there was the payment of pensions to former servants and others, including the former servants of the late Queen Marie Leczinska, which Antoinette insisted on continuing.

The health of the inferior servants was an ongoing concern

that necessitated the employment of an apothecary and two surgeons. These were in addition to the "body apothecary" and surgeon for the household, who tended the Queen herself and her officers. The purveyance of foodstuffs, the care of glassware and silver, the storing and cleaning of robes and court dresses—not to mention shoes, bags, fans, gloves, undergarments and hats—employed many dozens of people. The regulations put in place by Abbé Terray called for linen clothes, napkins, chemises and lace to be replaced every three years (later changed to five, then seven years as successive controllers attempted to enforce more stringent economy); clerks of the linen cupboard had to make certain these regulations were honored, and that the discarded items were disbursed appropriately.

Oversight of these long-range matters went on while the daily, hourly services were performed without which the household could not run smoothly. The making of the Queen's bed, for example, had to be completed while she and her entourage were at Mass. Once the Mass-bound procession had left the apartments, the waiting women hurried in with clean sheets and pillows, and, opening the huge double curtains that surrounded the bed, stripped off the old linen and put it into huge baskets lined with green taffeta to be taken to the laundry. Then four liveried footmen were called in to turn the mattresses, which were too heavy for the waiting women to lift. Once the footmen had withdrawn, new white sheets were put on the bed and the covers arranged. So skilled were the waiting women at this task that they accomplished it in five minutes, and dusted the furniture and tidied the mess left after the dressing and coiffing of the Queen as well, with one of the ladies-in-waiting sitting in a large armchair looking on to make certain everything was done properly.[4]

Fortunately, one of Antoinette's ladies-in-waiting, the Comtesse de la Tour du Pin, left a long and detailed account of her life at Versailles. She was born Henriette-Lucy Dillon, the daughter of an Irish soldier who commanded a regiment in the French army and his French wife, a great beauty named Lucie de Rothe, also one of Antoinette's ladies. (Antoinette, the Countess recalled, "was always ready to be captivated by glitter" and Lucie was lovely and glittering, though tragically she died young.) A number of Henriette's other relatives held court positions, and because of these connections, her marriage to the Comte de la Tour du Pin de Gouvernet was celebrated in the chapel at Versailles. She obtained her appointment as lady-in-waiting, but first had to be formally presented, a ceremony that made great demands on the grace and poise of a young woman.

Her aunt the Princesse d'Hénin took Henriette to Paris to a dancing master, one M. Huart, who was accustomed to preparing women for their formal presentations. "It is impossible to conceive of anything more ridiculous than those rehearsals of the presentation," the Countess wrote in her memoirs. "M. Huart, a large man, his hair very well dressed and white with powder, wore a billowing underskirt and stood at the far end of the room to represent the Queen." M. Huart showed Henriette when to remove her glove and bow to kiss the hem of the Queen's gown, how to walk with dignity down the length of the room, how to curtsey gracefully despite the encumbrance of her robe and gown. "Nothing was forgotten or overlooked in these rehearsals, which went on for three or four hours. I wore a train and the wide paniers of court dress, but above and below was my ordinary morning dress, and my hair was only very simply pinned up. It was all very funny."

The day of the presentation came, and Henriette was dressed in her special white gown embroidered with pearls and silver, and wore around her neck "seven or eight rows of large diamonds" which Antoinette had lent her for the occasion. More diamonds sparkled in her hair. "Thanks to M. Huart's good coaching," she recalled, "I made my three curtseys very well. I removed my glove and put it on again not too awkwardly. Then I went to receive the accolade from the King and his brothers, the Princes," and other dignitaries. Years afterward, the Countess still remembered how embarrassing and exhausting the ceremony was for her. Even though many of her relatives were present, and even though the Queen's affection for her late mother predisposed her to welcome Henriette, she still felt as if she were running a gauntlet, "being stared at by the whole court and being torn to shreds by every critical tongue." "One became the topic of every conversation and on returning to the 'jeu' in the evening . . . every eye was upon you."[5]

It was not long, however, before Henriette learned to feel at home among the Queen's ladies. She stood with the others each Sunday in the salon next to Antoinette's bedroom, waiting for the signal to enter for the ceremony of the grand toilette. The salon was always full, she recalled, there were usually at least forty women waiting there, often more. "Sometimes we were very closely packed," she wrote, "for our paniers took up a great deal of room." When the Princesse de Lamballe entered the bedchamber, and then the first lady-in-waiting and the mistress of the robes, the women knew that the ceremony would soon begin. In a few moments a footman came to the bedchamber door and called in a loud voice for *"Le Service."* At this the ladies entered.

"As soon as the Queen had greeted each of us in her charming, kindly way, the door was opened and everyone admitted. We stood to the right and left of the room in such a manner as to leave a clear space at the door and in the center of the room." Often the women had to stand in rows two or three feet deep, their paniers crushed and their gowns wrinkled, until the entire group moved off toward the chapel. One day Henriette encountered the British ambassador and, knowing the English custom, shook hands with him. Antoinette happened to see her, and, as "she had never seen this English form of greeting before, found it very amusing. As jokes do not die easily at court, she never failed to ask the [ambassador] on the many occasions when we were both present, 'Have you shaken hands with Mme de Gouvernet?'"

The Sunday morning audiences went on until 12:40, when the footman again advanced to the door and announced "The King!" At this Antoinette "would go to meet him with a charming air of pleasure and deference. The King would incline his head to the right and the left, and speak to a few ladies whom he knew, though never to the young ones." His extreme short-sightedness meant that he would only recognize those who stood very near him, Henriette recalled, and it was evident that he felt encumbered by his heavily embroidered coat, sword and hat.

The procession to the chapel was at its most elaborate on Sundays, and foreign visitors liked to come to Versailles to witness it if possible. The first gentleman of the bedchamber led the way, the Captain of the Guard following him, then came the King and Queen, who walked slowly enough to enable them to speak a few words to each of the courtiers as they passed them. "Often, the Queen would speak to the foreign ladies who had been presented to her in private, to artists and to writers. An inclination of the head or a gracious smile was noted and carefully stored against future need." Behind the King and Queen came the highest ranking ladies, with those of lesser rank bringing up the rear. "We walked four or five abreast," Henriette wrote, "the young ones trying to be on the outside and those who were considered to be in fashion—among whom I had the honor to be included—taking great care to walk close enough to the line of courtiers to be able to catch the pretty things whispered to them as they passed."

To pass through the long Galerie des Glaces without stepping on the train of the lady in front took considerable skill. One never raised one's feet off the parquet, but rather glided along, swanlike, never looking at the floor but mindful of avoiding the yards and yards of velvet and taffeta and silk that swirled everywhere and threatened to cause an accident. Once the gallery was safely crossed, each lady "threw her train over one of her paniers and, making sure she had been seen by her servant who would be waiting with a large, gold-fringed, red velvet bag, she rushed to one of the side galleries of the chapel, trying to find a place as close as possible to the gallery occupied by the King and Queen." The red velvet bag contained a missal and other necessities.

When Mass and dinner were over, Henriette and the other ladies were able to take their leave, though etiquette required them to pay brief calls on Provence and Artois and the royal aunts before retiring to their own rooms. Henriette enjoyed visiting Artois, whose youth and good looks held considerable allure. "Great efforts were made to please him," she recalled, "for to succeed was a guarantee of fame." After these obligatory calls the ladies were on their own for a few hours, and returned to their own apartments where they took off their stiff formal gowns, dined and socialized. Rest was impossible because of the stylish high coiffures, but they could at least sit down and relax until shortly before seven in the evening, when the card games began and the ladies-in-waiting had once more to be in attendance.

"We had to be there before seven," the Countess wrote, "for the Queen entered before the chiming of the clock. Beside her door would be one of the two curés of Versailles. He would hand her a purse and she would go around to everyone, taking up a collection and saying: 'For the poor, if you please.'" Each lady was expected to donate a silver coin, each man a gold louis. Often this small collection came to as much as 150 louis, which the curé would distribute among the neediest of his parishioners.[6]

Without minimizing the artificiality of the royal court, the stiffness of its manners, the awkwardness of its dress, the Countess's memoirs nonetheless reveal its moments of extraordinary beauty and graciousness. Many years after her period of service, when the glories of Versailles were long past, she and others brought to mind the shimmer of the silken gowns and the glitter of diamonds, the magnificence of the huge palace theaters, all gold and glass, lit by hundreds of chandeliers, the splendid ballrooms transformed by papier-mâché greenery and silk flowers into forests, the gallantry of the men and the allure of the women. The suppers, the Countess recalled, were the quintessence of this exquisite hothouse culture. The guests, carefully chosen for their cultivation, wit and worldliness, their ability to be at ease in polished company, arrived at half-past nine.

"All the toilettes, all the elegance, everything that the beautiful, fashionable society of Paris could offer in refinement and charm was to be found at these suppers."[7] There was fine food, scintillating conversation, brilliance and glamour nuanced with flirtation and enticement. Music played, wine flowed, there was laughter, life was very sweet. The talk went on until long past midnight, when the candles burned down and the women, hiding their yawns behind their jeweled fans, were escorted back to the tiny closets allotted to them to snatch an hour or two of sleep before morning.

❧ 11 ❧

THE Scottish philosopher David Hume, who visited Versailles ten years before Louis XVI began his reign, was enraptured by the palace. "I eat nothing but ambrosia, drink nothing but nectar, breathe nothing but incense, and tread on nothing but flowers," he wrote in his ecstasy. The grandeur of the place had clearly befuddled his senses. In actuality Versailles was a vast cesspool, reeking of filth and befouled with ordure.

Peasants from the surrounding villages brought their garbage to the palace and dumped it in the gardens. Indoors, the walls, woven hangings and costly upholstery gave off an unpleasant sooty smell; the chimneys drew badly, and the rooms were full of smoke from November until August. The odor clung to clothes, wigs, even undergarments. Worst of all, beggars, servants, and aristocratic visitors alike used the stairs, the corridors, any out-of-the-way place to relieve themselves. "The passages, the courtyards, the wings and the corridors," a contemporary wrote, "were full of urine and fecal matter. The park, the gardens and the chateau made one retch with their bad smell."[1]

English travelers accustomed to the "neatness" of royal and noble houses in their own country were repelled by the "unclean manner" in which the "noble apartments" at Versailles were maintained. The paintings and statues were neglected, the furniture was allowed to become dirty and shabby. People were careless about their bathing and grooming. "I shall never get over the dirt of this country," Horace Walpole grumbled, and he had traveled extensively.[2] The approach to Versailles, the English agreed, was magnificent, along wide roads shaded with stately trees. But the squalor inside was unspeakable.

One afternoon, not long before she became Queen, Antoinette and her sister-in-law the Comtesse de Provence went to call on Victoire. On leaving Victoire's apartments the two women paused in a courtyard to look at a sundial. From a second-story window someone flung a pail of waste water into the courtyard, and the two Princesses were drenched. Possibly the drenching was no accident, for the window was in Madame Du Barry's apartments and her servants had no love for the dauphine. But more likely than not it was just one of many such incidents, quite unintentional and too commonplace to record.[3] It was no wonder Antoinette kept fresh flowers in her rooms and burned flower essences in china perfume-braziers and ornamental oil pots; it was to drive away the stinks that beset her.

There were dogs and cats all over Versailles, many of them wild. The mayhem and dirt caused by Antoinette's dogs has already been mentioned. But Louis too kept dogs, and had a large and capacious dog kennel in the main reception room of Fontainebleau. This was a miniature palace in itself, made of oak painted white with gilt pilasters and moldings, and decorated with painted sprigs of flowers. Each dog had three mattresses inside, upholstered in red velvet.[4]

Madame de Guéménée, a favorite of Antoinette and governess of Louis's sisters Clotilde and Elisabeth, was always attended by a great many small dogs. "She offered to them a species of worship," Mercy told Maria Theresa, "and pretended, through their medium, to hold communication with the world of spirits."[5] Whatever their value for psychic communication, the little pack must have made her apartments unlivable.

Contributing to the dirt and disorder were the wide array of people, many of them uncouth and unsavory, who wandered freely through the palace and its grounds.

Virtually anyone could enter the palace. Some effort was made to keep out people who had recently had smallpox, but everyone else was admitted. The only requirement was that the men possess a hat and a rapier, and these could be rented from the concierge. Parisians with muddy boots tramped through the elegant salons and down the long galleries, admiring the furnishings

and objets d'art, touching them, coveting them. Though there
were servants everywhere, contemporary accounts do not mention
guards who watched the transient visitors to prevent them from
stealing small treasures or cutting the golden tassels from the curtains to sell once they got home.

We may safely assume that the palace held a free-floating population of light-fingered thieves who preyed on the courtiers and
lived on their gilded pickings. On the evening of Artois's marriage, a masked ball was held in celebration. A number of "richly
dressed" burglars were admitted to the ball, and proceeded to relieve the guests of their watches and purses, their snuffboxes and
jewelry.[6] Antoinette's wedding ring was stolen from her in 1771
(though she believed she had lost it when washing her hands) by a
woman who used it "in sorceries to prevent her having any children." The thief confessed her malevolence to the curé of the
Madeleine de la Cité many years later, and the curé sent the ring
to Madame Campan's husband with an explanatory note. He of
course gave it to Antoinette, who was happy to have it back and
made no effort to discover or punish the thief.

Ambassadors and other dignitaries from foreign courts
brought their entourages to Versailles, complete with slaves, camp
followers and exotic pets. Entertainers of all sorts, from the actors
and musicians of the Paris theaters to the bear-keepers and animal
trainers who made their living on the boulevards, came to the palace to perform. Even the prisoners of the chain gangs, on their
way to service in the galleys at Brest, were marched through the
town of Versailles—though their route was eventually changed
during Louis XVI's reign because the kindhearted King was free-
ing too many of them and they were a hazard to the community.[7]

Madmen and idiots were not excluded from Versailles, provided their behavior was not violent. Madame Campan recorded
how Antoinette "put up with the most troublesome importunities
from people whose minds were deranged," and was reluctant to
order them taken away.

One such madman was a pale, thin nobleman from Bordeaux,
a man whose "sinister appearance," Campan wrote, "occasioned
the most uncomfortable sensations." His name was Castelnaux,
but he was generally referred to with derision as "the Queen's
lover," for such he declared himself to be. Taciturn, humorless,
and vaguely threatening, Castelnaux shadowed Antoinette every-

where she went, and for ten years and more she tolerated his presence on the fringes of her life. As his status gave him the entrée at court, he was able to attend every ceremony during the day and evening, and indeed he was invariably present, sitting as close to the Queen as he could when she went to Mass, staring at her throughout dinner, placing himself directly in her line of sight during the evening card-playing and never taking his eyes from her face. When she went to the theater, he was there, when she stayed at the Petit Trianon he was there as well, walking endlessly around the garden, at the edge of the moat. Rain never deterred him, or ice-cold winds, or searing heat; like some ghostly sentry, he was always at his post near the Queen's side. When the court moved to Fontainebleau or Marly he always anticipated its move, so that he could be waiting for Antoinette when she arrived. When she stepped down from her coach, Campan says, his melancholy face was always the first she saw.

After many years "the Queen's lover" ceased to be a joke and became, in Campan's words, "an intolerable annoyance." Antoinette still would not let anyone restrain Castelnaux, but she did talk with a celebrated attorney to see whether he could persuade the madman to give her some peace. The attorney did his best, talking to Castelnaux for nearly an hour and then returning with good news: the madman had agreed that, "since his presence was disagreeable to her, he would retire to his province." The Queen was relieved—briefly. Half an hour later Castelnaux was back, requesting an audience with Madame Campan. "He came to tell me," she wrote, "that he withdrew his promise, that he had not sufficient command of himself to give up seeing the Queen as often as possible." She reported the conversation to Antoinette, who took the news philosophically.

"Well, let him annoy me!" she said, "but let him not be deprived of the pleasure of being free!"[8]

Castelnaux was no menace to the health or hygiene of the palace, but other perpetual hangers-on were. Prostitutes solicited in the courtyards and public rooms, knowing that they would be tolerated as long as they kept out of the royal apartments themselves. Ragged, barefooted children, many of them homeless, ran up and down the great staircases carrying messages, stole food from the kitchens and snatched what sleep they could in the stables and outbuildings. Hungry ex-servants, down at heel and far from clean, stood about in groups, hoping to hear of openings in the household and looking enviously at their more fortunate peers who wore the King's livery. Cleanliness was impossible with such people constantly underfoot, and in any case the servants were more concerned about their prerogatives than about carrying out the humble tasks of sweeping and cleaning, washing the floors and removing offensive refuse.

If the environment of the court was unhealthy, it was also full of inconvenience. With its hundreds of servants, it was an unwieldy mechanism, and inefficient. At times it broke down altogether. On one occasion the court was in the process of moving from Choisy to Versailles. The move did not disturb the routine of the King's hunt, which went on as usual. Antoinette decided to follow the hunt in a coach, with her three aunts. When the coach came to a river, however, the aunts became worried that it might overturn, and insisted on getting out even though they were in "an extremely boggy place." Antoinette got out too, and began the long trek back to Choisy. There were no servants to rescue her or her aunts—all the servants had gone on ahead to Versailles—and the walk proved to be long and very wet. She lost one of her shoes in the mud, and the rest of her clothes became very bedraggled. Fortunately she was able to dry herself at a hearth fire, though her clothes were scorched. At last she went on to Versailles, where she hoped the servants would have prepared the palace for the return of the court. But her apartments had somehow been neglected, the rooms were not heated, and she soon came down with a cold.[9]

Inconvenience was a way of life for the courtier. Living in cramped, dark quarters, keeping very long hours, forever jostling for space in the overcrowded salons, surrounded by "an appalling crowd, that makes a most fatiguing racket," as one of them wrote, the denizens of Versailles suffered for their status. They dared not relax, or look tired, or reveal how bored they were. To be agreeable was a necessity, to smile when one's tight brocade shoes pinched and one's scalp itched and one's rival was gaining in favor. An experienced official passed on this advice to a novice: "You have to do three things: say nice things to everybody, solicit every post that is likely to become vacant, and sit down when you can."[10]

The goal of every courtier was to amass offices, privileges, and ultimately wealth. But there was a heavy price to be paid. He or she had to stand for hours in the *oeil-de-boeuf*, the "bull's-eye" chamber next to the King's bedroom lit by a single round window, waiting to be noticed, to be admitted to the inner sanctum, or to overhear some bit of gossip or news that might help him advance himself. He had to take part in tedious spectacles. At one ball the courtiers learned the intricate choreography of a dance in which they formed the letters of Antoinette's name. He had to flatter, to persuade, to cajole his superiors while battling to keep his inferiors in their places. And above all, he had to be patient, often for years, with no guarantee that he would ever gain the rewards he sought.

Nonetheless, there were compensations. Those not privileged to dine with the King and Queen or the great personages went to the *Grand Commun*, the huge communal dining hall at the palace where good food was to be had amid equally good company. Society at the *Grand Commun* was pleasant and enlightening. One met there artists, scholars, writers. Politics and current affairs were endlessly discussed, topical issues debated. Intrigues were hatched, ambition ignited. Grievances were aired. "It was the fashion to complain of everything," wrote the Comtesse de La Tour du Pin. "One was bored, weary of attendance at court. The officers of the Garde du Corps, who were lodged in the chateau when on duty, bemoaned having to wear uniform all day." A popular subject was how soon they could get away to Paris to dine and attend the theater. "It was the height of style to complain of duties at court, profiting from them nonetheless and sometimes, indeed often, abusing the privileges they carried."[11]

The courtiers complained about the expense of maintaining themselves in the proper style, the cost of wigs (the best ones made of human hair, far superior to the cheap ones made of horsehair or goat's hair), the high prices of the best hairdressers, the interminable fittings of gowns and waistcoats, the ever-changing demands of fashion. No one ever had enough money, it seemed; debts mounted up, yet it was dangerous to economize, for the courtier who spent the most money, even though it had to be borrowed money, had the best chance of recouping it once he managed to attain the favor he sought. To owe one's tailor or shoemaker hundreds of thousands of livres was expected in a person of taste. To retrench financially was to invite ruin.

The scramble for advancement led to intense narcissism, and to myopia. No one bothered to scrutinize his competitors too closely. In this atmosphere, imposture flourished.

In the last years of Louis XV's reign a pretty young girl of fifteen or sixteen managed to swindle a good many people by posing as the King's mistress. How she got the idea, and whether anyone besides herself was in on the scheme, is obscure, but what is clear is that by seducing some of the royal pages she was able to gain access to the King's apartments. Once she had this entrée, she was able to persuade people that she was indeed on the most familiar terms with King Louis and that she could use her influence over him to their benefit. Hungry for any extra advantage, however slight, the edgy courtiers paid eagerly for her influence— and were bilked.

In a short time the girl amassed some sixty thousand francs, plus many perquisites and favors. She sent for a surgeon to attend a woman in labor and persuaded him that he was delivering the King's bastard and so he should consider himself honored. No doubt she cheated tradesmen and dressmakers in the same fashion. Appearances were what counted, and the girl gave every appearance of being what she claimed to be. After all, the King's taste for pretty young girls was well known, and this girl was very pretty, and, according to Madame Campan, who knew her, of such a "modest demeanor" that no one suspected her of deceit. In the end she even convinced the haughty Adelaide and the soft-hearted Victoire of her genuineness.

But then, somehow—the details are tantalizingly vague—she was exposed as an imposter. She was only eighteen then, though much older in worldly wisdom. Clever to the end, she tried to save herself from punishment through another fabrication. At the tender age of fourteen, she said, she had been seduced by a priest, who forced her to pose as the King's mistress in order to enrich himself. The priest was suspended from his offices, but was later able to prove his innocence. The girl was sent first to the Bastille, then to another prison. Her brief, and for a time lucrative, career was over.[12]

Another trickster had a much longer career—and did much more damage. Cahouette de Villers, whom Madame Campan described as "very irregular in conduct, and of a scheming turn of mind," also posed as Louis XV's mistress and, after he died, as a familiar of Queen Antoinette. Cahouette's husband was a royal treasurer, but as he did not have the right of entry to the Queen's apartments, she set out to become the mistress of a man who did: Gabriel de Saint-Charles, intendant of the King's finances.

Cahouette went to Versailles every Saturday with her lover, stayed in his apartment, and learned everything she could about the court, and especially about the Queen. As she was a reasonably good painter, she hit on a plan to approach Antoinette directly, by painting her portrait. She copied a portrait done by another painter and presented it to Madame Campan's husband, who was Antoinette's librarian and one of her secretaries, but he, "knowing her conduct," refused to pass it on to his mistress.[13] The Princesse de Lamballe, however, was more accommodating.

Through her lover Saint-Charles, Cahouette next got hold of some documents signed by Antoinette, and learned to copy her execrable and distinctive handwriting. More accomplished as a forger than she had been as a painter, the woman wrote herself a number of letters and notes putatively signed by the Queen, and filled them with personal touches and familiar endearments. She then showed the letters to friends and acquaintances, claiming that her friendship with Antoinette was a "great secret" just as her relationship with the late King had been. Naturally her reputation grew, as someone favored with the Queen's intimate confidence. The Queen, it was whispered, had a "particular kindness for her," and even entrusted her with the purchase of things for her private use.

Cahouette forged letters in which the Queen asked her to procure jewels and other costly items from Parisian shopkeepers; she had only to show these letters to the jewelers and tradesmen to be given whatever she asked for—and infinite credit besides. Eventually, not content with this, Cahouette approached the Farmer-General, M. Beranger, who controlled the tax revenues, and showed him a forged letter in which Antoinette asked her to procure two hundred thousand francs for her—funds that she badly needed, but that she was reluctant to ask her husband for. The Farmer-General, thinking that by doing the Queen the good turn of giving her the funds he might obtain some far greater advantage from her in return at a future time, gladly gave the imposter the sum she asked for.

Amazingly, even this colossal swindle went undetected for

quite some time. Eventually, however, M. Beranger began to wonder whether he had been duped. He made tentative inquiries—very discreetly, for there was always the possibility that Antoinette's request had been genuine and he risked exposing her secret. What he learned from these first inquiries emboldened him, however, and he finally went to the Paris police. They were able to follow Cahouette's trail of unpaid bills, pawned finery, and unsubstantiated boasts. The imposter was unmasked, and sent to prison, and her poor husband was forced to replace the two hundred thousand francs. The forged letters, found among Cahouette's effects, were sent to Antoinette. She and Madame Campan examined them one by one, and found to their dismay that the forgery was remarkably convincing. The only difference between the Queen's writing and the forger's was that the latter wrote a little better, with "a little more regularity in the disposition of the letters."

Still another imposter was more subtle. The Countess of Walburg-Frohberg, a Swabian married to a minor court official, masqueraded as an intimate of several important personages, from the Minister of Foreign Affairs to the Queen's chief equerry. She too had letters to back up her claims, and her victims were only too eager to believe that they were genuine. From her rented rooms in the Hotel Fortisson, in the town of Versailles, the Countess held a miniature court of her own, receiving visits from petitioners who paid her to plead their cases with the great. It was a nearly foolproof scheme, since those who came to her had no way of discovering whether or not she had the ear of the people she claimed to know so well. All they could do was to continue to pay her—and to hope for the best.

The Countess overstepped herself, however, when she pretended she had a right to join a royal cortege in her coach. She was recognized and questioned, and the lieutenant of police opened an inquiry into her doings. Soon all was revealed. The Countess had been sly enough, though, to leave nothing incriminating behind. The police had only her victims' word that she took money from them; she claimed, to the contrary, that she had used her influence on their behalf purely out of kindness, that no money had changed hands at all. She was elusive—and dangerous, for unlike Cahouette de Villers, the Countess of Walburg-Frohberg knew a great many secrets, and was in a position to embarrass some very important people. Afraid that she might become vindictive and ruin reputations if she were to be imprisoned, the police let her go on condition that she return to Germany. As far as is known, she did not return to Versailles—at least, not under the same name.[14]

These impostures succeeded, not only because the courtiers and would-be courtiers were gullible, but because they wanted desperately to succeed. The mythology of the court was for some stronger than its actuality, and the mythology dictated that the ambitious, the hard-working, the well-connected, would eventually win offices and wealth. Versailles cast a spell over those who lived and served and visited there. And while they were under its spell, they breathed nothing but incense, drank nothing but nectar, ate nothing but ambrosia—and imagined that they crushed roses underfoot.

12

I N October of 1774 the spies that kept watch on all the younger members of the royal family reported that Theresa,
Comtesse d'Artois, was very likely pregnant. Her period
was six days late, and her husband had been more attentive
to her than usual for the past several weeks.

"There is half a suspicion and much rumor about the supposed
pregnancy of the Comtesse d'Artois," Antoinette informed her
mother. The signs in themselves were not conclusive, as Theresa
was irregular, but Antoinette knew that her brothers- and sisters-
in-law were doing their best to produce heirs as quickly as possible, the intensity of their endeavors accelerated by the advent of
their brother's reign. Louis was King; if he died without a male
heir Provence would rule; unless *he* fathered a male heir Artois
would become King. Aside from the rivalry of the individuals, the
future of the dynasty was at stake. No one felt this more keenly
than Antoinette, who, though she knew perfectly well that her
childlessness was her husband's fault and not her own, decided
voluntarily to curtail her riding each month during the last ten
days before her period in hopes of increasing her fertility.

It was a futile, even a pathetic gesture. General Krottendorf
continued to arrive on schedule, and Antoinette's sister-in-law
Theresa continued to be late. By December Theresa was sure she
was pregnant, and for once the short, unprepossessing, long-nosed
Countess was able to upstage her lively and attractive sister-in-
law.[1]

Antoinette was predictably pained by the event, though characteristically she showed only gracious happiness for Theresa. "Something which I have always suspected and feared has happened," Mercy wrote to the Empress in Vienna. "It is that the Queen, struck by this event, and reflecting on her own condition, finds with reason a very grave subject for pain, and I see with apprehension that her majesty is inwardly affected in a most agonizing fashion." Theresa's pregnancy quickened Antoinette's old grief about her marriage. Would Louis ever face the reality of his incapacity and let himself be treated? Early in December he had a long conversation with Antoinette's doctor, and discussed the brief if painful operation that he needed to make him capable of ejaculation. He got as far as discussing it, but no farther; when the surgeon spread out his sharp steel instruments, the King practically fainted, and changed his mind about going ahead with the operation.

Antoinette, it seems, did not press him on this most delicate of subjects. And yet they both were aware that their continued childlessness, apart from giving rise to ridicule and undermining Louis's authority, was likely to lead to sordid schemes among the courtiers. An impotent King could not be influenced through mistresses, but the King's wife, sexually frustrated and full of hidden resentment for her husband (or so it was supposed) could be controlled through a lover. The courtiers watched Antoinette closely to see whom she favored. Would it be a young and handsome soldier, a foreign diplomat, a seasoned, middle-aged courtier?

All these types and more were at hand. There was Count Balint Esterhazy, an impossibly handsome Hungarian officer whose family was impossibly rich and who claimed among his ancestors Attila the Hun. Antoinette helped him pay his debts and acquire a regiment. There was the Duc de Lauzun, a funny, sly Gascon with an inflated ego and a large fund of amusing stories. Antoinette found him entertaining, embraced him as a friend—and wound up having to send him away when he mistook friendship for lust. There was the fifty-three-year-old Swiss, Baron Pierre-Victor Besenval, a lieutenant colonel in the Swiss Guards, who sang topical French songs and was full of heavy flirtatiousness. Besenval too was rejected, and so was the Comte d'Adhémar, a dandy who, like Antoinette, played the harp, and the Prince de Ligne, fortyish and cosmopolitan, who was an Austrian at home in the Hofburg and whom Antoinette enjoyed because he reminded her of her childhood. The Prince was an easy companion because he made no effort to seduce her and indeed praised her purity, finding "her soul as beautiful and white as her face."

The gossips watched, and waited for Antoinette to slip from virtue. When she disappointed them, they arrived at a vicious explanation: the Queen did not take a lover, it was said, because she had one already—the Comte d'Artois.

The young Artois, barely seventeen in the winter of 1774–5, had become quite insufferable. He was extremely pleased with himself, and it showed. He had managed to father a child, a feat that neither of his older brothers had been able to match. He was handsome, while his brothers had none of his appeal. He had dash and style; he was popularly known as "the Prince of youth." All the women at court, even some of those old enough to be his mother, came to pay their compliments to him and vied for his smiles and his attentions. He was at the center of the Queen's group of favorites, he was admired and envied. With his wife absorbed in her pregnancy, Artois spent every spare moment with Antoinette—or so it appeared to the spiteful courtiers. He never left her side. They went to the races together; he drove her about in his daring open carriage called a "devil." It was almost as if he, Artois, and not the heavy-footed Louis, were King.

Artois even mimicked the kingly role, walking in front of Louis though etiquette forbade anyone to precede the King, making insolent remarks in his presence, pushing him and stepping on his feet—in short, making a conspicuous nuisance of himself. And Louis did not respond with regal indignity, as he should have; instead he was weak and apathetic, which seemed to confirm the suspicions that Artois was cuckolding him, and that he, pathetically unable to perform toward Antoinette as a husband should, was compliant in the affair.

Young as he was, Artois had already earned a widespread reputation as a rake and a libertine, with mistresses in Paris, visits to costly courtesans, rumored seductions of court ladies and frequent bouts of drinking and wild gambling. A liaison with his royal sister-in-law would fit right in with this pattern of life.

And what of Antoinette? She was no better than he was, so the gossip went. Hadn't she held an orgy one night at Marly, after the King had gone to bed?[2] Didn't she wear dresses with names such as "Masked Desire" and "Indiscreet Pleasures"? Didn't she insult and mock the elderly ladies of the court, just as Artois mocked Louis? And didn't she show her brazenness in riding vicious-looking horses, riding astride like a man and wearing a man's green pantaloons under her English riding coat?

No one could prove that Antoinette and Artois were lovers— and of course they were not. Yet there was something different about her. Her enemies put it down to illicit love; more perceptive observers might have seen in it a kind of desperation.

The Antoinette of good resolutions, of self-imposed study and reading had vanished. So had the Antoinette whom Mercy found to be timid and fearful, dependent and passive. A new self had emerged, a self that was brittle, frenetic, hardened by a constant surfeit of pleasures. The new self became preeminent soon after Antoinette became Queen, but her newfound eminence alone was not responsible for it. Instead the transformation owed much to the pressures of ceremony, the inescapable reminders of her barrenness—of which her sister-in-law Theresa's pregnancy was only one—and her emancipation from the tutelage of the Comtesse de Noailles and Mercy.

Obsessive spending was one symptom of this emerging identity. Day after day Antoinette spent lavishly, excessively, on the Petit Trianon, on gowns and coiffures and feathers, on her friends, who received costly court appointments and pensions, and on jewels. The spending spree reached new heights in the early months of 1775. The Queen developed a passion for feathered headdresses. Crests of feathers, some of them two or three feet high, became the fashion. Visitors to Versailles found themselves in a "forest of feathers," and a new term was coined— "featherheads"—to describe Antoinette and her giddy coterie.

Feathers were costly enough, but diamonds were prohibitively expensive. Yet Antoinette had to have them, indeed craved them. Diamond earrings, bracelets, more bracelets—nearly a million livres' worth within a few months. And there had to be elegant occasions to wear all this finery. The court balls in the winter of 1774–75 were exceptionally splendid. No expense was spared in the decoration of the theaters and salons where the balls were held, or in the preparation of elaborate costumes for the dancers. Tyrolean, Indian, antique French costumes were demanded. The servants in the department of the King's pleasures worked for days on each extravagant production; one particular gown that

Antoinette ordered, ornamented with antique lace from the time of Henri IV, kept the seamstresses up all night.[3] In all, the balls for the first three months of 1775 cost more than a hundred thousand livres, chiefly, the officer in charge of them noted, "because of the quantity of gold embroidery which was used for the gowns and the quadrilles."

When the expense sheets were shown to the King and Queen, they defended the extravagance. They "did not find this expense to be too high at all," they said, "for amusing the entire court throughout the entire winter."[4] Louis's Finance Minister Turgot, however, took a different view.

An austere and abstemious nobleman, Turgot did not trouble to hide his disdain for the spendthrift habits of the Queen and her circle. As Controller-General of Finance, he was wedded to economy, as the King declared himself to be. And to honesty, as few at court were. Only by restricting spending, he declared, could the country's economy be restored to health. This policy had brought results in the Limousin, where Turgot had been intendant; it would work just as well for all of France, provided the King and Queen were cooperative.

In his distaste for court expense, Turgot articulated a widespread grievance. Many of the French, particularly the businessmen and artisans, resented both the waste and the inefficacy of the monarchy and its political servants. Versailles to them was nothing more than a costly frivolity, where pampered wastrels enriched themselves at the expense of hard-working tradesmen and laborers. And Versailles was only a symptom of an entire system, social and governmental, which exploited the many for the benefit of the worthless few. Turgot was not the most radical exponent of this view, but he was among the most candid. He was blunt in his disparagement of the monarchy and its traditions, traditions that belonged, he said, to the "barbarous centuries" and should not be dragged along into the present. Nothing short of a thoroughgoing reform of the finances would salvage the state; this meant stringent economies, coupled with a commitment to levying no new taxes and taking out no new loans.

King Louis needed Turgot, not only to enforce the cutting of expenses but to bolster his own sagging self-discipline. Louis meant well, his intentions were of the best. He meant to promote austerity, not extravagance. But he was proving to be too weak to impose his will on those around him, especially his wife. His regal posturing, his loud declarations about the need to exclude women from government, his long hours of desk work had ceased. He had tried, in the first months of his reign, to devote himself to the labor of kingship. But he lacked the toughness to keep up the labor for long. By the time winter came, and with it the Queen's elaborate balls, Louis had resumed his preferred pastimes of hunting, construction and lock-making. He relied on Turgot to do his work for him, just as his grandfather had relied on Choiseul, even though he realized that his Finance Minister was at heart the enemy of monarchical government.

"M. Turgot's ideas," Louis said, "are extremely dangerous." Yet his goal, fiscal solvency, was the same as the King's, and his methods, it seemed, were necessary. He was given a free hand.

Turgot imposed restrictions on court spending, limited the powers of the guilds, and abolished the *corvée*, the right of the nobles to demand free labor services from the peasants on their estates. In so doing he was attacking outworn customs from the "barbarous centuries." But he went further. He attacked the barbarous network of customs restrictions that impeded the movement of grain throughout the kingdom, thus creating for the first time a free market in grain. The harvest of 1774 had been scanty, and the free movement of grain was expected to alleviate the near-famine conditions by leading to a lowering of bread prices. But in practice the opposite happened. Wealthy speculators bought up all the grain, and drove up the price of bread far beyond what the poor could afford. They blamed Turgot, who earned the hatred not only of the starving people but of the horde of customs officials deprived of their livelihoods. The courtiers too hated him for curtailing their expenditures, as did the nobles and the guild members.

Hatred turned to fear when the severe grain shortage, exacerbated by Turgot's policies, led to rioting. Townspeople plundered the bakeries, peasants attacked the flour mills and even waylaid boats carrying cargoes of flour. Criminals took advantage of the chaos to rob and pillage at will. The turmoil in Paris at the beginning of May 1775 was swift to escalate and the Paris police, many of whom were sympathetic with the rioters, were unable to restore order.

The unrest spread to Versailles, and the courtiers panicked.

An angry crowd, made up of residents of two dozen small villages in the vicinity of the town, stood at the palace gates shouting "that they had no bread, that they had come to get it, and showed pieces of barley bread which was very inferior" though it had cost them two sous.[5] They also complained because the marketplace of Versailles had been ordered closed. Turgot had gone to Paris, to deal with the crisis there, and in his absence the young King took charge. "You can count on my firmness," he wrote in a hasty note sent off to the Finance Minister, and indeed he showed firmness—combined with alertness and common sense. He sent a detachment of guardsmen to the marketplace, and ordered it opened under their surveillance. He sent the captain of his bodyguard to speak to the crowd. Meanwhile the Mayor of Versailles, without consulting the King, ordered the bakers to lower the price of good quality wheaten bread to two sous, the price the rioters demanded.

At Versailles all was over in a few hours, with no bloodshed. The presence of the guardsmen had a calming effect, bread was made available at a reasonable price (much to the King's embarrassment; he accused the Mayor of "a stupid maneuver"), the King's fortitude put heart back into his courtiers. "I shall not go out today," he wrote to Turgot in Paris, "not from fear, but in order to let things calm down." In Paris, however, Turgot sent regular troops, including cavalry, against the rioters. Louis advised restraint but the minister, convinced that the riots were part of a political plot and not the protest of hungry and frustrated people, ordered the troops to attack and they shot and bludgeoned at will. With cannon on the ramparts and hangings in the streets, the disorder subsided, yet it left Parisians furious. They blamed Turgot and his royal master as well, and their bitterness was to endure.[6]

Mercy went to see Antoinette, and found her upset by the reported violence of the crowds. She was accustomed to nothing but adulation from the people. Despite the critical songs and the venomous libels written about her, she believed that the Parisians felt affection for her. Certainly they showed affection when she attended the Opera, cheering her, sometimes for a quarter of an hour, and cheering still more loudly to see that they moved her to tears. She knew that stories circulated in the capital about her generosity toward her servants and toward victims of injustice.

She knew that when early in his reign Louis dismissed the Chancellor Maupeou, thus reversing his grandfather's enlightened policy toward the parlements, the Parisians burned Maupeou in effigy. "Let us avenge our charming Queen," they cried, "of whom this wretch has dared to speak evil and write libels."[7] Parisian shops did a brisk trade in royal trinkets and ornaments: porcelain medallions celebrating "Louis le Populaire," engravings, books, crude portraits. An English visitor to Paris saw two expensive porcelain figurines in a china shop, finely executed, representing Louis playing the harp and Antoinette with her embroidery in her lap.[8]

To be sure, there were caricatures for sale ridiculing the Queen's gigantic coiffures and feathered crests. But the attitude they represented was far from universal. One published collection of headdresses, whose intended audience was admirers of Antoinette, included this poem:

> Behold the coiffure of our Queen,
> Whose perfect taste is therein seen.
> 'Twere well her style to imitate,
> Herself in acts both small and great.
> For should you copy her good deeds,
> You will inspire our love, respect,
> And like her, sow the seeds
> Of charity towards God's elect.[9]

Antoinette believed that she and Louis were admired, loved, even worshipped by the Parisians, despite the evident suffering of the poorest among them and despite the harsh taxes they struggled to pay. Now she was forced to confront their fearsome anger, and it unnerved her.

It unnerved her even more in that her husband's coronation was imminent.

Preparations had been under way for this great event since the previous summer. The coronation would be in Rheims cathedral, following ancient tradition; Kings of France had been crowned there since the time of Louis VII in the twelfth century, and Clovis I had been baptized there by Saint Remi in 496. But there had been no coronation in over half a century, the cathedral needed repair and new buildings had to be built to house the courtiers and dignitaries of Louis XVI's swollen court. Carpenters and stonemasons labored over the work for many months, while at the same time tailors and seamstresses and embroiderers worked to produce the elaborate vestments for the clergy and the robes and mantles and vests to be worn by the King and the peers.

All this was very costly. Even though Turgot pared down the expense, and Louis ordered additional retrenchment—he told the Paris merchants not to spend any money on coronation festivities and instead to use it to relieve the poor—the total bill came to about a million livres.[10] Maurepas, cautious and circumspect, suggested that the ceremony be postponed. But this would mean canceling orders given to goldsmiths, jewelers, clothiers, lace-makers and drapers, not to mention ensuring more cost at a later date, for the road from Paris to Rheims would have to be repaired not once but twice. At the risk of angering an already outraged public, the decision was made to go ahead with the coronation.

The response was on the whole enthusiastic. To be sure, when the dozens of glittering carriages passed along the road to the cathedral, carrying the peers and clergy and functionaries, and the members of the royal entourages, laborers knelt along the roadside and entreated them for bread. But they did not riot, or throw stones at the carriages, and the spectators cheered when the King passed by.

The coronation ceremony itself was most impressive, the solemnity of it as imposing as the spectacle. Before an immense crowd, the clergy and lay peers gathered, the Bishops in full pontificals and the peers in vests of cloth of gold with ducal mantles of violet cloth lined with ermine. Two Bishops led in the King, splendid in violet boots with red heels, a cloak of violet velvet and an ermine cape, all his garments decorated with golden fleurs-de-lis. Despite the length of the ritual, and the stifling heat, which made Louis perspire freely and visibly as he knelt in his burdensome vestments, the spectators watched and listened intently, frequently bursting into acclamations. They saw the Archbishop of Rheims take the Holy Ampulla containing the coronation oil from the Master of Ceremonies and anoint the King with it on his head, breast, shoulders and arms. They heard him promise to prevent violence and injustice, exterminate heretics and rule his people justly. They listened while the Archbishop intoned the prayers.

"May the King have the strength of the rhinoceros," he said, his words echoing throughout the ancient building with its high clerestory and brilliant stained glass, "and may he, like a rushing wind, drive before him the nations of our enemies, even to the extremity of the earth."

Louis was handed the golden sceptre, nearly six feet long, and the hand of justice, a mighty golden staff encrusted with jewels, and was crowned with the crown of Charlemagne, its rubies and sapphires glowing in the candlelight. Then he was led to the throne, and the Archbishop made him a profound bow, and then shouted, *"Vivat Rex in aeternum!"* "May the King live for ever!" At this the great church doors were opened, and the people who had been waiting outside for hours in the heat rushed in, "and instantly made the roofs resound with shouts of 'Long live the King!' which were reechoed by the crowd of persons engaged in the ceremony, who filled the enclosure of the choir like an amphitheater."

People began to applaud, the applause grew until it filled the cathedral. It went on and on, becoming thunderous, and as it continued the fowlers loosed dozens of caged birds, which fluttered up through the vast space under the vaulted ceiling, their freedom the symbol of France's freedom under the rule of a beneficent King.[11]

It was too much for Antoinette. Moved to tears, she had to retire to the inner rooms prepared for her, and the crowd, watching her, was pleased by her show of emotion. When she returned their applause swelled. According to the Abbé Veri, a rather jaundiced observer of royal affairs and an adviser to Maurepas, the crowd applauded more loudly for Antoinette than they did for Louis—but in the Abbé's view their applause gave an entirely false impression of public opinion. Flatterers there were in plenty, he wrote in his journal, but the coronation was little more than "formalities and decoration." In truth the French looked sourly on the expense of the ceremony, and waited impatiently for the government to deal seriously with its financial burdens.[12]

All of Antoinette's touching loyalty to Louis and her natural optimism came out in her letter to Maria Theresa about the coronation. She wrote that it was "perfect in every way," that "all the world seemed delighted with the King," and that the ceremony seemed to her to bind the monarchy and the people with even more intimate ties of emotion and obligation. "I could no longer restrain myself; my tears flowed in spite of me, and the people liked this. I did my best throughout the whole time to return the greetings of the people, although it was very hot and the crowds were very great. But I did not mind my weariness." Above all Antoinette was surprised and pleased that the same hungry folk who had stormed the granaries and shouted their dissatisfaction at the gates of Versailles could receive their King with such great enthusiasm.

"It is an astonishing thing, and a very happy one, to be so well received two months after the revolt, and in spite of the dearness of bread, which unfortunately still remains. It is an amazing feature in the French character, that they will let themselves be led away so easily by bad counsels, and yet return again so quickly."[13] Antoinette was right, the French were volatile, but not because they were "led away" by troublemakers. They loved the monarch yet hated the monarchy, with its expensive trappings and sycophantic entourage. Louis they hoped would be another Henri IV, a hero to his people, a savior to his country. But Louis's ministers, and their disruptive policies, were detested. And the detestation was growing.

Meanwhile the little Comtesse d'Artois was nearing the time of her expected delivery. She had not suffered much during her pregnancy, and if her husband's dissipation and habitual infidelity affected her at all she did not show it. "She is happy enough not to fear her delivery," Antoinette wrote to her mother toward the end of June 1775. "It is true that she is such a child that she is overjoyed because she has been told she would not be given any black medicine." What the dreaded "black medicine" was Antoinette did not say, but clearly Theresa's pleasure in preceding the Queen and her own sister in childbearing swept aside any fears for her safety. Antoinette must have dreaded the coming birth, for her own marriage was as hopelessly barren as ever and she knew that she would have to undergo the humiliation of being present at Theresa's delivery.

By custom all the members of the royal family and the courtiers attended the birth of a prince or princess. When Theresa's labor began Antoinette took her place in the birth chamber, and watched, outwardly solicitous, inwardly in pain herself, as the midwives and doctors did their work. Theresa had an easy time. The labor was not prolonged—"only two or three strong pains" toward the end—and the baby was a healthy boy. The mother put her hand on her forehead and cried out, "My God, how happy I am!"

Antoinette was completely mortified. "I need not tell my dear Mama how I suffered in seeing an heir who isn't mine," Antoinette wrote to Maria Theresa six days later. "But I still managed not to forget any attention due the mother and child."[14]

The courtiers were informed of the birth of a boy, the Duc d'Angoulême, and the noise of rejoicing in the galeries and salons where the public waited carried throughout the palace. Antoinette lingered with Theresa until the latter was washed and put to bed. Then, making an effort to look as calm as possible, she returned to her own apartments, passing by the crowd of spectators and guessing their thoughts. A delegation of fishwives from Paris dogged her footsteps, following her through the long corridors and "calling out to her in the most licentious expressions, that *she* ought to produce heirs."[15] She quickened her steps, and hurried in to her inner sanctum where Madame Campan waited. There she wept, freely and bitterly, while her bedchamber woman did her best to console her inconsolable sorrow.

13

IN April of 1777 a tall, well-built man of thirty-six, wearing a plain cloth suit of outdated cut and color, got down from a modest carriage and entered an inexpensive Paris hotel. He had only a single servant with him, and very little luggage. Passers-by might have taken him for a traveling schoolmaster or clerk, except that his mobile features seemed to express extraordinary intelligence and his alert, somewhat protuberant eyes exceptional discernment. He wore a toupee over his bald pate, and his own long hair was gathered into a very thin queue at the nape of his neck. His servant addressed him as "Sir," but he announced himself in the hotel as Count Falkenstein, which title created a certain amount of bustle and deference—not to say frank surprise—in the hotel staff.

Count Falkenstein was none other than Antoinette's oldest brother Joseph, Holy Roman Emperor and co-ruler of the Austrian lands with his mother Maria Theresa. He was traveling incognito, to save expense and, more important to him, to avoid fuss and etiquette. He liked to be free to go and come as he pleased, without fanfare. He was by nature simple and direct, even rudely blunt, and unnerving in his frankness; whenever possible he preferred to cut through formality and artifice to find the reality behind it. He knew that he would see more of reality traveling as Count Falkenstein, and it was important that he discover as much about his sister's situation, and about France, as he could.

The sullen and moody youth had grown into a sharp, hypercritical man, curmudgeonly and unpredictable. He had not remarried after the death of his second wife Josepha, he answered to no woman save his august mother and she closed her eyes to his numerous liaisons. More worldly than his father had been, Joseph was at the same time fiercely idealistic, skeptical of the prevailing social order with its ranks and hierarchies, distrustful of monarchy and contemptuous of aristocrats. He had opinions on everything, not excluding topics about which he was poorly informed. He liked to shock people and expose their complacency. He liked to stir things up. To be sure, he had his vulnerable side. Flattery disarmed him. As his mother wrote, "he loves to shine." And there was an undertone of affection beneath his bluff exterior, though as one who knew him very well wrote, he feared involvement, and kept both love and friendship at bay.

No doubt Joseph wanted to visit Antoinette, for he seldom did anything he did not want to do. Yet he also made the journey to France at his mother's urging. She was desperately worried about her daughter, now twenty-one and still childless after seven years of marriage and three of those years as Queen. Scandalous rumors about her had been reaching Vienna for a long time, and even Mercy admitted, in dispatches that sometimes went on for fifty pages, that Antoinette was extravagant, that she had a taste for disreputable companions and louche amusements, and that she gambled heavily and recklessly nearly every night. Her contempt for the courtiers and her devotion to a clique of intriguing favorites had led, Mercy said, to an unprecedented situation. During the winter of 1776–77 Versailles had been all but deserted. People had stayed away in droves, partly as a protest against Antoinette's ill-advised exclusivity and uncontrolled behavior. Clearly the Queen was doing damage to herself and to her adopted country, and her husband was unable or unwilling to stop her.

Joseph might have more influence over her. He was her older brother, he had been fond of her as a child and could give her fraternal advice. Besides, it was in his interest as a ruler to keep France allied with Austria; Antoinette's behavior, and still more her failure to give France an heir to the throne, threatened that alliance. Joseph had plans to annex territories in Bavaria and the Low Countries. Should the French government oppose him, these plans would have to be abandoned, and Austria would also become more vulnerable to her ancient enemy Frederick II of Prussia.

Nor could the long-term effects of Antoinette's childlessness be ignored. Every court in Europe was concerned about the French succession. The birth of the Duc d'Angoulême meant that, for the present at least, the King of Sardinia (the infant Duke's grandfather) could expect to see his descendants become Kings of France. The King of Spain, a descendant of Louis XIV, might become a pretender to the French throne if Louis and Antoinette had no children. Savoyards, Spaniards, Prussians, Saxons, all sent spies to Versailles, beyond the authorized spies of every country who held diplomatic rank, to monitor the status of the succession. The fecundity of the royal couple was vital to the peace of Europe, and certainly to the well-being of Austria.

Count Falkenstein had himself driven to Versailles and entered the palace by a secret staircase. His reunion with Antoinette, whom he had not seen since she was a child of fourteen, was touchingly warm. They talked in private for several hours, and Antoinette, with her customary candor, told him everything he wanted to know about her pastimes, her favorites, and her intimate life with Louis. It must have been a relief to her to be able to speak freely to her brother, even though she knew he was bound to disapprove of how she lived. To unburden herself, to admit the actual state of her marriage and her humiliation because of it, must have been cathartic.

She told him how she had suffered during her sister-in-law's delivery, and how she was hounded by the taunts of the fishwives and by the mocking songs people sang about her and Louis ("Everyone whispers/Can the King, or can't he?/ The sad Queen is in despair"). Attempts were being made to tempt Louis to take a mistress, an actress at the Comédie Française; he spent so few nights with his wife that the courtiers, ever alert for opportunities, thought that his head might be turned by another woman.[1] Interfering people offered aphrodisiacs and fertility aids; there were fears of malevolent influences, spells or witchcraft that prevented conception. Only a few months earlier, when Louis and Antoinette were returning from the chapel along one of the galleries open to the public, a cleric had thrown himself down in front of them, blocking their path, and pressed into Louis's hand a paper containing "the secret of perpetuating his august race." The man was ejected, and the King laughed. But he read the paper, which recommended that he eat mandrake root (a traditional aphrodisiac) or apply it directly to his troubled flesh.

As Antoinette talked, weeping from time to time in her distress, Joseph began to realize what a tangled problem his sister's marital relations had become. What ought to have been a healthy physical union, mutually pleasurable and mutually lustful, had from the outset been overlayered with tensions and psychological quirks arising from Louis's slight deformity and both partners' sexual innocence. The pressures associated with the succession had made the problem worse and worse over the years. The royal physicians, too eager to please to give blunt advice, had been no help whatsoever. None of them was bold enough to tell Louis clearly that his phimosis was the problem, that it could be corrected, and that until it was he would not be able to ejaculate.

No doubt the doctors were reluctant to cause pain to the cowardly Louis, and so they gave vague and contradictory judgments, some saying that the "difficulty" would resolve itself in time without their intervention, others wrapping themselves in equivocations. (One gave his sage opinion that "there are many drawbacks to having it [the operation] performed and many drawbacks to not having it performed.") Half-believing that time alone might bring about a miraculous spontaneous cure, the couple had experimented naively from time to time, but their failures had made them both feel ashamed and inadequate. Only a few days before Joseph's arrival they had tried again, and Antoinette wrote to her mother that she had "greater hopes" and was "convinced that the operation is no longer necessary."

But it was clear to Joseph that these hopes arose from ignorance. Louis was able, Joseph discovered through his candid conversations with both husband and wife, to "have strong, well-conditioned erections," but not to complete the act. "He introduces the member, stays there without moving for perhaps two minutes"—probably wincing with pain all the while—"withdraws without ejaculating but still erect, and says good night." Such was the sad ritual the couple played out, painful for Louis and frustrating for Antoinette, and on it their hopes were based. "This is incomprehensible," Joseph wrote to his brother Leopold, "because with all that he sometimes has nightly emissions, but once in place and going at it, never, and he is satisfied; he says plainly that he does it all purely from a sense of duty but never for pleasure."[2] Antoinette, he added, lacked the passion to demand more from Louis—and apparently she lacked the common sense to ask any of her women, even Madame Campan, whom she trusted, what was missing in their lovemaking. Louis too, it seems, had no one in whom he could confide, and was so isolated from the other men of the court, more from shyness than because of his exalted rank, that he could not discuss his plight with any of them.

Joseph was privately contemptuous of the "two complete blunderers," and told Leopold he wanted to whip Louis "so that he would ejaculate out of sheer rage like a donkey," but for once he understood the need for tact. He befriended the timid King, explained the facts of life to him and, in the end, got him to promise to have the dreaded operation that would make a man of him. He cornered Antoinette and advised her to entice Louis into her bed in the afternoon, when he still had energy; in the evening, after a huge meal, he would be no good to her. Joseph did not spare his sister's feelings. Her entire security depended on her having a son, he told her. Preferably more than one. Barren queens had a way of being put aside, buried away in convents or exiled to undesirable country houses. She listened and nodded, her eyes big with fear. He felt assured that she would heed his advice.

Antoinette took her eccentric brother to meet everyone of consequence at the palace. He was present at the *lever* and *coucher*, at the elaborate Sunday ceremonies, he attended elegant suppers and gambling parties. Where Joseph was concerned Antoinette forgot modesty. She boasted of his intelligence, his knowledge of military affairs, his austerity and lack of pretentiousness. The courtiers looked askance at "Count Falkenstein," with his plain suit the color of fleas *(puce)*. Flea-color had been in style at Versailles briefly two years earlier; there were many shades, from "old flea" to "young flea" to "flea's head" and "flea's thigh." Joseph's shade of flea did not provoke admiration. Besides, the fashionable world had long since moved on to newer shades: Paris mud, indiscreet tears, dandies' guts. They took offense at his rudeness, and ridiculed his fluent but idiosyncratic French. He was looked on, Madame Campan wrote with icy primness, as a prince "rather singular than admirable."

They liked him better than they had liked Antoinette's younger brother Maximilian, who had made a short visit to Versailles in 1775 and failed utterly to impress or charm them. They applauded Joseph's taste in actresses (he sampled the Parisian demimonde) and did not mind, though his mother and sister certainly did, that he went to visit Madame Du Barry at Louveciennes. But they smiled at his preference for plain food and almost monastic living (he slept on a small uncomfortable bed in his inexpensive Paris hotel, and would not stay in the palace, preferring a lodging-house at Versailles), and they resented the curiosity he showed about the workings of government and especially about financial affairs. He investigated the expenses of the court, took notes on finance and quickly arrived at highly critical opinions. Madame Campan noted how Joseph collared her father-in-law and lectured him vehemently for over an hour, "without the slightest reserve," about the government—no doubt with emphasis on its shortcomings.[3]

For his part, Joseph was thoroughly put off by the overdecorated courtiers and their dissipated amusements. He teased Antoinette about using too much rouge. One day when she was putting on more rouge than usual, before going to the theater, he "advised her to put on still more; and pointing out a lady who was in the room, and was, in truth, highly painted, 'A little more under the eyes,' said the Emperor to the Queen: 'lay on the rouge like a fury, as that lady does.'" Antoinette told him in private to blunt his rudeness, although, as Madame Campan remarked in an aside, Joseph's cutting comments "agreed very well with the sneering spirit which then prevailed."[4] The trailing plumes, mountainous headdresses and ingenious styles appeared laughable to the curmudgeonly Austrian, who derided them vociferously and criticized Antoinette for leading the French into such grotesque aberrations of taste.

Joseph's views on the royal family were cruelly negative. The obese and sour Provence he found "nondescript and very frigid," his wife vulgar and scheming. Artois, whose uncontrolled carryings-on at the racetrack made him appear worse than worthless in Joseph's eyes, was dismissed as a "fop" whose wife was "an absolute imbecile." (Imbecile or not, Theresa had by this time borne two children and would soon have a third.) Joseph did not comment on the royal aunts, who were very much at the periphery of things by this time, but Adelaide took a liking to him. On the pretext of showing him some portraits, she persuaded him to visit her, whereupon she embraced him once they were alone and said that an embrace at least "should be permitted to an old aunt."[5]

Whether he was blinded by a brother's affection, or whether

Antoinette's fresh loveliness and ingenuous charm simply won him over, Joseph ended by feeling sympathy for his little sister despite her lapses of judgment and her wayward amusements. He saw clearly that she lived in a constant state of nervous tension. She often burst into tears, her weeping exhausting her and leaving her drained. She was often sad, but she had an imperiousness that rarely deserted her, and when she wanted something she had a large arsenal of weapons to use to get it, from bullying to guile to wheedling to tears and tantrums. She trained her most potent weapons on her husband, who had to withstand her emotional scenes and who rarely said no to her.

"Her situation with the King is very odd," Joseph told Leopold in a letter. "He is only two-thirds of a husband, and although he loves her, he fears her more; our sister has the kind of power to be expected from a royal mistress, not the kind a wife should have, for she forces him to do things he doesn't want to do."[6] Louis was so childlike that he needed firmness at times, and was bound to look to any woman he cared for for mothering. This was not Antoinette's fault, but it did skew their relationship and gave her an unwarranted amount of power over him. It also allowed her, paradoxically, to prolong her own childhood and indulge herself, since he offered her no mature companionship and exercised no restraint over her.

"The Queen is a pretty woman," Joseph told Leopold candidly, "but she is empty-headed, unable as yet to find her advantage, and wastes her days running from dissipation to dissipation, some of which are perfectly allowable but nonetheless dangerous because they prevent her from having the thoughts she needs so badly." Antoinette was amiable enough, but she "thought only of having fun." She was "tied down by no etiquette," she "ran around alone or with few people without the outward signs of her position, she looked a little improper." In short, "she was not doing her job," either as a queen or as a woman, and this was bound to lead to bad consequences in the future.

Fortunately, Joseph concluded, his sister was a thoroughly virtuous woman. The worst of the slanders associated with her, that she had Artois and any number of other men, and probably women as well, as lovers, was obviously untrue. "Her virtue is intact, even strict," Joseph told Leopold, "but less through forethought than inborn disposition; in a word it has been all right until now, but in the long run she will find herself resourceless and things may go badly; that is what I have been telling her, but although I am perfectly satisfied with her friendship and her sincerity—she listens, she agrees—the whirlwind of dissipation which surrounds her prevents her from thinking of anything but going from pleasure to pleasure."

Worst of all, it was clear that Antoinette would keep up her shallow pursuit of diversion and amusement as long as there were people around her to egg her on, and there were "armies" of such people. "All the people who surround her encourage her in this frenzy," wrote the disgusted Joseph. "If she listened a little less to the people who urge her on . . . she would be perfect. The desire to have fun is powerful in her, and since people are aware of it, they prey on that weakness, and those who give her the largest amount of, and the most varied pleasure are listened to and treated well."[7]

Still, in the midst of the "whirlwind of dissipation" Antoinette was true to her character, which was generous, honest, and on the whole without vices, except for her gambling, which horrified Joseph in its extravagance and frequency. She threw away large sums at faro, she was thoroughly reckless and heedless. But she did not cheat (as many others did), and she did not make scenes (as Artois did), or try to take revenge, or sulk, when she lost.

The heart of the problem, Joseph realized, was Louis. Tall and robust, his round face blemished by smallpox scars and his small, myopic eyes giving him a porcine appearance, at twenty-three Louis was as strong as an ox. He liked to wrestle with the courtiers, nearly strangling the Prince de Ligne and severely injuring the corpulent Duc de Coigny and others. His advisers never knew when he might turn playful, seizing the coal shovel and using it to lift up the nearest page, bounding around the room like a six-year-old and tickling the elderly valet de chambre, who started like a hare and darted away, making Louis laugh. He played alongside his young pages, delighted when they snatched the wigs from the heads of solemn officials or drew mustaches on the upper lips of servants sleeping in the corridors. He played practical jokes, then, laughing loudly, "fled the scene of battle with as much speed as a young army." At his *lever* and *coucher*, he amused himself by making faces at the noble who handed him his shirt, "bobbing aside, avoiding the garment, and letting himself be pursued with it." No matter how many distinguished visitors were present, Louis seemed to have no dignity, he liked to be chased around the room half-naked, his raucous laugh making him seem imbecilic.

He wanted the best for his country, he knew France faced extremely serious problems and he had compassion for his people. But he lacked the mental rigor to tackle the difficulties head-on, and the physical energy to sustain the labor of ruling day after day. He was hopelessly indolent and by the spring of 1777 he had lapsed into a perpetual apathy. "He leads a very uniform life without curiosity," Joseph told Leopold, "without overall views." His ministers governed everything. "The King is only an absolute sovereign when he passes from one form of slavery to the next," was Joseph's judgment. "He can always change his ministers, but he can never, unless he is a transcendent genius, become the master of the way his government is run. You can imagine how the state's business is done; as for me, I can see clearly that all the detail which is connected to personal intrigues is taken care of with the greatest attention and interest while the important business of the state is completely neglected." The expense of the royal household ran to one-sixth of the total government budget—a fact that shocked Joseph and made him distrust the current Controller-General of Finance, the Swiss banker Jacques Necker.[8]

During his few months in France Joseph saw and did a great deal. He took in the sights of Paris, visiting the important institutions, the prisons, the workshops, the picture galleries. He traveled extensively in the provinces, interested in agriculture and animal husbandry and village life. Through it all he kept up his simple habits and his sober diet. He became something of a celebrity. The courtiers laughed at him—they laughed at almost everyone—but the Parisians liked him and were sorry to see him go. Louis gave him valuable gifts on his departure, Gobelins tapestries, Savonnerie carpets, a service of Sèvres porcelain. Antoinette gave him a watch with her portrait on it, and extracted from him a promise to visit her again. He rode off as he had come, wearing his plain puce suit and riding in his modest carriage. Antoinette was sad for a time, but the courtiers felt relieved, for his scornful scrutiny had not been easy to bear and they were developing a prejudice against Austrians.

Antoinette's behavior changed after Joseph left. She went less often to Paris, she gambled less, she tried to improve her mind, resuming her reading of books she had put aside for years. Artois, her companion in frivolity, was away on a tour of the provinces, and in his absence it was easier for her to discipline herself. But her reform was brief; by the fall she was gambling again, her reading forgotten, amid scenes as "tumultuous and unseemly" as ever.

There was, however, one monumental difference. Soon after Joseph's departure Louis braved out the operation he had feared for so many years. And afterward, when he had healed, he made love to his wife for the first time.

"I am in the most essential happiness of my entire life," Antoinette wrote joyfully to her mother at the end of August. "It has already been more than eight days since my marriage was perfectly consummated; the proof has been repeated and yesterday even more completely than the first time."[9] Her first impulse had been to send a courier to Vienna, but then she realized that such a dramatic move would cause speculation and gossip, and she wanted nothing more than to enjoy her happiness in private. She hoped to become pregnant right away, and was disappointed when she did not. Still, there was hope that she soon would be, and that hope sustained her. Maria Theresa was beside herself with delight to learn that Antoinette was a wife at last, though she immediately began giving her advice—no riding astride, no carriage rides, no excessive worries over the troubles of servants or friends. "A first pregnancy is always important for the others," the Empress cautioned. "If you start with a miscarriage, it is the end and must be avoided. Given your constitution, I should not fear that you were liable to them, but once you get used to them, there is no remedy."[10]

Maria Theresa still wrote vigorous letters, but age and illness tormented her and kept her from all but the least taxing activity. Her mind was alert, she kept up with the reading and writing her rule demanded, though much was delegated to Joseph. But her legs and ankles no longer supported her heavy frame, she needed help to walk any distance, and her hands and arms were stiff with rheumatism. She could no longer climb the steps to the top of the Glorietta, her garden retreat at Schönbrunn, and had to be raised and lowered by a mechanical device, a large sofa upholstered in green morocco with mirrored sides that was winched up and down. She often had herself carried to the vault in the Capucin church where Francis lay in his coffin and where, she told one of her servants, he was becoming impatient to hold her next to his cold side.

In March of 1778 General Krottendorf failed to make his appearance. When he still had not arrived by the end of April, Antoinette was certain she was pregnant. For a moment the venomous tongues ceased to wag—but only for a moment. They soon found fresh matter for gossip: if Antoinette was really pregnant, who was the child's father? Not Louis, not after all this time. Artois? One of the circle of the Queen's admirers?

Despite the slanders, Antoinette rejoiced. She and Louis knew that they had succeeded at their most important task, and they were drawn closer together. Theresa with her three children was put into the shade; the Duc d'Angoulême was sickly in any case, and his sister was a tiny and weak infant who might die at any time. The third baby was too young as yet to invite speculation as to its hardihood. Provence and his wife were still childless, and, people said, were likely to remain so.

Antoinette hoped and prayed that her child would be a boy, a strong, healthy boy who would grow up to be King. She took care of herself and him, eating well (though she normally ate very sparingly), going for walks every morning and evening, spending her time following such soothing pursuits as embroidering and making netted purses. She felt well, except for a "feeling of stifling" that came over her now and then. Her accoucheur—nepotism was rife at Versailles; he was the Abbé Vermond's brother—was said to be the best available, though as events proved, he lacked sound judgment where his patient's welfare was concerned.

The summer of 1778 was extremely hot, and Antoinette, queasy and stifled, spent entire days shut in her rooms, escaping the heat. She emerged in the cooler evenings to take walks on the terrace below her apartments with Artois and Provence and their wives. The court was full of tension that summer, for since March France had been at war with England and now the warfare threatened to spread to the Hapsburg domains. Joseph, in Vienna, had seized lands in Bavaria on a specious pretext and predictably, Frederick II was threatening to invade Austria, posing as the avenger of the wrong done to the Bavarian Elector. Less predictably, the French Foreign Minister Vergennes deserted Austria, condemned Joseph's action, and showed no willingness to come to

Austria's aid if and when Frederick invaded. Maria Theresa feared the worst. "I am overwhelmed," she wrote to Mercy. "I do not know how to live. Nothing but my faith sustains me . . ."[11] To Antoinette she wrote in a sterner vein, pressing her to use all her influence to prevent the Austro-French alliance from dissolving.

Elderly and incapacitated as she was, the Empress was at her most characteristic in the letters she wrote to her daughter at this time. She insisted that Antoinette become a politician, manipulate Louis, and checkmate Maurepas and Vergennes. At the same time she preached to her about wifely duty and gave endless advice about motherhood: Antoinette should obey her accoucheur absolutely; she should not wrap the baby up too tightly once he was born; she shouldn't let him get overheated, or overfed; she should find a good healthy nurse for him, though such women were unheard-of in Paris.[12]

Antoinette, coping with heat, pregnancy, and her demanding mother, also had to cope with her husband's crisis of confidence. The looming conflict with Austria distressed Louis, he wanted to please his wife but felt helpless to control his ministers. Maurepas, elderly but spry and mischievous and perversely eager to cause trouble in the royal marriage, was no help to him at all. Louis came to Antoinette in tears and confessed that he could do nothing. When he tried to exert his will, the ministers argued with him, he said, silencing him and making him doubt himself. "You see," he told his wife, "I have so many faults that I cannot answer a word."[13]

Antoinette had no experience in dealing with politicians, but she knew how to dominate, how to win an argument. It was not easy to silence her. She told Louis that she would stand by him in his meetings with the ministers and help him make his points and see that his policies were carried out. She did more than that; she confronted Maurepas directly, accusing him of intriguing with Prussia and of evading the King's orders to the contrary. "I will no longer be put off with such evasions," she told him. "I have kept patience until now, but things are growing serious." Startled, the minister tried belatedly to ingratiate himself with the Queen, but failed. For once her warmth and charm were not in evidence. She was adamant, and she was cold.

The situation was complex, for in February of 1778 France had committed herself secretly to supporting the American colonies with munitions and money in their battle with England. The American cause was extremely popular—Benjamin Franklin, the colonists' ambassador in Paris, was lionized and fashionable women showed their loyalty by wearing hats in a new style called "The Insurgents"—but France could hardly afford to embroil herself deeply in a global war.[14] She valued her remaining American colonies, particularly the French West Indies with their abundance of sugar, coffee and cotton, and she did not want to risk losing them in a naval confrontation with the British. However, if such a confrontation came, Vergennes wanted France to be free of continental entanglements, in particular free of any obligation to go to the defense of Austria. Hence the rapprochement with Frederick II.

In coming to the aid of Louis Antoinette did herself no good at court, and in the long run she did not help the Austrian cause either. Maurepas was all smiles in her presence, but criticized her behind her back. Her enemies—which is to say, most of those who were not her few favorites—began referring to her as *l'Autrichienne*, with the emphasis on the last syllable (*chienne* means bitch). As France geared up for war, with soldiers assembling in camps in Brittany and Normandy and ships being fitted out and manned at Brest, her fears for Austria, her family and their domains increased. Her brothers Joseph and Maximilian were commanding troops, putting themselves in danger. Joseph wrote her reproachful letters. "As you do not wish to prevent this war," he said loftily, "we shall fight like brave men."[15] Maria Theresa stepped up her demands. Antoinette did all she could, but like Louis she was ultimately ineffectual.

Frustrated and in anguish to realize that she was failing in her responsibilities, she broke down and went to Mercy for help. Usually she kept the polished diplomat at arm's length, retaining her composure when she was with him and maintaining a polite distance. Now all her defenses were down. She confessed to Mercy, in tears, that "her deep trouble"—by which she meant her inability to protect the alliance symbolized by her marriage—was leading her to think seriously about her future life. No doubt the approaching birth of her child was having the same effect. She was contrite, she felt the need to examine her shallow life and her unworthy companionships. "I have never seen the Queen so depressed," Mercy told the Empress in his next dispatch. Antoinette asked his advice, and he gave it to her. He also urged her to tell her mother the unfortunate truth about Louis's weakness (which she knew already from Mercy's candid secret reports), and to try again to get the better of Maurepas not by overt confrontation but by flattery and dissembling. Antoinette, who could dissemble well enough with Louis when she wanted to, drew the line at pretending friendship toward Maurepas. She could not "pretend graciousness to a man she despised," she told Mercy, no matter what was at stake.

The crisis eased. Though the state of war continued to exist, by fall the threat of imminent battle retreated. Once again Antoinette put all her energies into preparing for the birth of her child. She declared herself ready to give up her old life and start fresh. "I want to live as a mother, nurse my own child, and devote myself to his education," she declared. She would install the baby on the ground floor of the palace, where he would be near the terrace where she herself liked to walk. In time he would take his first steps on the terrace, he would join his cousins, Theresa's children, in games and festivities at the Petit Trianon. Best of all, his birth would help to solidify once again the fragile bonds between Vienna and Versailles.

14

Louis could not wait for his son to be born. He watched over Antoinette tenderly, visiting her apartments many times a day, loaded down with gifts and eager to reassure himself that all was well with her. He did his best to ignore the ever increasing stream of scurrilous songs and ribald poems that circulated in the court and capital, denying his paternity and slandering his wife. It was impossible to keep this sort of ephemera away from the Queen, damaging though it was to her peace of mind. In mid-December, with the delivery expected any day, an entire volume of songs ridiculing Antoinette and several court ladies was thrown into the palace through the *oeil-de-boeuf*. (The author was caught but not punished.) Throughout the kingdom, however, songs of thanksgiving were sung in the cathedrals and prayer vigils were kept for the safe delivery of the Queen. Versailles, rarely crowded in recent years, was full for once. Nobles who lived in Paris installed themselves at the palace to await the great event, to profit from it if they could, to witness it if they were lucky.

When the labor pains began, early in the morning of December 19, the royal family, the Princes of the blood and great state officers all moved into the Queen's apartments and waited in the rooms adjacent to her bedchamber. They had to be present at the moment of birth, and custom required that anyone else who so desired should be admitted as well. The outer rooms of the apartments began to fill up with courtiers and officials, relatives and hangers-on.

In the bedchamber the accoucheur Vermond and his assistants busied themselves around the special "labor bed" where the Queen lay. Huge tapestry screens surrounded the bed, secured with ropes by the King's orders. No breath of air stirred in the overheated room. The huge high windows were sealed shut with caulking, and paper had been pasted over them to prevent any draught. As the labor progressed the order was given for the royal family and officials to be admitted. They came in, and ranged themselves around the bed. The Princesse de Lamballe was there, as the Queen's friend and superintendent of her household, as was Antoinette's closest confidante Yolande, Comtesse de Polignac. Mercy too was asked to attend, though he was extremely ill at ease; childbirth made him squeamish.

For some eight hours the witnesses kept their places, while Antoinette endured ever stronger contractions. She did her best to be brave. Had not her indomitable mother undergone more than a dozen births without flinching? Did not German women pride themselves on their ability to undergo pain without complaint? She had witnessed Theresa's labor, now Theresa was forced to witness hers, and to feel mortified in her turn. Provence too, and Artois were watching for the child who would displace them in the succession. Undignified and wretched as she was, writhing in the high bed under the eyes of her relatives, Antoinette must have felt pride and a sense of triumph as the pains increased in intensity and frequency. "The Queen showed great courage," Mercy afterwards wrote laconically in his report to Maria Theresa.

Her courage all but deserted her, however, when the accoucheur announced "the Queen is giving birth" and at once, according to Madame Campan, "torrents of inquisitive persons" poured into the bedchamber from the adjoining rooms in a noisy and tumultuous rush. They pressed against the tapestry screens and jostled the indignant officials, they shoved up against the furniture, they made movement impossible. The spectators were "so motley a crowd," Madame Campan recalled, "that anyone might have fancied himself in some place of public amusement."[1] Everything seemed to happen at once. Antoinette's pain reached an agonizing crescendo, the room felt hotter than ever and so close that it was hard for her to breathe. She was aware that the baby was being born at last—and, gasping and panting, she looked over at

the Princesse de Lamballe who had agreed to give her one sign if
it was a boy, another if it was a girl. The sign was given: a girl!

The room began to go black. The noise became a roaring in
the Queen's ears. Two eager Savoyards who had climbed up onto
the furniture in order to get a better view saw that the baby was
female, that the accoucheur was distracted and in a panic, and
that the Queen, lying still on her lace-trimmed pillows, had
fainted. Her mouth twisted oddly. The Princesse de Lamballe,
never very stalwart in a crisis, fainted also and had to be carried
out through the crowd.

"Give her air!" shouted the panic-stricken Vermond, realizing
that he was on the point of losing his patient. "Warm water! She
must be bled in the foot!" The baby must at this moment have
taken her first breaths and gasped out her first little cry, but no
one, afterward, could remember hearing it. All the concern was
for the Queen, who had just disappointed her subjects by failing
to give them a dauphin. The King rushed to the nearest window
and, using all his great strength, flung it open, tearing open the
seal and causing ice-cold air to rush into the room.

There was no basin of hot water ready to bleed the Queen
into, but the accoucheur ordered the chief surgeon to lance the
royal foot without it. The surgeon opened a vein, "the blood
streamed out freely, and the Queen opened her eyes. The joy
which now succeeded to the most dreadful apprehensions could
hardly be contained." Hastily the valets de chambre cleared the
room of the noisy rabble, dragging out those spectators reluctant
to leave by the scruff of their necks. Courtiers embraced one another and shed tears of joy, and Vermond, enormously relieved,
ordered that the baby be wrapped in blankets and taken to her
governess, the Princesse de Guéménée.

Though contemporaries did not note it Antoinette must have
been gravely disappointed that her child was not a boy. Her
daughter could not inherit the throne, she would have to have a
son. No doubt she wanted more children. Still, having gone
through the ordeal once, it cannot have been pleasant to realize
that she would have to undergo it again, and soon, in order to
accomplish the minimum expected of her. Louis's proclamation
announcing the birth of his daughter, who was christened Marie-
Thérèse Charlotte and was known as Madame Royale, stated that
"this visible mark of Providence makes me hope for the complete

accomplishment of my desires and those of my people, the birth of a dauphin."[2] Antoinette felt compassion for the child. "Poor little thing," she said when she took her into her arms for the first time, "you were not wanted; but you will be my very own the more for that; a son would have belonged to the state."[3] Possibly Antoinette, who had confessed to Mercy many years earlier that in her childhood she had never really felt loved, was drawn especially close to the tiny child on that account.

Twenty-one cannon shots thundered in Paris to salute Madame Royale, and a huge bonfire was lit in the square in front of the Hôtel de Ville with fireworks at night. Processions, services of thanksgiving, music and special theatrical performances all marked the birth. In the poor quarters of the capital open-air feasts were held and people glutted themselves on the King's meat and bread and on the wine that flowed from the public fountains. It was an orgy of satiety in a season of shortages and famine; glad of the King's bounty, the poor forgot for a few days their resentment against the Queen and listened with satisfaction to the bulletins from Versailles about her recovery. Her health was "satisfactory," her belly "supple and not at all painful." She was nursing her daughter normally and eating cereal and biscuit, even a little chicken. Her good spirits were reportedly back within a week after the birth, and six weeks later she and the King made another formal entry into Paris to receive the city's congratulations.

The streets were cleared, the house fronts decorated to receive their majesties. Officials wore their finest coats and guardsmen their smartest livery. The speeches were laudatory, the fanfares thrilling. Outwardly, Paris was rejoicing. But a shadow overhung the royal entry. The unpopular war with England was bleeding the shopkeepers and tradesmen, the laborers were not earning enough to get by. Bread was dear. Antoinette might be the heroine of the hour, but the stories of her escapades at the Opera balls, the rumors of her numerous lovers of both sexes made her contemptible to many Parisians, and as her ornate carriage passed along the streets the crowds were thin and in some places silent. In the public mind the Queen was associated, not with monarchy and motherhood, but with dissipation and expense.

Only a few months after Madame Royale's birth Antoinette was pregnant again, and of course she and Louis hoped for a son.

But overexertion caused her to miscarry, and her hopes were
crushed. She was also fearful, according to Madame Campan, realizing that if they knew of her miscarriage her subjects would be
very likely to blame it on her dissolute life. The miscarriage was
kept secret from the courtiers and the public—and also from
Mercy and Maria Theresa. The Empress was hounding her
daughter incessantly about the need for a dauphin. Every letter
from Vienna brought a scolding, a warning, an urgent demand.

Then at the end of 1780 the demands ceased. Momentous
news arrived from the Hofburg: the great Empress Maria Theresa
was dead. Typically, she had worked until almost her last hour,
knowing that her worn out, clumsy body could not last much
longer. In the intervals between writing to her children and running her share of the government, she had taken time to sew her
own shroud and to make herself a dress to be buried in.

Antoinette had not seen her mother for ten years, but she
grieved for her as if they had been living in the closest intimacy.
Dressed in her mourning black, she shut herself in her most private rooms and had everyone except Yolande de Polignac and the
Princesse de Lamballe sent away. She found comfort in talking
about the Empress, not as a beloved parent but as a beleaguered
yet triumphant sovereign; the sad truth was, Antoinette had never
known her mother very well.[4]

At two years old, Marie-Thérèse Charlotte was an attractive,
fresh-faced little girl with large eyes and her mother's clear skin.
She showed signs of having a difficult temperament, she was not
an amiable child. Antoinette, determined not to let her become an
imperious brat, overly conscious of her status and ungovernably
haughty, reduced the number of servants around her child to a
minimum and ordered them to raise Madame Royale in an atmosphere of simplicity (as far as was possible in a palace). It was the
servants, not the Queen, who provided the hour-by-hour care of
little Thérèse, but Antoinette visited Madame de Guéménée's establishment frequently every day and kept herself informed about
every tooth the baby cut and every word she spoke. When her
teething brought on a fever, Antoinette sat by her bedside for
hours at a time, frowning with concern over "the sweetness and
patience of the poor little thing in her suffering."

Early in 1781 Antoinette finally became pregnant again, much
to her relief and that of her husband and the entire country. When

her brother Joseph, now sole ruler of the Hapsburg domains, made a brief visit to Versailles in August he was very pleased to find his sister in good health and her pregnancy well advanced. Two months later, on October 22, she gave birth to a boy. This time precautions were taken to protect both mother and child from the smothering crowd of onlookers. Only a dozen or so relatives and officers were allowed to be present in the bedchamber, besides the accoucheur and his staff.

"So deep a silence prevailed in the room at the moment the child first saw the light," Madame Campan recalled, "that the Queen thought she had only produced a daughter; but after the Keeper of the Seals had declared the sex of the infant, the King went up to the Queen's bed, and said to her, 'Madame, you have fulfilled my wishes and those of France; you are the mother of a dauphin.'"[5]

As Louis spoke, the tears rolled down his face. Forgetting his habitual awkwardness, he went around the room and took everyone by the hand, chattering joyously on about "his son." There was pandemonium in the antechambers when the news was announced. Strangers embraced each other, laughing and weeping at the same time. "Even those who cared least for the Queen," Louis wrote in his brief account of the birth, "were carried away by the general rejoicing."[6] The newborn infant was almost an object of worship. Madame de Guéménée took charge of him, sitting in an armchair with wheels that was perambulated gently toward her apartments. People followed the armchair, gazing reverently at the tiny bundle in her arms and reaching out to touch the chair as if it were a holy relic.

All the tradespeople of Paris sent delegations to Versailles to honor the dauphin's birth. Each delegation, wearing distinctive costumes and accompanied by musicians, carried an object representing their occupation. The chimney sweeps carried a make-believe chimney, with a small boy emerging from the top. The butchers carried a side of beef, the blacksmiths an anvil, the bootmakers a small pair of boots intended for the little dauphin. The tailors brought a small uniform made for the baby in the appropriate regimental colors. When the gravediggers appeared, however, bearing an infant-sized coffin, the royal family was offended and the police had to intervene.

The formal celebrations in Paris in honor of the dauphin's

birth were not held until he was three months old. Fearing the dark mood of the Parisians, and recalling how scant their cheers for Antoinette had been when Madame Royale was born, the Mayor and city officials tried to keep the spectators from massing before the Hôtel de Ville, center of the festivities. Free food, wine and entertainment were offered in various parts of the city in hopes of keeping the crowd dispersed. The people behaved themselves, though they cheered far more loudly for the King's coach as it passed along the streets than they did for the Queen's. After a banquet there was a fireworks display in the evening—somewhat spoiled by bad weather—and two days later a huge masked ball was held where some thirteen thousand people danced and stuffed themselves with rich food all night long.

At last there was an heir to the throne. Yet if the succession problem was solved, France's other dilemma, how to deal with the huge national deficit, was growing worse.

From 1776 to 1781 the national finances had been guided by the Genevan banker Jacques Necker, a wealthy parvenu who was considered quite vulgar by the overrefined courtiers. Necker was believed to be a financial genius, a businessman with a Midas touch who could make the economy thrive as he had made his own investments thrive. He had a wide acquaintance in banking circles, where he enjoyed the confidence of his peers. It was hoped that he could transmute this confidence in himself into confidence in the French government, and in fact he did—though the long-term results of this success were disastrous.

Necker faced enormous difficulties. Economic recession had been the norm in France since the last years of Louis XV's reign, and the recession had meant lower tax yields, and hence smaller resources with which to meet the growing expenses of government. Compounding the problem was the fact that there was no central treasury, no single state bureau where hordes of bookkeepers toiled over massive account books tallying income received and monies paid out. Such record-keeping was in the hands of independent financiers who bought the privilege of serving as payer, receiver or treasurer to a particular government department. Taxes were collected by independent financiers as well, who were members of the company of Farmers-General. Thus the task of supervising state finance was fragmented and decentralized, and menaced by the unhealthy practice of allowing public money to pass through private hands. For the financiers who bought state offices naturally expected to profit from them, and the route to profit lay in using the King's money to finance personal enterprise. There was no central bank to provide stability and to anchor the economy, only a crowd of businessmen who, like Necker, sought to strike the optimum balance between the health of the government and that of their own bank accounts.

Necker waded bravely into the Augean stables of public finance and tried to clean them out, but made little headway. He was not devoid of reforming ideas, and had his tenure lasted past 1781 he might have been able to make beneficial changes in both fiscal policy and practice. But during his five years in power he was under great pressure to finance the American war, and to gather the needed funds he used the most expedient method: raising loans. It was here that his reputation was an advantage. He was able to attract investment on an unprecedented scale—some five hundred and twenty million livres—by offering lucrative terms and promising to repay in less than twenty years. It was a mark of Necker's success that the Dutch, who traditionally invested in Britain, channeled some of their funds into France for the first time during his ministry.[7] The debt service on these gigantic loans strained the economy; annual interest was in the hundreds of millions of livres. Beyond this, the loans stimulated bankers and financiers to a frenzy of speculation, and what slender means came into the royal coffers was quickly lent to the government again by the payers, receivers and treasurers who were put in charge of it.

Necker was trusted and admired by the public, but was forced out of government in 1781 by Maurepas, who informed the King that the other ministers had threatened to resign unless Necker was sent away. The dismissal was very unpopular, all the more so because the Controller-General had published an optimistic (and thoroughly misleading) work on the state of the public finances, the *Compte rendu au roi*, which claimed to show that there was a small surplus in the King's accounts. The *Compte rendu* was widely read and even more widely discussed; few other than Necker's enemies realized that it omitted to tell the whole story, and covered up the growing deficit. Consequently, Necker remained popular and continued to be a highly vocal critic of the government after his dismissal.

In September of 1782 a shock wave rippled through the court and spread out from it in ever widening circles. The Prince de Guéménée, one of the greatest of the court nobles, married to an intimate of the Queen who was governess to the royal children, was forced to declare himself bankrupt. His debts, when finally totaled in later years, amounted to some thirty-three million livres. He owed hundreds of thousands of livres to other courtiers—for it was common practice for the office-holders of Versailles to lend one another money, secured by the future income from the debtor's offices. He owed bankers, financiers, nobles, jewelers, tradesmen, wig-makers, tailors, servants, even the well-to-do peasants who lived on his estates in Brittany who had entrusted their savings to his administrators. Everyone had lent him money on the strength of his name, his powerful connections, his expectations. His possessions and those of his wife in land, houses, jewels, all the rich accoutrements of a privileged life, seemed endless. But they were in fact heavily mortgaged, ultimately so heavily that the entire edifice of debt collapsed, leaving some three thousand creditors to seek desperately to recover their losses while cursing the Prince and Princess. Madame de Guéménée, eccentric and extravagant, hostess of so many ruinous gambling parties, was especially resented.

It was a shock, it was a scandal. More than that, the Guéménée bankruptcy was a rent in the gilded curtain of court life. It exposed, for a moment, the precarious system of loans and speculations, risks and expedients that lay behind the facade of splendor. If such a man as the Prince de Guéménée could fall from grace, if his high connections and ancient name could not ultimately protect him, then everyone else was vulnerable. Credit, extended and overextended, was the life blood of the court and its inhabitants. The more a man owed, the wealthier he was presumed to be. Yet somehow the Prince's credit had run out, and no one, not his friends, not his relatives (who were selling off their jewels and paintings and horses as fast as they could in an effort not to be dragged down with him), not even the King, had intervened.

Was it possible, people asked themselves, that the credit would not go on forever, and if so, what should they do to protect themselves? Everybody owed everybody else money. What would happen if, one day, all the loans were called in at once?

For a moment the myth that sustained Versailles was shattered, the myth that wealth and glory came to those who served the King patiently, borrowed heavily against their future prospects, and showed the world an image of success while waiting for genuine success to arrive. The courtiers trembled and held their breaths.

There was no prison sentence for the Prince de Guéménée, though his notary did not escape justice. While hundreds of lesser figures suffered ruin, the Prince merely retired to his lands in Navarre, and his wife quietly left court for Brittany, taking her dozens of little dogs with her. Louis and Antoinette maintained a discreet silence about the couple's unfortunate fate, treating it more as an embarrassment than a scandal. After all, they too were enormously in debt, as were all the members of the royal family. Artois was estimated to owe some twenty-one million francs, and Antoinette continued to order gowns and jewels, and to refurbish the Petit Trianon, as though she knew no limits.

Weeks went by, the bankruptcy proceeded, the courtiers scrambled to find new sources of credit. Eventually the crisis passed. But they felt less secure than ever in their dealings with one another and with the dizzying world of the financiers. With each new transaction they wondered how long it might be before their own credit, and perhaps even that of the government, ran out.

15

AT twenty-seven Antoinette was at the height of her beauty. Her candid blue eyes looked benevolently out at the world, their delicate tint set off by her masses of ash-blond hair and by a complexion so perfect in its radiant freshness that portrait painters despaired of capturing it on canvas. She had become quite plump, with a very large bust and a double chin, but her arms were beautifully shaped and her hands and feet small and dainty. The majesty of her bearing was unequaled. "She walked better than any woman in France," wrote the painter Elisabeth Vigée-Lebrun, "holding her head high with a majesty which made one recognize the sovereign among all her court."

Maturity and motherhood had softened her vivacity and added depth to her expression. She was as warmly affectionate as ever, but in repose her face held sorrow. She was growing older, blessed with two children whom she adored, but burdened with a husband who was more ungainly boy than man, who offered her no real companionship and who was increasingly dependent on her to help him make decisions and to keep up his limited courage.

She was very much alone. To be sure, Yolande de Polignac was some comfort, a friend she could cry with, confide in, and hug to her when she needed to feel a friend's warmth. But Yolande was not enough. To be fulfilled Antoinette needed a man's love, and at twenty-seven she finally found it, gave in to it, and became a changed woman.

Tall, patrician, poetically handsome, Axel Fersen was a young

Swedish nobleman who had been groomed from birth for a life of distinguished court service. His father, Field Marshal Frederick Axel Fersen, was an important figure in Swedish politics, and the son was expected to imitate if not surpass his success. A dutiful, well-behaved young man, at sixteen Fersen was sent abroad with a tutor to study at the best military schools in Europe and to polish his manners at foreign courts. He stayed for a time in Brunswick, went on to Turin, studied at Strasbourg. He paid a visit to Voltaire at the latter's estate at Ferney, and was amused when the elderly celebrity received him dressed in an antique scarlet waistcoat, a shabby old wig and a faded dressing-gown. ("But we were struck," Fersen noted in his diary, "with the beauty of his eyes and the liveliness of his glance.")

Inevitably, Fersen visited Versailles, and met Antoinette, who was then dauphine. Later, at a masked ball, she talked to him for some time before he realized who she was. She must have been quite taken with him, not only because he was singularly handsome, with classic features and an almost feminine beauty, but because he was intelligent and, as a contemporary remarked, "he thinks nobly and with singular loftiness." There was a dignified melancholy about Fersen that touched a chord in the isolated Antoinette; like her, he had an undertone of sadness. And like her, he disliked formality and pretense. "All his art is in his simplicity," the Comte de Tilly wrote of Fersen, and Antoinette prized simplicity highly.

His grand tour complete, Fersen returned to Sweden. In 1778 he was at Versailles again, however, and this time he noted in his diary that Antoinette was "the prettiest and most amiable princess that I know." In his Swedish cavalry uniform of blue doublet, white tunic and tight chamois breeches he must have been a sight to warm any young woman's blood, and by the end of his stay Antoinette was clearly infatuated with him. Enthusiasm for the cause of the American colonists was then at its peak, and Fersen determined to go to America and fight against the British. When he said his good-byes it was noticed that Antoinette "could not take her eyes off him," and her tears pooled unspilt.

The departure was a false alarm. The expedition Fersen intended to join was postponed, allowing him to return to Versailles once again. He was appointed colonel in the regiment of the Royal Deux Ponts, and this, plus the Queen's obvious partiality to him, made all the other young men at court jealous of Fersen. Finally in the spring of 1780 he embarked for America, as aide-de-camp to General Rochambeau, who commanded the expeditionary corps of the French army in aid of the American colonists.

The rigors of the American campaign toughened Fersen, while his knowledge of English made him invaluable to the French soldiery. He was delegated to negotiate with General Washington (whom he found "very cold" despite his "gentle and honest face," and his "air of a hero"), and at the end of the war Washington made him a member of the Order of Cincinnatus.

In June of 1783 Fersen returned to France, older, thinner, and covered with glory. The French and the Swedes showered him with military honors and promotions, he was idolized and admired. He renewed his visits to Versailles, and once more became a member of Antoinette's inner circle. And something more. Over the course of that summer an intimacy began between them that, then or later, almost certainly became physical.[1]

The idyll lasted only a few months, but they were crucial. Fersen, who had been in the market for a wife and had had in mind two candidates to fill the position, suddenly decided not to marry after all. "I have made up my mind," he wrote to his sister Sophie. "I cannot belong to the one person to whom I should wish to belong, the one who really loves me, and so I wish to belong to no one."[2]

He could not belong to Antoinette, but he could secure a post for himself that would ensure that he would be at Versailles from time to time on a regular basis. He obtained command of the Royal Swedish regiment in the French army. From now on he could expect an itinerant life, combined with periods of time spent at the Swedish court and at Versailles. The Swedish King Gustavus took him along on his travels, but wherever he was, Fersen wrote to Antoinette.

Theirs was certainly not a conventional romance. Their times together were always brief, they had to be exceedingly discreet. Fersen had other liaisons while he was apart from "the one who really loved him," as most men and many women of his class did, yet they were lustful adventures, not love. He never married. Antoinette remained special to him. To her, his love was a revelation and a source of joy even in his absence. Present or absent, he remained in the background of her life, never out of her thoughts for long.

Thérèse was six years old and the dauphin three when Antoinette gave birth to her third child and second son, Louis-Charles, Duc de Normandie, in March of 1785. The pregnancy had not been an easy one, but the labor was swift and the birth without complications. Another son was very welcome, he assured the continuity of the dynasty should some accident remove his older brother. In Paris the customary formalities were observed to celebrate the birth, the bonfires and illuminations, the public feasts and fountains running with wine. But when the Queen came to the capital six weeks later, she was very coldly received. Parisians, who in recent years had been plagued by shortages of fuel and the rising cost of bread, and who were currently suffering because of a prolonged drought, were in no mood to cheer the "Austrian bitch" in her elaborate gilded carriage. The cannon boomed from the Invalides, the guardsmen stood smartly at attention, but the people did not cluster to acclaim the Queen.

More and more they were blaming her for the food shortages, the fiscal crisis, the renewed aggression of Austria which threatened to embroil France in war. Emperor Joseph was proving to be ambitious and bellicose, and Antoinette was widely believed to be his tool at Versailles. And the stories of her extravagance were causing more and more resentment. While the current Controller-General, Calonne, was struggling merely to pay the interest on the huge outstanding loans made to the government, millions were being spent on the personal household expenses of the Queen, and on her sycophantic favorites. Every bookshop in the Palais Royal sold pamphlets recounting in salacious detail how the Queen squandered money on her lovers, male and female, how she craved more and more luxury, how her wardrobes bulged with sapphire-studded gowns and her closets held chests full of priceless diamonds.

Everyone had heard of her private retreat at Trianon, and of the little hamlet she was having her architect construct there. It seemed a perverse extravagance, for the Queen to create a village for her own amusement while in many parts of France real peasants in real villages were in dire want. In her make-believe village stood eight small thatch-roofed cottages, their plaster walls cleverly painted with cracks to make them look weathered, their gardens full of vegetables and fruit trees. Nearby were barns, a poultry yard, and a mill. A farmer named Valy was brought in to live in the farmhouse and look after the livestock. Cows were pastured in a small field, and milked into porcelain tubs in an exquisite little dairy. The Queen had her own cows, named Brunette and Blanchette, and white goats and white lambs, rabbits and cooing pigeons and clucking hens. There was a note of pathos at the miniature hamlet, amid the abundant charm; it represented an almost childlike vision of a simpler, happier world. But the Queen's critics saw nothing of this. To them the village was one more in a long list of frivolous purchases. They called it "Little Vienna," and made fun of Antoinette indulging in her rustic pleasures.

They were infuriated to learn, shortly before the birth of the Duc de Normandie, that yet another palace had been acquired for the Queen: St.-Cloud, a very large and commodious mansion set in a garden of cascades and fountains. St.-Cloud was situated on rising ground across the river from the Bois de Boulogne. It had belonged to the Duc d'Orléans, who sold it to the King, who made it over to Antoinette as her own property, to use as she saw fit. The money to buy St.-Cloud came in part from the sale of other royal lands, but the people, who had no way of knowing this, assumed that more millions of livres had been added to the deficit in order to gratify the Queen. They began calling her Madame Deficit, and denounced her more vehemently than ever. In the Paris Parlement, Antoinette's detractors shouted that it was "impolitic and immoral" for a valuable royal palace to belong to a foreigner, and a foreigner noted for making expensive improvements to her dwellings. (Antoinette did order alterations to the facades of St.-Cloud and remodeled the private apartments, and the alterations were not complete until 1788.)

In truth Antoinette wanted St.-Cloud for her children, in particular for the dauphin whom she felt was too confined at La Muette. The nursery was expanding. The new baby made three royal children and she intended to have more. Thérèse she liked to keep near her at Versailles—Mercy complained that it was awkward to accomplish necessary business in Antoinette's presence because her daughter was always underfoot, distracting the mother and disrupting conversation—but the boys needed their own establishments. St.-Cloud would be perfect, its park and grounds spacious enough for them to roam freely in and its location, nearer Paris than Versailles, would be convenient. There was enough room to accommodate Louis's sister Elisabeth as well, who in 1785 was twenty-one and was becoming a much loved friend and companion to Antoinette. In addition, Versailles, already dilapidated under Louis XV, was decaying rapidly. Necessary repairs would take upwards of a decade, the King was advised, particularly if payment for the costly work had to be spread out over a period of years. St.-Cloud might thus become a necessity. Still, the Queen's newest acquisition was much resented.

Even more resented was the family she had singled out for conspicuous advancement: the Polignacs.

Yolande de Polastron, Comtesse de Polignac was a soft-eyed, mild and delicately beautiful woman with an attractive serenity that had a calming effect on the restless and occasionally frenetic Antoinette. She was much admired for her exquisite manners, her skin "with the whiteness of a narcissus," her lovely brown eyes, good teeth and charming smile, even her "little pink fingertips."[3] She may have had something of the attraction of an older sister to Antoinette, for she was six years the Queen's senior. Married to Comte Jules de Polignac, a soldier of good family but only modest means, Yolande might have tried to advance herself through intrigue as so many did at Versailles. Instead she seemed content with what she had. When Antoinette first saw her at a palace ball, and admired her "angelic face" and good figure, she told the Queen candidly that she rarely came to Versailles as her husband's income was not sufficient to support the expense of court life. She dressed simply, talked softly and sweetly, and in general was in refreshing contrast to the grasping people around her. Antoinette was much taken with her, and by 1777 they were fast friends.

Yolande's detractors were quick to claim that her apparent lack of ambition and her artless charm were merely a clever ruse, that they hid a ruthless and acquisitive nature. Some claimed to see behind her mild expression the evidence of "her shameful villainy." But Madame Campan, who despised guile, saw none in Yolande. She was of "retiring character," the bedchamber woman thought. Presumption and affectation were foreign to her, she "beamed with grace." Sometimes, Madame Campan wrote in her memoirs, Yolande spent several hours with her while waiting for Antoinette, "and talked frankly and ingenuously of all the honors and dangers that she saw in the kindness shown to her."[4]

As usual, Antoinette's kindness took the form of lavish generosity. Count Jules de Polignac was given the post of first equerry to the Queen, solving all financial difficulties and making him a wealthy man. Yolande and Jules were given spacious and well located quarters in the palace—a great rarity and a coveted privilege. In time Yolande took the place of the scandal-tainted Madame de Guéménée as governess of the royal children. And all the couple's relatives prospered as well.

Antoinette and Yolande became inseparable when the former was in her early twenties and the latter approaching thirty. Throughout her twenties the Queen remained devoted to Yolande, "a friend of whom I am infinitely fond," as she put it. "When I am alone with her I am no longer a Queen, I am myself!" The spiteful gossipmongers invented lies about the two women, saying that they were lesbians and even that Yolande acted as a procuress for Antoinette, providing her with young women. There was an extraordinary closeness, at least on the Queen's side, but it had nothing to do with sex. Antoinette's heart belonged to Fersen, and Yolande had for years been the mistress of the difficult, occasionally violent Comte de Vaudreuil, a literary dilettante and inveterate intriguer.[5] "The Queen can no longer do without this young woman's company and tells her all her thoughts," Mercy commented, and his description was probably the most accurate one.

Yolande may not have been scheming to advance herself, but many of those around her certainly were, and for them her friendship with the Queen was a golden opportunity. They constantly "wrenched from the Queen favors which caused complaints among the public," Mercy wrote. Members of the Polignac circle were given a disproportionate share of the pensions, offices and appointments handed out at court; those excluded from the favored group, including men of older lineage and longer service (and even, on occasion, greater merit), were angry and resentful. The number of the Queen's enemies grew larger. Antoinette was persuaded to reward people merely because Yolande or her husband liked them or were related to them. Often she rewarded those, such as the Duc de Vaudreuil, whom she herself disliked.

The list of Polignac appointees was a long one. Diane de Polignac, Yolande's sister-in-law, was lady of honor to the Countess of Artois. (Ugly, vindictive, with a razor-sharp wit and a fierce intelligence, Diane was called "the Red Moon" because of her ruddy complexion.) Francois-Camille, Marquis de Polignac (uncle of Yolande's husband Jules) became first equerry to the Comte d'Artois and drew a sizable pension besides his large salary and valuable perquisites of office. Louis-Héraclius Victor, Vicomte de Polignac, was appointed to a governorship and given a large pension. His daughter became lady-in-waiting to King Louis's sister Elisabeth. Auguste-Apollinaire de Polignac, a Cluniac monk, received a pension and another Polignac cleric, Camille-Louis, was paid a double salary as Bishop of Meaux and Abbot of St.-Epure. Lesser branches of the family were given gifts and annuities worth tens of thousands of livres.[6] Jules de Polignac's friend (and Antoinette's reputed lover) the Duc de Coigny became wealthy as first equerry to the King and the Duc de Vaudreuil was made chief falconer.

Yolande's husband was the most conspicuous beneficiary of the Queen's largesse. He was in charge of her stables, and in 1780 was created a hereditary duke. Large cash gifts followed in subsequent years. Not satisfied with this wealth, he flagrantly abused his office to pillage the royal treasury, charging the Queen's accounts for the purchase of a hundred and fifty additional horses, for many more stable servants and increased purchases of supplies and fodder. Each extra expense made money for Jules, for in each instance the actual amount he paid out was far less than the amount for which he billed his royal mistress.[7] With the profits of his swindle he acquired several valuable houses, spent lavishly on their furnishings and lived in princely fashion.

To be sure, the Polignacs and their satellites were not the only courtiers to prosper under the Queen's special patronage, merely the greediest and most conspicuous. The Princesse de Lamballe, before Yolande de Polignac eclipsed her, enjoyed nearly a million livres in fees, salaries and grants, and saw to it that her brother was also extravagantly rewarded. But the Polignacs, as a group, obtained 2.5 million livres in cash and nearly half a million in pensions and salaries—truly a prodigious sum given the fact that the entire household budget of the court in 1776 was some thirty-six million livres. When the Polignac wealth is compared to the two livres a day earned by the average Parisian laborer it seems even larger, and even more superfluous. The enemies of the monarchy were outraged. While the honest workmen of Paris sweated for their bread, they complained, the gilded idlers of the court were growing richer and richer—and all because of the wicked Austrian bitch.

The Parisians' dark view of the Queen was intensified in the late summer of 1785, when the details of a prolonged and very damaging scandal involving the Cardinal de Rohan, Grand Almoner of France, a fabulously expensive collar of diamonds, and a clever swindler began to come to light.

The central figure in the scandal was the Cardinal, a worldly, witty and gullible man in his fifties. As Prince de Rohan he belonged to the highest nobility of France, as Cardinal he participated in the highest councils of the Church, as Grand Almoner he held one of the most visible posts of honor at Versailles, where he was often to be seen going to and from the chapel and presiding there in his scarlet silk robes. His vices were equally grand and visible. His boundless vanity led him to squander money on his own magnificence, buying elaborate painted coaches and keeping a huge retinue of servants in scarlet liveries trimmed with gold lace. His lust was said to rival that of the late Louis XV, and like Louis he kept a large and well stocked harem—in addition to his numerous conquests among the women of the court. Antoinette's brother Leopold summed him up succinctly by saying that he was "without religion or morals."

Antoinette had been hearing complaints about the Cardinal ever since her earliest years at the French court. Rohan had been sent as ambassador to Austria in the early 1770s, and no worse envoy to the hard-working, highly moral Maria Theresa could be imagined. He offended the Empress by riding, booted and spurred, through the middle of religious processions, by setting up a private brothel and by turning his ill-mannered servants loose on the Viennese. He ran up gigantic debts, led the heir to the throne astray with stories of the high life in Paris, and had the temerity to smuggle in silk and sell it, contrary to the customs regulations, at his mansion. Maria Theresa called Rohan "a bad lot," "perfectly incorrigible." In her letters to Antoinette she urged again and again that he be recalled, as he was dishonoring France and alienating the Austrians. Besides, she added, he was fundamentally ignorant of affairs, a frivolous man of no substance and trivial interests. Toward his sexual exploits—he had managed to bewitch, if not to seduce, all the women of Vienna, "young and old, beautiful and ugly"—she felt nothing but disgust.[8]

Maria Theresa's excoriation of Rohan left a strong impression on her daughter, and when Rohan returned from Vienna and in time became Grand Almoner she refused to have anything to do with him. Her antipathy was so pronounced that everyone noticed it—and as usual those who hated Antoinette whispered that it was only a pretense, and that Rohan was in truth another of her secret lovers. The Cardinal himself, however, knew that her coldness was genuine and saw in it a formidable barrier to his further advancement.

This, and his intrinsic gullibility and lack of judgment, made Rohan a ripe victim for charlatans and swindlers, and Versailles was full of these. Among the most celebrated was Giuseppe Balsamo, a magician and hypnotist who called himself the Comte de Cagliostro and made extravagant claims about himself and his abilities. He said, and many believed him, so powerful was his hypnotic persuasiveness, that he was several thousand years old, that he had overcome illness and death and could help others overcome them, that he could cure any ailment, create wealth and confer power in worldly affairs. He posed as the Grand Copt of the order of Egyptian Masonry and enrolled many credulous followers in his lodges.[9] Rohan believed that the magician could unblock his path to advancement at court, could reconcile him with Antoinette and make him one of the King's ministers.

But there was yet another, equally crafty charlatan in the Cardinal's circle. She was Jeanne de Saint-Rémy, who called herself Comtesse de la Motte-Valois. Jeanne's father had in fact been a descendant of the Valois Kings, but had died penniless, leaving his two children to be raised by their peasant mother who beat them and exploited them. Jeanne had grown into a clever imposter who, together with her soldier husband, posed as an habituée of the royal court and pretended to enjoy the Queen's friendship. An accomplice, Retaux de Villette, forged Antoinette's signature on letters that Jeanne used to enhance her credibility. She obtained an introduction to the Cardinal, and eventually became his mistress. When he confided to her his ambitions to become a royal minister and above all to enter the Queen's good graces, Jeanne saw a way to become very rich.

She told Rohan that she would use her influence with her "friend" the Queen on his behalf, and after a time convinced him that she was succeeding in breaking down Antoinette's prejudice against him. He was overjoyed—and wanted her to arrange an audience for him. A genuine audience with the Queen being an impossibility, Jeanne staged a make-believe meeting, hiring a Paris prostitute to impersonate the Queen. Rohan, who was beside himself with eagerness, did not question the odd circumstances of the "audience" Jeanne told him she had arranged, which was to be held at midnight in the gardens of Versailles. In the dark the Cardinal believed that the pretty veiled woman who handed him a rose and murmured cryptically "You know what this means" was in fact Antoinette. He probably also believed, given his monstrous conceit, that she was in love with him.

The Cardinal could not wait to give proof of his devotion to his sovereign lady, and Jeanne was not slow to convey to him the Queen's requests. She asked him for money, first sixty thousand livres, then more. And then a unique opportunity arose for Jeanne to enrich herself beyond her wildest dreams.

For years the crown jeweler, Böhmer, had been trying to persuade Antoinette to buy a fabulous necklace he had made, a heavy collar of diamonds with long hanging pendants. In all, the necklace contained some five hundred and forty gems, and was worth 1.6 million livres. It was inconceivable that anyone but the Queen could afford such a costly bauble—yet Antoinette had lost her taste for diamonds and could not be persuaded to buy the necklace. Böhmer heard of the Comtesse de la Motte-Valois, and of her vaunted intimacy with the Queen. Through an intermediary he approached her and offered her a thousand louis if she could convince Antoinette to buy the neckalce. Seizing her opportunity, Jeanne told the jeweler that the Cardinal, acting for the Queen, would make the purchase, which he did soon thereafter. The necklace was handed over to Rohan, who gave it to Jeanne, never doubting that she would deliver it to her friend Antoinette. (In fact she gave it to her husband, who went to England to dispose of the diamonds one by one.) A few months later, when Böhmer demanded payment, the truth of the swindle came to light.

Antoinette learned, first to her surprise and then to her horror, that Böhmer had delivered to her, via Cardinal Rohan, a necklace she had never ordered, and that the first installement of the payment for that necklace was past due. Rohan, she declared, had used her name "like a low and inept forger." He was a liar and a cheat. Everyone knew he was deeply in debt; out of desperation he had taken advantage of his court position to try to bilk the Queen.

Rohan was summoned to the King's cabinet to face his sovereign and several officials. Antoinette was also present. Louis questioned him, and as it became clear that he had been deceived by the clever Jeanne, he grew pale and looked as if he would faint. He protested that "a lady called the Comtesse de la Motte-Valois" had taken advantage of him. He promised the angry Antoinette that he would pay for the necklace—an impossibility, given his debts and the enormous bill from Böhmer—and insisted that he thought "by carrying out this commission he was paying court to Her Majesty."

Nothing Rohan said was sufficient to exculpate him. In front of the entire court, then assembled for the procession to the chapel for midday Mass, the Cardinal was arrested and taken off to the Bastille. Jeanne was arrested the following day and, though she denied her guilt and tried to convince her accusers that Cagliostro had been Rohan's ally in stealing the necklace, she too was unconvincing. The police inquiry uncovered damning evidence against the Countess. She and her husband, before his departure for England, had grown rich overnight, buying cartloads of furniture, engaging a large staff of servants, entertaining lavishly. Only the sale of the diamonds could explain this sudden wealth, therefore Jeanne had to be guilty.

Contemporaries interpreted the scandal according to their prejudices. The police were convinced that Rohan was guilty of nothing more than gullibility. Rohan's enemies blamed him, and saw Jeanne as his accomplice. But the majority of people, at court and outside of it, blamed Antoinette. She was extravagant, she loved diamonds; therefore it followed that she must have staged the entire affair of the necklace in collusion with the Cardinal, who was probably her lover. His arrest was merely a ploy to make her look innocent, when in fact she was the one who belonged in the Bastille.

Rohan was tried at the end of May 1786 and Antoinette, who by this time was seven months pregnant with her fourth child, fully expected that he would be found guilty, if not of theft, then of knowing participation in fraud. The trial was a great *cause célèbre*, with Rohan's partisans wearing hats of "cardinal red" and proclaiming that their hero was being persecuted like the early

Christian saints and martyrs. Pamphlets sprang up, predictably blackening Antoinette and championing Rohan. Suddenly the reprobate Cardinal was seen as a guileless innocent, victimized by the wicked Queen; his former lovers (a group that included many of the great ladies of the court) were among his loudest defenders, grateful to him for having destroyed their love letters just as the investigation began. Rohan had become a symbol, he represented all those who saw themselves as injured by Antoinette's extravagance. To take his side was to strike a blow against the Queen, and there were many eager to injure her in any way they could.

Among them were the lawyers of the parlement, who demanded that Rohan be acquitted, and the judges, who treated him like a prince. After eighteen hours of deliberation the complaint against the Cardinal was dismissed. Jeanne, alias the Comtesse de la Motte-Valois, was sentenced to be branded and imprisoned (she escaped ten months later), her absent husband was condemned to the galleys. Cagliostro was exonerated.

Thousands of people cheered the Cardinal when the verdict was made known, and more cheers went up when he emerged from the Bastille. Louis made him give up his court post as Almoner and forced him to leave Paris for his abbey at Chaise-Dieu, but his legal vindication overshadowed these minor humiliations. More important, a major insult had been delivered to the Queen.

16

CARDINAL Rohan was acquitted on May 31, 1786. The following day Antoinette wrote a *cri de coeur* to the Comtesse de Polignac.

"Come and weep with me, come and console your friend. The judgment that has just been pronounced is an atrocious insult. I am bathed in tears of grief and despair."

Antoinette was nearly eight months pregnant, and throughout her pregnancy she had been under great strain. The investigation into Cardinal Rohan's culpability, the worsening fiscal crisis, the endless calumnies printed about her by her numberless enemies demoralized and weakened her. For the past month she had had to restrict her activities somewhat, complaining that she did not have the physical strength to maintain her usual routine.[1] There must have been women at Versailles who watched the progress of the Queen's pregnancy with apprehension, shaking their heads and remarking that such a tense and troubled gestation would result in harm to the child.

Antoinette worried over her children, just as she worried over her husband who, year by year, found it harder and harder to cope with all that was awry with his government and looked to her for solace and advice. Her daughter Thérèse, whom she called Mousseline, was now seven years old, a miniature lady dressed in flowing robes, her hair curled and carefully if simply dressed. Mousseline was a temperamental child, with a selfish streak, much attached to her mother; Antoinette took pains to prevent her from giving herself airs. To this end, she brought another little girl into the Princess's household, the daughter of one of the maids, and gave orders that this child, whom she renamed Ernestine, should be treated in exactly the same way that Mousseline was. The two girls wore the same clothes, ate their meals together, took their lessons together. No special deference was shown to Madame Royale, and far from resenting this loss of superiority, Mousseline became very fond of Ernestine and loved her like a sister. One imagines the two children playing with their bewigged dolls, with doll-sized plumed hats, taffeta gowns and high-heeled satin shoes supplied by Rose Bertin.

Antoinette's older son, the dauphin, was now nearing five years old, a sad figure in his sailor suits and long baby curls. His spine was twisted, one shoulder was much higher than the other, and he was small for his age. He seemed exceptionally vulnerable to fevers and debilitating diseases, and he did not put on weight like a healthy child.[2] He had developed a serious look, perhaps because of the pain he had to endure, perhaps because he was introverted by nature. He knew that his spinal deformity—which worsened markedly as he grew older—worried his mother. The sight of him brought tears to her eyes, according to the Princesse de Lamballe; when Antoinette supped with her son, she wept so freely that she could hardly eat.

The youngest child, the fifteen-month-old Louis-Charles, Duc de Normandie, was as robust and healthy as his brother was sickly, a round-faced, apple-cheeked baby whom Antoinette called her *chou d'amour*, or sweetheart. He had inherited her vibrant good health, she called him "a true peasant child" and took delight in his precocious intelligence and good temper. If her older son was the cause of an abiding sorrow, and deep concern, at least the younger one proved that she could bear healthy offspring and she expected him to flourish. When one day she went to visit him and found a doctor applying leeches to his tender flesh, she was so shocked that she fainted. The little Duke did have one weakness: his nerves were delicate, and any sudden unexpected noise—the barking of a dog, the rumble of carriage wheels—upset him.

As her pregnancy entered its final weeks Antoinette had the rare pleasure of a visit from a member of her family. Her brother Ferdinand, who was a year older than she was and had been her favorite brother in childhood, came to France with his Italian wife in mid-May and remained until mid-June. In the midst of her troubles Antoinette must have been glad to see him, though it cannot have pleased her to have him witness her humiliation at the hands of the Paris parlement in the Rohan affair, or to know that he was hearing all the slanderous things being said about her. She must have told him how she was innocent of blame in the scandal over the diamond necklace—"that horror," as she called it—but Ferdinand could hardly take a step without encountering pamphlets and cartoons and broadsheets insulting to his sister.

Paris was full of lurid accounts of the Queen's love affairs and her sordid dissipations. Old stories were revived, of her orgies in the gardens of Versailles and her nefarious plot to make a drunkard of her husband so that she and her lovers could deceive him more easily. References to "Madame Deficit" and "the Austrian bitch" were everywhere. Not content to steal the infamous diamond necklace and then try to blame the Cardinal, the Queen, it was alleged, had actually paved the floor of the Petit Trianon with precious gems which she crushed under her red heels. Caricaturists mocked the obese King and his spendthrift wife, showing them gorging themselves at a sumptuous banquet while all around them their pinch-faced subjects held their empty stomachs and gazed hungrily at the food.

The libelous pamphlets made their way into the palace, where disgruntled servants handed them out freely and sometimes even had the effrontery to leave them in the royal bedrooms or under the King's napkin when he sat down to dine. Gossip flew. The Queen was pregnant with the Cardinal's child, or Fersen's. She was bankrupting the country by sending hundreds of thousands of francs to her brother in Austria and spending three hundred thousand livres a year on clothes and mammoth hats.[3]

Spreading slander against the Queen had become a fad, as much in style as the "Henri IV ruffs" sprouting at the necklines of fashionable garments in the summer of 1786 and the new color called "goose-droppings" that was all the rage. Some Parisians took the King's zebra as their model, and at once everything they wore, from coats and waistcoats to stockings, had to be striped. There was no end to the new fads: coiffures called "porcupine" and "baby's cap," "pomegranate," "periwinkle" and, with a nod to the fledgling United States, "Boston" and "Philadelphia"; powdered hair worn in preference to wigs; "republican" dress (flat shoes instead of heels, skirts worn without paniers for women, round hats and frock coats for men); hats in the form of cherries and turnips and head-scratchers trimmed with diamonds. A notable change had to do with buttons, which were traditionally of gold or silver, sometimes studded with precious gems. This year the style called for steel buttons instead. "Steel fever" infected the well-to-do, who wore not only steel buttons but steel buckles on their shoes and steel braid on their uniforms. Steel watch-chains hung across their "republican" vests, and even their ancestral swords were replated with steel.

Fashion reflected politics, and in politics the craze was for everything English. So women asked their coiffeurs to dress their hair à la "English Park" or "Huntsman in Covert," read English novels and danced to English tunes, chose dishes and silver services that were "English in shape," and drove English carriages. Some young men at Versailles affected to speak French with an English accent and "made a study of all the awkwardness of manner, the style of walking, in fact, all the outward signs of an Englishman, so that they could adopt them for their own use." The highest compliment one could be paid was to be mistaken for an Englishman.[4]

Surrounded by opprobrium, Antoinette prepared to enter labor for the fourth time. On July 9 a daughter, Sophie Hélène Beatrice, was born. Little attention was paid to the birth, still less to the baby once her sex was disclosed. She was small and delicate, the midwives whispered that she was deformed. No doubt Antoinette murmured consolations and endearments to the tiny child but she too must have been dismayed at her size and imperfect shape. Sophie did not look like a healthy baby, and in her first days of life she did not thrive.

Antoinette had not fully recovered from the birth when one of her least favorite relatives arrived in France for a month-long visit. It was her sister Christina, thirteen years Antoinette's senior and very much the meddling, critical older sister. Christina had always been Maria Theresa's well-behaved, perfect daughter, blessed with exceptional intelligence, and blessed too with a happy marriage to a man she chose for love, Duke Albert of Teschen. Her life had not been unblemished by sorrow—she had lost at least one of her children in infancy—but she seems to have been the sort of resolute character who takes such losses in stride and has little sympathy for others who are more sentimental. At forty-four, Christina had become a domineering matron who, no doubt, saw it as her duty to force Antoinette to see the error of her ways.

The visit began badly, with Christina presenting Antoinette with some "mean-looking boxes" as a gift and lording it over her in a way the latter found "extremely bothersome." "The renewed acquaintance of the two sisters," Mercy informed Emperor Joseph in Vienna, "was not entirely without difficulties." Antoinette felt fragile, both physically and emotionally. The last thing she needed was an annoying relative trying to tell her how to live her life. She enlisted Mercy's help in avoiding her sister, keeping her away from the palace as much as possible and making certain that when unavoidable, Christina's visits were brief.

She was in any case preoccupied with little Sophie, who did not put on weight and, after six weeks, was still as small and as feeble as a newborn. Neither mother nor baby were doing very well; Antoinette confessed to being slow to recover her strength, and was glad to see the last of her sister and brother-in-law at the end of August. Once they had gone, she let down her guard completely and became ill with a high fever and severe sore throat for several weeks.[5]

At thirty Antoinette was growing stout. Corsets compressed her waist to a trim twenty-three inches, but Madame Eloff, the court dressmaker, measured her bust at nearly forty-four inches and her dimensions were clearly ample. Thirty was a perilous age and aristocratic ladies rarely owned to being over thirty, though it was understood that after they reached that unmentionable age they could no longer dance or wear fresh flowers next to their fading complexions. ("To a bourgeois a duchess was never over thirty," the sixty-year-old Duchesse de Chaulnes once remarked.) To camouflage her generous proportions Antoinette invented a new style of *robe de chambre* called the "Aristotle," which was voluminous enough in its Grecian folds to drape the figure flatteringly.[6]

She spent more time than ever in the small circle of her family and female attendants. It was neither safe nor pleasant to go to Paris, where her elegant heated boxes at the Opera and Comédie Française remained empty. At the theater there was always the risk that the audience would respond with applause to any reference to "the cruel Queen" in a classic drama, while operas offered even more opportunities for insult. Instead of seeking entertainment in Paris, Antoinette spent her evenings with her older children, keeping herself amused by playing billiards and solving the riddles in the *Mercure de France* (she was very good at these) or retiring to the "Gilded Cabinet," where her harp and harpsichord were kept, to play and sing with Madame Vigée-Lebrun (whose artistic talents extended to music) and the composer Grétry. Her singing was tuneful if undistinguished, and her harp-playing had become very fluent through years of practice. According to Madame Campan, Antoinette had become "able to read at sight like a first-rate professor."[7] One court observer, the Swedish ambassador, thought that Antoinette spent more time than she had in the past at her prayers and at Mass—no doubt praying for the health of her fragile youngest daughter.

There was very little society for her to mingle in. Versailles continued to be sparsely populated, and the number of the Queen's enemies had grown considerably during the affair of the necklace. Cardinal Rohan was connected by blood or marriage to most of the great families of France, and his relatives shunned the woman who, in their view, had wronged him. Yolande de Polignac, for years Antoinette's closet friend, had cooled toward her. Antoinette believed that Yolande had been "subjugated" by the Rohan faction, and though she still summoned the Duchess to comfort her in her worst hours, she no longer felt comfortable visiting Yolande's house, knowing that if she did she might well find enemies there. She knew better what to expect at the house of the British ambassador, the Duke of Dorset, where the musicians played lively Scottish reels and where she could forget the restrictions on dancing imposed at Versailles and enjoy herself.

Fersen had returned to Sweden, Louis was poor company at the best of times, and was usually away hunting or closeted with his locks and his map collection. Antoinette spent many hours alone, busying herself at the Trianon milking Brunette and Blanchette, stroking her white goats and sheep, overseeing the sale of the eighty pounds of oranges her orchard produced each year. Perhaps she turned the pages of a few light books (*Memoirs of a Young Virgin*, *Confidences of a Beautiful Woman*, and *Anecdotes of Conjugal Love* were some of the titles she kept at the Trianon), more probably she wept and prayed and surveyed her face in the mirror, noting the pouches that were filling out under her eyes and the deep creases that ran from nose to chin.

She felt beleaguered. Her subjects despised her, pamphleteers attacked her in print, her enemies shunned her and struck at her behind her back, her erstwhile friends were growing distant. One day in September of 1786, Madame Campan found Antoinette in her bedroom at Trianon, in tears after reading some vicious letters.

"Ah, the wicked men, the monsters!" she said through her tears. "What have I done to them. . . . I wish I were dead!"

Orange-flower water and ether were brought—the remedy kept handy for the Queen's fits of nerves—but Antoinette ignored them.

"No," she told her attendants, "if you love me, leave me; it would be better if I were dead!" The servants left, but Madame Campan stayed while Antoinette hugged her and sobbed.

In October, the court left as usual for Fontainebleau, the old decaying palace in the midst of the wild forest of Bière with its huge rocks and thick dark woods. Each fall the vast trek was made, hundreds of wagons and carts and carriages trundling along the muddy roads, dragged by thousands of weary horses. (The King and principal courtiers alone requisitioned over two thousand horses to transport themselves and their baggage.) Beyond the personnel of the court, there were furnishings and tapestries to be transported—some four hundred tapestries in all—by the officials and the servants of the Garde Meuble du Roi. These filled wagon after wagon, along with the accoutrements needed to hang them and clean them and protect them from the dust and jolts of the roads. Then there was the kitchen equipment, and the bedding, the food stores and wines and coals and the tall traveling wardrobes every gentleman and lady possessed. Added to these were the wagons filled with actors from Paris, along with their scenery, their painters, designers and laundresses, and the tailors, embroiderers and wig-makers who created their costumes. New plays were traditionally presented at Fontainebleau before the King and Queen, and this season promised to be no different— except in expense. In all, the move cost some six hundred thousand livres, and Calonne, already hard pressed to meet ordinary expenses, had to borrow to finance it.

Once the travelers reached the palace, they found it more dilapidated than ever. Apart from the Queen's newly redecorated bedroom and gaming room, the former a restrained masterpiece of design in delicate silver and gold ornamentation, the latter redone in "Pompeian" style, with the walls painted in imitation of Pompeian artwork and chairs and tables copied from Roman models, the apartments ranged from shabby to uninhabitable. Large areas of the palace were moldy and rat-infested; once elegant wall coverings and floors of inlaid woods were rotted and stained from the rain that leaked through holes in the roof. Fewer than two hundred of the rooms were fit to be occupied, which meant that most of the courtiers had to be lodged, uncomfortably and expensively, in the adjacent village.

Once the rooms were meted out, the tapestries hung and usual court routine established, life at Fontainebleau proceeded pleasantly. And in the view of at least one observer, Necker's daughter Germaine, now Madame de Staël, it was Antoinette who was the center of attention. "It was above all around the Queen that the waves of the crowd surged," she wrote. Everyone was eager for her attention, "their eyes were glued to the steps of the Queen."[8]

Her every word, her every gesture were touched with grace and kindness. She was never overly familiar, yet she gave every appearance of having forgotten her exalted rank in her pleasure at being with the people around her. This, however, was in public. In her own beautifully decorated apartments, and in the children's rooms where the tiny Sophie struggled for life, the Queen was sorrowful, especially on the many wet days when it was impossible to ride or to go for long walks in the forest.

As usual, Louis spent his days at Fontainebleau hunting, in fair weather and foul, and enjoyed visiting the nearby forest of Compiègne, his favorite haunt as a boy. He loved Fontainebleau, and had recently ordered extensive renovations begun on one wing of the palace to create more livable quarters for himself and his children. He knew that the court's annual visit to Fontainebleau was costly, and becoming more costly year by year, but he was reluctant to give it up, even though Calonne had recently made it plain to him that the country was on the brink of financial ruin.

The Finance Minister had come to him in August with a dismal message. The treasury was empty, investment had slackened, trade was stagnant, Calonne said. Public confidence in government was at its lowest ebb in memory, and, worst of all, for this year of 1786 expenditures promised to exceed revenue by well over a hundred million livres. It was no good proposing small savings to be made here and there (though it would help if the King gave up his trips to Fontainebleau), or finding new temporary expedients to push back the fatal repayment dates. Nothing short of extensive, thoroughgoing reform of the state would in the long run do any good.[9]

Louis had been hearing dire warnings of this general kind for at least ten years, and had so far avoided having to come to terms with them, but Calonne's message compelled attention, and must have troubled the King throughout his stay at Fontainebleau. The good of his subjects was more on Louis's mind than usual, for earlier in the year he had made an eight-day journey to the Normandie coast and had been received there with great enthusiasm. Cheering crowds welcomed him to Cherbourg, where vast defensive works were being built for protection against England, and to Caen and Honfleur and Havre. When he heard cries of "Long live the King!" he joyfully shouted back "Long live my people!" and at the end of his trip he announced that he was "the happiest King in the world." It was refreshing to encounter French men and women who were not Parisians, who did not share the Parisians' scorn for monarchy. It was also refreshing, and unpleasantly revealing, to savor the approval of the public knowing that it was meant for him alone—in short, to travel without the Queen.

At thirty-two Louis was uglier and more unprepossessing than he had been as a boy. His squat, fleshy body was that of a "good rough stout man," in the view of one of the gardeners at Versailles, and not that of a King. Madame La Tour du Pin thought that "he looked like some peasant shambling along behind his plough."[10] Although his strength was still prodigious, he seldom used it, and he stuffed himself so gluttonously at meals that his fat made it hard for him to move. Triple, even quadruple chins dominated his moon face, his skin was deeply scarred and pitted and his small yellowish eyes, which were in a perpetual squint because of his short sight (spectacles were not worn at court), looked dully out on a narrowing world.

He was somewhat less timid than he had been as a boy, but no less gauche. The idea of bold, direct action in any sphere was foreign to him, he needed to be led, persuaded, coaxed into action—and into speech, being, as Antoinette said euphemistically, "by nature taciturn." (It was something of a triumph for him to embolden himself to shout "Long live my people!") He had lost his taste for childish pranks and practical jokes, and his intellect, always eccentric, had blossomed with maturity. His retentive mind was a storehouse unexpectedly rich. He could recite long passages from the plays of Racine, sometimes interrupting the nightly *coucher* with lengthy and surprisingly expressive dramatic recitations. He had a very good reading knowledge of English, and, according to Madame Campan, could translate difficult passages from *Paradise Lost*. He was an expert on the genealogy of the Bourbons, and of the great families of the nobility. His knowledge of geography was extensive enough to permit him to draw up navigation instructions for an explorer about to sail around the world. And he had a good memory for names and numbers, sometimes irritating his ministers by pointing out minute duplications or other minor errors in the accounts they presented to him and insisting that they be corrected. On his favorite subject, which was hunting, he could be amazingly voluble, and his knowledge of forest lore was impressive, if rarely displayed to anyone besides his huntsmen.[11]

Over the years he had retreated more and more into the privacy of his apartments at Versailles, which reflected his interests and tastes and where he found peace.

One entered these apartments to find displayed a number of engravings, all dedicated to the King and some showing the canals built during his reign of which he was especially proud. A stairway led upward to another room which housed his collection of geographical charts, globes and map cabinet. Here he liked to draw maps, and the room was strewn with uncompleted sketches and half-finished charts, some with color washed in, some without. Nearby were records of all the royal hunts, showing the dates and times of each hunt, and the number of game killed. Totals were given for each month, each season, and each year of his reign.

The tools and instruments in the turning and joining room Louis had inherited from his grandfather, who had enjoyed working in wood. The library held treasures from past centuries—the manuscript books of Anne of Brittany and Francis I, the prayer books and expensively bound volumes that had belonged to the later Valois kings and Louis XIV—and books published during the present reign. There were in addition many folio volumes of the debates of the English Parliament and a manuscript history of all the French plans, made over several centuries, to invade England. In the library Louis kept boxes of state papers, sorted by country, and a few salacious "histories" of the reigns of Catherine the Great and Paul I of Russia.

Without doubt the King's favorite room, and the one in which he spent the most time, was his forge. Here he had two anvils and a large number of iron tools, and with them he worked on his locks. There were locks of every sort and description, from small common locks to intricate secret locks to ornamental locks gleaming with gilt copper. There the master locksmith Gamin was to be found, serving as the King's teacher. Gamin judged his royal pupil to be "good, forbearing, timid, inquisitive, and addicted to sleep. He was fond of lockmaking to excess," the master locksmith said, "and he concealed himself from the Queen and the court to file and forge with me. In order to convey his anvil and my own backwards and forwards [to and from other royal residences], we were obliged to use a thousand stratagems."[12]

Also in the forge was Louis's favorite servant Duret, who sharpened his tools for him, cleaned the anvils, and kept the apartments in good order. Duret was very fond of his clumsy and ungainly master, and liked to do him small favors. In his private apartments Louis allowed himself the luxury of wearing the spectacles that court etiquette forbade elsewhere, and it was Duret who fitted them and adjusted them to the King's myopic sight.

The locks, the tools, the heavy anvils were trundled along the muddy roads to Fontainebleau along with the other household goods. No doubt the Queen disapproved. She wanted Louis to spend his evenings in the grand salon and at her new Pompeian-style gaming tables, not to secrete himself with Gamin and Duret and his locks. But she could not always have her way. Indeed, the older she grew, the less often she could count on things going to her liking. Louis was who he was; she could tell that he was troubled, and that he needed his privacy, and she knew that sooner or later the full burden of his troubles would fall on her shoulders.

17

WHILE the court was at Fontainebleau Calonne approached the King with a reform plan.

Instead of the present complicated taxation system, he proposed to institute a land tax, to be levied not in coinage but in goods, at harvest time. No individual or group would be exempt from this tax, and it would be administered by the landowners themselves, through elected assemblies of their own—under the supervision of the royal intendants, as agents of the King. Crown revenues would be increased through the imposition of new duties and through more efficient management of the royal lands. To stimulate the stagnant economy, internal customs barriers would be instituted, and the *corvée*—the right of landowners to exact unpaid labor services from the peasants on their estates and the right of the King to demand compulsory service repairing roads—commuted to a money payment. (Turgot had abolished the *corvée* in the 1770's, but the abolition had lapsed with his tenure of office, and the reimposed *corvée* had been in force for over a decade.)

Once his reform program was in place, Calonne told the King, it would be possible to raise short-term loans, to be secured by expected new revenues. And to give potential lenders even more cause for confidence, Calonne proposed a convocation of some hundred and fifty "notables"—noblemen, bishops, mayors and civic dignitaries from all over France—who would lend their prestige to the reforms and restore confidence in the government's ability to solve its financial difficulties.

Calonne's plan went forward, and the Assembly of Notables convened on February 22, 1787. Almost from the outset, however, the strategy went awry. The notables refused to back the Finance Minister's reforms, or even to consider them, and after six acrimonious weeks the King dismissed Calonne. Vergennes, on whom Louis had relied for so many years, had died in February and to replace him Louis, who was in great anguish of spirit, appointed the elderly Archbishop of Toulouse, Cardinal Loménie de Brienne.

The upheaval in the government upset Louis greatly, and he turned to Antoinette for solace. After Vergennes's death he came to her apartments and wept, calling himself a worthless bankrupt and in despair over the mountain of debt that was growing higher each day. When Calonne's scheme failed because of the recalcitrance of the Notables, the King was in a fury. "That scoundrel of a Calonne!" he roared. "I should have had him hanged!" He punctuated his outburst by smashing a chair, then lapsed into a brooding silence.

His ministers let him down, his subjects were uncooperative, even defiant. And by summoning the Assembly of Notables, he had all but admitted that he and his ministers could not govern effectively without at least the appearance of popular consent.

Loménie de Brienne, well intentioned and capable, hoped to be able to work with the Notables where Calonne had failed. He proposed compromises in the nature of the land tax, and assured the members of the Assembly that the royal family would reduce their household expenditures in order to bring the deficit down. But the Notables were adamant. They were feeling their power, having brought about the fall of Calonne and sensing that their very existence as a body empowered (however vaguely) to speak for the community of the King's subjects represented a significant shift toward some form of representative government. They called on the King to summon the Estates General, and demanded that a permanent body of auditors be appointed to supervise the management of state finance. Too late, Loménie de Brienne saw that no compromise was possible. On May 25 he dissolved the Assembly.

Axel Fersen was at Versailles when the closing ceremonies took place. He watched them, noting in his diary how imposing the Notables looked in their robes and gowns of rank and office, and adding that the Assembly had done little to lower the deficit or improve the outlook for the future. Certain reductions in the expenses of the royal household had been ordered—a lowering of courtiers' pensions, and of the budgets of the Queen's stable and the King's hunting establishment, for example—but no deep systemic changes, and only the latter could ultimately salvage the situation.[1]

Fersen was at Versailles often, though in his role as liaison between the French and Swedish courts he had to spend a good deal of time at the court of Gustavus III as well. Sweden and Russia were at war; as Colonel of a Swedish regiment Fersen had military obligations to fulfill, along with his duties in France as commander of the Royal Swedish. He was accustomed to a rather hectic and unsettled life, but in the spring of 1787 Antoinette was preparing to give him a home base of sorts. She ordered alterations made in her apartments so that Fersen would have a place to live during his official visits to Versailles. The most conspicuous feature of the lodging created in the Queen's apartments was a Swedish stove, installed at some expense and necessitating the demolition of part of a wall and an expanse of flooring. This remodeling was recorded in the Service of the Royal Buildings, and Fersen referred to it cryptically in his diary. (On April 7, 1787 he noted the existence of a "plan for lodging upstairs," and two weeks later he wrote of "what she has to find me for living upstairs." The stove and its newly created alcove were mentioned the following October.[2]

Even if Fersen and the Queen had not been lovers—and by this time their relationship was long past its intense, incandescent early stage and had become mellow and mature—it would have been advisable to lodge Fersen at Versailles, for he was there nearly every day when in France. He went riding near the Trianon three or four times a week, and Antoinette rode out alone to meet him there. While riding in the park they could enjoy at least some degree of privacy, but, the court being what it was, they were watched, and prying eyes took note of how often they met and how long they stayed away. "These meetings caused a great deal of public scandal," wrote the censorious Comte de Saint-Priest, Minister for the Royal Household, "in spite of the favorite's modesty and restraint, for he never showed anything outwardly and was the most discreet of all the Queen's friends."[3] The minister was a reliable source of gossip, though he had no objectivity whatsoever where Fersen was concerned (the ever gallant Swede had seduced his wife) and he had little love for Antoinette, as she had tried to have him replaced. Still, Antoinette was clearly imprudent—or perhaps by this time she had ceased to care very much what people said about her.

She did care, though, when her lack of circumspection caused her husband pain. One day while out hunting, Louis was handed a packet of letters. He read them at once, sitting down on the grass and becoming so absorbed in what he was doing that he forgot the hunt completely. His equerries tactfully retired; when they returned they found the King in a terrible state, so distraught that he could not even mount his horse. His moon face was tear-stained, his small yellow eyes red-rimmed. The equerries hurried him into a carriage and took him home. It turned out that one of the letters was an indictment of Antoinette for infidelity with Fersen. Apparently it contained something more than the commonplace gossip that had been making the rounds of the court for years, and that Louis had heard often enough before, something truly upsetting.

"They want to take from us the only friend we can rely on," Antoinette said sorrowfully when Louis told her what had happened. Probably disingenuously, she suggested that they banish Fersen from Versailles, but the King would not hear of it. Hurt as he was, he too relied on Fersen and needed him more than ever in this season of crisis.

Whatever Louis may have believed about his wife and the handsome Swede, this was no time to torment Antoinette with accusations. Her baby daughter was dying.

Little Sophie lay in her cradle, fighting for breath, her weak lungs failing. Antoinette kept watch beside her, in tears over her "poor little angel," heartbroken and powerless to save the tiny child who was growing more feeble by the day. On June 15 Sophie became dramatically worse, and four days later she was dead. Antoinette shut herself away at Trianon, with Louis and her sister-in-law Elisabeth. "Come," the Queen wrote to Elisabeth, "we shall weep over the death of my poor little angel. . . . I have need of your heart to console mine." While the mother grieved, surgeons opened the small body and examined the organs. As expected, the lungs were found to be "in a very bad state."

Antoinette grieved—and clutched her older son to her with

dread. He too was sickly, his malformed spine prevented him from running and playing like a normal child, and his perpetual seriousness was unnatural. In her worst moments Antoinette feared for his life; now that one of her children was dead the horrifying possibility seemed to move closer that another of them might die—and the most important of them, the heir to the throne.

But there was to be no leisure to indulge private anxieties or private grief. The monarchy was in crisis, and the King was unable to face the crisis squarely, much less take action to remedy it. Panic-stricken, tearful and irresolute, Louis turned to his wife to rescue him from the quagmire into which he was sinking, knowing that she would be stalwart where he was timid.

Stalwart she was—but untutored in the intricacies of governing. She was intelligent, she had opinions, she was not afraid to confront the ministers and state her opinions boldly. But courage and common sense were woefully inadequate; what was needed was leadership and expertise and a rigorous commitment to fundamental change. And Antoinette could offer none of these things. She was far too unpopular to exercise leadership, even if her gender (and her temperament) had not been obstacles. She had no expertise to offer. And she was her mother's daughter: the concept of fundamental change was foreign to her. If there were problems with finance or with popular discontent, then her common sense told her that the ministers must be to blame. Change the ministers, and all would be well.

Fersen described the state of affairs at Versailles very well. "The King is weak and suspicious," he wrote. "He trusts only the Queen and it appears that it is she who does everything. The ministers often go to see her and keep her informed of all business." It appeared that Antoinette was trying to take over the government. People said what they had been saying for years, that the King drank and that his wife saw to it that he stayed drunk so that she could "make him sign anything she wanted." But Fersen knew the truth. Louis had no particular liking for drink. He wasn't drunk, he was frightened. He was hiding behind his wife.[4]

Behind her facade of resolution and courage, Antoinette was miserable. "My happy days are over," she told Madame Campan, "since they have made me into an *intrigante*." She knew that she was being criticized for meddling, she knew that she was hated.

There were even audible murmurs of disapproval among her servants. One day she heard one of the musicians in the chapel remark that "a Queen who does her duty will remain in her apartments to knit." Hearing this, she told her bedchamber woman, she felt a pang. "I said within myself, 'Poor creature, you are right; but you do not understand my situation; I yield to necessity and my unfortunate destiny.'"[5]

All her enemies now stepped up their campaigns against her. Libelous pamphlets sprang up, cartoons proliferated. Spiteful Adelaide, the King's aunt, now living in retirement with her sister Victoire at Bellevue, made a point of collecting the venomous literature circulating about the Queen, and gathered all the spiteful gossip she could, then spread it widely, both in print and by word of mouth. Louis's brother Provence, pleased by all the turmoil and hoping that his talents and abilities might be recognized at last, took it upon himself to tour the country, displaying himself to his brother's subjects in true princely splendor, very nearly usurping the King's role. During his tour he complained that the Queen had prevented him from joining his brother's council. But for Antoinette, he seemed to be saying, he could put his gifts to good use in the service of the country. While strutting magnificently in public, in private Provence was writing pamphlets, verses, scurrilous stories about Antoinette and her erstwhile circle of friends, all designed to spread discontent and improve his chances of gaining power.

Caught up in the maelstrom, Antoinette sought to find peace in the eye of the storm. She spent time with her children, hovering over her firstborn protectively. She went riding with Fersen as often as she could. She took lessons in English from Madame Campan, and for a few brief weeks she even studied German, her mother tongue, but gave it up, "finding all the difficulties which a Frenchwoman, who should take up the study too late, would have to encounter."[6] She had become too much a Frenchwoman—in her own phrase, "a Frenchwoman to her fingertips."[7] A traveler returning from Senegal brought the Queen a black child as a gift. Instead of making him a page, which would have been the conventional thing for her to do, she took him into her household and instructed a servant to look after him. He was baptized Jean Amilcar, and was supported, as were the other adoptive children she took in from time to time, from her budget.

That budget was shrinking, thanks to the efforts of Loménie de Brienne. Nearly two hundred of the Queen's servants had been dismissed for reasons of economy, and to save still more money, Antoinette ceased to hold dinners and balls. She began to conserve her elaborate wardrobe, ordering old gowns mended and old slippers resoled. These were token gestures, hardly worth making given the immensity of the deficit. Still, they had some impact on the day-to-day running of the court, where the shortage of money was so desperate that, as Mercy wrote, "they do not know how to meet the slightest expenses."

Meanwhile the political atmosphere was becoming more and more unsettled and fluid. After dismissing the Assembly of Notables, Loménie de Brienne found that he could not overcome the opposition of the Paris Parlement, which refused to register the reforming edicts. Signs of dissatisfaction were everywhere, in the meetings of the new Paris political clubs and discussion societies, in the angry broadsheets plastered on walls, in the mass meetings held in many parts of the country. When Loménie de Brienne was appointed, the other ministers had resigned, creating more havoc at the center of power. Clearly the existing mechanisms of government were inadequate. An entirely new mode of procedure had to be found, a new forum in which the crisis could be discussed and, if possible, controlled. In their enthusiasm for things English the French looked with approval on the English Parliament—and realized that France too had once had such a body, the Estates General, which had not met for nearly a hundred and seventy-five years. Why not revive it?

The critical clamor reached a peak in August of 1787 and the King angrily banished the Paris Parlement to Troyes in hopes that the move would force the members to be compliant. The political clubs too were banned—which set off renewed protests. The unrest was beginning to coalesce around the Paris Parlement and its defiance; instead of being merely one among thirteen parlements, the Paris Parlement was coming to stand for all opposition to the government. The opinions of Parisians—who hated Loménie de Brienne—loomed large. And the King's wealthy dissolute distant cousin Philippe, Duc d'Orléans, who had always been popular among Parisians, now began to appear to be the chief spokesman for the opposition.

Orléans had never been content with the role allotted to him.

He had ability, but as a member of the younger branch of the Bourbons he was never allowed to let that ability shine. He had hoped to become high admiral of the royal navy, but his one opportunity for naval glory, at the Battle of Ushant, ended in undeserved disgrace. He subsequently obtained a minor army command, but won no distinction. He was in a sense the natural focus of opposition to the monarchy—political dissatisfaction traditionally coalesced around Princes of the blood—and as the monarchy became enmired in difficulties he emerged more and more as the champion of the people in the cause of less oppressive government and a respite from chaos.

To Orléans's enemies he was a vain, selfish rake who cared for nothing but his own sordid pleasure. "He corrupted everything within his reach," wrote Madame La Tour du Pin, who despised him. Antoinette made fun of him, calling him "colonel-in-chief of the empty heads" (Les Têtes Légères) after his regiment (Les Chevau-Légers). But to his friends and companions in debauchery he was merely a rich, self-indulgent and uninhibited young man who liked to play. Lord Herbert was among Orléans's guests in 1780, and left a record of how the host and his guests spent their time during a few carefree days. First they went boar-hunting, then visited Orléans's estate at Mousseaux, where "we dined a pretty numerous, noisy company, there being some females of the party. After dinner we amused ourselves by flinging one another into the water, at last by stripping naked and hunting the hare through wood, water, and so on."[8] The Duke was no intellectual, he had little depth of character and no self-discipline. But in the turmoil of the late 1780's he saw his chance to seize power, and was determined to make the most of it.

The resistance of the exiled parlement had begun to affect France's position abroad. Unrest in the Dutch republic threatened to lead to a Prussian invasion, and the French were expected to go to the aid of their Dutch allies should the Prussians attack. Meanwhile Britain was poised to declare war on France, should the French intervene militarily in the Dutch affair. With Vergennes no longer on hand to guide the conduct of foreign relations, and with the recalcitrant parlement refusing to register the edicts that would, in the short run at least, bring in new revenues there could be no question of French intervention, in the Low Countries or anywhere else. The country's defenses were all but paralyzed by the general lack of funds.

Paris was in chaos. Angry crowds formed, seeking outlets for their grievances. Noblemen's carriages were seized and halted, and their occupants insulted. Songs were sung about "Louis the Crack-Brained." "Madame Deficit" was excoriated. Straw-stuffed figures of Loménie de Brienne, Calonne, Yolande de Polignac were burned to wild applause. The crowds were preparing to burn the Queen in effigy too when the police stepped in and prevented it. The King received a letter from his cousin Orléans. Unless the Paris Parlement was recalled, the Duke wrote, France would experience a "fatal conflagration which will be hard to extinguish."[9]

By September it was clear that the parlement had won. A more forceful King, a more effectual chief minister might have found a way to overcome the opposition, but Louis XVI and Loménie de Brienne could not. The parlement was recalled, and Parisians, interpreting the recall as a triumph for their views as put forth by their champions, burst into celebration. In the Place Dauphine, rue du Harlay and other streets near the Law Courts, people massed to cheer their heroes. There were bonfires and exploding fireworks, torchlit meetings and processions. Night after night, Paris was illuminated by the revelers, their singing filled the narrow streets. The King and his courtiers stayed out of the city, which had become an enclave of defiance, a vital node of resistance to the authority of the throne.

In October of 1787 a cultivated British visitor to France, Arthur Young, was present at a dinner party where the unsettled state of the country was the primary topic of discussion. "One opinion pervaded the whole company," he recorded afterwards, "that they are on the eve of some great revolution in the government, that everything points to it." The "confusion in the finances," the enormous deficit, the crying need for a meeting of the Estates General ("yet no ideas formed of what would be the consequence of their meeting"), the lack of ministerial talent sufficient to do more than offer palliatives, the King who was well intentioned but lacking in sufficient "mental resources" to govern decisively, the court "buried in pleasure and dissipation": all these pointed toward a momentous change.

And there were two other factors, Young wrote, which his

dinner companions stressed. One was "a strong leaven of liberty, increasing every hour since the American revolution." The other was "a great ferment amongst all ranks of men, who are eager for some change, without knowing what to look to, or to hope for." The ferment, leavened by the idea of liberty, was not likely to be dampened, no matter how the immediate crisis resolved itself. And meanwhile, as Young noted, there was the imminent question of whether, and when, the government would go bankrupt, and what would happen when it did? "Would a bankruptcy occasion a civil war," he asked, "and a total overthrow of the government?"[10]

A month after the conversation Young recorded occurred, Louis XVI summoned the members of the Paris Parlement to Versailles for a Royal Session. The purpose of the special meeting was to persuade the parlementaries to give confirmation, or "registration," to an edict allowing the government to borrow four hundred and forty million livres so that it could go on functioning. The atmosphere was tense in the great chamber where the King, in full majesty of purple robe and ermine cloak, gold lace and heavy gold chains, addressed the assembled body. It must have been hard for him to face them at all, still harder to address them knowing their resentments and knowing too that, after the events of the previous summer, they were feeling their power.

They were magistrates, nobles, many lawyers—and among them was the troublesome Orléans. The procedure at a Royal Session called for the King to request the registration of an edict or edicts, then to permit debate on the merits of the proposed laws. Under the circumstances some debate was to be expected, but the vitriolic quarreling that erupted must have surprised Louis.[11] The parlement was not uniformly opposed to either the King or his proposals; members battled back and forth over whether or not to go along with what was asked—and thereby give tacit support to monarchical authority—or refuse, underscoring their own independence.

For seven hours the debate raged, while the King listened in unhappy silence. Antoinette was not near by to support him, Loménie de Brienne was unwell, there was no one to advise him on this unprecedented occasion. Finally, seeing that the parlementaries were unable to agree, he decided to assert his power. He ordered the keeper of the seals to register the edicts, even though the parlement had not voted to do so.

From out of the mass of bickering delegates Orléans spoke up. He told his cousin that what he was doing was illegal.

Louis raised himself to his full height. "I don't care!" he shouted. "That's up to you . . . yes . . . it is legal because I wish it!"

Trembling with rage, yet abashed by the insubordination he faced, the King shambled out of the hall, the angry shouts of the parlementaries ringing in his ears. In his rush to get away from them he forgot to dissolve the Royal Session. But he did not forget, once he reached the safety of his apartments, to order the exile of his rebellious cousin of Orléans.

18

Toward the end of 1787 the elderly principal minister Loménie de Brienne began to cough blood. He was sixty years old, and his battles with the Assembly of Notables and Paris Parlement had drained his energies. His relations with Antoinette were very good, but he had a difficult time with the ever vacillating, frequently obstinate King, who was alternately fearful and obstreperous in his attitude toward his crumbling government.

An enlightened man with a brilliant mind, and an exceptionally capable administrator, the Archbishop lacked force and firmness. Like his royal master, he had not been gifted with the power to command. What effectiveness he might have had had in any case been undercut by the blows to the royal authority suffered under Calonne, and by the widespread perception that the King could no longer govern without the cooperation of the Paris Parlement.[1] Far from being trusted, Loménie de Brienne was hated and reviled, though in fact he had a clear grasp of the nature of France's complex crisis and was not devoid of intelligent proposals for reform. But as the year closed he was yielding more and more to the pressures of his office, and his health was beginning to betray him.

One of the pressures that weighed on the principal minister was France's military impotence. In mid-September the Prussian army had crossed the Dutch frontier and in succeeding weeks had systematically brought all of the Dutch provinces under its control. Lacking funds to pay the soldiers, no French army could march to the defense of the Dutch, and many doubted whether France could defend herself if attacked. Once the most feared military power in Europe, France had been reduced to near helplessness.[2]

Count Alvensleben, an envoy of the new Prussian King Frederick William II (Frederick II had died the previous year), came to Versailles not long after the Dutch defeat and was profoundly dismayed by the situation he found there. The glittering surfaces of Versailles and the shallow narcissism of its occupants repelled him. "Everything here is in ceremony, in formal dress, in veneer, in phrases, in national gasconnades, in tinsel, in intrigue," he wrote in his report to the Prussian King. "Substance always gives way to form. Twenty-five million united egoists, and vain of their union, despising all other nations. . . . and everybody up in arms if any attempt is made to remedy the evil and destroy the abuses."[3]

Coming as he was from the rather austere Prussian court, the Count was bound to be startled by the surface opulence of Versailles. But in his report he emphasized more the prevailing attitude of the French than their materialism. "France is like a young man whom one cannot free of his debts, because the more money he has the more credit he gets, and the more credit he gets the more he squanders." Reform was unthinkable as long as the obsession with extravagance went unchecked. "It is as impossible for France to put order into her affairs and consequence into her plans as it is for water to go against the current," the Count wrote. "If credit were revived, the squandering, the disorder, the magnificence of attire, the abuses, and the arrogance of conceit will go on with head raised and the people will be more ground down than ever before."[4]

It was not only that the government needed reform, the entire nation needed to be regenerated, preferably by a king with the will, the power and the perseverance to sweep away the old abuses and to provide moral leadership. But Louis was not such a king. He spent as much of his time as possible away from the palace hunting, and when he was present, he was either "capricious, short-tempered and curmudgeonly," Alvensleben wrote, or else he was immature and foolish. The Count was not the only visitor to Versailles to remark on the King's childishness during Mass in the palace chapel, when he customarily sat next to his brother Artois and the two talked and laughed loudly like adolescents during most of the service.

The new year 1788 opened with a fresh salvo from the Paris Parlement. The members protested the King's "illegal" act in forcing the registration of the edicts during the previous November, and tried to assert their authority in declaring unlawful the King's right to arrest and imprison any subject without trial.[5] When in response Louis attempted to undercut the parlement's procedural authority by substituting an appointive "plenary court" where laws would be registered the parlementaries again asserted their views, in a forceful statement of the "fundamental laws" of the kingdom. Only the parlements, they proclaimed on May 3, had the right to register laws, and the King could not replace them with newly invented substitutes. And no new taxes could be imposed without the authorization of the Estates General.

It was the boldest language used to date by members of the opposition, and Louis, after months of inaction, took action, suspending the Paris Parlement and arresting two of its most radical members. Immediately a firestorm of protest erupted. The twelve provincial parlements objected vociferously, and in many cities throughout France there were riots. In Toulouse, Rennes and Dijon the rioters ousted the civic authorities; in Grenoble, royal troops were assaulted by the townspeople and a mass meeting was held where the summoning of the Estates General was demanded. Then, to add to all the upheaval, a more ominous event occurred. Just as the grain in the fields was ripening, with the harvest not far off, a freak hailstorm felled the stalks, destroying half the crops in the kingdom. Now, in addition to all the unrest, before long there would be famine to cope with as well.

All in all, Antoinette wrote in a letter to her brother, Emperor Joseph, it had so far been "a very vexatious year." "God grant," she added, "that the next one will be better."

She had been vexed by many things: her "anxieties and agitations" about the government; her fear that, if France were forced into war, Louis might have no choice but to summon an Estates General too quickly, "before tranquillity is perfectly re-established"; the continuing effort to cut back on expenses; her ever-present worries about her children.[6] Mousseline had had a severe fever and Antoinette had stayed by her bedside for two nights—on one of the nights Louis joined her—praying and watching for signs of improvement. ("The poor little thing said such tender things to us," she confided to Joseph, "that she made us cry.") Mousseline was nine years old, and "beginning to become a person," her mother told another correspondent. She was beginning to leave childhood behind, and was capable of being good company.

The weak health of the dauphin was a constant source of anxiety. He was bedridden, a near cripple, feverish and thin. Antoinette tried in vain to find justifications for his worsening state. His adult teeth were coming in, she wrote to the Emperor; his teething might be causing his fevers. Then too, one ought to keep in mind that the King had been weak and puny as a child, and now he was one of the strongest men in the kingdom. The dauphin was only six years old and might grow out of whatever ailed him. Hoping that a change of air would do him good, Antoinette sent her son to Meudon for a month, and when he came back to Versailles he seemed slightly improved. But he still had intermittent fevers, his spine was still deformed and he remained puny and unhealthy. All in all, though he had some good days, the bad days were more frequent, and Antoinette, watching him, knew in her heart that there was not much reason for hope.[7]

Summer arrived, and in Paris the life of the boulevards went on as pleasantly as ever. Pleasure seekers gathered in the warm evenings to stroll along the broad walks under the huge trees, the roads were filled with carriages, the tables crowded at the outdoor cafes and gardens, where musicians played and people paused to rest and refresh themselves. A visitor from England admired the "cheerfulness and whimsical variety of the spectacle, the confusion of riches and poverty, hotels and hovels, pure air and stinks, people of all sorts and conditions, from the Prince of the blood to the porter." Ordinary Parisians put on their best silk breeches and ruffled shirts and came in groups to stroll or dine, dandies paraded on horseback, fashionably dressed women sat at the little tables surrounded by their admirers. Footmen, enjoying an evening's liberty, sat and drank beer, old soldiers lounged and smoked, and talked of long-ago campaigns, shopwomen in their chintz gowns flirted with hairdresser's assistants who courted them, hat in hand.

"The buildings [are] very good," the English traveler went on, "the walks delightful, and most of the places of amusement adjoin." There were amusements in abundance, from plays and acrobats to dwarfs and giants, magicians and rope-dancers. A wax museum drew many spectators, where for two sous one could see "the King, the Queen and the dauphin, sitting under a baldaquin, and a bit in front of them, seated at a table, three personages representing Voltaire, Rousseau and [Benjamin] Franklin." The late Frederick II of Prussia was there too, "a piece very well executed, and they say taken from the original." There were puppet shows and concerts, freaks and dancing dogs. And there were many things to buy, cakes and fruit and flowers, prints and fans and lapdogs. Peddlers ran along the roads, ignoring the cheap crowded fiacres but jumping up on the steps of the fine painted carriages to offer their wares to the elegant ladies and gentlemen inside.[8]

There was much political talk, and the street orators held forth on the evils of the tax burden. "Republican" dress was conspicuously in evidence, as were powdered hair and steel buttons, but for the most part the worries of the day were forgotten. People complained, however, about what was contemptuously called the "wall of captivity"—the wall beyond the boulevards erected four years earlier to facilitate the collection by the tax farmers of duties on goods coming into the city—that blocked the view of the countryside and "increased the corruption of the air, by obstructing every breeze from the country, occasioning the death of thousands of feeble and asthmatic persons." The tax farmers were hated, for their wall as for their ill-gotten wealth and the corrupt system of government it represented. And as the evening advanced people became more voluble, talking, as they now did at all times and in all places in Paris, about the deficit and the Estates General.

On August 8 the King announced that the Estates General would meet on May 1 of the following year, 1789, an announcement intended to restore the government's shaky credit. The treasury was empty, and the financiers, who had no faith in Loménie de Brienne, would not lend any more. A week after the first announcement came another: the treasury would no longer honor its debts with cash payments, but would issue promissory notes instead, bearing five percent interest.

Notes from a bankrupt treasury were worthless, the very issuance of the notes was an admission that the government's credit was at last completely exhausted. Parisians panicked.

"Anxiety and fear sat upon every countenance," a contemporary wrote. Creditors large and small called in their debts, attempting to amass as much cash as possible before the entire economy collapsed. Dreading a catastrophe of massive proportions, people once again took to the streets, rioting in protest against the "forced loan" represented by the valueless promissory notes and demanding the dismissal of Loménie de Brienne. The Archbishop, now hopelessly discredited, had lost control of the situation.

Louis retreated into passivity, and Antoinette, greatly worried, sent for the only man she could trust to give her sound advice: the Comte de Mercy.

Mercy had by this time been in France nearly twenty years, and he was nearing sixty. He knew the workings of the French government as well as anyone, he had observed it at close range in person and through the eyes of his numerous spies. He was astute, jaundiced, realistic. And he was ready to be of service to the Queen at this juncture.

Antoinette and Mercy knew, as indeed all France believed, that there was only one possible replacement for Loménie de Brienne, only one man whom the financiers trusted and who could therefore gain a desperately needed extension of credit. Jacques Necker, out of the government for many years, would have to be brought back in. Antoinette had already convinced the principal minister that he should yield the financial responsibilities to Necker. But, she told Mercy, she was not at all certain that Necker would accept the office of Controller-General so long as the failing Loménie de Brienne remained in his post at the head of the royal council. But if the Archbishop stepped aside, who would take his place? She needed Mercy's advice and diplomatic skill.

"We must have someone," she wrote to Mercy on August 19, "especially with M. Necker, he needs someone to slow him down. The person above me [that is, King Louis] is not capable of doing so and as for me, whatever may happen, whatever people say, I am only in the second rank and, in spite of the confidence the first has in me, he often makes me aware of it."

Mercy did his best, but Necker refused to come into the government under the nominal leadership of Loménie de Brienne. After nearly a week of negotiating, during which the unrest in Paris continued and the ill effects of the collapse of the treasury spread, Mercy convinced the Archbishop to resign. There would be no principal minister to replace him, Necker would rule all. There would be no one to "slow him down," though it soon became apparent that Necker did not intend to introduce reforms. The Estates General was due to meet in a little over seven months, and he would await the deliberations of that body. Meanwhile he sought—and found—credit. Overnight the treasury acquired the wherewithal to prolong its functioning.

Antoinette had presided over the crucial change of ministers, yet far from taking pride in her competence, she was shaking with fear. "I tremble—excuse this weakness, for it is I who have brought about [Necker's] return," she wrote to Mercy. "It is my fate to bring bad luck; and, if his infernal machinations fail once again, or he diminishes the King's authority, I shall be hated even more."9 Even if Necker survived in office, and made no mistakes or miscalculations, she feared that the tremendous tension under which he had to work might kill him. Clearly she had suffered, and was still suffering, caught in the middle between her ineffectual but proud husband who "often made her aware" that she was his inferior and the ubiquitous critics who chastised her no matter what she did. Even her old nemesis Adelaide, Louis's strong-willed aunt, had tormented her. Adelaide came to see Antoinette during the last days of Loménie de Brienne's ministry and, witnesses said, reduced her to tears. After the interview, the Queen "was seen with her eyes red as if she had been crying."10

The return of Necker had an immediate and startling effect. The government's stock rose, people celebrated publicly, and there was a fitful resurgence of gratitude toward the King and Queen. It appeared that the King had finally bestirred himself and taken a necessary step toward improving the finances, and to his subjects this seemed a good omen for the future. Yet the celebrations in the last days of August marking the advent of Necker had an ugly side. Eyewitnesses described how the rejoicing turned to rioting, and the rioting escalated alarmingly.

"I walked out in the evening," wrote John Villiers, later Earl of Clarendon, "and saw the whole of the Place Dauphine in a blaze, from the burning [in effigy] of the Archbishop, and the illumination of the windows; one huge sea of heads covered the whole Place, and thousands, and tens of thousands, were wrapt in confusion, noise, and violence." Guardsmen marched through the streets, ten deep, some mounted and some on foot, fighting with the people, "who repelled their drawn swords with clubs and showers of stones."[11]

It seemed to Villiers, as to others, that the Parisians no longer had any reverence for authority, that they despised the military ("which once they revered and trembled at"), and felt themselves to be in possession of a power more fearsome and more vast than any the government claimed. Yet Paris had a police force of only some fifteen hundred men, most of them untrained, to defend its six hundred thousand citizens. In subsequent months the daring, unrestrained crowds stoned the carriages of aristocrats, yelled insults at women and attacked the servants of the wealthy. Their hatred of all privilege, their resentment of the nobles, especially the courtiers, for living in splendor at public expense emboldened them. And as the months passed, and the weather turned so cold that the Seine froze and the roofs of the houses were buried under deep falls of snow, their hatreds and resentments increased.

The winter of 1788–89 was one of the coldest within memory. Week after week the temperature remained below freezing, the river was a solid block of ice and long icicles hung from the statue of Henri IV near the Pont Neuf. Peddlers tramped their routes, singing out "Fresh salmon!" "Old boots!" "Mushrooms!" "Ribbons!" "New songs!" and a hundred other cries while flailing their arms to keep warm, but there were few buyers. The cold and the snow kept people in their houses; the filth flowing in the gutters turned to ice, and as the snow was too deep to permit the carters who normally collected it to haul it away, the refuse heaped up, and stank horribly.

In the Saltpetrière, the vast workhouse where seven thousand poor women and girls, foundlings and the sick were sheltered, the inmates sat at their workbenches and sewed with frozen fingers. One ward of the oldest hospital in the city, the Hôtel-Dieu, was set aside for receiving the shivering poor who feigned illness in order to be admitted. But this ward had room for only four hundred people, and there were many thousands in need of food and a refuge from the cold.[12] At the Foundling Hospital, run by the Daughters of Charity, the infants wailed in their cradles. In this chilly season thirty or forty newborns were left on the nuns' doorstep every night, and many did not live until morning. Despite the terrible weather, hardy folk still came on Sundays to see the open-air animal fights in the rue de Sèvre, which were always held, winter and summer. But the numbing cold soon drove them from the arena of combat.

Every winter the poorest of the country people drifted into Paris, day laborers and homeless peasants who hoped to find enough work to feed themselves until spring. They crowded into cheap lodgings, two and three to a bed, scavenging when there was no work, giving up their children to the Foundling Hospital when they could no longer feed them, begging when they had to. Paris also attracted the blind, who braved the streets in pairs and trios, tapping the cobblestones with their sticks, their copper bowls held out to receive alms. But in this harsh winter it seemed as if there were many more blind men appealing for aid, many more cripples sitting on church steps or huddled in doorways with outstretched palms. And as the bitter cold continued, their wretchedness increased.

Axel Fersen, who was in France throughout the winter, recorded his impressions. "We are having a very severe winter," he wrote, "freezing for three weeks; the cold has been up to 13 degrees and at midday 2, 3 and 4 degrees. For a week past there has been four inches of snow in the streets of Paris and the roofs are covered. The river is frozen, which hampers the provisioning of Paris, so that they fear a famine; it is also feared in the provinces. There is very little wheat, and what there is they cannot grind because of the lack of water, for there has been no rain since August."[13]

With the river turned to a solid block of ice and the roads made impassable by snow, the city was cut off. No barges came up the Seine filled with wood, and so there was no fuel to heat the houses. No grain boats came in at the quai du Louvre, and supplies of grain fell drastically. Without grain, the bakers could not bake bread, and bread was the staple in the diet of the poor. The markets were periodically flooded out, much good food was swept away and what remained was sold for high prices. "There is great misery in spite of the numerous well-ordered measures taken by public and private charity to alleviate it," the Spanish ambassador reported. "It is to be feared that it will get worse and that the coming year will be a calamitous one."[14]

The specter of famine was terrifying. Everyone knew that grain supplies were low because of the previous summer's hailstorms, and now the cold was complicating the situation. Whenever there were shortages, speculators moved in to take advantage of the high demand, which sent prices still higher. The King, always compassionate, visited the poor in the villages near Versailles and gave some of the treasury's borrowed money to alleviate their want. He and Necker bought supplies of grain abroad and brought it to Paris at enormous expense, then installed hand mills to grind the flour. (While the weather remained below freezing, the water mills could not operate.) But whatever the government tried to do, it was never enough. The lottery of twelve million francs which the King himself had instituted to benefit the farmers ruined by the hailstorm was forgotten; instead, Parisians repeated again and again how Orléans had sold some of his finest paintings and donated to the hungry the eight million francs they brought.[15] Antoinette's charitable efforts were hardly noticed.

The longer the freezing weather went on, the more people were thrown out of work. Transport was at a standstill, nothing could be bought or sold. With the grain market deserted, all the small businesses in the neighborhood—eating houses, taverns, inns, brothels—were shut down. The laundry boats could not operate. Workshops and factories in the Faubourgs St.-Antoine and St.-Marcel closed, leaving thousands of men unemployed. Those who had come to the city in search of employment found themselves with no prospects. And at the same time, the price of bread was rising, from twelve sous in November to fourteen sous in December and still higher as the new year opened. At the best of times the average Parisian spent half of his or her income on bread. With no work, and bread prices rising sharply, starvation loomed.

Wolves howled in the dark forests that ringed the ice-bound city, and Parisians, gathering in fear around their cold hearths, said their prayers and waited for spring.

19

FOR weeks the twelve hundred deputies to the Estates General had been converging on Versailles, buying up every room in every lodging in the town, swarming over the palace grounds, eager to catch a glimpse of Necker or the royals, meeting in little knots to talk and speculate and frown over the coming session. Hundreds of deputies demanded to see the Petit Trianon, the Queen's special pleasure-house about which they had heard and read so much. They tramped through the little farm, peered into the miniature dairy, startling the cows and goats and scattering the chickens. The keepers on guard at the Trianon were interrogated: where were the Queen's apartments, they demanded to know, the ones decorated with diamonds and sapphires and rubies?[1]

In the evenings the deputies gathered in wine shops and coffeehouses to argue and debate, and to sing the newest popular song:

> In his time Sully the great
> Saved the kingdom and the state
> Necker is as great as he
> Savior of France he shall be!
> Alleluia!

There was but one topic of conversation: the Constitution the Estates General would devise. For months the politically conscious part of the populace had been thinking, reading, and talking of little else—except the weather, and the shortages of food, of course. But now it was May, the bleak winter had given way to the warm showers and mild days of spring, and the ferment of ideas was well advanced.

"It is all a delirium," Fersen wrote. "Every one is an administrator and talks of nothing but 'progress;' in the antechambers the lackeys are busy reading political pamphlets, ten or a dozen of which appear daily; I do not see how the printing-offices suffice for them all."[2]

Many of the pamphlets were about America, the new nation across the water where, it was widely believed, a determined group of progressive thinkers had created an ideal commonwealth free of the wastefulness and corruption that weighed France down. America showed the way. At a single stroke the American colonists had established a new society, on their own sovereign authority. They had thrown off the English King who restricted them, the privileges and titles that separated them one from another. Liberty and equality were the only principles they worshiped, representative government their only ruler. The deputies admired the Americans and their government—a number of the younger nobles among them had fought on the side of the colonists against the British, and were known as *"les Américains"*—and expected that the forthcoming meeting would accomplish the transformation of France into a state not unlike the United States—albeit with a monarch, whose powers would no doubt be much reduced.

It was an idealistic vision—and one that tended to dissolve when confronted with the hard realities of self-interest. For as one deputy, a lawyer, wrote, everyone was "in favor of innovations tending to a free government," yet everyone understood the concept of "free government" differently. The provincial nobility no longer wanted to be inferior to the courtiers, the lower clergy wanted to share in the wealth of the Bishops and Archbishops, and the great nobles wanted everyone to be ruled by the King except themselves, his natural peers and companions. What the rest of the French wanted was anyone's guess, although it was clear that they wanted Necker in charge of reforming the finances and they did not want any more interference in government affairs by the Queen, or any of her greedy friends. Some hoped that the King would step aside and let the Duc d'Orléans take his place.

Traditionally the Estates General was constituted from among the three social orders: the First Estate, or clergy; the Second Estate, or nobility, and the Third Estate, men of consequence and property who were neither clerics nor nobles. But the precise numbers of deputies to be drawn from each group was not fixed. Necker, in a crucial meeting of the royal council held at the end of December 1788, had argued that because the First and Second Estates would most likely vote against reform, and in opposition to the monarchy—just as the members of the Paris parlement and Assembly of Notables had done—it would be prudent for the King to woo the deputies from the Third Estate, and to make their numbers as large as possible so that he could rely on them to out-vote the clergy and nobles in any vital show of support. Antoinette was present at the council meeting and she too favored enlarging the numbers of the Third Estate deputies.

Thus when in January the instructions were issued for the deputies to be chosen, the King ordered that there be selected nearly twice as many deputies from the Third Estate (some 621 in all) as from the First and Second Estates, which had 308 and 285 respectively. He also recommended that the deputies compile lists of specific grievances for the general body to consider, a traditional procedure in the past.

These lists, or *cahiers*, disclose a wide range of concerns. "We beg His Majesty to have pity on our farmland because of the hail we have had," reads the *cahier* from Ménouville, a village in the Paris basin. "We state that salt is too dear for poor people." The peasants of Ménouville complained that there were stones blocking the main road that forced travelers to tramp through their cornfields, "doing a lot of harm," and wanted the King to understand that their crops meant everything to them, as they were unable to produce sweet hay and thus could not raise livestock. But broader issues were mixed in with the pressing local troubles. "We state that there should not be any tax men," the villagers decided, and that "there should be no militia duty, because this ruins many families." "We inform His Majesty that our goods are too heavily burdened with seigneurial and other charges." The *cahier* concludes, "Given and decreed today 25 February in the presence of us, undersigned inhabitants of this parish."[3]

The townspeople of Gisors in Normandy, after saluting "the best of Kings," and offering him their "gratitude, respect, love and submission," made known their opinion that the King had no authority to impose taxes "except by the general agreement of the assembled nation." The nobles of Roussillon in the south echoed this sentiment in their *cahier*, stating "that to the nation legally assembled in the Estates General belongs exclusively the right to grant subsidies, to regulate the use made of them, to assign to each department the agreed necessary funds, and to demand an account of them." They extolled "the liberty of the citizen" as "the most precious of all possessions and most sacred of all rights," but insisted that the privileges of the nobles must be maintained, as they were "of the essence of monarchic government."[4]

Each of the three estates sent in hundreds of *cahiers*, drawn up by nobles and townspeople, villagers and clergy. The ecclesiastical grievance lists called for reform of the church as well as the state, to give parish priests a greater voice in the governance of church affairs. Virtually all of the *cahiers* were deeply and sincerely monarchist; their authors could not conceive of a state without a king, and not only a king but a ruling dynasty. That the powers of the King should be circumscribed, and those of the three orders of his subjects extended, seemed good and right. But no *cahier* even hinted that the King might step down (though some of Orléans's most ardent supporters certainly hoped for this), or that the monarchy might become a republic.

On May 4, the day before the Estates General was to hold its first session, the deputies met at the church of Notre Dame to walk in procession to the cathedral of St. Louis. Preceded by heralds on white horses, and by the clergy of Versailles, the deputies of the Third Estate marched in two long lines, past cheering crowds. They wore suits of plain black cloth with short silk mantles, and with black tricorn hats to match. The etiquette of dress had been prescribed in detail; the deputies of the Third Estate were prohibited from wearing any conspicuous adornment, even plumes in their hats. Behind them came the deputies of the Second Estate, most of them noblemen, all of them in black silk coats embroidered with gold thread and mantles trimmed in gold, gold vests, and black breeches. Silk stockings and lace ties completed their uniform, and their hats had white plumes. The parish priests who formed the majority of deputies in the First Estate were also in sober black, but the Bishops wore scarlet robes and the Archbishops were in violet. The higher clergy formed an escort for the Holy Sacrament, carried by the Archbishop of Paris under a canopy.

Immediately behind the deputies came the King, a glittering figure in his robes of cloth of gold sparkling with jewels, a huge diamond in his hat. He was not wearing his customary benevolent expression, one observer thought—possibly because, although there were loud cheers of *"Vive le Roi!"* there were even louder shouts of *"Vive le Roi d'Orléans!"* and *"Vive notre père!"* ("Long live King Orléans! Long live our father!").

Louis was still recovering from a shock. Only days before, he had been supervising some repairs being made at the palace, climbing up onto some scaffolding where the laborers were, forty feet above the marble courtyard. He took a clumsy step—and would have fallen to his death had one of the workmen not grabbed his clothes and saved him. With typical generosity the King had rewarded his rescuer with a pension of twelve hundred livres, to be paid on condition that the man not change his profession. The accident was a bad omen, as was the slow wasting of the dauphin; that both should occur now, just as the country was poised for a great change, seemed ominous to many.

Equally ominous, in the view of the court conservatives— among whom were Artois and the senior Princes of the blood, the Dukes of Condé and Conti—was the meeting of the Estates General itself, and its constitutional agenda. A few months earlier the three Princes had petitioned the King to dismiss Necker, and to silence the republican thinkers and pamphleteers who were pushing the country toward democracy. Popular rule, in any form, was dangerous, the King's brother told him. It could lead to nothing but chaos and violence. Antoinette too was deeply worried about the outcome of the upcoming meeting of the Estates. According to Mercy, she "tried to coax her august husband into being a little firmer," but he plodded stolidly ahead, leaving to Necker the task of guiding and shaping the forces of change while he put his trust in his subjects' love for him.

In reality the King was isolated, and his isolation was weakening him politically. "It is as yet impossible to tell how far the effects of this madness will go," Mercy wrote as the deputies gathered at Versailles, "but to judge by the sort of solitude in which the sovereign finds himself, by the weakness and fear in his ministry, by the audacity with which even the Princes of the blood oppose the monarch, one must consider the entire subversion of the monarchy as entirely possible."[5]

On the King's left, behind the Princes and royal Dukes, was Antoinette. She had aged, her ash-blond hair was noticeably thinner and threaded here and there with white. She was still, as one visitor had written the previous August, "a fine portly looking woman," but her expression was sad, and her face careworn.

Over the past year and more she had taken on herself much of the burden that was properly her husband's. According to Mercy, she was "entirely occupied with the arrangements regarding the interior, the economies, the reforms, the parliamentary discussions." She attacked these issues as they presented themselves, handling crises, meeting with ministers, reading documents, generally working to solve whatever difficulties Louis's incapacity presented her with. She applied herself to these matters "without any method or prearranged plan," Mercy observed, and the result, predictably, was confusion and frustration—made worse by Louis's maddening secrecy.[6]

With only partial information to work from, and guided, Madame Campan thought, by "persons more ambitious than skillful," Antoinette was often frustrated in her efforts to apply herself to government. "One day," Campan recalled, "while I was assisting her to tie up a number of memorials and reports, which some of the ministers had handed to her to be given to the King, [she] sighed. . . . 'Every woman who meddles with affairs above her understanding, or out of her line of duty, is an intriguer and nothing else," the Queen told her chamberwoman. "The Queens of France are happy only so long as they meddle with nothing, and merely preserve influence sufficient to advance their friends and reward a few zealous servants."[7]

The effort it cost her to involve herself with the ongoing tasks of government, the eccentricity of the King, the worsening condition of her dying son all preyed on her, exacerbating her usual nervous state. She was "so acutely distressed that her temperament was much affected by it," Mercy thought. And now the Estates General was about to convene, and no one knew what might come of it.

Antoinette had recently put a great deal of effort into writing the speech Louis was to deliver the following day at the formal opening of the meeting. The draft that she produced is revealing;

as always, she saw the situation in simple terms. The King's subjects were in a rebellious mood, and they needed to be reminded
that it was their duty to obey the King. "To the burden of the
taxes and the debts of the state, there has been added a spirit of
restlessness and innovation that will bring about the greatest disas-
ters if it is not promptly checked," her draft reads. "I hope that
this assembly will show the obedience which [is] as necessary to
the people's happiness as it is to the conservation of the monarchy."[8]

It was a speech worthy of Maria Theresa's daughter, and indeed Antoinette's life had come to resemble that of her tireless
mother in recent months. Like the Empress, Antoinette spent
hours mulling over letters, reports, and memoranda. Unlike her,
however, Antoinette had no talent for organization, or for efficiency, or for politics. Where wisdom and effective leadership
were called for, she offered only anxiety and diligence. And she
knew perfectly well that her talents were limited, and this must
have saddened her.

Now as she rode through the streets of Versailles, her head
held proudly, acutely aware of the silence with which the spectators greeted her, she must have suffered, though she tried not to
reveal her suffering. (Several observers noted that while the King
was "repeatedly saluted as he passed," the Queen received only
"deep and universal silence.") She had been frustrated in her
efforts to convince her husband to hold the meeting of the Estates
General far from Paris, preferably forty or fifty miles away, so
that the Paris crowds and the Parisian rebelliousness would not
influence the deputies unduly. But he had taken Necker's advice
instead of hers, and decided to hold the meeting at Versailles, in
the shadow of the palace and only a few hours' walk from the city.
And this was the result, this coldness, this hostility. Madame La
Tour du Pin thought that the Queen looked "sad and cross," angry at the limitations and restrictions she encountered all around
her, and at the attitude of her subjects, sad because of the constant
wounding of her sensitive nature.

Suddenly a group of shabbily dressed women, catching sight
of the Queen in her elegant carriage, dressed in her gown of silver
tissue, her hair sparkling with diamonds and nodding plumes,
cried out loudly "The Duc d'Orléans forever!"

The brazen cry shattered the silence. Antoinette, startled,

gasped and nearly fainted. "She was obliged to be supported," Madame Campan wrote, "and those about her were afraid it would be necessary to stop the procession." No doubt orange-flower water and ether were produced. But the bad moment passed. The Queen recovered herself, "and much regretted that she had not been able to command more presence of mind."[9]

The procession went forward as if nothing had happened, the drummers continued to keep the cadence and the military bands played. Most of the spectators knew nothing of the slight incident in the Queen's carriage, their attention was elsewhere. When the procession at last reached the cathedral, Antoinette took her place with the other members of the royal family under the purple velvet canopy, looking serene and dignified. But during the long Mass, one observer thought he detected "on the Queen's mouth an expression of anger," despite her poise and "intrepid assurance." The King, largely oblivious to what his wife was going through, sat on his velvet chair and dozed.[10]

On the following day, the deputies assembled in the morning in a hall behind the Hôtel des Menus Plaisirs, in the rue des Chantiers. It was a vast room, with a vaulted ceiling, intricate plasterwork moldings, and huge Doric columns lining a broad center aisle. On both sides, tiered balconies overlooked the expanse below. At one end was a raised stage, where a throne had been placed for the King, under a high baldaquin of purple and gold.

The deputies arranged themselves by order, with the clergy to the right of the throne, the nobles to the left, and the Third Estate at the back of the hall, facing the throne. The balconies quickly filled with spectators, eager to witness the spectacle, eager to hear the King's address to the deputies and Necker's. The work of redesigning the French government was about to begin.

But first there would have to be a roll call. It took several hours for the names of all twelve hundred deputies to be called and inscribed, but finally it was done, and at noon the King made his entrance, followed by the other members of the royal family. Louis's rotund body was encased in the robes of the Order of the Holy Ghost, richly embroidered and thickly encrusted with diamonds. Beside him, Antoinette was a splendid figure in a silver spangled gown and violet mantle, a fillet of diamonds in her hair. As soon as the royals entered the deputies stood, and shouted

"*Vive le Roi!*" and they listened attentively as the King began his speech.

He had discarded his wife's draft, and spoke, loudly though gracelessly, of his deepest feelings. "The day my heart had been awaiting has finally come," he said, "and I am amid the representatives of the nation I take pride in ruling." The deputies had come together to address the financial condition of the kingdom, he said, and to reestablish order. His own power was great, yet his concern for his subjects was equally great. "Everything you may expect of the most loving interest in the public happiness, all that can be asked from a sovereign who is also his people's best friend, you may, you must expect from my feelings." His intentions were of the best, his love for his people unbounded. His voice, the deputy Adrien Duquesnoy thought, was "harsh and brusque," but his sentiments were tender and noble, and his brief speech was interrupted by applause several times. ("I tried to see why," Duquesnoy wrote, "for certainly there were no grounds for it.")[11]

The King sat down, and Necker began to speak. The deputies leaned forward to hear his words—and soon realized that they were to be disappointed. The wonder-working financier, the vaunted savior of the state, had nothing to say about reform, nothing about a constitution, only platitudes in praise of the King and his kind condescension in allowing the Estates General to meet. Necker's voice gave out, and one of his assistants read the rest of the interminable speech, which seemed to many of the onlookers to last two or three hours and to consist chiefly of bookkeeping details. Clearly, Necker had not wrestled with the complex problem of the finances and had no specific policies to recommend. Or he had—and the King had forbidden him to present them.

Antoinette sat below the King, her countenance a mask of gravity and, some thought, hauteur. Yet she was ill at ease. "The Queen's great dignity was much commented on," wrote Madame La Tour du Pin, who was present at the opening session, "but it was plain from the almost convulsive way in which she used her fan that she was very agitated. She often looked towards that part of the Chamber where the Third Estate was sitting and seemed to be trying to seek out a face in the ranks of that mass of men among whom she already had so many enemies."[12]

Whose face the Queen may have been seeking is unknown. She may not have been looking for anyone at all, only trying to distract herself from the tedium of Necker's endless speech. Or she may, more likely, have been thinking about her son, and about how, as soon as the session was over, she would rid herself of her finery and hurry to Meudon to be with him.

20

THE dauphin was dying. His eyes were dull in his
thin face, his legs were so weak he could not walk without being supported on both sides. He was in the hands
of his governors and valets, who kept him isolated at
Meudon, hoping that the fresh country air would revive him.
With his increasing weakness and listlessness had come a change
in his attitude toward his mother. He turned away from her, refusing to speak when she was in the room—and to make the situation infinitely worse for the sorrowful Antoinette, she was not
allowed near him except for very limited periods of time.

Spiteful servants and courtiers whispered that she preferred
her younger son, the sanguine, rosy-cheeked Duc de Normandie,
which wounded her. "She is very much altered," an English traveler thought who saw her in mid-May of 1789, "and has lost all
her brilliancy of look." He had last seen her less than a year earlier, and the change was remarkable. She was "more gracious than
ever," he found, but "the whole tenor of her conversation was
melancholy." She told the Englishman that she "had much on her
heart," and he understood.[1]

Both parents went often to Meudon, the King interrupting his
hunts to visit his son. The meeting of the Estates General was not
going well. Instead of engaging with the serious matters of finance
and administration the deputies were in dispute over procedural
questions. But the grave illness of the heir to the throne took precedence over this, and as the boy languished, his deformed ribs
crushing his lungs and vital organs to virtually choke the life out
of him, Louis and Antoinette gave him most of their attention.

215

The end was prolonged. Day after day the grieving parents arrived, conferred with the doctors—who could do little beyond numbing the pain of their royal patient with sleeping draughts— sat for a while by the boy's bedside, and then left again for Versailles. On June 2, with the dauphin clearly in extremis, special prayers were ordered in all the churches. The following day the King spent six hours at his son's bedside and when he left, at ten o'clock at night, Antoinette stayed on. The death vigil ended at one o'clock the next morning. The Prince was dead—and immediately the Queen was sent out of his bedchamber so that the physicians could perform the requisite autopsy on his deformed body.

Etiquette dictated all: that the King and Queen be kept away from the corpse, that the body, once opened (the vertebrae were found to be "decayed, bulging and displaced, the ribs curving and the lungs attached to them"), be displayed in its velvet-lined coffin draped with silver cloth, that the heart be carried to Val-de-Grace by the Duc d'Orléans's son for separate interment, that the boy once destined to become Louis XVII be conveyed to St.-Denis for burial. First, however, he lay in state for several days, surrounded by banks of wax candles and by monks chanting prayers day and night. His crown, his sword, his knightly orders were laid on the coffin. On June 8 the funeral was held, with several dozen prelates and as many court gentlemen in attendance, along with twenty-eight deputies from the Estates General, all of them members of the Third Estate.

The urgent business of the Estates General was imposing itself on the royals' private grief. On the day the dauphin died, Sylvain Bailly, the Paris deputy who had been chosen as spokesman for the Third Estate, came to Versailles to deliver a message to the King. Bailly was polite. He expressed the sympathy of the deputies on the dauphin's death. But, he added, he and others needed to arrange an audience with the King as soon as possible. Through his servants, Louis made known his acquiescence. He would speak to the deputies in two days. When Bailly and the others returned to Versailles on June 6 for their audience, they found the King in low spirits, dressed in mourning. "Are there no fathers in the Assembly of the Third Estate?" he asked sadly.

The Estates, Bailly explained, were deadlocked, they could not reach a consensus on how to undertake the first task facing them—namely, how to verify the deputies' credentials. Necker had ordered each of the three Estates to meet as a unit to carry out the verification of its own members. The nobility had complied, the clergy wanted more discussion before agreeing to comply. But the Third Estate refused on principle to meet as a separate entity; if they did so, it was felt, they would be setting an undesirable precedent for future voting. Fearing to be outvoted two to one if the three Estates voted *en bloc*, the Third Estate held out for voting "by head"—i.e., with each deputy allotted one vote, and all twelve hundred deputies polled as a group. The verification should also be carried out by the entire body of the Estates.

Since May 28 discussions between the three Estates had been proceeding, with the royal ministers present. But after a week no progress had been made, and Bailly and the others looked to the King for leadership. Necker, ill and ineffectual, was losing the confidence of the deputies, though Parisians continued to idolize him. The Third Estate—which began calling itself "the commons," after the English House of Commons—was becoming restless and worried. Some of its members feared that the nobles were not acting in good faith, but were planning to subvert the Estates General and entrench their own privileges still further. Meanwhile the hungry Parisians were rioting, the price of bread was rising and famine threatened. Public order had become a chimera. Everywhere Bailly and his colleagues looked, the country was out of control, while the King persisted in his hesitant, benign apathy. As soon as his son's funeral was held, he and Antoinette retired for a week of seclusion at Marly.

While the Estates General wrestled with its internal problems, the Parisians' patience with the deputies was waning, and their denunciations of the privileged classes were growing more and more shrill. At the Palais-Royal, where new political pamphlets appeared every hour—or so it seemed—orators preached violence against the government, and were met with thunderous applause.

"Down with the rich!" "Liberty!" "Democracy!" The shouts were exultant—and urgent. Though the King held back from taking decisive action, Necker was not hesitant, merely prudent. He knew that, beyond the uncoordinated groups making up the Paris police, the only guarantors of order were the soldiers, yet he was

receiving reports that the soldiers might not obey their commanders if called upon to fire on rioting citizens.

Much was being asked of France's soldiery in this time of turmoil. They were guarding grain convoys, standing guard on market days, quelling disturbances. They were becoming tired and
dispirited, and like their civilian brethren they were impatient and
angry at the lack of leadership emanating from Versailles. Many
were loyal, but many others were wavering in their loyalty, sensing, as they were in a unique position to do, that the government
faced imminent collapse.[2] The regiment of French Guards stationed in Paris, some thirty-six hundred men, might under other
circumstances have been able to preserve order, with the support
of the police and of other regiments brought in from nearby
towns. But as it was, many guardsmen were rapidly becoming
infected with republican fervor. With each passing day their obedience was eroding, and their commanders cautioned the chief
minister that the men could not be counted on in an emergency.

The emergency was upon them, or so the deputies concluded.
On June 10 the Third Estate urged the nobles and clergy to put
aside their separate identities and unite with the majority in confronting the danger presented by a turbulent citizenry and an unresponsive government. Five days later most of the clerical
deputies had joined the commons; two days after that, the swollen
Third Estate proclaimed itself the National Assembly, and
marked the beginning of its daring claim to sovereignty by declaring that all existing taxes were illegal.

There had been a vacuum at the center of power. The bolder
and more active of the deputies had taken steps to fill it. But the
King, goaded out of his passivity at last by Antoinette, Artois and
others (Mercy thought that Louis should disband the Estates General immediately and advised that "violence may be the only possible way to save the monarchy"), finally decided to assert
himself. On June 18 he decided to hold a special royal session of
the Estates General five days hence, on the twenty-third, when he
would propose a reform program. Because the meeting hall required special preparation for this Royal Session, the deputies
could not meet there, and were told on the morning of June 20
that their scheduled meeting could not take place. Troops guarded
the door of the hall and, because it was raining, the deputies took
shelter in a nearby indoor tennis court.

Feeling ill-used, suspicious of the nobles and, now, of the monarchy, filled with a sense of their own recently declared sovereignty, the National Assembly voted to continue to meet, whatever the circumstances (that is, even if the King ordered them not to), until they had "established the constitution of the kingdom on solid foundations."

This monumental step was quickly followed by more unrest as, following the royal session on June 23, Necker resigned, leading to noisy demonstrations, more defections of deputies from the First and Second Estates to join the National Assembly and, most worrisome, mutinies of companies of the French Guard. Louis was concentrating more and more troops around the capital, among them foreign regiments that he hoped would prove loyal.

Versailles was full of chanting, shouting crowds, cheering for Necker (who, after Louis and Antoinette jointly appealed to him, agreed to return to office), abusing and even assaulting those deputies who had not joined the National Assembly. The aged Archbishop of Paris was nearly stoned to death because he declared himself to be an opponent of the commons, and several of his servants were wounded. "Three or four madmen lead the whole thing," Fersen wrote dismissively, but in truth the crowds were enormous and largely leaderless. They gathered, coalesced around the chanting of a slogan or around a symbol—such as a bust of Necker—and gained momentum as they tramped through the streets, their tone angry or exultant depending on the most recent turn of events.

By June 27, having ordered reinforcements to join the troops already massing around the capital, and more troops to protect Versailles, Louis had done all he could. Their strength corroded by continuing mutinies, the regiments were at best a flawed bastion between the court and the energized multitude. The newly constituted National Assembly had at least a chance of gaining control of the situation. The King ordered all those deputies who still clung to their delegated identities to join the National Assembly.

Versailles was jubilant, there were fireworks and people illuminated their houses in celebration. But at the palace, Antoinette, Artois, and dozens of others in the King's immediate entourage were in grave distress. Reason tottered, hysteria spread. Antoinette alternately wept and harangued her husband. Didn't he know that Orléans was bribing the hungry Parisian workmen of the faubourgs to rebel and overthrow the government? Didn't he realize that Necker wanted to depose him and become a dictator? Where was his pride, where was his loyalty to his family, to the dynasty that had ruled France for so many centuries? Why didn't he order the soldiers to massacre every rioter, to capture the National Assembly and imprison the deputies, to burn the rebellious faubourgs if need be? If he wasn't prepared to do these things, Antoinette cried, then they had better leave Versailles, perhaps leave France altogether, as Artois was preparing to do.

Weeping, pleading, commanding—even begging. Antoinette used every emotional stratagem she knew, yet Louis remained immobile, save that on July 1 another twelve thousand troops were ordered to march to Paris. Everyone around the King saw, or imagined that they saw, the approach of catastrophe, yet he remained resolutely, stolidly confident that the worst would not happen, that somehow, through the people's sacred link with their sovereign, calm would be restored and the work of reform could proceed. He believed this, even if his intuition told him that he and his family were in danger; he denied his intuition, and went on denying it, day after day.

Meanwhile in Paris, the grain shortage was so severe that thousands of hungry people stood outside the bakeries all day waiting for bread, only to be told that there was no bread, or to be sold a handful of sour crusts. Each morning there were fresh rumors that all the bread was gone, or very soon would be. And what bread there was was blackish and coarse, all but inedible. "Swallowing it scratched the throat," Bailly recalled later, "and digesting it caused stomach pains." What flour remained in the grain markets was of the worst quality, yellow and smelly, and the bread made from it was hardly bread at all, but "rock-hard lumps" that could be cut only with an ax. Even so, people fought like snarling wolves over the scraps. "There was frequent bloodshed," Bailly wrote. "Food was snatched from the hand as people came to blows. Workshops were deserted, workmen and craftsmen wasted their time in quarreling, in trying to get hold of even small amounts of food."[3] Hunger and fear drove many to the edge of sanity, they craved revenge on those who had made them suffer.

And so when, on July 12, word spread outward from the Palais Royal that the King had dismissed Necker, the pent-up vengeance and hatred were loosed. All morning and into the early afternoon, people streamed into the streets, outraged that their champion had been sent away, angry over a rumor that the King had had the meeting hall of the National Assembly mined in order to blow it up, provoked by the dragoons and hussars that clattered into the Place Louis XV and by the Swiss Guards standing behind their artillery in the Champs Elysées.

In the Palais Royal, the young journalist Camille Desmoulins made an impassioned speech, accusing the Parisians of cowardice and shaming them into resisting the tyranny to which they were being subjected. He and others shouted "To arms! To arms!" Heedless of the danger from the soldiery, an immense crowd marched to the gardens of the Tuileries behind a bust of Necker, screaming and shouting, their clamor tremendous and frightening in its intensity.

Suddenly they were met by a regiment of German soldiers, the Royal-Allemand. At their head was the Prince de Lambesc, horseman extraordinaire and distant cousin of the Queen. Drawing his saber, he urged his mount forward, driving a path through the wall of bodies, knocking over women and children and cutting down an unarmed guardsman who had joined the citizens' procession. The savage attack brought forth cries of anger, and more shouts of "To arms! To arms!" It was nearly evening, and after a brief scuffle the Royal-Allemand, in need of reinforcements to confront so immense a horde of rioters, was withdrawn.

Stories of the ferocious Lambesc were told and retold in the neighborhood of the Tuileries, in the wine shops of the Palais Royal and in the faubourgs where the starving laborers gathered in purposeful knots to curse the government. All the troops had been withdrawn from the city, but they still ringed the suburbs in their tens of thousands, ready to march in and massacre the citizenry, already being starved into submission. The massacre must not happen. The people had to be armed, to defend themselves.

On the following morning, July 13, the bourgeois electors of Paris—who after electing their representatives to the Estates General, had claimed governing authority in the capital—set up a permanent governing committee for the city. To keep order a new civic militia was formed, the garde bourgeoise, to be composed of forty-eight thousand men. People were burning the hated customs barriers and breaking into gunsmiths' shops to obtain weapons.

More members of the French Guard joined the armed civilians. Paris was rapidly passing beyond royal control.

At Versailles, informants brought word of the most recent happenings in the capital. Artois went to his brother and tried to convince him that his policy of tolerance and moderation was inviting rebellion.

"I have thought it over," pronounced Louis. "To resist at this moment would be to expose the monarchy to peril; it would lose us all. I have retracted my orders; our troops will quit Paris. I shall employ gentler means. Do not speak to me about a *coup d'au-torité*, a mighty act of force. I believe it more prudent to temporize, to yield to the storm, and above all to bide my time, for the awakening of the men of good will and the love of the French for their King."[4]

The King's sentiment was noble, his policy fatal. Emboldened by the fact that no troops were being sent into the city—yet still fearful that they would be at any moment—more and more Parisians were putting everyday concerns aside and undertaking the work of defending themselves and finding food for themselves. The stores of grain were thoroughly and systematically looted, while the search for arms continued.

On the next day, July 14, the city was full of new rumors. The soldiers were on the point of attacking in force, it was said. The governing committee urged Parisians to erect barricades in the streets to hinder the attackers. All those without arms gathered at the Hôtel des Invalides, demanding that the governor in charge turn over to them what weapons he possessed. When he refused, the crowd muscled its way past the gates (the defending guards did not fire) and looted the cellars, where some twenty-eight thousand muskets and ten cannon were stored. Now they had arms—but there were no cartridges, or very few, and only a small store of powder. These, it was generally believed, were kept in the dark bastion that guarded the Faubourg St.-Antoine, the Bastille.

The squarish medieval castle built of yellow stone, whose thick round watch-towers loomed eighty feet high, had been built in the fourteenth century on the site of what was then one of the main gates of the city. Both architecturally and in function the Bastille was an anachronism, a "great, heavy and clumsy" structure as one English tourist thought, which had long outlived its usefulness. Another found it "horrible to look at." Used as a warehouse for military stores and as a prison for small numbers of elite prisoners—aristocrats guilty of sexual offenses, outspoken journalists (Voltaire had been imprisoned in the Bastille twice, Diderot and the Marquis de Sade once each), printers of dangerous books and pamphlets—the fortress was spacious and even comfortable by the standards of most eighteenth-century prisons, but it had acquired a sinister reputation.

Behind the ancient towers, it was said, were torture cells where enemies of the King languished interminably. People unlucky enough to be imprisoned in the Bastille never came out again, or so it was popularly believed (though Cardinal Rohan had been imprisoned there only briefly following the diamond necklace affair). Tourists shown around the outer courtyards reacted with a frisson of horror, detesting the "accursed mansion" whose gloomy walls were an embodiment of absolutism at its most threatening.

Antiquated and underused as it was, the Bastille was a powerful symbol, and the crowd that approached it on the morning of July 14 did not know that there were plans to demolish it before long.[5] They knew only that they needed ammunition, and that as members of the newly created garde bourgeoise they represented the city's only means of defense.

Hordes of unemployed workmen from the neighborhood of the Bastille rushed to join the crowd from the Invalides, which included a number of professional soldiers who had mutinied from the French Guard. The defenders of the fortress, a feeble garrison of eighty-two old soldiers and a contingent of thirty-two Swiss, were known to be reluctant to fire on the demonstrators, yet there were cannon displayed on the ramparts, aimed at the heart of the multitude. A delegation from the new municipal government tried to persuade the Bastille's nervous governor, the Marquis de Launay, to capitulate and hand over his store of powder and cartridges to the Parisians. But De Launay resisted for hours, even after the attackers managed to lower the outer drawbridge and hundreds of people rushed in to fill the courtyard beyond it. Shots were fired, whether by the defenders or the attackers will never be known for certain. Men began falling on both sides, and in the noise and tumult fresh efforts to persuade De Launay to capitulate were futile.

Finally, when some sixty of the former French Guards, supported by hundreds of armed civilians and four cannon, tried to breach the walls De Launay ordered the inner drawbridge opened.

Cheering and shouting, the besiegers ran into the courtyard, snatching muskets out of the hands of the defending soldiers—many of whom had tried to indicate their sympathy with the citizens, turning their muskets upside down and waving white handkerchiefs—destroying records and papers, rushing into the cavernous old chambers of the fortress searching for prisoners. Only seven prisoners were found, which must have surprised the attackers. Four were criminals convicted of forgery, who had been transferred to the Bastille from overcrowded quarters elsewhere. Another was the Comte de Solages, imprisoned at his family's request as guilty of incest. Another was a mad Irishman (possibly driven mad by his captivity), and the last another madman who called himself Major White, and who claimed to have been confined in the Bastille for nearly thirty years.

The decrepit Major White, with his dazed look, his white beard nearly a yard long, his matted hair hanging in trailing pigtails, was the sort of prisoner the besiegers had expected to see in hundreds. He could hardly talk, and when he was led out into the sunshine, an eyewitness wrote, he walked in amazement as if he were blind, his "face directed toward the sky." It was a touching sight, many who saw the old man must have been in tears.[6]

The fortress was despoiled of its cannon and cartridges and powder. And then the work of revenge began.

The captured soldiers were hauled to the Hôtel de Ville, forced to run a gauntlet of blows, threats and insults. Several of the men were set upon and murdered, all went in fear for their lives, dodging stones and knife-thrusts. The Swiss were especially harassed and menaced. The Marquis De Launay, blamed for the deaths of nearly a hundred men during the attack, was surrounded and butchered. His mutilated body was repeatedly stabbed and shot, one man cut off his pigtail as a keepsake. "His head! Cut off his head!" The head was partially severed with a sword, then finished off with a pocketknife. Then the grisly trophy was stuck on the end of a pike and paraded before cheering spectators.

The story spread quickly. The old, impenetrable fortress in

the Faubourg St.-Antoine had been captured by the valiant citizens of Paris, defenders of liberty against the tyranny of the King. Dozens—no, hundreds of prisoners had been freed. The dungeons of the Bastille had been full of them, it was said, wretched victims of injustice, dying in the fetid darkness. And the brave conquerors of the prison had freed them all. In the Place des Morgues lay the bodies of those slain in the assault, mourned by their grieving relatives. They were heroes, all of them, the living and the dead. They would hearafter be known as Conquerors of the Bastille, that hardy corps of cobblers and cabinet-makers, merchants and soldiers, masons and tailors who had dared to capture the grimmest monument in Paris, inaugurating, so the British ambassador thought and so tradition would hold, "the greatest revolution that we know anything of."

21

ON the day following the assault on the Bastille, Artois ordered his servants to prepare for a hurried departure from the country. He intended to leave that very night, taking his children and his mistress and leaving behind all but the most portable of his valuables. He did not intend to wait for more violence to break out in Paris, and he knew that he could not trust his foolish brother the King to see reason at last and instruct the army to fire on the rebels in the capital. Emigration offered the only hope—perhaps the only hope for the future of the Bourbon line. He said his good-byes, waited for nightfall, and left.

Others followed Artois's lead. The Prince de Condé, the Duc and Duchesse de Polignac and their children, the Abbé Vermond, these and dozens of others, including many who had been Antoinette's closest associates and friends, made swift and sudden departures for less troubled realms. Those who did not leave were preparing to leave, mentally and physically. Terrifying reports reaching the court from Paris spoke of armies of rioters, fifty thousand strong, ready to march on Versailles with muskets and cannon. The courtyards of the palace were full of people, shouting criticisms of the Queen, threatening to pull down the throne, demanding that the royals show themselves on the balcony, with their children.

Madame Campan mingled with the crowd. "I heard a thousand vociferations," she wrote. "A woman, whose face was covered by a black lace veil, seized me by the arm with some degree of violence, and said, calling me by my name, 'I know you very well; tell your Queen not to meddle with government any longer; let her leave her husband and our good Estates-General to work out the happiness of the people.'"

Another demonstrator seized the bedchamber woman by the other arm and said, "'Yes, yes; tell her over and over again that it will not be with these Estates as with the others, which produced no good to the people. . . . There will not now be seen a deputy of the Third Estate making a speech with one knee on the ground; tell her this, do you hear?'"

When Antoinette came out on the balcony in response to the crowd's demands, Madame Campan was very much afraid for her. The voices grew more shrill and menacing. Where was the infamous Duchesse de Polignac, people wanted to know. She had to be somewhere near the Queen, "working underground, mole-like." But, they added, "we shall know how to dig her out!"[1]

It was as much the tone of these remarks as their meaning that alarmed the Queen's confidante. The threats were murderous, the criticisms edged with a thirst for vengeance. Even though the King, earlier that day, had gone to the meeting hall of the National Assembly (which many in the crowd, it seems, still referred to by its former name) and announced that he had removed all possible provocation to the rioters in Paris by withdrawing the troops from the vicinity of the city, they were far from content. Pulling back the soldiers was only a beginning, all the labor of reform still lay ahead—and meanwhile the price of bread was reaching new heights. As for the deputies to the National Assembly, many were frightened by the growing autonomy of the Parisians, even as they suspected the motives and feared the supposed secret maneuvers of the King. He seemed benevolent, but those who were known to dominate him—chiefly the Queen—were not. And if the dreaded army of rioters did come in their thousands to Versailles, who was there to stop them?

In Paris, the governing committee appointed Bailly Mayor of the city with the veteran of the American war, the Marquis de Lafayette, as commander of the garde bourgeoise (which was soon renamed the National Guard). Would Lafayette's men protect the monarchy, and the persons and property of the deputies, in the event of more violence? No one could say with certainty.

On the sixteenth of July, the King, the Queen and the ministers gathered in Louis's apartments to make a crucial decision. Should the rest of the royal family follow Artois into exile, or should they stay at Versailles, with all the risks that that entailed? Delegations from Paris had been arriving to see the King for the past several days, asking him to come to the city to reassure the people and to do what he could to restore calm. If he elected to stay, he would have to face the volatile Parisians, at the risk of his life. Yet if he left, he would look weak and cowardly, and he might never be able to return.

The arguments went back and forth, the various possibilities were debated. If the King decided on flight, he could take refuge in Metz, the venerable fortress town some two hundred miles to the east of Paris. Yet getting there would be difficult, as many provincial towns were in revolt in imitation of Paris and the countryside too was beginning to erupt in violence. And if the royal family reached Metz, what then? Louis had no money, no provisions, only the valuables he could carry. Antoinette, who argued strongly for the flight to Metz, insisted that Louis could rebuild his eroding authority quickly, by rallying the army to reconquer the kingdom on his behalf. Yet she knew how passive he could be, he was not the man to lead an army or inspire a counter-rebellion.[2]

"Well, gentlemen," the King said at length to his councillors, "we must decide; am I to go or to stay? I am ready to do either." The ministers were against the risks inherent in flight, Provence and the Maréchal de Broglie, War Minister, urged Louis to stay. He deferred to the judgment of the majority.[3]

Antoinette was displeased. There was no doubt in her mind that her husband was doing the wrong thing. All the clearsighted members of the family, all the sensible courtiers were leaving. Half the rabble of Paris might at any moment descend on Versailles, ransack the palace, kill her and Louis and their children. It was madness to stay and let this happen. She prepared to leave, gathering her jewels in a single box small enough to carry and burning many of her official papers lest they fall into the wrong hands.

She was still grieving the loss of her son, now she grieved the loss of her friends and intimates, whose departures she watched in sorrow. She sorely missed Yolande de Polignac, who made her escape from Versailles dressed as a chambermaid and sitting, as servants usually did, on the outside of her coach. Yolande had been, earlier in her life, Antoinette's closest friend, and even though a rift had developed between them in recent years the Queen felt bereft when Yolande departed. The petty intrigues that had divided them were in any case dwarfed by the momentous events of the past weeks, and by the imminent danger felt by nearly everyone at the palace.

The danger was acute. On the same day that the question of flight was discussed in the King's apartments Antoinette received a special courier in secret. He was an old man, over seventy, a wealthy Frenchman living in Brussels sent posthaste to Antoinette to deliver a letter from her sister Christina. Christina had written four pages to Antoinette, but because the aged courier was warned that his life would be at risk if he were to be discovered carrying a letter addressed to the Queen, he committed the entire letter to memory and burned it. Then he set out for France. When he arrived safely in Paris, he reconstructed the letter from memory and delivered it in person to Antoinette at Versailles, "telling her that the feelings of an old and faithful subject had given him courage to form and execute such a resolution."[4]

With her friends gone, Antoinette had few confidantes. Her sister-in-law Elisabeth was a loving friend, but her two other sisters-in-law were hardly any comfort to her. Artois's wife had always been a cipher, and Provence's wife, who was "given to drink," was inclined to create "disgusting scenes." Adelaide was a spiteful critic, and Victoire, once plump and cheerful, now kept to her apartments and worked at her sewing behind a canvas blind which screened her from the curious. Altogether the royal family gave Antoinette scant companionship and little peace, particularly as there were political factions forming around the King's brothers which led to quarrels and heightened tensions.

The departure of Yolande de Polignac meant that the Prince and Princess required a new governess to supervise the servants of their households and oversee their education. Madame de Tourzel was chosen, a widow of forty who was staunchly loyal to the monarchy. Antoinette wrote out a long memorandum for the new governess, describing each of the under-servants of the royal children in detail.

The heir to the throne, now aged four and a half, had in his household three under-governesses, one of whom, Madame de

Soucy, was "a bit severe with the child" but "very faithful," and another of whom, Madame de Villefort, "spoiled him." The eight chamberwomen Antoinette stigmatized as being guilty of "bad talk in the chamber," and the cleric assigned to teach the boy his alphabet, the Abbé d'Avaux, was "not all he ought to be;" until recently the Abbé had been tutor to both children, but the Queen had been forced to find a replacement for him as tutor to her daughter. The Prince's doctor, Monsieur Brunier, was "jokey and familiar" though something of a scandalmonger.

As for Madame Royale's household, there were two "first women" and seven chamberwomen, evidently more discreet in their conversation than the dauphin's women, and Madame Brunier, the doctor's wife, who had looked after the Princess since her birth. Madame Brunier was loyal and zealous, a cheery woman if greedy and somewhat coarse. Her daughter, Madame Fréminville, was "a person of true merit," mature and responsible. She had three children of her own, but devoted herself to Thérèse, earning her complete love and trust. It was Madame Fréminville who took over her education from the disappointing Abbé d'Avaux. As for the rest of the servants, Antoinette wrote, there were only some menials, "utterly insignificant beings," who were not worth mentioning by name.[5]

All the palace servants were fearful on the morning of July 17, when they learned that the King was going to Paris. Antoinette was almost certain that he would be taken prisoner once he reached the city. She made her plans accordingly, ordering her traveling vehicles prepared and writing out a speech she would deliver to the National Assembly in the event that she found herself alone. "Gentlemen," she planned to say, "I come to place in your hands the wife and family of your sovereign; do not suffer those who have been united in heaven to be put asunder on earth."

She rehearsed the speech again and again, Madame Campan remembered, "her voice often interrupted by her tears and by the sorrowful exclamation, 'They will never let him return!'"[6]

Louis was amazingly calm, everyone else was agitated. He knew that he was risking his safety on the affection of his subjects, but as always he trusted in that affection, and believed that he would be all right. He had rescinded the order that had begun all the turmoil in the capital, he had recalled Necker. By remaining at

Versailles instead of running away, as so many others had done, he showed his trust in his subjects, and his good will. Surely they would not take advantage of him or harm him. Just in case, however, he made his will before departing, and named Provence as Lieutenant-General of the kingdom, with full authority to act for him in his absence.

At ten in the morning the King set out for the capital, with twelve bodyguards, thirty deputies from the National Assembly and an escort from the town guard of Versailles. Outside Paris Lafayette's National Guard awaited him, to lead him to the Hôtel de Ville. The Parisians turned out in their thousands to watch as their sovereign was led along, one observer wrote, "like a tame bear." The crowd was orderly, yet Louis must have been alarmed to see that every single person, man or woman, layman or cleric, held a weapon. Some had muskets, others swords, still others held an array of improvised weapons—scythes, sickles, carpenter's chisels, iron spikes affixed to the end of long sticks, sledge hammers, anything potentially lethal. When the King got out of his carriage at the city hall, "he had to pass through an alley of men," wrote the American Tom Paine, then in Paris, "who crossed them over his head under which he had to pass, impressed perhaps with the apprehension that someone was to fall upon his head."

Inside the Hôtel de Ville, Louis listened to speeches and made a speech himself. The Mayor, Sylvain Bailly, gave him a cockade in the revolutionary colors of red, white and blue to wear in his hat (red and blue were the colors of the city of Paris, white the Bourbon color), and he obligingly put it on. He showed himself to the crowd once again, now wearing the emblem of their cause, and they shouted their approval. Soon afterwards he was on his way back to the palace.

Antoinette had been waiting all day for news of her husband, closeted in her private rooms with her children. Outside, the long corridors and huge salons were hushed; "a deadly silence reigned throughout the palace," wrote Madame Campan, "fear was at its height. The King was hardly expected to return." When he finally did return, he embraced his wife and children with the fervor of a man who had been away for a very long time. "Happily no blood has been shed," he told them, "and I swear that never shall a drop of French blood be spilled by my order."

But blood was being shed, all across France. The assault on

the Bastille had inspired uprisings in many towns. Crowds stormed fortresses, city officials were driven out and new municipal governments formed on the model of the one in Paris, with committees appointed to alleviate the scarcity of grain and citizen militias organized. In some towns the transition was peaceful, but often it was not. Violent riots broke out at Rennes, at Rouen, at Strasbourg. At St.-Germain, only a few miles from Versailles, hungry villagers hanged all the millers. And in the countryside, where the price of bread was half again as high as in the capital, and where rumors spread wildly of a government plot to create famine and of "brigands" being sent out to harry the villagers and create havoc, hysteria led to anarchy.

Afterwards, it became known as the "Great Fear." Terror spread with the rumors: the brigands were coming to destroy the crops, to pillage the barns and rape the women. The brigands were burning villages, slaughtering livestock, harassing peasants. In some places the brigands were said to be Austrians, elsewhere they were imagined to be Spaniards or Sardinians. In the popular imagination, all France was under assault. Soon people imagined that they actually saw, on the horizon, hordes of armed men bent on mayhem. (What they may actually have seen were bands of itinerant laborers or beggars or mutinous soldiers.)

Madame La Tour du Pin was staying with her husband at the town of Forges-les-Eaux in Normandy, in the last days of July. Her lodgings overlooked the high road from Neufchâtel and Dieppe. One morning, very early, she heard a mass of people rushing into the square below her window, "all of them showing every sign of desperate fear. Women were weeping and wailing, men were raging, swearing, threatening, some were raising their hands to heaven crying 'We are lost!'"

In the midst of the frightened crowd was a man on horseback in a torn green coat, shouting that "they will be here in three hours; they are pillaging everything at Gaillefontaine [a town five miles away]; they are setting fire to the barns."

The noblewoman went out into the street, joined the crowd and tried to convince them that the rumor was false. But the town curé, as terrified as his flock, sounded the tocsin and created more alarm. Finally both madame and her husband volunteered to ride to Gaillefontaine to prove that there were no ravaging bands of brigands to fear. After an hour's ride they reached Gaillefontaine where a man armed with a rusty pistol challenged them and asked them whether or not the pillagers had reached Forges-les-Eaux. When they replied in the negative, he took them to the town square and shouted to all the people gathered there, "It isn't true! It isn't true!" For the moment, the great fear receded.[7]

Incidents of rural violence proliferated. People armed themselves, took refuge and waited for the dreaded marauders to arrive. When they failed to materialize, the armed villagers went in search of them, and became marauders themselves, burning the chateaux of landowners, destroying feudal records as symbols of the hated taxes they paid to their overlords, in some instances looting and murdering. Tax offices were broken into, prisons opened and the prisoners released. Their authority undermined by the chaos in Paris, the inactivity of the National Assembly and the passive compliance of the King, local officials could do little to restore order. And with no effective force to check the mayhem, it fed on itself, and on fresh rumors of counterattacks from the rebels, who were said to be hoarding supplies of grain so that the villagers would starve and poisoning the wells they drank from.

Versailles too was full of rumors and grim stories, of crimes in the countryside and mounting vengeance against the nobles in Paris. "All bonds are broken," Fersen wrote. "Riots are taking place in all the cities of the kingdom, but they seem to be only a parody of what is going on in Paris." And in Paris, no one was allowed to leave the city, yet every day people evaded the ban and departed in droves. "By winter, unless quiet is restored, it will be deserted," Fersen thought. "All is confusion, disorder, consternation."[8] Emigration became a necessity, to many military officers, a point of honor, now that the National Guard was assuming control. Soldiers who remained in France with their regiments received stern letters from emigré officers accusing them of cowardice and of betraying the monarchy.

Antoinette, anxious and fretful, was continually alarmed by reports of disorder and what increasingly seemed like anarchy. The King's authority was all but annihilated, laws were disregarded, discipline broken down. There was no government, merely committees exercising limited power within limited jurisdictions. "The city of Paris is now really the King," Mercy wrote—but if Paris was King, what was Versailles? And what was to become of the royal family?

"We are surrounded by nothing but difficulties, misfortunes and unhappy people," Antoinette wrote to Yolande de Polignac on August 12. "Everyone is fleeing." "My health is fairly good," she added, "although necessarily a bit weakened by all the continual shocks which I have undergone." She told her friend that she spent the day in her apartments, shut up with her servants and children, receiving no one but the messengers who continually brought her bad news.

Every day brought word of new riots, of atrocities, of radical political steps being taken by the National Assembly, which was rapidly becoming the de facto locus of sovereignty. On the night of August 4, the Assembly took the remarkable step of abolishing many feudal rights—thus overturning, in a matter of hours, a network of social and economic relationships centuries old. Many nobles stepped forward to surrender their privileges, carried away by the fervor of the moment and fearful of the agrarian unrest. On August 26 the Assembly decreed the Declaration of the Rights of Man and the Citizen, which furthered the subversion of royal power by setting forth the inalienable rights of individuals and claimed political equality and liberty for France. Antoinette may or may not have read, or heard repeated, its lofty phrases—that government exists for the benefit of the governed, and not of those who govern, that nature has made all men free and equal, that resistance to oppression is the right of every free citizen—but she certainly knew their import.

Everything she heard made her fearful for her own safety and that of her family. On August 30, a man was arrested in Paris on charges of conspiring to attack the palace with a band of several hundred insurgents. Day after day, demonstrators crowded the palace courtyards, making audible threats, ridiculing the monarchy, calling for the destruction of the nobles. There was no safety to be found inside the palace, as many of the servants were known to be paid spies of the politicians in the National Assembly or of the agitators in Paris. "The majority of the domestics of the royal family had been gained over by the factious spirits," wrote Madame de Tourzel, whose memoirs chronicle the private lives of the King and Queen and their children after August of 1789. "They had become their spies, and gave a most exact account of everything that transpired, as well as of the persons admitted to the royal circle."[9]

Privacy was a thing of the past—even letters were opened and read. ("Don't answer this," Antoinette warned Yolande de Polignac in one of her letters. "Only write what may be read [by others], for everything is ransacked and nothing is safe.") She was still able to wander through her fantasy village and visit her miniature farm and dairy. A visitor to court saw her there one day at the height of summer. She was alone, wearing a plain linen dress with a lace cap. She thought she was unobserved, yet even without an audience, the traveler wrote, she held her head proudly and walked like a queen. Her outward assurance was deceptive, however, for in letters she confessed herself "sad and afflicted," and in need of the affection only her absent friends could provide. Still, she never lost heart. "Believe always," she told Yolande, "that adversity has not diminished my strength or my courage." "We must hope that one day there will be calm again."[10]

On August 25, the feast day of St. Louis, a large deputation from Paris came to pay their respects to the King and Queen as was customary on this day. But this year the ritual was different. Sylvain Bailly marched at the head of the delegation, followed by Lafayette and his entire staff. A group of fishwives was also present, with a bouquet of flowers for the King.

"The Queen received them all in state in the green salon next to her bedroom," wrote Madame La Tour du Pin, who had returned to Versailles from Normandy.[11] Unlike Louis, who had been willing to wear the tricolor cockade and show himself in sympathy with the Parisians, Antoinette made no concessions to the changing times. She wore her diamonds, her rubies and her emeralds, taken from the little traveling box in which she now kept them, and glittered defiantly as the Parisians entered the room. Her expression showed none of her usual graciousness; in fact she was angry, and she let her anger show, which Madame La Tour du Pin privately judged to be a grave mistake. ("She was incapable of gauging the importance of an occasion, she allowed her feelings to be seen without reflecting what the consequences might be.")

The usher announced, "The City of Paris!" and the delegation came forward. "The Queen waited for the Mayor to go down on one knee, as was customary," wrote the Duchess, "but M. Bailly made only a very deep bow as he entered. The Queen replied with an inclination of the head which was not sufficiently friendly." Bailly then made a short and eloquent speech, assuring Antoinette of the devotion the Parisians felt for her, and referring tactfully to the general fears of a food shortage.

Antoinette listened impassively, her displeasure evident. She knew what people were saying about her in the capital, how some accused her of engineering the shortage of bread and the high price of flour, how they repeated a vicious anecdote in which, after being told that the people had no bread, she allegedly said, "Then let them eat cake!" It was an old story at the Bourbon court, first told about the wife of Louis XIV and later about the reigning King's Aunt Sophie. There was no truth in it. But it gained plausibility with constant retelling, and in the popular mind it made Antoinette a monster.[12]

Lafayette stepped forward to present the staff officers of the National Guard to the Queen. Here Antoinette's anger visibly flared. Her cheeks grew red and everyone could see, the Duchess wrote, "that she was under the stress of some very strong emotion." She managed to stammer a few words to the men "in a shaking voice" and nodded her head to indicate that the entire delegation was dismissed. All the Parisians felt snubbed. They left, according to Madame La Tour du Pin, in a very bad humor, angry with the haughty Queen who had treated them so shabbily and "resolved to take their revenge."

22

EVERYONE knew that the danger lay in Paris. If the King would not emigrate, he ought at least to move the court and the National Assembly farther from the turbulent capital. Compiègne would do, or Soissons. Anywhere that could not be reached within hours by an angry crowd incited by a newspaper report, an orator, a conspirator, a rumor.

In September, with the town of Versailles itself in the grip of a crime wave, Louis thought seriously of leaving. Antoinette had been ready to go for months. Now the children's governess, Madame de Tourzel, was told to ready herself to leave "without any preparation, if circumstances should so require."[1] Yet no destination had been decided on, and the provincial towns were in turmoil, the countryside scorched by violence. Soldiers were deserting and emigrating. The King must be pardoned for wondering whether there was safety to be found anywhere.

And in any case, he declared, his "feeling heart" forbade him to abandon his recalcitrant subjects. "All Frenchmen are my children," he had told Artois shortly before the latter left for the border. "I am the father of a big family entrusted to my care. Ingratitude and hatred are arming against me, but the eyes are merely clouded, the minds misled, the heads troubled by revolutionary torment."[2] Once the clouds blew past, the minds recovered their good sense, the heads cleared, all would be as before. He had only to wait, like a patient father, and all would be well.

In the meanwhile, the government was in limbo. Necker was preoccupied with schemes to sell bonds to fill the empty treasury. No taxes were being collected, there was disorder throughout the kingdom, and the National Assembly had yet to draft a constitution. The King's role was unclear, though it was evident that his actual authority had dwindled. Paris, as ever in the vanguard of change, reorganized itself on September 18, setting up a central ruling body, the Commune, and giving a great deal of autonomy to each of the sixty municipal electoral districts of the city. Each district was henceforth to have its own assembly, its own committees to regulate police, judiciary, military and food services. The city was a miniature kingdom, where the subjects were sovereign. (Although only men could vote, and not only were women excluded but workers and servants and soldiers as well, the non-voters could attend the discussions and make their voices heard.)

The subjects were sovereign, but they were hungry; the grain crop recently harvested, though bountiful, had not yet reached Paris. And the King was taking threatening steps, ordering the Flanders regiment to Versailles, strengthening the bodyguard, equivocating rather than cooperating when the National Assembly presented him with their decrees. The Parisians were hungry, they were impatient with the sluggish pace of change outside their city, above all they were suspicious. Why was the King creating a new military bastion at Versailles, if not to launch an attack on Paris? Why was there no grain, if not because the Queen, who hated them, was trying to starve them? And why was the Queen's brother, Emperor Joseph, making peace with the Turks (as the newspapers and the orators informed them he was), if not to turn his armies against the Parisians and all other friends of liberty in France?

"We need a new dose of revolution," announced one of the Paris newspapers. We need to bring the King and his court to Paris, proclaimed another. The King was being controlled by his wicked wife, and by the aristocrats who wanted to bring to a halt the progress of liberty. Unless King Louis was safe and secure among his Parisians, the aristocrats might spirit him away in secret, then run the government without him. And their first step would be to crush the revolution in the capital.

Their fears at fever pitch, incited by the rousing champions of liberty who spoke in the cafés of the Palais Royal, encouraged by agents of the Duc d'Orléans, who aspired to replace his cousin, on the morning of October 5 hundreds of women (and men dressed as women) gathered at the Hôtel de Ville and began to walk toward the high road to Versailles. Dozens, hundreds more people fell in step behind the women, who were shouting "Bread! Bread!" and calling for the return of the King to his capital. Soldiers of the National Guard fell in with the marchers, some fifteen thousand of them, ignoring the commands of their General Lafayette, who ultimately gave in and followed the swelling crowd.

The women led the way, brandishing kitchen knives, skewers, brooms, their shouts all but drowning out the drums of the National Guard.

"Hang the Queen, and tear her guts out!" they screamed.

"How shall we divide her up?"

"How I'd like to rip her belly open and tear out her heart!"

"I'll have a leg!"

"I want the innards!"

The women held out their aprons, wrote a lawyer who saw the procession pass, "as though they already carried in them what they had promised themselves, and in that attitude they danced."

The rain that fell more heavily with each mile they marched, the muddy road they marched along, wet through, their aprons soaked and their shoes heavy, hampered them not at all. They sang, waved their knives and broomsticks, exhorted one another to hold firm to their purpose of hanging the Queen and making cockades out of her entrails. With every mile the threats became more venomous, the suggested torments more obscene.

A servant brought word of the advancing horde of marchers to Antoinette at Trianon. She sent a hasty note to her husband, who was hunting at Meudon, and then hurried back to the palace. There all was "general disquiet and consternation," the page Hézècques recalled afterward. The King was not expected to return for hours, the courtiers were terrified, and, as usual, no one was in charge. Late in the afternoon the dull roar of thousands of tramping feet and shouting voices could be heard. Only the few hundred men of the royal bodyguard were on duty to repel the crowd as it streamed into the Place d'Armes in front of the palace gates. Some of the demonstrators invaded the meeting hall of the National Assembly, where the women, their "hunting knives or half-sabers hanging over their skirts," climbed on the benches, screaming for bread, booed and mocked the deputies and pretended to flirt with the president, Mounier. The commotion was indescribable, with muddy-skirted women singing, talking and shrieking their demands while the deputies tried in vain to carry on their business. Guns were going off in the streets, the noise and confusion were dizzying.

At length Louis returned from his hunt, tired and bedraggled, and agreed to receive a delegation of the Parisians, along with Mounier. The meeting was businesslike, the King blamed the National Assembly (which, he said, had "tied his hands") for the shortage of food in Paris and promised to do what he could to remedy it the following day. While conversing with the deputation, however, he must have been distracted by the shouted abuse audible from the courtyard below the windows, and by the mounting panic among the servants and courtiers. He still hoped, Madame Tourzel believed, "by kindness to recall the wandering spirits to himself," but he had just enough sense to order the huge iron outer gates of the palace shut. (Shutting them took hours; they had been open for a hundred years or more, and were rusted into position.) Ministers, advisers, military officers pleaded with him to call out the Flanders regiment, or at least to move some cannon into position to threaten the demonstrators—who, of course, had cannon of their own. But he refused, and in any case, the soldiers could not have been counted on to actually fire on the crowd if ordered to do so. Lafayette and his National Guard, traveling more slowly than the civilians, were still on the road; the Versailles National Guard had joined the crowd.

The beleaguered royal bodyguard was no match for the thousands who kept up their milling and shouting long after nightfall. Finally, in desperation, Louis ordered that six light carriages be made ready to carry him and his family and servants to safety. But the carriages were stopped by the demonstrators long before they could reach him. Fortunately, at this juncture—it was now near midnight—the Paris National Guard arrived. Lafayette, exuding calm, apologized to the King for his inability to control his soldiers and then garrisoned two thousand of them in the palace, promising to guarantee the safety of the royal family. With the two thousand guardsmen in place, and a few of the bodyguard on duty as well, Louis felt more secure, even though there had been some fighting and fifteen or sixteen men of the bodyguard had been killed.

It might have been possible for the King and Queen, with their children, to slip out of the palace in disguise some time during the night, under Lafayette's protection. No one will ever know. Instead they spent an anxious night, frightened by rumors that the Paris National Guard was unreliable, exhausted by the day's tensions. Antoinette went to bed at two o'clock in the morning, protected by the men of the bodyguard outside her bedchamber and by four of her women who sat against the door on the inside. One of the four women was the sister of Madame Campan (Madame Campan herself was away from Versailles that night), and afterward she told the Queen's biographer what happened just before dawn.

At about 4:30, she said, the women were startled by "horrible yells and discharges of firearms." What they heard was the angry crowd invading the palace, incited by several guardsmen who shot and killed two of their number. One of the women ran to rouse Antoinette. Madame Campan's sister opened the door, and saw one of the bodyguard "holding his musket across the door, and attacked by a mob, who were striking at him; his face was covered with blood. He turned round and exclaimed, 'Save the Queen, madame; they are come to assassinate her.'"[3]

Quickly, she bolted the door again, then ran to Antoinette.

"Get up, madame," she cried, "don't stay to dress yourself, fly to the King's apartments."

Antoinette got up, threw a petticoat over her nightgown and ran to the door which led to the *oeil-de-boeuf*. It was locked, but frantic knocking brought one of Louis's servants, who opened it. Louis was not in his apartments, he had gone to look for Antoinette. He soon returned, however, and Madame de Tourzel brought in the children. Everyone, probably including Fersen, who later wrote that he was "witness to it all," clustered in the *oeil-de-boeuf* and waited in terror as the Parisians swarmed through the palace. The King's sister Elisabeth, Provence and his wife, Adelaide and Victoire, the ministers, servants and officials, all huddled in the dim room—it was not yet daylight, and there was a dense mist in the air—listening to the fearful shouts and cries of pain and triumph, the musket fire and clash of swords. The bodyguards were loyal, but the National Guard gave way before the tidal wave of rain-soaked, furious bodies pouring in from the palace courtyards.

Then Lafayette arrived from the nearby mansion where he had spent the night, leading a battalion of grenadiers from Paris who managed to intrude themselves between the crowd and the door to the *oeil-de-boeuf*, rescuing the trembling victims inside. The royals and their entourage were safe for the time being. Yet the demonstrators, forced outside, could not be dispersed. The pale early morning light revealed them, "a crowd of almost naked women," one witness wrote, "and men armed with pikes, threatening the windows with terrifying cries." It was a sight to horrify even the most hardened soldier. People waved axes, cudgels, long knives. The severed heads of two of the murdered guardsmen were stuck on poles and displayed aloft. Not a few in the crowd had blood on their clothes, on their hands and faces. And they had been thwarted in their desire for more blood—the blood of the Queen.

Louis found his courage and went out on the balcony above the crowd, but his calming words were unheard.

"The Queen! The Queen!" the people shouted.

Someone had brought Antoinette a yellow and white dressing gown to wrap over her nightgown. She stepped out on the balcony beside Louis, her posture regal as always but her hair disheveled and her face very pale. She held her daughter and son by the hand.

"No King! No children!" The King and the children retired to the *oeil-de-boeuf* once again, leaving Antoinette at the mercy of the Parisians.

"There she is, the damned whore!"

"We want her head, never mind the body!"

"Long live the Duc d'Orléans!"

Antoinette, courageous and dignified, took the edge off the hostility (nothing could have subdued it entirely) by her quiet presence, and by the grace of her curtsy. Amazingly, no one shot at her or threw a tile or a stone. In a moment Lafayette joined her, and took her hand and kissed it.

"*Vive la Reine!*" cried a voice or two. "*Vive Lafayette!*"

Poised between awe and bloodlust, the crowd let the Queen step back into safety. The chanting continued, but now the chant was changed.

"To Paris! To Paris!"

The King, called back on the balcony, acquiesced.

"My children, you want me to follow you to Paris. I consent, but on condition that I shall never separate from my wife and children." He retired to make his preparations.

It took more than seven hours for the long, straggling procession to return to Paris. The National Guard led off, each guardsman with a loaf of bread skewered on the end of his bayonet. Then came fifty wagons loaded with grain plundered from the palace, and behind the wagons was the royal carriage, its occupants constantly harassed by a burlesque escort of fishwives, prostitutes, the rabble of the Parisian streets, singing and cavorting madly all around them, drunk on power and on wine from the royal cellars. "Several of them rode astride upon cannons, boasting, in the most horrible songs, of all the crimes they had committed themselves, or seen others commit," wrote the Marquis de Molleville, who went along in the mass emigration from Versailles to Paris on October 6. "Those who were nearest the King's carriage sang ballads, the allusions of which, by means of their vulgar gestures, they applied to the Queen."[4] Carried away by "paroxysms of brutal joy," deprived of sleep for nearly two days, badly nourished and under the strain of a powerful excitement, the women howled their triumph.

"Cheer up, friends," they shouted to the villagers who watched the wild procession pass. "We shall no longer be in want of bread: we bring you the baker, the baker's wife, and the little baker boy!"

As a macabre prank they took the severed heads of the two guardsmen to a wig-maker's shop and forced the poor man to groom and powder the bloody hair. Now the heads, mounted on pikes, were waved proudly above the marchers, along with long poplar branches torn from the trees in the park of Versailles. "At some distance," Molleville wrote, "this part of the procession had a most singular effect; it looked like a moving forest, amidst which shone pike-heads and gun-barrels."

Behind the forest of pikes walked the dispirited royal troops, the bodyguard and the Flanders regiment, some of the men wounded. Then came the carriages of some hundred deputies to the National Assembly, followed by another hundred carriages filled with courtiers, clutching their valuables and fearing what might be in store for them once they reached the capital.

On through the afternoon this "grotesque saturnalia," as one newspaper account called it, proceeded, crossing the Seine at Sèvres and filing on in the gathering dusk past the villages on the outskirts of the capital. The occupants of the royal carriage, their nerves constantly buffeted by the verbal assaults and threats of the marchers, deafened by musketfire, no doubt hungry and thirsty, as the little dauphin said he was, must have been nearly beside themselves by the time they reached Paris.

During the journey, Madame Campan wrote, the royals "heard incessantly a continued noise of thirty thousand muskets loaded with ball," which were charged and discharged in token of joy for the happiness of conducting the King to Paris.

"Fire straight!" people called out—yet often the musket balls struck the ornaments of the carriages, narrowly missing the King and Queen and their children. The smell of the powder was suffocating, "and the crowd was so immense, that the people, pressing the coaches on all sides, gave them the motion of a boat."[5]

Antoinette said little, but her face, which bore the "marks of violent grief," told all. She sat beside her husband, her jewel box near by, no doubt doing what she could to comfort her daughter and son. Lafayette rode beside the carriage, his presence offering limited protection, but she felt more anger toward him than gratitude. She may well have felt resentment for Louis, for being so stubbornly opposed to emigration, for overruling her pleas that they take refuge away from the palace on the previous day, for stupidly putting his trust in his "good people" who had come so close to murdering them all.

Now they were being forced to leave their home, to put themselves at the mercy of a horde of howling strangers who delighted in bloodletting. They were no longer King and Queen of France, they were merely the baker and the baker's wife, refugees from safety, on their way to the dangerous city where the merciless people ruled all.

23

EVEN before the royals left Versailles a courier was despatched to Paris to warn the governor of the Tuileries that the court was on its way. The courier arrived, breathless and agitated, and delivered his message. But there was little that the governor could do. The sprawling old palace was a shambles, its dingy corridors and smoke-blackened chambers far too dilapidated to be made ready at a few hours' notice for royal inhabitants. No King had inhabited the Tuileries in nearly seventy years—though Antoinette had kept a pied-à-terre there, earlier in the reign, for very occasional use after an evening spent at the theater. The present occupants were a down-at-heel rabble of aging retainers, retired officials and artists who had once done work for the court. The governor hastily chased them out, but not before the first of hundreds of carts and carriages began arriving from Versailles, filled with trunks and boxes and with the seven hundred–odd people who made up the royal household.

Six years earlier a report on the Tuileries had been compiled and sent to the King. It made dismal reading. The palace was little more than a "cluster of hovels." The royal apartments "no longer really exist," the compilers wrote, having been partitioned off to form smaller rooms which the occupants had sorely neglected. "Unless something is done about it they will not be able to offer His Majesty's family even a moment's shelter." Predictably, nothing had been done. And now, without warning, the cluster of hovels had to be made livable, food and fuel, furniture and lodgings had to be provided, a new court established.

The chaos of the first few days was unimaginable. There were no beds, no hangings, few candles and fewer fires. There was only one mirror—a small one used by the King. People slept where they could—on old warped billiard tables, on benches, on piles of clothes, on the floor. During the day they wandered, shivering, through the chilly rooms and along the dim corridors, trying to avoid drafts where the wind blew in through broken windows, snatching meals at odd moments and waiting for something like order to be reimposed. They were in a stupor, wrote the page Hézècques in his memoirs, uprooted as they were and surrounded by inconveniences, frightened by the hooting, jeering crowds of people who filled the palace gardens and courtyards, calling ceaselessly for the King and Queen to show themselves.[1]

An English visitor to the Tuileries on October 8 watched Louis and Antoinette struggle to maintain their dignity as they received the foreign ministers. "The palace seemed in the utmost disorder," he wrote later, "was crowded with all sorts of people without distinction. . . . The King was much dejected and said little. Her majesty's voice faltered and the tears ran fast down her cheeks as she spoke, and all their attendants seemed impressed with the deepest melancholy and concern." Decorum was impossible amid the screams and shouts from outside, and it was clear to the Englishman that all the new inhabitants of the palace were deathly afraid that the Parisians would swarm in and threaten them, even murder them, as they had murdered the guardsmen at Versailles. All the gateways and doors were protected by Lafayette's militiamen, with artillery, yet no one felt safe inside. The Tuileries was "a prison disguised under the name of palace," as Hézècques thought. The Parisians, not the soldiers, were the jailors. "The blind and headlong will of the populace directs all."[2]

Day after day more wagons and carts arrived from Versailles, bringing furnishings, bedding, porcelain and chandeliers. Workmen began to repair the walls, restore the crumbling masonry and the peeling paint. The smell of gilding was everywhere, as unpleasant as it was pervasive. The courtiers tripped on ladders and buckets as slowly, day after day, they resumed their duties. By the end of the month the interior of the Tuileries was beginning to take on, at least superficially, the appearance of Versailles. Fine paintings were hung on the walls of the state rooms, curtains sparkling with gold covered the warped window embrasures, crystal chandeliers lit up the gloomy corners, where faded tapestries hung waiting to be cleaned. The King's smithy was brought in, piece by piece, and set up for him to use, and if his bedchamber at the Tuileries did not match the splendor of his state bedroom at Versailles, with its hangings of purple and gold brocade and its costly porcelain candelabra, at least he had his anvil and his locks to console him.

Antoinette's apartments were transformed from a state of near ruin to something like splendor. Fersen was surprised, when he saw them, at how luxurious they were, given the dirt and disorder everywhere else. He moved into a hotel in the rue Matignon, near the palace, in order to be on hand when Louis and Antoinette needed him, and gave up his commission in order to devote himself fully to their service. Whether he and Antoinette continued to maintain a romantic liaison is impossible to say, though contemporaries assumed they did.[3] She was clearly distraught, he, to judge from his letters, busy and concerned, above all, about the restless populace and its growing appetite for violence. He foresaw disaster for the monarchy, he could not imagine how the misguided King or his maligned Queen (whom he called "an angel of goodness") could escape the popular lust for mayhem.

Merely to be abroad in Paris was to fear for one's life in October of 1789. No one could predict with certainty what the aroused crowds might do. Each day brought fresh alarms, news of conspirators arrested, of rioting and plundering in various parts of the city, of additional guardsmen brought in to protect the palace. For several nights in a row ominous chalkmarks were discovered on houses, and the occupants, fearing that they had been singled out for massacre, spread panic in their districts. "We are living in the midst of constant fear," wrote one German diplomat. "The populace is not yet satisfied." Vengeful acts continued: on October 21, a crowd formed outside the shop of a baker, blaming him for the shortage of bread though he had in fact been up all night making as many loaves as he could. The shop was destroyed, the baker seized and taken out to the Place de Grève where he was hanged, then decapitated. The head was stuck on the end of a pike, and the trophy paraded through the streets in what was coming to be a grotesque ritual.

All Paris was under arms, the police and guard, overwhelmed, kept up their pursuit of agitators and lawbreakers. The day after the murder of the baker two of his murderers were hanged, and on the following day at least two others were brought to justice. Antoinette, full of sympathy for the baker's widow, and finding that, contrary to rumor, the poor woman had not died of fright on being shown her husband's severed head, sent her six thousand francs out of pity.

"I am all right, on the outside," Antoinette told a correspondent soon after taking up residence at the Tuileries, "but my heart is wounded as never before."[4] She was in constant anguish, frightened for her husband and children, distrustful of the Assembly, in despair over her future. She tried to keep up a show of courage—or at least of brittle hauteur—but often her fears were too much for her. Her voice broke, the slightest disturbance made her weep. "We are lost," she had told Madame Campan just before leaving Versailles, "dragged away, perhaps to death: when Kings become prisoners, they have not long to live."[5] A prisoner she certainly was, though in a gilded cell, her casket of diamonds still secure in her possession, her finery brought intact to the new residence. She understood the reason for her captivity. The Assembly, Lafayette, the Parisians all expected that the royals would try to leave the country, and this they were determined to prevent. Many of the nobles, however, believed that the King's escape was only a matter of time, and that once he left, as one highborn lady told the American Gouverneur Morris, "it would set Paris in a flame."[6]

Antoinette wanted desperately to leave, if a way could be found to circumvent the vigilance of their captors. It was suggested to her that she and the dauphin might be smuggled out of the palace in disguise, to make their escape on their own, but she was reluctant to leave Louis. Besides, there was talk of a counter-revolution, of troops being massed to overturn the Assembly and the municipal government in Paris. Louis was secretly in contact with the other European sovereigns, assuring them that, despite his public show of cordiality toward the Assembly, he had no intention of conceding any of his powers to its members. He asked his cousin, King Charles IV of Spain, for money and made the same request of Antoinette's brother Emperor Joseph. With their aid, order might yet be restored, and the monarchy returned to authority. If this happened, some argued, it would be best for Louis and Antoinette to stay in France—though their lives would clearly be in peril in the early hours or days of a counter-coup.

In any event, it was advisable to keep up appearances. Court ritual must go on unperturbed by the alarming scenes just outside the palace windows. The ceremony of the King's *lever* and *coucher* were celebrated, the Queen presided over her evenings of card games, and entertained guests in her small if luxuriously appointed apartments. Both monarchs dined in public just as they had at Versailles, surrounded by their servants in splendid livery, the King overeating more prodigiously than ever, the Queen nibbling at her chicken and sipping nervously from her water glass.

The Tuileries became the social mecca of Paris. At Antoinette's evening card parties were to be found not only aristocrats but commanders of the Bourgeois Guard, Assembly deputies, prominent citizens and obscure soldiers; she had "obliging things" to say to them all. Her courteousness was oil spread on troubled waters, in her small way she created an oasis of harmony amid discord. Yet the Tuileries inevitably became a social battleground, where all the nobles who had not emigrated came to demonstrate their loyalty to the monarchy and their opposition to the Assembly. They made an exaggerated show of reverence to the King and Queen, provoking the republicans by wearing white cockades (instead of the red, white and blue revolutionary cockades sold on every Parisian street corner), the women sporting huge bouquets of white lilies or bunches of white ribbon in their hair. To wear the Bourbon white was to invite a brawl, or at the very least a challenge to a duel, even within the walls of the palace. Outside in the streets, sentinels stopped anyone not wearing the tricolor, and an offender with a white cockade was lucky to escape with only a severe reprimand.

And if the social elite wanted to come face to face with the royals, ordinary Parisians were even more curious to see them in the flesh. The Tuileries, like Versailles, were open in the afternoons to anyone who could afford an entrance ticket; on Sundays, when entrance was free, the crowds were so huge that the palace servants could hardly enter and leave the rooms or go up and down the staircases to perform their duties.[7] Initially, Hézècques recalled, the King was treated with some degree of respect and was not mobbed. But as the months passed, what respect there was melted away. "No royal could appear at a window without being insulted," he wrote, and whenever they went to Mass, which meant walking across the terrace and exposing themselves to the noisy throng waiting in the gardens, people clapped, booed and shouted themselves hoarse. Most of the shouting was derisive, angry or obscene, but not all; there were invariably some partisans of monarchy, some shouts of *"Vive le Roi!"* and even, on occasion, *"Vive la Reine!"*[8]

Madame Campan described how a crowd of women gathered under Antoinette's windows and demanded that she come out and show herself to them. With her usual bravery, she faced them, and "engaged in a dialogue with them." One of the women tried speaking to her in German, and when the Queen said she didn't understand it, the entire group broke into applause and yelled, "Bravo!"

They grew more daring, and began asking for the ribbons and flowers she was wearing in her hat. Obligingly she unfastened the ornaments and passed them out. The women seized them eagerly, snatching them out of each other's hands as trophies and beginning a new chant.

"Marie Antoinette for ever! Our good Queen for ever!" they shouted, keeping up their cheering for half an hour, long after the Queen had left them and gone back inside.[9]

They were not so much pleased at Antoinette's affability and generosity as astonished at it, for everything that they heard and read about her made her seem a monster of depravity and cruelty. For years Antoinette had been slandered by pamphleteers and rumormongers, but in the summer and fall of 1789 her detractors grew more vicious than ever, emboldened by the Assembly's decree in late August granting freedom of the press. Caricaturists drew her as a winged harpy with a forked tail and long curved talons, with diamond earrings dangling from its ears. Orators denounced her as the enemy of the French people, who had asked her brother to send his army against France and who had vowed in secret to burn Paris to the ground.

Hateful images of the Queen were to be found all over the capital, her long nose and sharp dark eyebrows, fat chin and cheeks were a familiar sight. Every ugly impulse was ascribed to her. Faithless to her husband, cruel to her people, she was consumed by lust and devoured by greed. One anonymous pamphlet called her "the Iscariot of France." "This Persephone wears the redoubtable head-dress of the Fourteenth Apostle," the pamphleteer insisted, "of the same character as Judas. Like him, she dips her claws into the plate to steal and squander the treasure of

France: her hard eyes, traitorous and blazing, breathe only flame and carnage. . . . Her nose and cheeks are pimply and empurpled by the tainted blood which is discharged between her flesh and her leaden hide, and her fetid and infected mouth harbors a cruel tongue."[10]

The Assembly followed the royal family to Paris in October, meeting temporarily at the Archbishop's palace and after a few weeks settling into permanent quarters in the riding school in the Tuileries gardens. Some deputies chose to return to their provinces, but the majority stayed to continue the exhilarating, enervating struggle to hammer out a government. They met three afternoons a week in noisy, often rancorous and unruly debate. Deputies polished their speeches at the salons and dinner parties of fashionable hostesses before delivering them on the Assembly floor, but frequently the fine phrases were drowned out by the "hallooing and bawling" of opponents of the speaker's position. The strongest orators, rather than the most sagacious ones, tended to carry the day. "Sometimes an orator gets up in the middle of another deliberation," one observer remarked, "makes a fine discourse and closes with a snug resolution which is carried with a huzza."[11]

Monarchists and not a few cultured republicans thought the deputies were incompetent, by and large, and worried that without a more effective governing body the country would before long fall prey to anarchy, civil war, or a seizure of power by a popular demagogue. Certainly the issues the deputies faced were very grave. They needed to find a means to control the wayward, power-crazed Parisians, and to keep the capital supplied with adequate food and fuel stores over the coming winter. They were threatened with challenges to their authority from Brittany and the Cambrésis, where the revolution was unpopular and the Assembly detested. They had to undertake the long-term tasks of forging a legal and institutional framework for the liberty they claimed. And, if this were not enough, they had to find immediate solutions to the urgent crisis in finance.

One member of the Committee of Finances estimated that the public debt had risen to nearly five billion francs in the last months of 1789, and Necker was hard pressed to find means to cover the interest payments. The Assembly reduced the royal pensions, saving millions of francs, but this was only a modest beginning at reform. Necker, while negotiating to buy grain from America and from England's Canadian provinces, was trying to persuade the Dutch financiers who had come to France's aid in the past to make huge loans once again, to be secured this time by the debt America owed to France. It was a grandiose strategy, perhaps too grandiose. The Finance Minister was floundering, critics murmured that despite his enormous reputation as a financial wizard, he was in truth as incompetent as the quarrelsome deputies.[12] As vain of his abilities as he was of his portly person, flattered by his social-climbing wife and by his witty, ugly daughter Madame de Staël, who was one of the most prominent hostesses in Paris, Necker was losing patience with the mercurial French. At one dinner party where the political discussion became vehement, a guest heard Necker mutter in disgust that the French were a "ridiculous nation," forgetting for the moment that he might be overheard by the servants.[13]

As the deputies debated, plots and counter-plots swirled around them, making their task more complex and putting their very existence in jeopardy. Rumor had it that unnamed persons were planning to massacre the King and Queen and all the nobles who had not yet emigrated. Disaffection in some provinces led many observers to envision a dismemberment of the kingdom, and eventual civil war. Monarchists and opportunists—including Provence—spun intrigues to abduct the King and then march on Paris with loyalist troops or foreign armies. Others wanted to force the ineffectual Louis to abdicate in favor of Orléans—who, though he had been sent to England to keep him from exploiting his popularity to make mischief in Paris, was still a potential threat to be reckoned with. Orléans was widely believed to have been responsible for the "October Days," when the King and Queen were forcibly brought to the Tuileries. Antoinette's brother in Vienna was convinced that the Duke was "himself the author of these upheavals in France." It was no longer clear that, as many of the deputies had once assumed, the ultimate political outcome of the revolution would be a constitutional monarchy. France seemed poised on the cliff-edge of disaster, and well-informed Parisians spent hours debating "whether the abuses of former times were more grievous than the excesses which are to come."[14]

At the center of all the turbulence was the Assembly's most

mesmerizing orator, Gabriel-Honoré de Riqueti, Comte de Mirabeau. Able to dominate the stormy debating sessions with his dark
charisma, Mirabeau committed all his considerable energies to
combatting everything that was worst about absolute monarchy—
its extravagance and waste, its support of parasitic courtiers, its
ineptitude and apparent contempt for the condition of the people.
"I am a mad dog from whose bites despotism and privilege will
die," the Count declared proudly, and like a mad dog he seemed
to hold everyone around him at bay. Mirabeau was grotesquely
ugly, with an ugliness so extreme that it was fascinating. His huge
head and deeply pitted skin, his deformed body and somber, even
demonic presence put him far outside the human norm, as did his
prodigious sexual gluttony and his equally outsize greed. "He is
an object of dread and contempt to all parties," wrote an Englishman who knew Mirabeau well, adding candidly that his distinguished friend was "ready to sell himself to any party who
thought him worth buying." Venal the Count surely was, and
coarse in his language, avid to violate every social convention. But
he was also immensely learned, a productive writer and translator
of the classics, with as intense a passion for books as for the pleasures of the flesh. It was largely Mirabeau's firmness, poise and
strength of will that kept the Assembly from collapsing or becoming hopelessly fragmented, and that guided the revolution along
its relentlessly democratic path.[15]

Mirabeau led the dominant party in the Assembly, the Patriots, dedicated to refashioning France and to pulling down the
old order, with the Assembly ascendent over the King. ("They
unhinge everything," Gouverneur Morris wrote of this group,
which he referred to as "Madmen.") Other factions were the
Blacks, or counter-revolutionaries, who wanted to restore the old
order in its entirety, and the Monarchists, who envisioned a division of power between the King and a popularly elected body or
bodies. (This group, rapidly dwindling in numbers and influence,
Morris favored, though he saw that they had a serious weakness in
that they had learned all they knew about politics from books, not
from experience, and hence were crude or naive in their approach
to gaining power.)[16]

Mirabeau was a Patriot, but an ambivalent one; while hating
royal excesses he did not hate the King, and was convinced that
France's best government would be an alliance between the King

and the people, with himself at the head of the popular wing. The
Assembly, which he referred to as "the wild ass," could never be
entirely dominant, in Mirabeau's view; it had to be led, bullied if
necessary, galvanized into action by a compelling personality. The
King was necessary, provided he was stripped of his absolute
powers and tamed by a constitution. Mirabeau told his friend
Comte de la Marck, a former ambassador of Maria Theresa and a
trusted intimate of the King and Queen, to inform the royals that
he was "more for them than against them" and to warn them that
they were in great danger. "Convince them," he said, "that they
and France are lost if the royal family do not leave Paris." He
drew up plans for an escape route, and envisioned Normandy as a
possible haven for the monarchy.

Antoinette wanted nothing to do with the grotesque and
amoral Mirabeau, who though he came from an aristocratic family
seemed to have lost his identity and adopted the behavior and
political attitudes of the lowest-class Parisians. She did not trust
him, despite La Marck's message, she felt certain Mirabeau was
concerned about no one but himself. Besides, Mirabeau's message
was only one among many. She had a personal letter from Catherine the Great, Empress of Russia, urging her to ignore the goings-
on in Paris and in the Assembly and stay above it all in regal
isolation.

"Kings ought to proceed in their career undisturbed by the
cries of the people," the Empress wrote, "as the moon pursues her
course unimpeded by the howling of dogs."[17]

There were many letters, secret messages, expressions of sympathy and dire admonitions. Madame Campan was there as always to read them to her, having taken up residence at the
Tuileries at Antoinette's urging. And there was Madame Thibaut,
the principal chamberwoman—"a person of great merit, and attached beyond measure to her majesty," according to Madame de
Tourzel—and Madame Tourzel herself, the capable governess to
the royal children. All these, and dozens of others, gave Antoinette constant signs of their support and encouragement in her
troubles. Her secretary Augeard urged her to get away from Paris
at once, and offered to abduct her himself some evening in a humble post-wagon drawn by two horses. She should dress as a governess, Augeard advised, and have the dauphin dressed as a little
girl. The first night they could stop at St.-Thierry, the country

estate of the Bishop of Rheims, and the following night at Augeard's own house at Buzancy. From there it was only a single post to the border. She was strongly tempted to follow the secretary's advice, but then thought better of it. Her would-be abductor was betrayed to the Assembly, arrested and imprisoned.

Meanwhile there were her children to look after, and her "bad leg," which had begun to cause her pain and inconvenience. Over the Christmas holidays she sprained it, not for the first time, and had to stay in her room, a semi-invalid, for nearly two weeks.[18] The presence of her son distracted her. "The little *chou d'amour* is charming," she wrote to the Duchesse de Polignac, "and I love him to distraction. He loves me very much too, in his fashion, when it suits him. I love to call him *chou d'amour*, to remind him of you and yours. Sometimes I ask him if he remembers you, if he loves you; he says 'Oui,' and then I hug him even more. He is well, he grows strong, and doesn't have tantrums any more. He goes walking every day, which does him a lot of good."[19]

Antoinette's nursery of children and foster-children became temporarily smaller when she sent the little Senegalese boy Jean Amilcar to a children's home at St.-Cloud. But Theresa's companion Ernestine was still a member of the family, spending virtually all her waking hours with the Princess, and the two girls were being prepared to take their first communion together early in the new year. They had grown so close, in fact, that the Queen was thinking of finding a child similar to Ernestine to be a companion for her son.

The winter months dragged by, the royal imprisonment went on. Each afternoon the King and Queen took their exercise in the Tuileries garden—Louis was not permitted to go hunting—the King escorted by six grenadiers of the National Guard, several household officers and a page, the Queen accompanied by one of her ladies and surrounded by guardsmen who stood so close to her that they could hear every word she said. Nearby, in a little railed-off garden of his own, the dauphin dug with a hoe and rake, while several grenadiers looked on.

Arthur Young saw them there one warm, drizzly January afternoon, and was struck by how ill Antoinette looked. "Her majesty does not appear to be in health," he told his correspondent afterwards, "she seems to be much affected and shows it in her face." A crowd of ticket-bearing spectators followed her, talking very loudly, scrutinizing her, hardly allowing her room to breathe—though some, Young noticed, took off their hats as she passed.[20] She felt her imprisonment keenly. "My soul is more agitated and troubled than ever," she confided to Mercy. She had begun to think of writing her memoirs, aware that she was living through significant events and determined to record her view of them. She saved letters, and began noting down "minute reports made in the spirit and upon the event of the moment," Campan says.[21]

She was determined to do all she could to survive the ordeal, and not only survive it, but triumph over it if she could. Her courage was more than equal to the challenge, and so was her character. But she was far from brilliant.

"The Queen," La Marck wrote, "has certainly sufficient intelligence and resolution for great actions, but I must confess that in matters of business, or even in conversation, she does not show that degree of attention and that logical sequence that is necessary to know in order to prevent errors and assure success."[22]

She was doing her best, but her best might not be good enough. And her strength, both emotional and physical, had begun to ebb. "They shall not destroy my courage," she vowed in a letter, "but I am suffering very much."

❧ 24 ❧

I N the spring of 1790 Paris was still in ferment. Drumbeats
sounded throughout the day and far into the night, and
every morning the militia bands heralded the dawn with
their shrill piping. No one could get any rest, for the continual marching and exercising of the soldiers, their interminable
evening parades and their "ostentatious bustle" in the streets at all
hours destroyed the peace of even the most sedate neighborhoods.
Living in the revolutionary city was "like living in a city besieged," a visitor wrote. The noise, the martial atmosphere, the
crowds, the shrieks, clamor and explosions from duels—which,
everyone agreed, were on the increase—kept tensions at fever
pitch. The pungent scent of the lilacs blooming in the Tuileries
gardens was lost amid the reek of gunpowder, smoke obscured the
blossoming chestnut trees and cries of alarm floated in the chill
spring air.

Fashion journals prescribed a "constitutional costume" for the
stylish woman, gowns in "colors striped in the national fashion."
Patriotism was chic. The loyal French woman was expected to
wear blue, with a hat of black velvet, hatband, and tricolor cockade. Moderates and aristocrats continued to display their politics
by not wearing the cockade, and continued to be regarded with
suspicion as a result, all the more so after the trial and execution
of the Marquis de Favras.

A member of Provence's Swiss Guard, Favras was accused of
acting as Provence's agent in an elaborate counter-revolutionary
plot to raise an army of thirty thousand men, kidnap the royal

family, and assassinate Lafayette and Bailly, Mayor of Paris. Letters from Provence were found on the Marquis when he was arrested by a suspicious Lafayette, and though Favras denied his guilt the Parisians had no doubt of it. His long trial had been one of the chief political diversions of the winter, with large crowds gathering each day outside the Châtelet, site of treason trials, to threaten the judges and shout "*A la lanterne!*" ("To the lamppost!"—meaning "Hang him from the lamppost!") The Châtelet courtyard was full of troops and guns, but there was no rioting. In the end the judges had ordered the Marquis hanged, an ignominious death for a nobleman (highborn criminals were by custom beheaded), and the Parisians had the satisfaction of watching him die in the Place de Grève.

Suspicion was in the air, the sentinels were kept constantly busy. Spying, always pervasive, now became suffocatingly so, made all the more urgent by the political turmoil. The Blacks and the royal ministers spied on the constitutionalists and the ultra-liberals, Lafayette and the deputies spied on the counter-revolutionaries, the Patriots spied on everyone. "The post is not safe," Fersen noted early in February, shortly after he returned to Paris. "There is such great inquisition, so many committees of search, and so much conspiracy, that no one dares either speak or write."[1] Despite the danger, communication went on, with Fersen serving as messenger, go-between, cipherer and secretary. There exist drafts of letters in Fersen's handwriting, with notes and corrections in Antoinette's hand, so he must have helped her compose the urgent requests for money and military support that she sent to the European monarchs.

Fueling the highly charged atmosphere in Paris were the political clubs that served in lieu of formal parties to focus ideas and policies, and to put forward candidates for office. Part debating societies, part news-gathering organizations, part philanthropic groups, the clubs—which often took their names from the monasteries or churches where they met—charged fees and dues and attracted Assembly deputies and middle-class Parisians. The Jacobin Club, so-called from its meeting place in the monastery of the "Jacobins," or Dominicans of St. James, was also known as the Society of the Friends of the Constitution, and attracted a variety of adherents, from deputies to liberal nobles to Parisians of modest means. The Jacobins were vigilant in denouncing local authorities if they neglected to enforce the Assembly's laws, and they spread discord by insisting that the King was making preparations to leave the country.

Lawlessness was everywhere. As the authority of the King tottered, that of the laws, moral and civil, seemed to crumble. Beyond the rioting and violence that had by now become endemic, there were mutinous upheavals in the army—commanding officers ignored and insulted, regulations disregarded, officers murdered before the eyes of their men. Petty crime flourished. Burglars ransacked the homes of the rioters while they were carrying out their grisly protests, and pickpockets did a brisk business among the crowds at the Tuileries. The Assembly voted itself the power to declare martial law, but the majority of the lawbreakers went unpunished. There were simply not enough police or National Guard to keep up with the mayhem, or to track down the perpetrators in its aftermath.

What shocked visitors to Paris, beyond the widespread criminality, was the immorality. "Paris is perhaps as wicked a spot as exists," wrote the American envoy Gouverneur Morris. "Incest, murder, bestiality, fraud, rapine, oppression, baseness, cruelty; and yet this is the city which has stepped forward in the sacred cause of liberty." The cause of the apparent paradox was not far to seek. "The pressure of incumbent despotism removed," Morris observed, "every bad passion exerts its peculiar energy."[2] Morris was hardly an innocent himself, with several French mistresses and a wide knowledge of the sophisticated world. But even he was appalled by fathers who kept their own daughters as their mistresses, and by the relative prevalence of incest generally. (Mirabeau was far from unique in having slept with his sister in his youth.) The revolution seemed to have accelerated the loosening of morals that was already far advanced.[3]

More urgent than the disintegration of morality was the disintegration of the economy. "Poverty and discontent are increasing," Fersen wrote in his diary. "Most of the workmen and artisans have come to beggary. The shopkeepers are earning nothing, for nobody buys. The best workmen are leaving the kingdom, and the streets are full of paupers."[4] There were no coins, or almost none; anyone who possessed coins hoarded them. With the royal treasury as ever in extremis, paper money had been issued in the form of state bonds backed by the sale of Church lands which had been appropriated the previous November. The bonds, or assignats, were exchanged, but not with confidence, and little or no credit was extended. The political assault on the old governmental and social system had had a severe and unanticipated result: with so many nobles emigrating, thousands of servants, craftsmen and small tradesmen whose livelihoods had depended on the orders and trade from noble households lost their livings. The royals' move to the Tuileries had also had its effect—because the King could no longer hunt, six hundred people were dismissed from the palace staff.

Ardent as many of them were for equality and liberty, the Parisians were suffering, and they blamed the Assembly for the severity of the economic upheaval. A group of eighty painters, tailors, woodworkers, shoemakers and the like addressed a petition to the King, lamenting their loss of business, the increasing food prices and the general misery inflicted on them in the name of political reform. "Sire, liberty and equality are chimeras which have broken all social ties, confounded all authority, destroyed order, disseminated discord, invited anarchy. . . ." They implored the King to remedy the abuses, and above all to "punish those seditious persons who in the name of being friends of the constitution, are its most cruel enemies."[5] Louis had received many such petitions by the spring of 1790, and their tone was becoming increasingly strident. To be sure, there were some enterprising businessmen who profited from the revolution, such as the contractor Palloy, who, having been commissioned by the municipal government to remove the debris of the demolished Bastille, made a fortune by selling the broken old stones as souvenirs. But Palloy was the exception, and the desperate manufacturers and builders and wig-makers who petitioned the King spoke for the majority of their peers.

Though action was urgently called for, Louis would not act. He sat inert in his apartments, he worked at his locks, he dozed, he stayed in his study for hours on end, reading newspapers and journals. When he was informed that the Assembly had discarded the old map of France with its provinces and decreed a new geographical division of the country into eighty-three departments, he amused himself in drawing up a map combining the old system and the new, and indicating the changes. He played billiards with Antoinette, chatted with his daughter, whom he adored, spent time with his son. He even played game after game of whist with Provence, though the latter annoyed him by continually giving him advice and talking politics. He ate like a glutton and slept long and heavily, sleep being the best refuge of all from the multiple distresses of his waking situation.

Though he was looking for aid from Spain, from the Hapsburg Empire, and from Swiss bankers Louis was publicly denying that he was a captive of the Assembly. He boasted that, once the weather improved sufficiently, he would take himself on a tour of the new departments. He gloried in the medal presented to him by the municipality of Paris saluting him as "the best of Kings" and "Restorer of French Liberty and the true Friend of his People." He had been told that there were new monuments erected in his honor in Lyons and Marseilles, and he wanted to see them, to receive the plaudits of his people. The revolution had made many changes, he seemed to be saying, yet France was still a monarchy, and he was still the monarch. At the urging of his ministers, Louis met with the Assembly and, in a remarkable speech—remarkable for its politics, not its rhetoric—proclaimed that he was himself the leader of the revolution.

This bold move was in keeping with Louis's eccentric but carefully thought out interpretation of his situation. As he saw it, he was in exactly the same position as King Charles I of England a century and a half earlier. King Charles had opposed the radicals in the English Parliament; eventually the conflict had deteriorated into civil war, and when the royalists lost the war, the King had lost his head.

"I am menaced by the same fate," he said. "The only way to escape from it is to do the opposite of everything that unfortunate monarch did." He read and reread the Earl of Clarendon's multi-volume *History of the Rebellion and Civil Wars in England*, and kept a portrait of King Charles on his wall. His preoccupation with the martyred King was reinforced by his advisers, formal and informal. He had been hearing about King Charles from the start of his reign, when Turgot had warned him that he might share the English King's fate. "Never forget, sire, that it was weakness that put the head of Charles I on the block. . . . You are considered weak, sire." Provence, Antoinette, his minister Montmorin all talked the same way. But by showing himself to be, not the enemy of the revolution, but the true friend of the people, he could avoid becoming a martyr. And if he avoided it long enough, in time his people were sure to come to their senses and recover from the temporary spasm of rebellion that shook them.

Meanwhile he was saddened by the polarization of the realm, by the defections and mutinies in the army and the plots and rumors of plots to kill him and his family. His loyal servants were his consolation. "I need to look at those which have remained faithful to me, by way of consoling my afflicted heart," he told Madame de Tourzel.[6] There were still many of these loyal servants—the two chief valets de chambre, Thierry and Chamilli, the numerous ushers and gentlemen of the bedchamber, the Grand Master of the Ceremonies, the Marquis de Brézé, the grand quartermaster of cavalry, the Marquis de Suze, and the first bedchamber gentleman, the Duc de Villequier. The soldiers of the bodyguard had gone, replaced by the National Guard whose members, unused to the court, were awkward at best and at worst, truculent and surly.

The guardsmen, along with millions of others, were outraged in April of 1790 when the Assembly made public the King's expenses. From 1774 to 1789, it was disclosed, the monarch and his court had expended the unimaginably huge sum of 227,983,716 livres on buildings, gardens, jewelry and other luxuries, pensions to favorites, entertainments. Nearly thirty millions had been paid to Provence and Artois for their costly establishments. Another six millions had gone to the Polignacs and other nobles, while only two hundred and fifty thousand had been paid out in charity to the poor. To be sure, one-half of the huge total had gone to pay the costs of war, and to support the army and navy. But twelve millions had been spent on the personal expenses of the King and Queen—to buy Antoinette's diamonds, people said—when only a small fraction of that amount would have eased the destitution in the capital and kept Paris supplied with bread.

The reaction to these disclosures was predictably harsh. Crowds in the Tuileries gardens sang the menacing revolutionary song "Ça ira," to which new and threatening lyrics were constantly being added:

> Ah! it will happen all right, it will
> The people are saying over and over
> Ah! it will happen all right, it will
> Despite the unruly ones all will be well!

Ah! it will happen all right, it will
Hang the aristocrats from the
   lampposts!
Ah! it will happen all right, it will
We'll hang all the aristocrats.

There was no end to the verses. "Despotism will die and liberty will triumph," "We'll have no more nobles, nor priests, only equality for all," and so on, with the "infernal clique" of Austrians consigned to the devil.[7]

Privilege and inequality were anathema. On June 23 the Assembly suppressed all titles of nobility. "No more Highness, excellency or eminence!" shouted one excited deputy. From there it was only a short step to calling for "No more King!"

No one saw this more clearly than Mirabeau, who for months had been offering to make himself useful to the King and Queen. Finally Louis had agreed to talk with him in secret, and they had struck a bargain. In return for paying the Count's numerous heavy debts, and giving him a pension of six thousand livres a month (plus a bonus of another million livres should the Assembly be permanently dissolved), Louis was to receive the full benefit of Mirabeau's powers of persuasion in the Assembly, and his pledge to commit himself to the formation of a constitutional monarchy.

Mirabeau was an impressive ally, though even the idealistic Louis must have realized that his motives were far from disinterested. He wanted wealth, and he expected to be given a place—as chief minister, perhaps—in any new royal government. It flattered the Count to meet with the King—and even more to meet the Queen, which he finally managed to do in July. But deep down he was ambivalent; his friend La Marck noted how he wavered between "an apparent desire to serve and inaction." Part of him wanted to save the monarchy, but an equally important part wanted to be King himself.

When Mirabeau finally met Antoinette she was at St.-Cloud. The Assembly had permitted the King and Queen to spend the summer there, provided they returned to the Tuileries to dine every Sunday and on other important occasions. The Count drove to St.-Cloud with his nephew, Victor, and told the younger man to wait for him at the palace gate. He was cautious about the prospective meeting, he couldn't be certain he was not being used in a counter-plot. But when he eventually returned to the carriage some time later, he was in a state of rapture. Antoinette had enchanted him and quite overawed him.

"She is very great, she is very noble, she is very unfortunate," Mirabeau told Victor in a voice that shook with emotion, "but I am going to save her." He saw in Antoinette the regal daughter of the great Maria Theresa, who had donned the mantle of her mother's dignity. She, not her ineffectual husband, was in charge, it had been her decision to summon him to a meeting. "The King has only one man near him," the Count declared, "and that is his wife." Convinced as he was of Antoinette's ability, he was equally convinced that she would soon have to emigrate. "The moment will come, and soon," he declared, "when she will have to try what a woman and child can do on horseback."

The first anniversary of the fall of the Bastille approached, and the National Guard, which had become a nationwide organization, chose this date for all its members, or Federates, to assemble in Paris in celebration. The Assembly approved a great Festival of the Federation, with tens of thousands of guardsmen from the departments gathering on the vast Champ de Mars between the Ecole Militaire and the river to swear an oath of loyalty to the nation. It was meant to be an apotheosis of liberty, this massing of provincial guardsmen, yet at the same time the festival was designed to demonstrate loyalty to the Church and the monarchy as the guardsmen were to hear an open-air Mass, celebrated by Talleyrand, Bishop of Autun, and the royal family was to take a prominent part in the spectacle.

The Champ de Mars was converted into a broad amphitheater surrounded by thirty tiers of benches for the onlookers. In the center of the amphitheater an Altar of the Country was erected, ornamented with figures and inscriptions. Here Talleyrand would celebrate Mass. The Ecole Militaire itself was transformed by canvas and streamers into a platform for the King, members of the Assembly and other notables. Opposite it was an enormous triumphal arch designed along classical lines, whose carved inscriptions extolled constitutional monarchy.

All this was created in only a few short weeks, in a frenzy of eagerness brought on by the rapidly approaching deadline and by a genuine outburst of patriotic zeal. In spite of the economic debacle, the shortages, the spying and the lawlessness, Parisians were gripped by a desire to celebrate all that had been achieved in the space of a single year. The excavations in the Champ de Mars became a symbol—like the tricolor cockade—of loyalty to the revolutionary government, and of hope for the future. Spontaneously people of all sorts joined the three thousand workmen toiling away to dig out the field, build the artificial hills, construct the altar and triumphal arch. And those who were not moved to pitch in and help were forced to do their share. Avid patriots roamed the streets impressing merchants, professional men, aristocrats of both sexes to dirty their hands and bend their backs on the Champ de Mars. Some said they even broke into convents, rousting out the monks and nuns and forcing them to take part in the common labor and to sing the "Ça ira."

The day of the festival dawned gray and threatening, and soon rain began to fall in torrents. The two hundred thousand spectators who had managed to secure seats or advantageous places to stand quickly became wet through, yet they waited patiently for the spectacle to begin, and every place was filled. Thousands of umbrellas made a multicolored canopy over the crowd, obstructing the view. Still, as the ranks of guardsmen, each group carrying its distinctive banner, marched past, followed by the line regiments and their officers, swords drawn, the sailors and cavalry, the rain was forgotten by all but the most tepid lovers of liberty. The marching and countermarching went on for hours, there were parades in every street all converging on the enormous amphitheater which became a single gigantic parade ground. The blue and white of the National Guards wove itself neatly in and out among the multicolors of the chasseurs and carabineers and hussars. Wet banners, drooping from their poles, were waved aloft as black clouds opened overhead and turned the parade ground into a sea of mud.

Still the spectators did not budge. The men waved their hats, some held up sabers and bayonets with loaves of soaked bread speared on their tips. Hundreds of people who had managed to get to the top of the triumphal arch sang and shouted and waved tricolor flags. On the Altar of the Country, three hundred priests in white robes and tricolor scarves stood in their places, waiting for the Bishop to arrive. An orchestra of over a thousand musicians trooped in and tuned up. Amid the shouting and singing, the thumping and shrilling of the military bands and the cacophony from the orchestra order was lost at times. Soldiers broke from their ranks and ran joyfully loose, joining hands to dance peasant dances, eating the ham, fruit and sausages people had tossed to them along the route of march. It was a very festive anarchy, almost playful, yet not without a hint of menace. Several of the priests were swept off the altar and forced to march up and down, muskets on their shoulders, grenadiers' caps on their heads. Wine flowed freely, orders were forgotten at times and some of the guardsmen, dripping with sweat and rain, forced their way past the sentinels into the special sheltered boxes where the ambassadors sat. Only the arrival of the Assembly deputies and the King brought all attention to the Ecole Militaire and put a stop to the merrymaking.

Artillery boomed a salute to the deputies, who marched in between two lines of flags. Then Louis made his appearance, in great state and with a colorful entourage. Beside his throne was a chair for the President of the Assembly, and above him was a space for Antoinette and the other members of the royal family, who were all cheered loudly as they took their places. Now the Bishop celebrated Mass, blessing the banners of the Guard units and leading the spectators in the traditional hymn of thanksgiving, the Te Deum. The oath-taking followed. One by one Lafayette, the officers of the Parisian National Guard, army officers and provincial guardsmen came before the Bishop to swear to uphold the nation, the law and the King. With "every sword drawn and every head raised," the King stood up and swore his solemn oath.

"I, King of the French, swear to employ the power delegated to me in maintaining the constitution decreed by the National Assembly and accepted by me." He reminded the massed thousands that he was "their father, their brother, their friend." He could only be happy if his subjects were happy, he said, his strength came from their liberty, his wealth from their prosperity. "Repeat my words, or rather the feelings of my heart, in the humble cottages of the poor," he shouted as the rain poured down all around him. "Tell them that, if I am not able to go with you to their homes, I want to be among them with my affection and the laws which protect the weak; to watch over them, to live for them, if necessary to die for them."[8]

Tears mingled with the rain, people shouted "Down! Down!" to those whose umbrellas blocked their view. "*Vive le Roi! Vive la*

Reine! Vive Monsieur le dauphin!!" Antoinette, wearing red, white and blue ribbons in her hair, held up her son to the crowd, and a fresh wave of shouting burst forth from thousands of throats. Finally the entire crowd repeated in unison their oath to be faithful to the nation, the law and the King. Trumpets blared, the spectators applauded, all was pandemonium as the soldiers once more broke into round dances and mingled with the crowd. Lafayette was so mobbed that he could barely move, screams and huzzas followed Louis as he made his way to his coach for the return to the Tuileries.

"For a few hours Louis became once again the idol of his subjects, the master of his empire," Hézècques wrote, recalling the festival. He was once again the people's champion, their enlightened ruler and friend. In the following days, throughout the banquets and balls and jousts on the river, the informal street dances and parties, the King's name was invoked with reverent fondness. Paris was the city of liberty, whose liberty-loving King dwelt in the shadow of his capital, the contented captive of his faithful French.

25

T HERE were plots astir to kill the Queen. A would-be assassin named Rotondo was found lurking in the inner gardens of the Tuileries, weapon in hand, waiting to assault Antoinette when she took her daily walk. No one knew how he penetrated the ring of guardsmen surrounding the palace, or how, once inside, he avoided detection for so long. Had the day not been rainy, and the royal promenade postponed, Rotondo might have succeeded.

The King's informers uncovered a conspiracy to poison Antoinette, and warned her to be cautious about what she ate. According to Campan, she took the warning calmly—or perhaps she was numbed by fear following the previous assassination attempt—and went to her doctor to get advice about antidotes. He told her to keep a bottle of oil of sweet almonds within reach, to mix with milk as an emetic, and to empty the bottle and refill it frequently lest the oil be poisoned. Madame Campan became concerned about the basin of sugar Antoinette kept in her bedchamber to sweeten her drinking water. Rotondo's escapade proved that anyone could gain access to the palace (had he bribed the guardsmen?) and many of the servants were presumed to be in the pay of the revolutionaries, or to hold strong revolutionary sentiments. To slip a toxin in with the sugar would be only too easy—and so Campan changed it three or four times a day.[1] Antoinette remarked wryly that her enemies would more likely kill her by calumny than by poison, but the plots and rumors of plots must have frightened her, making her realize how vulnerable the entire family was.

Several people claiming to be religious visionaries came to St.-Cloud and insisted on speaking to the King. They were turned away, but they kept coming back, and finally they were arrested. Both seemed slightly mad, and ultimately proved to be genuine. They had wanted nothing more than to urge the King to "put his trust in God and the holy Virgin, and so recover his authority."

Most of those who clamored to see the King, or to gape at the Queen, were harmless—as harmless as the silent, brooding Chevalier Castelnaux who was still Antoinette's shadow. But no one could be trusted completely, not when Paris was inundated with inflammatory pamphlets calling for the murder of the King and Queen. Murder, pillage, and arson were the common vocabulary of the journalists, who sold their papers throughout the city and even at the very door of the Assembly, a few minutes' walk from the palace. The most ferocious of the journalists was Marat, the doctor who had abandoned science for politics and whose indictments of the privileged fairly seethed with hatred. In the summer of 1790 he circulated a new pamphlet goading Parisians to seize Louis and the dauphin, to throw Antoinette and Provence in jail, and cut off the heads of six hundred people in authority. All taxation should be abolished, he insisted. Then and only then would the French be content—and safe from the enemies of the revolution, who were plotting to overturn it.

Fearing that Marat's vision of destruction was a harbinger of things to come, property-owning Parisians left the city, alarmed by the disorder, by the continuing economic collapse (the assignats were losing value at a frightening rate), and by the large numbers of vagabonds and deserters who streamed in from the provinces. The Assembly tried in vain to stem the exodus, but people left anyway, hoping to find stability away from the political maelstrom that was Paris. Yet many provincial cities too were convulsed by revolts and violent protests. At Toulon the dockyard laborers, enraged by rumors that they would not be paid, attacked the senior naval officer and were in the process of hanging him when a party of grenadiers came on the scene and saved his life. At Nancy, three regiments revolted and in the resulting chaos the arsenal was pillaged and hordes of townspeople rose in rebellion against the town authorities. In Lyons there were riots against the revolution—riots prompted, in part, by recent legislation which attempted to bring the Church under the control of the revolution.

The Civil Constitution of the Clergy, passed by the Assembly on July 12 and signed by a reluctant Louis ten days later, was the most audaciously radical legislation yet proposed by the deputies. It abolished the old episcopal sees and reduced the income of the Bishops—which in many cases was enormous—to a modest twelve thousand livres a year. Henceforth each of the eighty-four departements was to be a diocese, with its Bishop elected by the departmental assembly. Priests too were to be elected, by the assemblies of the districts in which they were to serve, and were to receive small stipends from the state. Broadly speaking, the Assembly's purpose in formulating the Civil Constitution was to eliminate abuses: the domination of the episcopate by the great aristocratic families, the wealth and extravagance of many higher clergy, the ignorance, immorality or venality of unworthy priests. The deputies argued that the Church, far from being a haven of spirituality, was a shamefully worldly institution whose wealth, stolen from parishioners, would be put to better use to serve the nation.

But to many of the French, the new law was nothing short of an attack on religion itself. Nine out of ten French men and women were Catholics, most of them devout, traditional believers untouched by the anticlericalism and skepticism of the Enlightenment. They went to Mass, said their prayers, attended to their devotions undisturbed by changes in government, and were outraged when the government presumed to make fundamental alterations in their religious lives. To turn the clergy into political servants was to make no allowance for conscience or piety—not to mention holiness. And it ignored the supremacy of the Pope, the spiritual leader of all Christendom, including revolutionary France.

The Civil Constitution alienated many who had eagerly espoused the principles of the revolution, and gave the counter-revolutionaries a strong new ideological weapon: from now on they could claim to be the champions of the Church as well as the monarchy, defenders of God and the faith against the godless revolutionaries.

The most tireless champion of the old order was Artois. Now in exile at Turin, surrounded by a growing number of fellow-exiles pledged to overthrow the revolutionaries, he was determined to take action, just as soon as he got the cooperation and backing of the other European sovereigns. He was encouraged rather than dismayed by an abortive rising in Languedoc by opponents of the revolution in May and June; he saw in it a portent of things to come, not a defeat. Even Louis's refusal to cooperate with him did not deter Artois, who busied himself traveling to the various European courts, meeting with his fellow exiles and sending out ciphered messages. (The messages were often hard to make out. "I have at last deciphered your letter, my dear brother," Antoinette wrote Artois in response to one such communication, "and it was not without difficulty. There were many mistakes.") He had never been more self-important, filled with a sense of mission, "always talking, never listening, being sure of everything," as Fersen wrote. By his side, his chief deputy, was Calonne, the former Finance Minister—and opponent of the Queen. And as the months passed, many others gathered around the Prince, to form what he hoped would become a powerful counter-revolutionary force.

Artois and his colleagues were anything but a comfort to Antoinette. She had little respect for her brother-in-law's abilities, she worried that he was making an already grave situation much more dangerous. Madame Campan believed that the Queen was fearful of Calonne, and dubious about the outcome of a counter-revolution led from abroad. "If the emigrants succeed," she told Campan, "they will give the law for a long time; it will be impossible to refuse them anything; to owe the crown to them would be contracting too great an obligation."[2] Yet she did not dare disown Artois and his efforts completely. He might become useful, and besides that, he had a spy within the bosom of the royal family: Princess Elisabeth.

The King's younger sister had become a source of friction. Opinionated, strong-willed, with a wry intelligence that made her skeptical of other people's motives, Elisabeth had become something of a thorn in Antoinette's side. She had no life of her own; Louis had neglected her welfare, failing to arrange a marriage for her. She had been a difficult child, "a little savage," according to Antoinette. The blunt, rude, untamed child had grown into a prickly woman, "neither pretty nor ugly," Antoinette's brother Joseph thought, who knew her own mind and spoke it frequently. She and Antoinette had always been friends, but now they clashed over politics. Elisabeth wanted her timid, inert brother

Louis to take bold action against the Assembly and the Parisians, Louis wanted to be left alone. Antoinette was the decision-maker, and Elisabeth tried to work on her, insisting that she cooperate with Artois, criticizing her for compromising her position in dealing with Mirabeau and Lafayette, urging her to stop temporizing and act the heroine. The two women remained fond of one another, but the sisterly bickering was an irritant to the already beleaguered Antoinette.

What Antoinette needed, she told Mercy, was not advice but money—lots of money. The Assembly had granted the King and Queen nearly thirty million livres to run their household (financed, like all other government obligations, by the sale of Church lands), but this was not enough, especially since Antoinette continued to order new gowns in abundance and new and costly furniture for the Tuileries. She needed money from abroad, secret funds she could draw on to pay for the escape she now saw as inevitable. ("We must fly," she had told Madame Campan a few months earlier. "Who knows how far the factions may go? The danger increases every day."[3]) Mirabeau had not been able to do much to help the monarchy. His most recent suggestion was that Louis fight the most radical of the revolutionaries with their own weapons, becoming a politician himself and organizing a party. Once he had this party behind him, he could leave Paris and set up a base of operations in some more congenial town. Of course, Mirabeau conceded, this might lead to civil war—which made Louis cringe. Mirabeau's counsel made the Queen angry. His plan, she told Mercy, was "mad from start to finish." "The monarchy is finished," she confided in another letter. And in another, "I fear having been very wrong about the route which we should have followed."[4]

There was no doubt in her mind any longer. Emigration was the only viable course of action—even though it would mean rejoining Artois and his coterie. Antoinette told Madame Campan about one scheme to escape from St. Cloud, where there were fewer guards and their surveillance was lighter. Louis would leave the palace with only an aide-de-camp of Lafayette's in attendance, plus his usual group of equerries and pages. Antoinette and her son would do the same, also escorted by only two of Lafayette's men, along with Madame de Tourzel. Elisabeth would get away on her own, or with the Princess Royal. They would leave at about four in the afternoon, as they often did, and would not be missed until eight or nine, when the long summer twilight closed in. Meanwhile "some persons, who could be fully relied on," would be waiting for them in a wood four leagues from St.-Cloud, with a large traveling coach, or berlin, and a smaller carriage for the attendants. Lafayette's men would be bribed or rendered helpless, the royals would climb into the berlin and be off.

Hours later, there would be panic at the palace, the royal apartments would be searched, and a letter from the King found—a letter to the Assembly, in which he announced his departure and gave his reasons for leaving. It would take another hour for the letter to be sent to Paris. And by that time the berlin and the smaller carriage would have six or seven hours' head start on any pursuers.[5]

Antoinette did not formulate this plan, but she approved of it, and no doubt urged Louis to carry it out. She failed. Louis would not budge. He was adamant, blunt and obscene. "Go fuck yourself!" he shouted to Lafayette when the latter tried to talk to him seriously and slammed the door on him. "The first bastard that talks to me about a plot or about emigration . . ." he yelled, finishing the sentence with a garbled obscenity. He was miserable, trapped in the Tuileries by the revolutionaries, trapped in inactivity by his own inertia and by his nearly phobic squeamishness about avoiding bloodshed. His wife nagged him, his advisers and well-wishers, his brothers and sister would not leave him alone. He knew, as he told Madame de Tourzel, that there were "French hearts which would have risked their lives a thousand times for the preservation of their sovereign." But when these champions approached him, they kept insisting that he do their bidding, or take violent action. And he couldn't. It was as simple as that. As Antoinette sadly concluded in a letter to Artois, "he sees his position differently from what it is."[6]

By the closing months of 1790, despite Louis's obstinacy, emigration had become a foregone conclusion. Antoinette had begun to plan and prepare for it in earnest, giving a great deal of attention to comfort and convenience and far too little attention to the dangers and difficulties of the journey. More than a year earlier she had ordered a huge *nécessaire*—a sort of traveling armoire—to have on hand "in case of precipitate flight." Into this heavy, bulky piece of furniture were now packed all the indispensable accoutrements of domestic life, toilet articles, cups, bowls, utensils, mirrors, boot-scrapers and toothpicks, billiard cues and gilded chamber pots. The *nécessaire* was to be sent on ahead, once final plans were made, to await the family at their intended destination. Clothing would have to be sent on ahead as well, and Antoinette wanted complete new wardrobes for herself and her children. But there was a problem: one of the wardrobe women, Mlle. Rocherette, was a staunch revolutionary, and if she received orders to provide so much new clothing all at once, her suspicions would be aroused. Then too there was constant scrutiny from the Assembly, and their informers, and from Lafayette's men. So Antoinette appointed Madame Campan to be in charge of ordering the items of clothing, with as much secrecy as she could manage.

Throughout January and February of 1791 the bedchamber woman slipped out of the palace, on her own, "almost in disguise" as she said, to visit dressmakers and seamstresses—being careful not to order too many things from any one of them, or to reveal any hint of whom the garments were intended for. She bought chemises and gowns, combing cloths and wrappers, gloves and slippers and quantities of lace. Antoinette had lost a good deal of weight, her dimensions had changed. The clothes ordered in 1791 would never have fit the buxom matron she had been only a year or two earlier. The children too had changed, of course. Thérèse was now a young lady of twelve, and the dauphin a sturdy five-year-old. Madame Campan had one of her sisters make the children's clothes, pretending that they were for her own relatives and sending the trunk containing them to her aunt in Arras; the aunt was instructed to take the trunk to Brussels and wait there with it for further instructions.[7] Beyond the well stocked *nécessaire* and the new clothes the royal family would need a traveling carriage—and here Antoinette's predilection to satisfy comfort over practicality was a serious miscalculation. She chose not the swiftest but the most spacious conveyance, the berlin, a vehicle like the one in which she had traveled from Vienna to Paris as a young bride. She ordered a berlin of exceptional size, practically "a small traveling house," according to a contemporary. It was ingeniously fitted out with a sort of larder, which could be stocked with all kinds of provisions, a cooking stove for heating meat or soup, even a dining table that could be raised up out of the floor. The seat cushions were removable; underneath were commodes. Only beds were lacking to make the carriage a second home. Encumbered with the royal family, their servants, several soldiers riding on the outside as bodyguards, plus all their baggage, food and other necessities, the berlin would be a heavy load even for six strong horses. And the horses would have to be changed every fifteen miles—a drawback, as horses were in short supply on all the roads. But this inconvenience was apparently not considered, or at least not seriously enough.[8]

Apart from the choice of vehicle, every other detail of the traveling arrangements was left to Fersen. He discovered that a Russian noblewoman, the Baroness de Korff, had recently made the trip from Paris to the frontier safely with her children and sister and several servants—a relatively rare feat, given the activities of the revolutionary "committees of search" and the exhaustive scrutiny of passports and other documents by village authorities. It occurred to Fersen that the royal family could use the Baroness's papers, or others just like them, and could disguise themselves as various members of the Baroness's traveling party. Madame de Tourzel could play the part of the Baroness, Louis could be her majordomo, Antoinette her children's governess. With the dauphin disguised as a girl, the two royal children could impersonate the Baroness's two daughters, and Princess Elisabeth her sister. The Russian ambassador, Simolin, offered to help Fersen arrange the deception and it was he who obtained the necessary documents from the French Foreign Minister Montmorin.

For protection once they neared the border the royal emigrants would need to rely on the army, and with mutinies commonplace this was likely to be problematic. Louis and Antoinette both felt that they could rely on the Marquis de Bouillé, a monarchist general who had managed to subdue the rebellion at Nancy. Antoinette wrote to Bouillé urging him to keep his troops in readiness at the frontier, but Bouillé told her in confidence that he could not be certain of his men; they were all "gangrened with the revolutionary spirit," he said, and might not remain loyal if they were called upon to protect the fleeing King.

Still, they would have to do. The situation was becoming worse by the day. Antoinette told the Spanish ambassador, whose help she sought, that her husband had no allies left. The European sovereigns, though concerned by the increasing political power of the republicans in the Assembly, were nonetheless gratified by the weakening of France, and were unwilling as yet to take any steps toward strengthening the Bourbon throne. Mercy had been recalled to Vienna, Necker had resigned and returned to Switzerland. Mirabeau, though still a loyal monarchist, had not shown himself to be a useful ally. Antoinette could not expect help from any of her relatives. The most powerful of them was her brother Leopold, the former Grand Duke of Tuscany who had become Holy Roman Emperor on the death of Joseph II. Unlike Joseph, who for all his eccentricities had been affectionate toward Antoinette, and concerned for her plight, Leopold was distant and unresponsive, and disconcertingly sympathetic to the more moderate ideas of the revolutionaries.[9]

"I had before me," the ambassador noted in a dispatch, "a desperate woman at the very end of her strength in dealing with the present situation." Others who saw the Queen thought she looked "very ill," and were shocked at the sight of her white hair and gaunt face. She kept her son near her as often as possible, and was always anxious to display him, as a sort of protective talisman. "They say here that he is her shield," wrote Lord Mornington, an Englishman who visited the Tuileries, "she never stirs out without him."[10]

The departure date was fixed for March 1791, but in February a series of incidents took place that forced a postponement. First, Adelaide and Victoire emigrated, leaving their house at Bellevue only hours before an angry crowd arrived, determined to prevent their departure. The two women carried passports granted by the Minister of Foreign Affairs and signed by the King, yet the National Guard pursued them and arrested them at the town of Arnay-le-Duc in Burgundy, keeping them there for eleven days until the Assembly, all but coerced by Mirabeau, decreed their safe passage out of France.

Next, incited by an epidemic of rumors that the King was about to follow his aunts into exile, and that the dauphin would soon be smuggled out of the country, an enormous crowd massed in the Faubourg St.-Antoine and began attacking the nearby castle of Vincennes, in the mistaken belief that the King meant to make his escape via an underground passage being dug to the castle from the Tuileries, a distance of under two miles. Vincennes was in fact under repair, the Assembly having ordered that it be restored for use as a prison, but the angry laborers from the faubourg, out of work and out of money, saw the fortress as a second Bastille and swarmed over it, dismantling it stone by stone. At a considerable cost in popularity, Lafayette ordered in the National Guard, and forcibly retook Vincennes, but not before another disturbance had arisen.

Among the shadowy counter-revolutionary organizations that had sprung up in recent months was a band of courtiers calling themselves the Knights of the Dagger, pledged to protect the King and, if possible, to get him out of Paris. When rioting broke out in the Faubourg St.-Antoine the Knights, some four hundred strong, strapped on their swords and rushed to the Tuileries to rescue the King and his family. There they encountered resistance, and were hewing about them and creating confusion and mayhem when Lafayette arrived and persuaded Louis—who seems to have been unaware that the Knights hoped to kidnap him—to call off the overzealous courtiers. Eventually a force of guardsmen disarmed and arrested them.

The rioting and rumor-mongering seemed endless, the shocks and outrages against the royals almost palpable. Emperor Leopold was said to be massing troops in Belgium. Antoinette was rumored to be having an affair with Lafayette, in hopes of alienating him from the goals of the revolution and enslaving him to do her fiendish bidding. The hated emigrés were said to be buying arms and raising armies, and sending their agents into France to subvert the revolution. The Assembly no longer referred to Louis as King but as "chief public functionary." The dauphin was "first deputy," Antoinette was "first deputy's mother."[11] And a new voice was being heard raised in anger against the despotism of the chief public functionary, the voice of a dapper little lawyer from Arras, Maximilien Robespierre, president of the Jacobin Club.

The assault on the Church, and in particular on those thousands of priests—some twenty thousand, by one estimate—who refused to take the oath of loyalty intensified. Lists of nonjuring priests were sold in the streets, and those whose names appeared on the lists were shouted down when they tried to say Mass. Some were beaten, threatened at pistol-point, or chased out of their churches. The brutality became worse when in March of 1791 Pope Pius VI denounced the Civil Constitution of the Clergy and suspended all clergy who had taken the oath.

Easter was approaching, and the royal family wanted to spend

Holy Week at St.-Cloud, away from the tensions of Paris. The servants were sent on ahead to prepare the palace, trunks were packed and orders given. The day before they were to leave the Tuileries Louis went to the palace chapel to receive the eucharist from his grand almoner, a nonjuring priest. Spies informed the Assembly of this act of disloyalty and the word spread immediately to the political clubs and outward into the working-class districts. At once there was a huge popular reaction, and by the following morning, which was Palm Sunday, placards appeared accusing the chief public functionary of breaking the law. An armed crowd grew on the Place du Carrousel in front of the palace. Ignoring the menacing Parisians, Louis, Antoinette and their children came out and entered the carriage, as Lafayette stood by with a troop of cavalry to escort them to St.-Cloud. The cavalrymen closed ranks around the vehicle. Then, as if on cue, the Parisians set up a terrifying shouting and catcalling, waving the weapons they carried and making the King, who had recently suffered a week-long attack of high fever and acute respiratory illness, turn pale.

At once the guardsmen too turned from protectors into a taunting rabble.

"Fat pig! Fucking aristocrat! Bugger of an aristocrat! You're not fit to be King! We want Orléans!"

They broke ranks and leaned in at the carriage windows, shouting at Louis that he was nothing but a public servant, and an overpaid public servant at that. He could not leave, they would stop him. They would shoot him if they had to. Some drew sabers and attacked the postilions, others violently assaulted the palace officials who came out to see what was going on.

Louis tried to muster his dignity, and demanded that the guardsmen open the gates of the inner courtyard, to let the carriage proceed. But they laughed at him, and laughed even more when Lafayette, after shouting at them and pleading with them until he was red-faced with exasperation, threatened to resign his post. Applause greeted the threat, and more insults to the King.

The crowd outside the gates was enjoying the spectacle, cheering the soldiers on, battering at the gates and chanting "Long live the National Assembly!"

A guardsman, his sword drawn, galloped straight at Louis. "You are a lawbreaker!" he shouted. "You harbor priests who have not taken the oath!"

"Miserable villain!" the King retorted. "Who appointed you judge of my conscience?"

Both Louis and Antoinette managed to retain their composure in the midst of this nightmarish scene, Fersen thought—though he was hardly an unbiased observer. "Both spoke with much firmness and coolness," he wrote in a letter to a Swedish friend. But neither they nor Lafayette nor any of the Guards officers could control the mutinous soldiers, who, egged on by the Parisians beyond the gates and elated by their own power, continued to hold the King and Queen hostage in their carriage for more than two hours. They stopped short of harming them physically, their torment was all verbal. Worst of all was the fear they inspired, the dread of harm, the knowledge that at any moment the guardsmen might elect to open the gates and abandon the entire family to the fury of the Parisians.

More soldiers arrived and joined the mutineers, shouting and swearing at the King, calling the Queen "a pretty bitch who thinks she can give us orders," taunting and jeering. A few grenadiers, Fersen noticed, were weeping.

"Sire, you are loved," they whispered to the pale Louis. "You are adored by your people. But do not go. Your life would be in danger. You are ill-advised, misled. The people want you to send away the priests, they are afraid of losing you."

Far from being moved by the loyalty of these men, the King responded angrily. They were the ones who were misled, he insisted. How could anyone doubt his intentions, or his love for his people?[12]

The milling and shouting, far from subsiding, seemed to gain strength as the hours passed. Finally Louis, realizing that he was beaten and that no municipal authority, no deputies, no troops were going to rescue him, gave the order for the carriage to turn around. When it reached the palace he and Antoinette and the children got out, and at once they were mobbed by the guardsmen—though some of the men assured him, "We will defend you" and followed him all the way inside and up the staircase to the very door of their private apartments.

"It is impossible to give any idea of what we had to suffer during Holy Week," Madame de Tourzel recalled in her memoirs. Threatened by the very men whom they counted on to protect them, all too aware of the vulnerability of the Tuileries and of Lafayette's waning influence, forced to attend Mass on Easter

Sunday at the parish church of the Tuileries, St.-Germain l'Au-
xerrois, where oath-taking priests officiated, Louis and Antoinette
were in an agony of anxiety. They had to get away, to escape the
menace that was closing in around them, to save themselves before the Parisians overwhelmed the Tuileries as they had Versailles, and slaked their thirst for vengeance in regicide.

❧ 26 ❧

I T was very late, the palace was settling into quiet. The sentries who guarded the gates, doors and windows stood silent, willing themselves to stay awake through the long watch of the night, aware that Lafayette must not find them dozing when he made his nightly visit to the Tuileries. On the long torchlit terrace fronting the gardens, guardsmen paced back and forth, alert for suspicious sounds and unexpected movements in the shadows.

It was known that the King had made plans to escape. Antoinette's wardrobe woman had gone to the Hôtel de Ville and told the authorities there about the suspicious *nécessaire* that her mistress had sent to Brussels on a flimsy pretext. The guards were cautioned, and told to double their vigilance. But a month had now passed since the spy had given her information, and no escape attempt had been made.

Inside the palace the long corridors were dim and still, the passageways deserted save for the soldiers who kept watch there, armed and in uniform, listening for any unusual sound yet lapsing, despite themselves, into a light trance. Nothing seemed different on this night, Monday, the twentieth of June. No one thought it significant that Count Fersen had visited the palace that afternoon, not leaving until six o'clock, or that after he left the Queen, walking in the gardens with her children, looked red-eyed as if she had been weeping. She often wept, after all, and Fersen was a very frequent visitor, having come the previous day and stayed until midnight, and the day before that.

No one thought it worth noting when, a little after eleven a woman and two little girls, one about twelve, the other five or six, emerged from the unguarded door to the Duc de Villequier's apartments—the Duke had emigrated—and stepped out into the courtyard. No one recognized the woman as Madame de Tourzel, governess of the dauphin and his sister, and it occurred to no one that the younger child, wearing a silk dress and bonnet made by the governess's daughter for use on this night, might be the heir to the French throne.

The trio walked unchallenged toward a line of hired coaches, approached one of the drivers—a very tall, handsome fellow who was chatting amiably with a stranger and idly flicking his whip— and entered his rather old-fashioned carriage. The coachman, who was in actuality Fersen, swung into his seat and drove off toward the river, passing along the quays in a wide arc and then, after about half an hour, stopping on the rue St. Honoré not far from the palace to wait for more passengers.

At about a quarter to twelve another woman slipped out of the palace, dressed inconspicuously in a plain morning gown and with the white cap of a servant covering her hair, and made her way to the waiting carriage. If she was noticed, she was not considered worth scrutinizing, though she was in fact the King's sister.

For the past dozen nights the sentries had become accustomed to seeing the bulky, portly form of one of the King's servants, the Chevalier de Coigny, go past them at midnight when his duties at the palace were completed. So they gave little more than a passing glance at the rather clumsy, heavyset man, so like the Chevalier in shape and dress and wig, who passed them and paused briefly to buckle his shoe before making his way out into the street and into the waiting carriage. His dark overcoat and round hat, and the walking stick he carried, were those of a lesser servant, not of a king.

The safe arrival of this fifth passenger was a great relief, for it meant that he had convinced Lafayette and Bailly, who came every night to check on security at the palace, that nothing out of the ordinary was happening. (Both men, by chance, had passed the waiting carriage in the rue St. Honoré, making the passengers tremble and shrink back into the shadows.)

It was some time before the sixth and final passenger made her appearance. She had dressed herself in the plain brown dress, short black cloak and black hat of a governess, pulling the dark veil of the hat down over her distinctive features before making her way out of the palace through the Duc de Villequier's apartments. Once past the sentries, however, she had got lost, and it took her longer than expected to reach the others. Finally, though, she saw the carriage, and knew the handsome driver, and climbed in.

"How glad I am to see you here!" her husband exclaimed, and embraced her. There were kisses, hugs and embraces all around, and then the driver touched his whip to the horses and they were off.

It was well after midnight, there were few people in the dark streets beyond the guardsmen and representatives of the city's sections deputed to keep order. Still, Fersen took the least frequented streets, avoiding well-lit areas, even though this meant slower progress. When the carriage reached the customs barrier, however, the unexpected happened. A marriage feast was in progress, by torchlight, with a large crowd of celebrants. Some of them were bound to be inquisitive. But Fersen was personable, the governess kept her veil over her face and the fat man pulled his round hat low. The wedding guests returned to their revels, the carriage was allowed to pass.

They made for Bondy, six miles outside of Paris, where the berlin, stocked with provisions and luggage, was waiting with fresh horses in harness. Here too were three of the bodyguard, dressed in yellow livery that Fersen had acquired from an emigrating nobleman, and two of the children's servants, Mesdames Brunier and de Neuville, who were to make the journey in a separate vehicle, a cabriolet.[1] The travelers got into the berlin, with the guards riding on the outside. Fersen took his leave, returning briefly to Paris before emigrating himself, to Belgium.

The two vehicles started off at once. Their route was to take them via Claye, Meaux, Chaintrix and Châlons to Pont-Sommevel, where a detachment of Bouillé's hussars under the command of the young Duc de Choiseul would be waiting to escort the passengers through Orbeval, Sainte-Ménéhould, Clermont, Varennes, Romagne, Bartheville, Dun, Mouzay, Stenay and Baâlon to Montmédy, their destination. At each of the towns, more soldiers would be waiting to increase the size of the mounted escort. Any resistance they might encounter past Pont-Sommevel would be nullified by the presence of the soldiers; therefore Pont-Sommevel was the crucial milestone in the journey. According to the timetable carefully drawn up in advance by Fersen, relying on what he knew of the Baroness de Korff's traveling time and on the information Bouillé's men had provided on the condition of the roads and the availability of post-horses, the berlin should reach Pont-Sommevel at two-thirty in the afternoon, between fourteen and fifteen hours after leaving Paris. Choiseul was to expect them by then. If they failed to arrive, he was to assume that they had been forced to abort their plans and await a more favorable time to make their escape.

Long before they reached Meaux the sky began to grow light, the village cocks crowed and fields and trees emerged into view. The travelers were becoming more and more lighthearted. Châlons and Pont-Sommevel, and safety, were only hours away. They had not been pursued, most likely they were not yet missed.

"When we have passed Châlons we shall have nothing more to fear," said the man in the round hat. He was looking forward to reaching Montmédy, where he would set up a new government, with himself once more in command. "You may be quite sure that when I am once firmly seated in the saddle, I shall be very different from myself as you have seen me up to now."[2]

The journey was going so well that the travelers were tempted to let down their guard, but they knew better. They had to remain who they were—the Baroness, her daughters, the nursemaid, the valet and the governess—until all possibility of risk was past. The berlin lumbered along the dusty roads, often trailing behind the lighter cabriolet, bouncing and jolting over stones and ruts and sinking into deep holes. At every hill the passengers had to get out and walk, and they were glad enough to stretch their legs, for no other stops were allowed except when necessary to change horses. They ate beef and cold veal from the well-stocked larder, they dozed when they could, they chatted hopefully about the house they had waiting for them in Montmédy, about Lafayette's dismay when he discovered them gone, about Provence and his wife who had also left Paris the night before, and were on their way to Montmédy by a different route.

They were clattering along a narrow bridge when suddenly the berlin lurched sharply, there was a tremendous jolt, and all at once the horses were screaming. The berlin had scraped the wall, and the resulting jerk had broken the harness and the horses had fallen. Repairs took an hour—during which the passengers must have waited nervously, trying not to attract too much attention—and by the time they were complete, and the berlin was jolting its way along again, the afternoon was well advanced. Clearly they would be very late for their rendezvous with the hussars at Pont-Sommevel.

Meanwhile at Pont-Sommevel, the young Duc de Choiseul was making a fateful decision. He had been waiting in the village with his hussars for the berlin to arrive, and it had not come. He continued to wait, even though his men were being harassed by the villagers, who were certain the soldiers had come to extort from them overdue rents owed to the local landowner. The peasants were armed, and growing angrier by the minute. They refused to believe that the hussars were waiting in Pont-Sommevel to escort a shipment of specie. How long was he to wait? His instructions had been vague on that point. Eventually, becoming impatient with the tense situation in the village and telling himself that the King must have changed his plans, Choiseul decided to withdraw his men. He sent couriers to inform the detachments in Orbeval, Sainte-Ménéhould and Clermont that they need not wait any longer. The King was not coming.

At five o'clock in the evening the berlin lumbered into Châlons, where the horses were changed. The post master, curious about the passengers in the expensive berlin, glanced at them—and glanced again. The fat man looked familiar. He *was* familiar. He was King Louis, dressed as an ordinary servant. Well then, let him be on his way, the post master must have thought. I won't betray him.[3]

Finally at six-thirty the passengers reached Pont-Sommevel, and looked out the windows eagerly, expecting to see the hussars. But there was not a soldier in sight, only knots of villagers, still armed, still suspicious about the unexplained goings-on in their village that day. Something was wrong. Where was Choiseul? Was the road impassable, had a bridge broken? Had they been betrayed? Should they wait for the Duke? They dared not ask questions of anyone in the village. They dared not even stop, except to change the horses. The valet and the governess consulted together, and decided to go on. After all, they had been assured that there would be soldiers at every post. They would pick up their escort at the next one.

But at Orbeval, an hour later, there were no hussars, only stone houses, barking dogs, and curious peasants. They sped on through, by now "in a state of violent agitation," as Madame de Tourzel wrote later in her detailed account of the journey. Montmédy, and Bouillé's troops, were now just over fifty miles away, but it would be dark before long and the country roads made for slow going. If they should meet with an accident, in the hilly road between Sainte-Ménéhould and Clermont, it might be hours before they were rescued. And the risk of discovery would be high. They had been promised an escort of troops who knew the roads, who could protect them under any circumstances. If the soldiers were not at Orbeval, they would have to be at Sainte-Ménéhould.

But here too nothing was as expected, and Antoinette, agitated even under the best circumstances, must have been extremely frightened. There were soldiers in the town, but they had been off duty for many hours, drinking and fraternizing with the townspeople. Their horses were unsaddled and stabled for the night. Only the captain, one Daudouins, was alert to the berlin's arrival. Trying to appear casual, he rode up to the vehicle and murmured, "The arrangements have been badly made. I am going away, in order not to arouse suspicion."

He rode off, and presumably managed to gather a few of his men together to form a small escort, for when the berlin and the cabriolet reached the staging post there were soldiers surrounding both vehicles. The post master, Jean-Baptiste Drouet, thought that there must be "some treasure" inside, to warrant such protection. He looked at the passengers. "I thought I recognized the Queen," Drouet recalled later, "and on seeing a man at the back of the carriage on the left I was struck by his resemblance to the effigy on the fifty-livre assignat."[4] Drouet, a former cavalryman, knew where his duty lay. He said nothing, but mounted his horse and rode off at once to warn the National Guard and raise the alarm.

The travelers, dismayed and uncertain, glad of their small escort but extremely worried about the next stretch of their journey—the last stretch, if all went well—set out for Varennes, the next stage. They knew that the district they were in was politically hostile to the monarchy. "All the towns in it," wrote Madame de Tourzel, "were ill-disposed." They were quite near the frontier, Austrian troops had been gathering just across it, and on the French side Bouillé's German and Swiss soldiers were a common sight and were greatly feared. The peasants, always watchful, had been on edge for months, and the recent movements of the hussars in the district told them that "something very odd was going on." The easiest route from Sainte-Ménéhould to Montmédy was through Verdun, but Verdun was not safe, so a more roundabout way had been chosen.

About ten miles beyond Sainte-Ménéhould a rider passed the berlin at full gallop, and shouted something as he went on by. No one understood his words, they were muffled by the noise of the carriage wheels. But his obvious urgency was worrisome, and the passengers looked at one another apprehensively. With the cabriolet preceding it the berlin rolled into the "upper town" of Varennes at eleven o'clock or shortly thereafter. Drouet and a companion who joined him on his ride from Sainte-Ménéhould were already there, having ridden far faster than the bulky carriages and by a side road through the woods, and they had taken the precaution of blocking off the bridge over the River Aire that led out of the lower town by overturning a cartload of furniture on it. They had also gone to find the Mayor of the town and the local commander of the National Guard, to tell them that the King was coming.

When the berlin arrived, Varennes was dark, but the local guardsmen were beginning to put themselves under arms, and lights went on in the houses as the clatter in the street woke people up. Drouet and his companion continued to spread the alarm, rousing people in the neighboring villages, who before long began to pour into Varennes in their hundreds.

The horses were lathered and drooping, and the postilions wanted to stop and rest them, there being no fresh team available. Louis, feeling keenly the danger they were all in, shouted to them to go on. The hussars became involved, and a noisy quarrel broke out.

Meanwhile Drouet had awakened the procurator of Varennes, Jean-Baptiste Sauce, who kept a chandlery in the lower town. He took charge, ordering the National Guard to position themselves at a point along the main street to wait for the berlin to descend from the upper town. Eventually it did, and the guardsmen stepped into view, their muskets pointed at the carriage.

Sauce and the Guard commander approached the vehicle and questioned its occupants.

Who were they, and where were they going? the two men wanted to know.

They were the Baroness de Korff, her children Amélie and Aglaë, their governess Madame Rochet, their nurse Rosalie and the Baroness's valet Monsieur Durand.

"And we are in a hurry," Madame Rochet snapped.

The two men asked to see the Baroness's passport. She handed it to them, and they brought it into the inn to examine it. Tense with fear, trying not to betray themselves by their nervousness, the passengers waited for the officials to return. By now the church bells were ringing, and a large crowd was gathering around the carriage. The hussars, far outnumbered by the National Guard, were thwarted and restless. More hussars arrived, and one officer came up to the window of the berlin to whisper that he knew a ford across the river, and would be happy to take the King across. But Louis, according to Madame Tourzel, "seeing the number of people around the carriage increasing every moment, and also that they were in a state of extreme exasperation, and being moreover afraid that his force was not strong enough and that he might therefore cause a massacre to no purpose, dared not give the order."

There was no need for drastic action, he reasoned. Bouillé was known to be at Stenay, only eight miles farther along the Montmédy road. All that was necessary was to get word to Bouillé that the berlin was in Varennes. The General could be there in a matter of hours, with an overwhelming force of cavalry. Louis thanked the officer and told him "to press Monsieur de Bouillé to use every effort to extricate him from his cruel position."[5]

Sauce came out of the inn at last, his face set and stern. The Baroness's passport was in order, but he and his colleagues thought it prudent to detain the travelers for a day. Drouet had after all been certain that the King and Queen were among the party. They could not take the risk of letting the berlin pass.

Sauce informed the Baroness and her companions that they would have to remain in Varennes for twenty-four hours, but that they were welcome to make themselves comfortable in his chandlery. They had no choice but to accept his hospitality, and followed him into his small dark shop and up the wooden stairs to his bedroom. There the two children collapsed on the bed, while the valet (he would not admit, when Sauce questioned him, to being the King) paced anxiously up and down.

The procurator sent for a judge who at one time had lived at Versailles and who would be able to confirm Drouet's identification. After a while the judge arrived, looked at the portly passenger, and without hesitation knelt reverently before him.

"Oh, sire!" was all he needed to say. The ruse was exposed, further denials were futile.

"Yes," Louis admitted wearily, "I am, indeed, your King. These are my wife and my children. We beg you to treat us with the regard which the French have always had for their King."

From Sauce's bedroom the word spread down the stairs and outside to the waiting crowd, which reacted with angry shouts. The procurator, uncertain what he ought to do, decided to do nothing, at least for the time being. Meanwhile the royal children were asleep and the King and his party were obviously in need of rest. Sauce left them to themselves until, at about three or four o'clock in the morning, two riders arrived from Paris.

In the capital the departure of the royal family had become known the previous morning, and at once the Assembly had met and ordered the arrest of the King. The Tuileries was sealed, and many of the palace servants—who knew nothing of the escape plans—were arrested. Lafayette redoubled the guards, the stock exchange and all the shops were closed in anticipation of a violent reaction. The Parisians, furious at the King for leaving, and even more furious at Lafayette for letting him slip away, broke through the gates of the palace and ran into the royal apartments. No one knew what to expect next, whether Louis would return at the head of a foreign army, or whether his departure ought to be taken as a form of abdication, as some of the Jacobins insisted. "People destroyed everything that bore the King's name or his portrait," Hézècques wrote. "The consternation became general."[6]

As soon as the Assembly had passed its decree Lafayette had sent out swift couriers along all the principal roads to search for the escapees. The berlin and its route had been relatively easy to trace, and Romeuf, Lafayette's aide-de-camp and the battalion commander Baillon discovered its trail; they had been riding only a few hours behind the royal party. Now they entered the chandlery carrying a copy of the decree ordering the King's arrest. One of them began to read it, but Antoinette, outraged that these two guardsmen who "were supposed to be entirely devoted to the royal family" should be so shamelessly disloyal, snatched the paper out of his hands and started to tear it to pieces. Louis stopped her—and she angrily threw it on the floor instead.

Now Sauce knew what to do. He would have to deliver the detainees to the two guard officers, who would return them to Paris.

Outside the chandlery windows people were shouting for the King to go. The hussars, standing guard in the street, were strictly forbidden by Louis to take any action that might harm the townspeople; they were powerless to prevent the insults and the jeering. The Duc de Choiseul, a tardy arrival in Varennes, managed to gain access to the King and urged him to take his son and ride swiftly, escorted by the hussars, to rendezvous with Bouillé. The National Guard—which hour by hour was massing in the town, thousands strong—would fire on the loyal soldiers, but the presence of the townspeople would confuse things, and there was a good chance that he would reach safety. Antoinette and the others could do the same, there were plenty of spare horses. But Louis demurred. Bouillé could not be far away now, rescue was coming. He would find an excuse to remain in Varennes until the general arrived.

He asked Sauce for a meal, and when this was prepared and eaten he asked that the children be allowed to sleep on a little longer. Antoinette tried to prevail on Madame Sauce, sitting with her and talking with her woman to woman. By permitting the King to continue on his journey instead of turning him over to Romeuf and Baillon, the Queen said, Madame Sauce would be "contributing to a restoration of tranquillity to France." Could she not prevail on her husband to let them go?

The procurator's wife was "moved," Antoinette told Madame Campan afterward. "She could not, without streaming eyes, see herself thus solicited by her Queen." But all she could say was, "Bless me, madame, it would be the destruction of Monsieur Sauce. I love my King; but, by our lady, I love my husband too, you must know; and he would be answerable, you see."[7]

It was by now full daylight, there were four thousand National Guardsmen and at least as many townspeople and villagers in Varennes, with more streaming in by the minute.

"To Paris! To Paris with them! Send them back! *Vive la nation!*"

The people knew, just as the King did, that General Bouillé was not far away, that the Austrians, whom the Queen had been subsidizing for years with French money, were just across the border. There must be no further delay. The royals had to be packed off to Paris before Varennes became the bloody focus of warfare.

No force was used against the royals, but Sauce became insistent. Louis ran out of excuses for delay. In desperation, one of the chamberwomen pretended to have a fit, clutching her stomach and throwing herself on the bed, weeping and imploring aid. She was ill, she needed a doctor. They could not leave her behind in such a state. But Sauce easily saw through this ploy and refused to permit any more delays.

Where was Bouillé? It was seven o'clock. Had the officer failed to reach him in Stenay? Or had Bouillé too been seized by the long arm of the Assembly?

Gradually Louis allowed his hopes to die. There would be no rescue. The escape plan had failed. He had had almost no sleep for nearly forty-eight hours, he had lost his will to fight. His children were drowsy, his wife, stricken and mute with anger. The clamoring crowd offered nothing but rebukes, they were eager to be rid of him.[8] Sorrowfully he made up his mind to go.

At seven-thirty the berlin rolled out of Varennes, back along the road to Clermont and Sainte-Ménéhould. Large numbers of National Guard escorted it, and hundreds of people surrounded it on its slow course, shouting *"Vive la nation!"* and waving their weapons. The occupants of the berlin, exhausted and defeated, were not permitted to close the shutters over the carriage windows. Their every act, their every word, was public.

Antoinette sat staring stonily ahead, her backbone rigid, her expression unreadable. She did her best to ignore the dirty faces that watched her through the windows, the dirty hands that reached in to touch her garments, the foul words flung at her from a dozen mouths. She, the daughter of an empress and the wife of a king, to be made the sport of coarse peasants! It was not possible, unthinkable. She shut her eyes and did her best to endure.

Across the Aire from Varennes, on the Stenay side, General Bouillé and his army arrived just in time to see the huge crowd and to hear the shouting and sense the excitement. They knew that the King and Queen were prisoners of the National Guard, on their way back to Paris. But Bouillé could not follow. The bridge was blocked, the only ford they knew of was too deep to cross. He had come too late. Well then, there was nothing to be done. He had to protect himself. Without hesitating Bouillé rode back the way he had come, toward the frontier and safety.

27

ALL the color had faded from Antoinette's once lovely face. Her pinched cheeks were pallid, her lips bloodless, her imperial blue eyes a grayish blue, and redrimmed with frequent weeping. Her hair was as white and lusterless as that of an old woman, and her body, once buxom and erect, had become stoop-shouldered and thin. She was aging. The constant strain she had been under for years had drained away her vitality, leaving her brittle and prematurely old.

Misfortune had wrought an "astonishing change" in her mistress, Madame Campan thought when she saw Antoinette after her return from Varennes. She suffered from insomnia, her nerves were constantly on edge, she was constantly, almost compulsively, apprehensive.

The return to Paris from Varennes had been a purgatory. The extreme heat, the choking dust of the roads, the savage voices howling and catcalling, the insults, the impudent man who spat in the King's face, above all the constant fear of death: these had preyed on the Queen's very sanity. For days the torment had continued, and when at last they reached the capital and returned to the Tuileries she discovered that her servants had been arrested, and that in her absence her apartments had been invaded and profaned by the angry Parisians.

She had only the slenderest of hope that the monarchy would endure in anything like its former status. The monarchist Mirabeau had died several months before the fateful emigration attempt. The Jacobins and the even more radical Cordeliers were gaining in strength. There were moderates in the Assembly, but they were struggling against their extremist colleagues and against the irrepressible Parisians, whose ferocity was rapidly becoming the driving force of the revolution. And the Parisians hated Antoinette passionately, and were calling for the deposition of the King.

Angered by Louis's attempt to leave the country, pinched by food shortages and the lack of employment, frightened by the falling value of the assignat, a crowd of thousands marched to the Champ de Mars on July 17 to sign a petition calling for an end to the monarchy. Violence broke out, two men thought to be agents of the government were hanged. At once Lafayette and Bailly brought in the National Guard, which opened fire. Some fifty people were killed, and many others injured. The massacre at the Champ de Mars ended Lafayette's popularity and widened the rift between the property-owning Parisians who feared anarchy in the city and the desperate, increasingly vengeful laboring classes and the very poor. The latter groups, alienated from the King, dissatisfied with the Assembly, inflamed by the radical press which seemed to articulate their darkest impulses, now boiled to avenge the men and women martyred on the Champ de Mars. Blood called for blood, they would have their turn.

But in September of 1791 it was the turn of the Assembly, which finally completed work on the constitution. Meant to enshrine the liberty the French had won for themselves, and to stand as the abiding foundation for the new France, purged of corruption and of privilege, the constitution represented in fact a political compromise and was fundamentally unsound. It retained the monarchy, shorn of its sacred quality and with the King reduced to "representative of the people," and possessing a suspensive veto—that is, he could cause the execution of any law passed by the Assembly to be delayed for five years. The National Assembly, which for all its flaws had passed the thousands of laws that created the new France, was to be dissolved and replaced by a Legislative Assembly with wide-ranging powers. To guarantee a fresh beginning, members of the National Assembly were forbidden to be elected to the Legislative Assembly—which meant that inexperienced men would fill the new legislative body.

Antoinette was contemptuous of the "monstrous constitution," and of the "collection of scoundrels, lunatics and beasts" who were to run the new government. But Louis, under duress, swore loyalty to the constitution, though afterwards he collapsed in tears.

His ceremonial oath-swearing over, he returned to the Tuileries and went into Antoinette's apartments via a private entrance. "He was pale," Madame Campan recalled, "his features were much changed. The Queen uttered an exclamation of surprise at his appearance." He looked quite ill, the bedchamber woman thought.

"All is lost!" he cried out. "Ah! Madame, and you are witness to this humiliation!"

His words were choked, he could hardly speak for the sobs that convulsed his fleshy body. He sat down heavily and dabbed at his eyes with a linen handkerchief. Antoinette "threw herself upon her knees before him," according to Madame Campan, "and pressed him in her arms." Quite stupefied, not knowing what to do, Madame Campan stayed where she was until Antoinette remembered her presence and in exasperation ordered her to leave the room.[1]

Antoinette was so offended by the constitution that, for a few hours at least, she considered escaping to Vienna. As far as she was concerned, there was no monarchy left. "These people will have no sovereigns," she said. "We shall fall before their treacherous though well-planned tactics; they are demolishing the monarchy stone by stone."[2]

Yet the constitution was celebrated in Paris with spectacles and celebrations. The Champ de Mars, so recently stained with blood, became once again a site of rejoicing when the constitution was proclaimed there to loud shouts of "*Vive la nation!*" Food shortages were forgotten as the municipality provided bread, meat and wine in huge open-air banquets, free to all. There were balloon ascensions and fairs, games and shows. The gardens of the Tuileries, so often host to furious, ranting crowds, were lit with thousands of glass lamps and turned into a fairyland by night. The palace itself, the squares, the Champs-Elysées were hung with lanterns and the Parisians, ever mercurial, surged happily through the streets, suddenly in a mood to forget their grievances and cheer the King and Queen.

But the mood of euphoria passed all too swiftly, leaving Antoinette once again feeling old, drained and overwhelmed. "Have pity on me!" she wrote to Mercy, "I assure you that it takes more courage to endure my situation than if I stood in the midst of a battle. . . . We have huge obstacles to overcome and great wars to wage."[3]

It seemed as if, at last, the powers of Europe were bestirring themselves to act, and great wars loomed. On August 27, 1791, just two months after Louis and Antoinette attempted to make their escape, Emperor Leopold and the King of Prussia, Frederick William II, joined in declaring that they regarded "the present situation of the King of France as a subject of common interest to all the sovereigns of Europe." In the joint Declaration of Pillnitz they swore to "act promptly" and "with all the force necessary" to restore Louis XVI's rights as King. To be sure, the other European sovereigns did not hasten to join their names to the declaration. Apart from King Gustavus of Sweden, the most passionate (and least practical) of Louis's champions among his brother monarchs, the other members of the royal fraternity were decidedly lukewarm. The King of Spain, though well disposed, had neither the money nor the troops to join in a counter-revolutionary invasion, and the English Prime Minister, William Pitt, was for the time being content to be merely watchful. Indeed none of the great powers had been willing to finance Louis's flight from Paris; funds had come from Fersen's personal fortune and from the tiny Order of Malta.

Still, the forces of counter-revolution were clearly swelling in size, if not in boldness. Now that Provence had joined Artois in exile (having succeeded in his escape where the King and Queen had failed), the emigré organization gained stature. The Elector of Trèves was host to the two royal brothers and their suites, allowing them to use his chateau at Schönburnlust and paying the costs of feeding and lodging their households. He also paid pensions to the exiled nonjuring priests and provided housing for the thousands of members of the bodyguard who now formed themselves into companies and prepared themselves to serve as the core of an invasion force. More emigrés joined the community every day, and though he was not prepared to fund them directly, Emperor Leopold sent Provence and his government in exile two million livres through his wife.[4] Louis also began sending his brothers funds; Artois received nearly seven hundred thousand livres from Louis between July of 1791 and February of 1792.

Antoinette was contemptuous of her brothers-in-law and their "confused and selfish" group at Coblentz. They had shown cowardice in running away from danger, she said, and they were traitors to their country. Provence in particular, she referred to as "Cain," who was doing his best to usurp his brother's birthright, exploiting Louis's danger for his own advantage. Now that the Emperor and the King of Prussia had issued their joint declaration, the emigrés were bound to become more of a problem, posturing and saber-rattling and giving the revolutionaries more cause to punish the royal family and circumscribe their movements.

They were already more closely guarded than they had ever been. "We are watched like criminals," Antoinette told the Duchesse de Polignac in a letter, "and such restraint is indeed horrible to endure." Their every move was scrutinized, they were watched even while sleeping, privacy was a thing of the past. Still Antoinette found ways to send ciphered letters to Fersen, and Leopold, and Mercy. She corresponded too with Antoine Barnave, a leader in the Assembly who had shown himself surprisingly sympathetic to the monarchy after spending time with the royal family on their return journey from Varennes.

"I have not a moment to myself, between the people I must see, the writing I must do, and the time I have to spend with my children," she confided to Fersen. Simply composing her secret letters, which were sometimes twenty or thirty pages long, and carefully ciphering them took many hours. Madame Campan wrote in her memoirs of the "great patience" the ciphering required. Both the writer and the intended recipient of the letter had to use the same book—in Antoinette's case, *Paul et Virginie*. The page and line of each letter or monosyllable were indicated according to an agreed-on code. Madame Campan helped Antoinette compose the cipher, and often made a copy of it, though she was not privy to its meaning.[5]

Then there was the difficulty of finding ways to smuggle the letters out of the Tuileries, sometimes in servants' pockets, sometimes inside articles of clothing or other unlikely places. Trustworthy couriers were hard to find; those that could be trusted were not always clever enough to avoid being caught by the police or committees of search.

Most of the letters Antoinette composed were appeals for military aid, appeals that became more urgent with every passing month. To Fersen, who was visiting the various European courts in an effort to impress upon the sovereigns the desperate plight of the French King and Queen, Antoinette wrote personal messages, addressing him as "most beloved and most loving of men," telling him that she loved him and that she could not live without writing to him, dangerous though this was. She urged him not to return to France for any reason, no matter what happened to her. His complicity in the escape attempt was known, and if he tried to cross the border into France he would be putting himself at the mercy of the revolutionary government. Much as she must have wanted to see him, she could not let him risk arrest.

"The Queen wrote almost all day and spent a part of the night in reading," according to Madame Campan. Beyond pleading with her brother Leopold, corresponding with agents abroad and trying to keep Provence and Artois from acting rashly, she received information from the various secret committees operating on behalf of the monarchy in Paris, groups that were the eyes and ears of the court keeping track of what the political factions in the Assembly were planning. Though Antoinette put no faith in these spies and intriguers, Louis employed more and more of them, using the funds the Assembly voted him to finance "secret measures" and to pay the informers hired by De Laporte, Intendant of the Civil List. If his own safety and that of his family could be bought, Louis intended to spare no expense to buy it, and began bribing radical deputies to the Legislative Assembly in hopes of improving his situation.[6]

All this made Antoinette profoundly weary. To Fersen she wrote of "the prodigious mental fatigue which afflicts me ceaselessly." Sorrow haunted her, and during the long sleepless nights she relived the unsuccessful journey that had ended at Varennes and tried to decide whom to blame for what had gone wrong. They had come so close to succeeding, after all. Others with better luck had followed their route and crossed the frontier safely. Her own hairdresser, Léonard, had ridden through Varennes only hours ahead of the royal berlin, carrying Antoinette's priceless jewels. No one had stopped him. Provence and his wife, taking only a slightly altered route, had been recognized at the last post before the border. But the man who recognized them was a monarchist; he had not only kept their secret but had driven them on to the frontier himself to ensure that they would not be apprehended.

If only the Duc de Choiseul had stayed longer at Pont-Sommevel, if only he had not sent word to the other detachments to leave their posts, if only one of the hussar officers at Varennes had ignored Louis's squeamishness about avoiding bloodshed and ordered his men to cut a path through the crowd. . . . If only they had taken along, as the Chevalier de Coigny had suggested, a retired post officer who knew the back roads. Time and again she relived the moment when, just outside of Varennes, the stranger had tried to warn them of the danger ahead. They had not understood him at the time, but afterwards, thinking back, both Louis and Antoinette realized that his words had been "You are known" or "You are discovered."[7]

Tormented by insomnia at night, harried during her waking hours, Antoinette had another fear to contend with. The pastrycook at the Tuileries was known to be "a furious Jacobin" who had been overheard to say "it would be a good thing for France if the King's days were shortened." The kitchen officials, who were fortunately devoted to Louis, tried to keep a close eye on him but could not be absolutely sure he would not try to poison the King's food. To be safe, Louis, Antoinette and Elisabeth, who ate together, touched nothing from the kitchen other than plain roasted meat—no breaded dishes, no sweets, no meat pies. A trusted servant bought bread and wine from shops and smuggled them into the palace, where Madame Campan locked them in a cupboard in the King's apartments. Because Louis refused to give up pastry altogether, the bedchamber woman was sent out to buy cakes and pies and pounded sugar from tradesmen, always being careful to disguise her errand and to buy from different suppliers each time.[8] The designs of the Jacobin pastrycook were thwarted. After three or four months of these precautions, the King and Queen heard from Laporte's spies that they need not fear poison any longer, for the revolutionaries had changed their strategy. There was no need to kill the ruler when they intended to abolish the throne.

Another winter had come, Paris shivered under severe frosts and the Queen's once lovely complexion withered in the cold, dry air. A joyless New Year's Day followed a joyless Christmas, and the news from Vienna and Brussels and Coblentz was bleak. The Legislative Assembly was proceeding aggressively to punish the emigrés by confiscating their property and to harass nonjuring priests by depriving them of their pensions. The King was no longer to be called "Majesty" or "Sire," and no one was to show him any of the traditional marks of honor, such as remaining standing in his presence or uncovering their heads. Louis, inert and withdrawn, nursed his wounds and read his journals and his library of works about Charles I, muttering that he was "abandoned by everyone."

Early one evening in mid-February of 1792 a tall, spare stranger with a large dog was let into the palace by a private entrance. It was Fersen, wearing a disguise and carrying important letters from the Swedish King. He had been fortunate to pass the frontier into France without incident, using false papers placing him under the protection of the Queen of Portugal. Luck remained with him; the guards were not only cooperative but polite, and did not guess that they were admitting the envoy of a foreign enemy. King Gustavus was doing a great deal for the beleaguered Louis and Antoinette. A few months earlier he had tried to launch an invasion of France via the Normandy coast, and was currently hoping to facilitate the escape of the royal family from Paris, while not abandoning hope that a second invasion plan for Normandy might still succeed. Fersen's mission was to persuade Louis—Antoinette, he knew, would be more than willing—to cooperate in their rescue.

Fersen made his way to Antoinette's apartments by the familiar route he had taken many times, fearing detection by the guardsmen but managing to avoid suspicion on account of his disguise and his dog. He was forewarned of the Queen's probable state of mind. Only days earlier she had had a secret meeting with the envoy of Catherine the Great, Simolin, and Simolin had told Fersen how she felt about the question of leaving Paris. It was the King and her son who needed rescuing, she had told the Russian envoy, she herself was not important. Her condition was so wretched, her anxiety so great that she had all but ceased to care about preserving herself. With tears in his eyes Simolin had recounted Antoinette's words. "I fear nothing," she had told him with a ferocious pride, "and I would rather run all possible dangers than live any longer in my present state of degradation and unhappiness."9

Fersen knew that he could count on Antoinette's courage, but he cannot have been prepared for the sight that met his eyes when he entered her apartments. There she was, a thin, tired, worn out woman who looked closer to sixty than to thirty-six. She was tense and pale, quite devastated by grief and overwork. No account survives of what they said to each other, but Fersen must have given her King Gustavus's letters, and urged her, with all the eloquence at his command, to insist that Louis avail himself of what might be their last opportunity for rescue. They talked for hours. Louis did not interrupt them. Fersen spent the night in her rooms.

The next day Louis informed the Count that he had made up his mind to stay on at the palace. He was after all under heavy guard, he did not like Gustavus's advice that he should escape alone, with Antoinette and the children remaining behind, and besides, he had given his word not to attempt to leave. ("The truth is," Fersen wrote in his diary afterwards, "he has scruples, having so often promised to remain—he is an honest man.") Once the allied armies began their invasion, which he counted on, he would agree to put himself into the hands of a party of smugglers who were expert at moving secretly, traveling with them through the forests north of Paris to where a detachment of troops would be waiting. Such was the extent of his planning. And he was deluded into thinking that, when the counter-revolutionary armies arrived, the revolutionaries would not dare to harm him as they would need him as a live hostage to save themselves from annihilation.

Louis talked to Fersen frankly, a sad figure in his old-fashioned wig and court dress, the red sash of the Order of Saint-Louis across his chest.

"Ah, ça! here we are alone and we can speak," he said. "I know that I am taxed with weakness and irresolution, but no one was ever in my position. I know that I missed the right moment; it was July 14 [1790]; I ought to have gone then, and wished it. But what could I do when Monsieur [Provence] himself begged me not to go, and Maréchal de Broglie who commanded said: 'Yes, we can go to Metz, but what shall we do when we get there?'"

Louis confessed that he had "lost the moment," and that since then he had never been able to find it again. He told Fersen his own view of what had happened on the disastrous escape attempt the previous year, and admitted that he knew nothing could be done to save the monarchy or unseat the revolutionaries except by force. But he now believed that he could never recover his full authority, no matter what happened. He would have to continue to cooperate with the Assembly, to use his veto power when he thought it necessary, and to wait for the other European monarchs to gather their forces.

Antoinette, who was present at this tête-à-tête, told Fersen that "there was no remedy but that of foreign troops, without them all was lost." Her efforts to cultivate allies among the deputies, the bribes the court had paid, their secret intrigues were leading nowhere. The deputies could not be trusted, and "all the ministers are traitors who betray the King."[10]

After several hours Fersen left the palace to make arrangements for his return journey. It was dark, he was not intercepted, and met his traveling companion who told him that a light carriage was ready and waiting. Returning to the Tuileries with the protection of a hussar officer he supped with the King and Queen and then said his good-byes. He saw that Louis was resolute in his determination to stay in Paris, and that Antoinette, who was just then occupied with a "detestable" letter from several of the Assembly deputies, would not be able to force him to leave. Both of them were enmeshed in futile intrigues and negotiations, they were sinking deeper and deeper into a dangerous quagmire, and the more they struggled, the more surely they were lost. Putting on his disguise and whistling to his dog, Fersen left the Tuileries at midnight by the main gate, convinced that his beloved friends were beyond help.

28

IN the middle of March 1792, some members came to a meeting of the Jacobin Club wearing red caps of an unusual kind. They were knitted woolen stocking caps, worn down low over the ears and coming to a point at the back of the head. The rest of the membership broke into applause at the sight of these caps, and at the next club meeting the president, secretaries and all the speakers wore similar ones, as did more than three hundred of the members. The next day red bonnets were to be found throughout Paris, in the faubourgs, along the boulevards, in the public squares and gardens, at the Palais Royal and the theater. In no time at all the red cap had become "the headgear of all French patriots," as obligatory as the tricolor cockade and more pervasive.

The red cap was the appropriate finishing touch in what was coming to be the revolutionary costume: loose-fitting trousers—in contrast to the tight breeches of the aristocrats—and a short jacket, wooden shoes, suspenders, perhaps a red sash at the waist, short, unpowdered hair—in contrast to the powdered wig of the privileged classes—and the tricolor cockade and red cap. Beards were frowned upon, the thing to have was a long, thick mustache that gave the face a fearsome appearance. Soldiers had always favored luxuriant mustaches, now civilians adopted them and in the countryside the phrase "the mustache men" (*hommes à moustache*) became synonymous with "the radical bandits from Paris."

The fad for red caps appeared just as Paris received one of the worst economic shocks to date. The assignats, which since the beginning of the year had been losing value at the rate of ten percent a month, reached a new low and as a result food became so scarce that old rumors of court plots to starve the people were revived. Food riots now became as commonplace and violent as political protests; Parisians were disillusioned and enraged to realize that the new constitution had not brought prosperity but its opposite. Their rage demanded new objects. It was not enough to hate and vilify the King and Queen, the privileged classes and the exploiters: now the public wrath was directed at the "enemies of the revolution."

The food shortages, the fiscal crisis, the divisions in the Assembly, the general state of disharmony and wretchedness all were perceived by the more vocal and aroused part of the populace as having a single sinister cause. The revolution was being betrayed. The proof of this betrayal was evident on all sides, but especially in the presence of Austrian troops just across the frontier. Who were the traitors? The Queen, primarily, and the King who had shown his deceitfulness in trying to escape, and the emigrés with their mock court at Coblentz and their conspiracies. The aristocrats, the monarchists, even the moderate deputies in the Legislative Assembly—all were traitors, to the extent that they were not actively furthering the progress of liberty. And the progress of liberty, it seemed to the furious Parisians, demanded war.

War was cathartic, it would purge France of its anti-revolutionary elements. War would regenerate the floundering revolution, focus it and bring it fresh glory. Never mind those contrary voices insisting that the armies of France were not prepared to fight, that they lacked officers and supplies, that the foreign regiments would refuse combat and that even the generals were reluctant to go into battle without more men, materiél and money. The traitors must be overthrown, the Austrian menace annihilated once and for all.

The Prussians, with their superb, some said invincible, army now joined the Austrians when the two countries became allied early in February 1792. Then on March 1 the prevaricating Emperor Leopold died and was succeeded by his bellicose son Francis II. The allied armies were soon on the move and the reigning political faction in the Assembly, the Girondins—so named because many of its members came from the department of the Gironde, in the Bordeaux region—pushed aggressively for war.

At the end of March France sent Emperor Francis a formal warning that unless Austria backed down from her combative stance war would be declared. Three weeks later Louis was placed in the ironic position of signing a decree committing his country to fight against the very forces he hoped would rescue him.

Meanwhile the red caps were all over Paris, and those who wore them were forming themselves into spontaneously organized gangs and assaulting the "enemies of the revolution." Priests, gentlemen, anyone who did not dress like a revolutionary sansculotte (a breechless, or trousered, citizen) was liable to be set upon, beaten and forced to put on a red cap. If the victim had the impudence to resist, or to spit on the red cap in protest, he was stripped naked and cudgeled with a thick hawthorn branch. The National Guard could not keep order, there were too many violent outbreaks, too many murders and robberies, especially in the faubourgs St.-Antoine or St.-Marcel, where middle-class people feared to go after dark. With macabre joy the Parisians danced in the streets when they heard that Emperor Leopold was dead, and celebrated wildly whenever one of their number appeared with a bloody head stuck to a pike. Cheering, dancing, singing the "Ça ira," they paraded in the Tuileries gardens shouting "Death to the King! Kill the Queen! Tremble, tyrants! We are the sansculottes!!"

They crowded into the Place de Grève on April 25 to watch an execution carried out by a new device, the invention of the Parisian physician and deputy Joseph-Ignace Guillotin. Dr. Guillotin's machine, a sort of giant chopping block with a heavy sharp blade that fell when released severing the victim's head, was intended to introduce social equality to the arena of punishment. In the past, criminals had been put to death in different ways, determined by their status: noblemen were granted the privilege of beheading—the quickest and most honorable method—while lesser men were hanged or tortured to death, their arms and legs broken and their pain-racked bodies fastened to a wheel. Now all men would die as formerly only nobles had, their heads "separated from their bodies in less time than it takes to wink."

Dr. Guillotin's device was celebrated in the popular press as an "ingenious and gentle" machine that would spare criminals great pain by dispatching them in a "prompt and expeditious" fashion. "The grandeur and elegance of the spectacle will attract many more people to the place of execution," announced *L'ami du peuple*. "More people will be impressed, and the rule of law will be more greatly respected."[1] The sight of the "blade of eternity" would embolden the criminal to make a more heroic end, and to keep his dignity. Dr. Guillotin was to be congratulated for conferring a boon on mankind, which in gratitude would name the new machine after its inventor, giving it the "sweet and charming". name of "Guillotine."[2]

The first human trial of the guillotine in April of 1792 was something of an experiment, which gave the many spectators an added frisson. The machine had been used on sheep and calves, and tested on human corpses brought from the charity hospitals. But no one could be certain that it would work as efficiently on a live criminal, and the wretched forger scheduled to be executed that day must have suffered the added torment of doubting the efficiency of the savage blade. Scientists speculated about whether the head might live on after it was separated from the trunk, whether the mind might go on thinking, the eyes seeing, the tongue wagging. But the forger's execution proved to be effortless and swift, and made a very good show, and the observers went off afterwards satisfied that they had witnessed a new and entirely satisfactory form of public vengeance.

The initial weeks of the war were going very badly. Day after day news came from the Austrian Netherlands of French soldiers retreating in the face of the enemy, giving up and deserting, showing insubordination and refusing discipline. The spirit of liberty, so cherished in revolutionary Paris and so carefully nurtured over the past three years, proved to be a destructive force in a revolutionary army. Soldiers took votes on whether or not to obey their officers, mutinied at will, and did not hesitate to eliminate "tyrant" officers when they tried to enforce their authority.

The army under General Dillon marched against Tournai, only to be turned back under heavy fire. The French fled in terror, claiming they had been betrayed and blaming Dillon. They mobbed him and tore him to pieces. The Duc de Biron's men too were in retreat. Lafayette knew better than to launch his troops against the Austrians; the best he could do, given his crippled, ill-equipped forces, was to take up a defensive position and wait for the enemy's assault. General Rochambeau resigned, General Luckner hung back and waited to see what would happen.

By the first week of May all hope of a French victory was gone. The generals urged the government to make peace. Two-thirds of the officers had emigrated; now many of the remaining ones were deserting their men and, with the men rebelling or melting away in large numbers, the entire army was crumbling. And the Austrians were advancing and would soon be on French soil.

In Paris wild fears and even wild rumors overrode all reason. People told one another that hordes of deserters would soon be swarming into the city, taking by force what little food there was and mowing down the citizenry. Priests who had refused to take the oath of loyalty were thought to be agents of the enemy, and were threatened with deportation to Guiana by à law of the Assembly. The King's household guard was sent away from the palace, and twenty thousand national guardsmen were brought from the provinces to the capital for protection. Louis used his veto power to oppose this transfer of guards—and was accused of conspiring with the enemy. Red-capped men tramped along the narrow alleyways in the heart of Paris, shouting that the Austrians were coming, calling people to arms to defend the revolution, breaking limbs and heads and spreading mayhem. Ordinary life was suspended, work stopped for no workman could afford the crazily inflated prices of bread and wine, vegetables and wood. After three years of excitement and uproar, it looked as though the city was about to be engulfed by a foreign army, its liberties crushed forever.

Such a catastrophe had to be the result of a massive and sustained betrayal, centered at the Tuileries. The Tuileries and its occupants had to be destroyed, before they completed the destruction of France.

On June 20, the anger of the Parisians boiled over and the ever-present crowd in the Tuileries gardens broke into the palace through an unlocked gate. The palace guards quickly gave way before the thousands of rioters, armed in the fashion which by now had become traditional with pikes, axes, clubs and knives. They carried banners reading "Tremble, tyrants, the people are armed!" and "Union of the Faubourgs St.-Antoine and St.-Marcel, we are the sansculottes!"

"The Austrian! The Austrian! Where is she? Her head! Her head!"

"Where is the fat pig?"

Doors were smashed in, locks broken, delicate furniture over-turned and trampled. The servants fled in panic before the onrushing swarm of sansculottes, who dragged a cannon with them into the palace and rampaged from room to room, shouting and swearing and demanding the hearts and entrails of the King and Queen.

More and more people swelled the throng of marauders, pour-ing in from all parts of the city—and still no force of guardsmen appeared to resist them. The Mayor, Jerome Pétion, did nothing. When the angry torrent reached the royal apartments the War Minister shouted, "Twenty grenadiers to protect His Majesty!"

"From all sides came the clatter of arms," wrote Madame de Tourzel, who was present when the Palace was stormed, "and the most outrageous remarks against the King." The crowd burst into the antechamber where Louis was. Elisabeth was with him, but Antoinette, who had tried to reach him, had been "dragged almost by force" to the dauphin's rooms by her frightened servants, who knew the danger she ran. Louis confronted the invading Parisians with courage, facing them down, answering their shouts of "Down with the veto! Ratify the decrees! Long live the nation!" with mild assurances that he too supported the nation and the constitution, and that he had sworn to uphold both.

"A man who has nothing with which to reproach himself knows neither fear nor dread," he said calmly, if rather senten-tiously, and he seized the hand of a man standing near him and put it against his embroidered waistcoat, over his heart. "See if it beats more quickly," he told the man.

But his words were drowned out by the continual shouting.

"Down with the veto! Ratify the decrees! Long live the na-tion!"

In exasperation Louis picked up a little bell and rang it in an effort to get attention. Several nobles, standing near him, waved their ivory sticks in the air and—"very politely" one observer thought—pleaded with the invaders to respect the law.

It was a curious scene, with hatchet-waving fishwives and craftsmen from the faubourgs arguing with their monarch. They accused him of lying to them, of deceiving them. "You have cheated us!" they screamed when he tried to protest. "Knots of rebels hustled the King," Madame de Tourzel remembered afterwards. "One wretch, armed with a pike, and with his eyes full of rage, advanced, making a sinister movement." Yet he did not strike the King, something held him back. A potentially murderous confrontation became a shouting match. The King accepted a bottle of wine from a butcher and drank the nation's health. He accepted a red cap from someone and put it on—with difficulty, because it was too small—and continued to wear it as the day went on. He listened, or appeared to listen, to the personal advice offered him by individual Parisians.

"Sire," one of them told the King, "your enemies are not in Paris, they are at Coblentz and it is time you realized that however much you would like to go and join them. The people, on the other hand, only want to see you happily going along with the constitution, and if you did this in good faith they would love you even more because, I repeat, they want to love you."

Louis listened to the man "open-mouthed, gaping at him wide-eyed," then told him that he would always remain faithful to the constitution.

"You are still deceiving us, Sire," the man replied, "but you had better watch out."[3]

All this time Antoinette had been restrained by her servants in her son's rooms, not knowing whether her husband was alive or dead. She held the little boy in her arms, weeping, "almost suffocated with her sobs." Then a message came from Elisabeth, telling Antoinette that Louis had not been killed, "that he was displaying the greatest courage," and that she would only do harm if she were with them. Meanwhile more Parisians broke into the outer room of the dauphin's suite and Antoinette hurried into the King's bedroom.

A delegation from the Assembly arrived at the palace to assess the situation, and tried to address the crowd, which ignored them. The deputies ranged themselves around Louis, and listened while one young man harangued him for nearly an hour, making what Madame de Tourzel called "absurd requests."

"This is neither the moment to make nor to grant such requests," the King told his subject. "Address yourself to the magistrates, the mouthpieces of the law; they will answer you."

After three hours of this Pétion finally arrived, but instead of bringing an armed force with him to put down the lawlessness he announced that all was well, the King had not been harmed and that his person had been respected. Then he went away again, leaving the King and Queen to the mercy of their tormentors.

One of the dauphin's footmen rushed breathlessly in to warn Antoinette that the outer hall was full of rioters who were smashing in all the doors and were just behind him. She hurried into the royal council chamber, where she faced the crowd, holding both her children close to her, pretending to ignore the torrent of catcalls and jeers and threats that erupted.

Protected by a ring of faithful grenadiers from the Filles Saint Thomas battalion, "who constantly opposed an impenetrable wall to the bellowing crowd," she sat down behind a table with her children on her right and left, and several Assembly deputies behind her. Santerre, the brewer from the Faubourg St.-Antoine who was one of the "Bastille men" and who had helped to organize the current demonstration, told the grenadiers to stand aside so that he might speak to the Queen.

"You are led astray, you are mistaken, madam," he told her. "The people love you and the King better than you think. Fear nothing."

"I am neither led astray nor mistaken," Antoinette replied with dignity. "And I know that I have nothing to fear in the midst of the National Guard." As she spoke she pointed to the soldiers.

For two hours the Queen was on display, with the brewer hustling demonstrators in and out of the room in shifts. Each group had the opportunity to see Antoinette and shout at her. A boy walked in carrying a bleeding calf's head on a pike. "Heart of the aristocrats" was written on an accompanying banner. Armed women shook their weapons at the Queen, she was called every obscene name in the Parisian vocabulary. She sat still, holding her children tightly, her face calm and her poise intact. Her evident fragility surprised some in the crowd, but even Madame de Tourzel did not hear any stray shouts of "Long live the Queen" amid the abuse. Santerre continued to usher people in and out of the council chamber, until at last the crowd dispersed and straggled slowly out of the palace, leaving a trail of destruction in its wake. A number of Assembly deputies lingered until the early hours of the morning, and Antoinette, letting out her anger at last, insisted on taking them through her son's rooms and showing them the hacked and splintered doors, the broken locks and shattered panels. There was evidence of the havoc everywhere, in the salons and on the staircases, even on the roof, and the Queen insisted that a full report of the damage be made.[4]

In the days following the assault on the palace the royal family braced for another onslaught by the Parisians. They knew now that they were undefended, there was no one, no force, they could look to to protect them. Somewhat to their surprise, the allied troops on France's northern border were slow to press their advantage. But they would invade eventually, and when they did Louis and Antoinette would face their greatest danger to date. The Assembly kept the scattered, demoralized revolutionary army in the field by printing three hundred millions more in assignats and raising fresh battalions of volunteers. And at the palace, where all was confusion and where Louis had retreated into morose silence, ministries changed every few weeks—sometimes every few days—and there was no stability.

"Our position is becoming ever more critical," Antoinette wrote to Mercy in Brussels early in July. "On one side there is nothing but violence and fury, on the other, weakness and inertia. We cannot count on either the National Guard or the army, we do not know whether we ought to stay in Paris or go elsewhere." As ever, the Queen was the one forced to make the crucial decision. Mercy advised her to take her family to Compiègne, then on to Amiens or Abbéville where stalwart monarchists stood ready to defend the sovereign.[5] The Landgravine of Hesse-Darmstadt offered to smuggle Antoinette out of Paris, but she refused to leave Louis and the children.

Every day ministers, diplomats, well-wishers begged the King and Queen to put themselves out of danger, and offered to make the arrangements, to ensure that loyal troops would be waiting to escort them to safety. Louis's own plan, to let himself be taken out of the capital through the forest by a band of smugglers, was still possible. Lafayette conspired to take over the government by force and warned the King that he must remove himself from harm's way at once. But Louis, though at times he vacillated and at least once made up his mind to attempt another escape, always returned to the same opinion in the end: he would stay in Paris, he had given his word, he would wait to be rescued by the Austrians and Prussians when at last they came.[6]

Antoinette was convinced that the radicals were planning to assassinate Louis. They were only waiting for the right moment.

The Cordeliers Club boasted that among its members was a secret society of tyrannicides who had sworn to kill everyone who attacked French liberty—and the King was the worst offender.[7] "The band of assassins is growing incessantly," the Queen told Fersen, "I still live, but it is a miracle that I do. They no longer want me—they want to kill my husband."[8] One frightened courtier brought Madame de Tourzel three stiff tunics made of twelve folds of taffeta, "impenetrable by bullet or dagger," which he had made for the King and Queen and the dauphin. The governess took the three cuirasses to Antoinette, who immediately tried hers on.

"Strike me," she ordered Madame de Tourzel, who had taken up a knife to test the garments, "and see if it penetrates." The idea horrified the governess, who said that she would do no such thing. Antoinette then took off the tunic and Madame de Tourzel put it on and struck it with the knife. It appeared to be impenetrable. Antoinette went to Louis and they agreed to wear the cuirasses "at the slightest symptom of danger."[9]

"Believe that our courage never deserts us," she wrote in cipher to Fersen. In fact it was not their courage but their endurance, their power to go on day after day in ever increasing danger, that was being tested. Antoinette worried once again about poison in their food, about the murderous bands that roved the outskirts of the Tuileries, shouting "Death to the King! Kill the Queen!" She shivered with fear when the orchestra in the royal chapel played "Ça ira" instead of religious anthems and when the very guardsmen outside her apartments shouted "Down with the veto!" when the King passed by.

On July 11, the Assembly, fearing imminent invasion and no longer willing to entrust the national defense to the King and his ministers, declared that a special state of danger to the country existed, and that any and all measures could be taken to save it. Two tense weeks later, the Duke of Brunswick, commander of the allied forces of Austria and Prussia, somewhat reluctantly lent his name to a threatening manifesto declaring the war aims of the allied army. Their purpose, the manifesto said, was to end the anarchy in France, to defend the monarchy and the Church, and to restore Louis to liberty and to the full exercise of his rightful authority. "If the Palace of the Tuileries is assaulted or invaded," the manifesto went on, "if the least violence, the least insult is directed at their Majesties the King and Queen . . . an exemplary and memorable vengeance will follow and the city of Paris will undergo a military execution."

The Austrians were on the march at last, and were sweeping through the country south of Lille. The Assembly had sent all the regular troops away from Paris—though the Swiss Guard moved in to camp in the courtyard of the Tuileries—and was attempting to raise fifty thousand more volunteers. Rumors flew that England was about to join the invasion. Red caps now crowned every head, every Parisian wore the tricolor cockade. A new group of sansculottes from Marseilles, some six hundred strong, swept into Paris and began provoking drunken riots during which several national guardsmen were killed. The men from Marseilles drowned out the "Ça ira" with a song of their own, a song full of élan and gore and with a thrilling chorus:

> "To arms, citizens!
> Form your battalions!
> March on, march on
> Let our fields be soaked in their impure blood!"

Soon everyone was singing the new "Marseillaise" and carrying weapons. Paris itself was becoming a battlefield, armed against the enemies both within and outside the gates. The forty-eight sections, or political wards, of the city were on the alert, ready to direct the assault. In the faubourgs, the cannon were loaded, the patriots in arms. On August 3, the sections voted to dethrone the King; if the Assembly had not deposed him within a week, they declared, the people would rise and carry out the task themselves, before the Austrians arrived to destroy the city and slaughter its inhabitants.

"Hurry, if you can, to bring us the help you promised us for our deliverance," Antoinette wrote in desperation to Fersen. She could not sleep, both she and Louis were up all night, "expecting to be murdered." Her distress and anguish were indescribable. "Everyone is awaiting the catastrophe soon to come," she told Fersen. Everyone knew that Paris, at its deadliest and most revengeful, was about to explode.

29

THE bells tolled solemnly, mournfully, ceaselessly. All the sections of the capital were on the march, the faubourgs under the brewer Santerre, the Left Bank, joined by the men of Marseilles and another contingent of guards from Brest. People ran frantically through the streets, a mixture of elation and fear on their faces. "Fly to arms! Fly to arms!" was the universal cry. It was a hot night, the night of August 9, and doors and windows were flung wide to the night air. The word had spread that all the houses were to be illuminated, and in street after street yellow light glowed from lanterns and torches and spilled out onto the dusty pavingstones.

Earlier that day the Legislative Assembly had once again rejected a petition from the provincial National Guard—the Federates—calling for the deposition of the King and election of a national convention. The Jacobins, together with other activists in the Paris sections, had long been planning to act on their own authority. Now representatives of the sections met at the Hôtel de Ville to take the government of France into their own hands. While the bells rang and the hastily assembled forces mustered, Paris reformed itself into an insurrectionary commune, and ordered the old municipal council dissolved. The Commander-in-Chief of the National Guard, the Marquis de Mandat, who had been entrusted by Mayor Pétion with protecting the Tuileries, was deposed and murdered, and replaced by Santerre. Pétion himself was replaced and put in detention.

Before dawn on the morning of August 10, the feast of Saint

Lawrence the Martyr, the men and women of the faubourgs began their march on the palace, thousands strong.

Inside the palace, no one could sleep. Informants had told the royal family that another popular assault was planned for the day of the tenth, and a plan of defense was in place. But apart from the Swiss Guard in the courtyard, a splendid body of nine hundred or so troops who were drawn up to form a cordon, and the eccentric noblemen who had enrolled as "Knights of the Dagger," there were no reliable defenders, and the courtiers knew it.

Madame Campan was at her post in the Queen's apartments, and wrote afterwards of everything she saw and did. Antoinette and Elisabeth, she recalled, did not undress or go to bed but lay down to rest on a sofa in a little room whose windows overlooked the courtyard. Antoinette was, as always, worried. Louis had refused to put on his padded vest, even though the danger was greater than ever, because he thought it cowardly to wear such protection when the troops had none. The two women could not sleep, and instead sat together on the sofa, "conversing mournfully upon their situation." Suddenly a musket discharged in the courtyard. At this they decided to join Louis in his rooms, and stayed there several hours.

Shortly before dawn Antoinette told Madame Campan that the Guard commander Mandat had been killed, and replaced by the revolutionary Santerre. Later, news arrived of the formation of the insurrectionary commune. Louis, unusually quiet and haggard, decided to review the National Guard troops, though he must have done so with a sinking heart. Badly dressed in a suit of violet velvet, waddling clumsily and all but tripping over his sword, his sparsely powdered hair sadly in need of brushing, Louis did his best to look kingly as he led his family past the ranks of guardsmen. A few men called out *"Vive le Roi!"* but Madame Campan, watching the review from a window, saw some of the gunners leave their posts, go up to Louis, and "thrust their fists in his face, insulting him in the most brutal language." Others booed him, and there were cries of "Fat pig!" The King, she saw, was as pale as a corpse, and after the review ended Antoinette confided to her that "all was lost, the King had shown no energy, and this sort of review had done more harm than good."

Madame Campan and her companions took refuge in the billiard room, standing on some high benches. Several hundred courtiers were there, all armed only with ceremonial swords and pistols. A few carried nothing but fire-tongs, which led to some joking despite the grim situation. Meanwhile the bands of fighters from the faubourgs were coming into view, "the sanguinary Marseillais at their head," and pointing their cannon at the palace. The gunners of the National Guard at once abandoned and unloaded their guns, and joined the assailants. Louis sent a message to the Assembly in the nearby Manège, to ask for whatever protection the deputies could provide. But the request was ignored. The deputies, knowing that their own authority had been swept away by the pre-dawn events at the Hôtel de Ville, did not bestir themselves to try to help the court.

Meanwhile an enormous crowd surrounded the Tuileries and the entire neighborhood, shouting and chanting, and the cannon from the faubourgs began to fire on the palace. Each barrage brought cheers and huzzas from the crowd, and the clanging bells and drumrolls all but deafened the palace defenders and made communication difficult.

A departmental official named Roederer, unwilling to stand by and let the royal family be mobbed, persuaded the assailants to let him have half an hour to talk with the King. Louis received Roederer in his bedchamber, with Antoinette by his side. Briefly Roederer explained that the guard could not be relied on, that the palace was all but defenseless. The only hope of safety lay in the Manège itself, with the Assembly. The royal family had no choice but to go there immediately.

Louis, sad-eyed and passive, did not protest. Antoinette did, and vigorously. The troops must be made to fight, she said. They must not give in. But Roederer, knowing how to appeal to her and where she was most vulnerable, told her that in advising resistance she was making herself responsible for the deaths of Louis and her children, not to mention all the courtiers and servants in the palace. Reluctantly she gave in and agreed to go to the Manège.

"Come, gentlemen," Louis said to his ministers, "there is nothing more to be done here."

Even as he spoke the palace defense was crumbling. Entire regiments of National Guards joined the crowd from the faubourgs. In the end only some six hundred loyal guardsmen were left, plus the Swiss Guard, "drawn up like real walls," Madame Campan thought, and the Knights of the Dagger.

Antoinette, mortified and defeated, could not imagine taking refuge in the Assembly chamber as anything other than a tactical retreat. "Wait in my apartments," she told the bedchamber woman as she left. "I will come to you, or I will send for you, and go I know not where."

Taking with her Madame de Tourzel and the Princesse de Lamballe—who had come back from Brussels some months earlier to be with her kinswoman and old friend—Antoinette went with Louis, Elisabeth and the children through the corridors and chambers to the terrace of the Feuillants leading to the Manège. The day was hot and humid, her face and neck were blotched with red. As she passed between lines of loyal guardsmen the crowd pressed in with such force that the soldiers could hardly restrain them. Hands reached out to snatch at her dress, unwashed bodies thrust close to her. When at last the group arrived in the Assembly hall, the Queen found that her watch and her purse were missing. She had been terrified when a giant of a man, "of great height and atrocious appearance," stepped out of the milling, shouting crowd and snatched her son as he walked along beside her, holding her hand. The man swung the little boy up into his arms. Antoinette screamed and looked as if she were about to faint.

"Don't be frightened," the huge Parisian told her. "I will not harm him." In fact he was protecting the dauphin by holding him above the crowd, out of reach. At the door of the Assembly chamber he lowered the boy and gave him back to his mother.

Roederer's half-hour had elapsed, and the Parisians resumed firing on the palace. The defenders, not realizing that the royal family had fled, resisted when some of the Marseillais attacked the Swiss. The entire battalion then fired into the mass of Parisians who were armed only with pikes and axes and knives. Hundreds fell dead and wounded, and the courtyard was briefly deserted. Then, however, an order arrived from the King: the Swiss were not to fire on the attackers. Louis did not want to spill French blood.

But it was too late. The comrades of the fallen Parisians, maddened with rage, rushed in to engulf the Swiss who were forced to fall back inside the palace. Hatchets broke down the doors, strong hands clawed at the windows. The Swiss held their ground, loyal to the King's order yet refusing to desert their post. "The populace rushed from all quarters into the interior of the palace,"

Madame Campan wrote, "almost all the Swiss were massacred." The assailants stabbed and clubbed them to death, cutting off their heads and carrying them as trophies, tearing off pieces of their uniforms to keep as souvenirs.

Shouting "Treason! treason!" the invaders routed out the occupants of the palace and slaughtered them, chasing them from room to room like merciless hounds harrying fleeing rabbits. Nobles were stabbed and their bodies were flung through the windows. The Knights of the Dagger, some of them men in their seventies, were mown aside and beaten to death. Faithful servants died where they stood, attempting to defend their masters; many in Antoinette's household died, believing they were protecting her from the onrushing crowd of murderers. "It seemed as if the people were struck with a sort of madness," wrote a Scotsman who was witness to the events of August 10. "It was impossible to describe all the acts of wanton horror."[1] Bodies were piling up in the courtyard, on the stairs, clogging the corridors. Those who could escape, taking refuge in secret passageways or hiding under the eaves, were the lucky ones. Many who jumped out of windows and tried to run away through the gardens were cut down in mid-flight, until the greenery ran red with blood.

So sudden and so brutal was the firestorm of slaughter that even the most dedicated Jacobins among the palace servants were killed. Spies, informers, revolutionaries were swept away along with page boys and aged laundry women, cooks and grooms and seamstresses. Furniture was broken and cushions ripped, tapestries hacked to pieces and paintings slashed.

Amid the maelstrom Madame Campan and several other women of the Queen's household cowered in the Queen's salon, waiting to die, when a band of Parisians burst in. Then a man in the long beard came up and put himself between the women and the butchers. "Spare the women!" he shouted. "Don't disgrace the nation!" The Parisians backed off. In the meantime Madame Campan, worried about her sister, went to look for her in another room where she thought she might be hiding. Several other servants of the Queen were there, among them a man "of great height and a perfectly martial physiognomy" who confessed to the bedchamber woman that he was "dying of fear." Footfalls were heard on the stairs outside, then a number of Parisians rushed in and began stabbing and decapitating everyone in the room, though the women threw themselves down on the floor and begged for mercy. Madame Campan ran towards the staircase, but as she reached it she "felt a horrid hand" thrust down her back and clutching at her clothes. Then a voice came from the bottom of the staircase.

"What are you doing above there?"

The man with the "horrid hand" loosened his grip, and answered only with a "hem!"

"We don't kill women," came the first voice.

"I was on my knees," wrote Madame Campan. "My executioner quitted his hold of me, and said, 'Get up, you jade; the nation pardons you.'"

She was spared, but forced to stand on a bench near a window and call out "The nation for ever!" at the top of her lungs.[2] Much later, after having witnessed the murders of her friends and fellow-servants, her gown bloodstained and her senses forever seared by all that she had seen and heard, she was permitted to leave the palace—only to be mistaken for a young Swiss guard in woman's dress, and threatened once again.

All day and into the night the horrors at the Tuileries continued. All the palace outbuildings were set on fire—except the Manège—including the barracks of the Swiss Guards, and the smoke from the burning buildings reached the Assembly hall where the King and Queen and their entourage were. To ensure their safety the royal family, along with Madame de Tourzel, the Princesse de Lamballe, and two or three others, were locked in a tiny room just behind the rostrum. From there they could see and hear the turmoil when angry Parisians stormed in to denounce the Swiss, and to report to the deputies that the palace was on fire. Louis and Antoinette were anguished by the knowledge that their servants were in mortal danger. "Each discharge of cannon made us tremble," Madame de Tourzel wrote, "the hearts of the King and Queen were lacerated, and we were plunged in profound sorrow as we thought of the fate that was, perhaps at that very moment, befalling those we had left in the Tuileries."[3] The dauphin was in tears, Louis was stoic though grieving inwardly, Antoinette, "full of propriety and dignified composure," according to one observer, gazed out at the deputies with regal calm, though her heart was surely breaking.[4]

Within hours of the first gunshots at the Tuileries the monarchy was dissolved. By Assembly decree the "executive power" was withdrawn from the King, the civil list suspended, a new national convention called for September 20 to govern the republic. Louis Capet and his family, it was decided, would be removed to the Temple, a medievel tower fortress on the grounds of an estate which had belonged to Artois, and imprisoned there to await the further pleasure of the Commune.

There were in fact two towers on the estate, one smaller than the other, and it was the smaller of the two that at first housed the royal family. The cramped, airless rooms with their stone walls and low ceilings were full of vermin, there was no linen on the hard beds and the stink was terrible. But the tower was secure, with a huge heavy oak door strengthened with sheets of iron. The massive old walls were ten feet thick. Eight municipal officers guarded the ground floor, soldiers kept watch on each of the four floors and a representative from the Commune was in the room with Louis and Antoinette at all times. After a few days the royal attendants—the Princesse de Lamballe, Madame de Tourzel and her young daughter, the waiting women and valets—were taken away to imprisonment elsewhere, which made the quarters less cramped, and the Commune did allow the family a certain amount of luxury in the form of six- or eight-course meals and a generous budget for clothing and furnishings.

Antoinette's room in the little tower was eventually made quite livable, upholstered in sky blue and with a sofa and armchairs in blue and white cloth. She had a dog with her, a Scottish terrier that had been a gift from the Princesse de Lamballe. (She named him Odin after a dog of Fersen's.) All her clothes, along with her cherished keepsakes and ornaments, the lovely furniture, paintings, hangings and artworks that had been in her apartments, had been burned or stolen in the assault on the palace. But now she was allowed to order a new wardrobe, and several dozen dressmakers were kept occupied sewing gowns and wrappers, petticoats and sashes, and coats of Florence taffeta. New slippers, hats, handkerchiefs and lace trimmings were ordered in abundance. It may even have given Antoinette a small measure of satisfaction to spend the Commune's assignats on finery—over a hundred thousand francs were billed for perfumes alone—believing as she did that any day the Austrian and Prussian soldiers would be in Paris.

She possessed what she believed to be a reliable itinerary for the invasion, and often told Madame Campan how "on such a day they would be at Verdun, on another day at such a place, that Lille was about to be besieged," and so on. She pinned her hopes to this calendar, and stood at the windows of the tower listening for the cries of the newsboys outside to learn the progress of the allied armies. And she was not disappointed. In the last week of August the fortress of Longwy fell, and soon afterwards Verdun came under siege. On September 2 Verdun surrendered, and in the following days Brunswick and his army moved resolutely, if slowly, westward toward Paris.

Paris responded with a convulsion of violence. Having convinced themselves that unnamed "royalist conspirators" were about to betray the city to the enemy, officials of the Commune decided to turn over the occupants of the prisons to the citizens of Paris for judgment, rather than waiting for the law courts to act. Over the next five days there was an orgy of indiscriminate slaughter. "People's courts" passed summary judgment on the occupants of the prisons, while hastily appointed executioners stood by with knives and swords to carry out the sentences immediately. Hundreds of nonjuring priests, imprisoned for their disobedience to the law requiring them to take the oath of loyalty, were butchered. Most of the remnant of the Swiss Guards, who had been taken prisoner on August 10, were murdered. The women's prison of the Salpetrière was emptied. Madame de Tourzel managed to save herself, with the help of some sympathetic guards, but the Princesse de Lamballe was not so lucky. She was summarily tried, judged guilty, and hacked to pieces; her severed head and genitals, displayed on pikes, were brought to the Temple and held up outside the Queen's window. When Antoinette saw the grisly display she fainted, and the terrible image of her mutilated friend must have stayed with her, tormenting her, for a very long time.[5]

The September Massacres brought a fresh wave of hatred for the imprisoned King and Queen, and savage crowds gathered outside the Temple as they had outside the Tuileries. The enfeebled Legislative Assembly gave way, on September 20, to the new governing body, the Convention, which promptly declared that September 22, 1792, would mark the first day of an entirely new calendar. Year I of the French Republic had begun.

And Year I began auspiciously, with a surprising victory of French troops over Brunswick's army at Valmy. Suddenly the tide of war was turning. The once demoralized revolutionary army found its heart, and the allied forces retreated. Over the next six weeks victory followed victory and the French invaded Belgium, forcing Antoinette's sister Archduchess Marie Christine and thousands of French emigrés to leave.

It was no longer possible for Antoinette to hope for foreign aid. She had no political allies, her friends and confidantes were scattered or dead. Her husband, though he possessed, in her words, "an abundance of passive courage," was resigned to the apparently hopeless situation. She still could take command, or so she thought. "As for myself, I could do anything," she told Madame Campan, "and would appear on horseback, if necessary. But if I was really to begin to act, that would be furnishing arms to the King's enemies." The outcry against her, a hated woman and an Austrian, would only worsen Louis's position in the eyes of his subjects. Under the circumstances she had no choice but to "remain passive, and prepare to die."[6]

She stood by Louis, defending him, refusing to criticize him, never allowing herself to be overtaken by bitterness or blame. She nursed him when he fell ill in November, suffering for ten days with a terrible fever, and caught the fever from him afterwards. She was patient with his moods, she understood only too well his passivity and shyness and it did not surprise her that, having discovered that the Temple contained a library, he spent hours reading Montesquieu and Buffon, Tacitus and Plutarch, *The Imitation of Christ* and the *Lives of the Saints*.

Louis devoured several hundred books within a few months, and when he was not reading he was tutoring his son in the Latin classics. His apartment in the Great Tower, to which he was moved at the end of September, was sparsely furnished with a bed that had once belonged to Artois's Captain of the Guards, a small bureau, four straight chairs and an armchair, a table, and a mirror hanging from the chimney. The stone walls were covered with handpainted wallpaper depicting the inside of a prison. The fireplace was welcome, for the autumn nights were very cold, but there were revolutionary slogans everywhere, and these galled Louis. The full text of the Declaration of the Rights of Man and the Citizen had been painted in large letters in his antechamber, surrounded by a border of red, white and blue.[7]

Though he never entirely lost his gluttonous appetite, Louis lost weight in the Temple. His porcine face grew thinner, his shadowed, defeated eyes became more deep set. There were lines of sorrow and disappointment around his mouth, and his expression was full of melancholy and reserve. Bertrand de Molleville, who saw the King often during the summer of 1792, was convinced that he had made up his mind to die, preferably by assassination. The memory of Varennes and its humiliations soured him on making another escape attempt, and he dreaded that unless a murderer carried him off he would suffer the unbearable ignominy of a judicial murder at the hands of his subjects, just as Charles I had. "He wished to die by the hand of an assassin," Molleville recalled, "that his murder might be considered as the crime of a few individuals, and not a national act." Yet now, imprisoned as he was and under heavy guard, no assassin could come near him, and many in the Convention were calling for his death. "I am not lucky," Louis told Molleville in a terse understatement. His political enemies had taken to referring to him as "Louis the Last."

On November 18 one of those who knew the King best, the locksmith Gamin, betrayed him.

For twenty years and more the locksmith had worked by the King's side, teaching him his craft, sharing his private smithy, coming to know him, one suspects, as no one else did. Gamin had seen Louis at his most relaxed, and at his happiest. He knew well the unshaven, sloppily dressed overgrown boy who retreated to his smithy to escape the responsibilities demanded of an elaborately coiffed, elaborately dressed king. Now Gamin revealed something which he knew would condemn his former master irredeemably in the eyes of the Commune. He said that while at the Tuileries Louis had ordered him to build a secret iron chest for storing documents he wished to conceal from the revolutionary authorities.

In the shambles of the palace the iron chest was found, and for two weeks a committee of delegates to the Convention sifted through the forty cartons of papers discovered inside. Most of the

documents were unobjectionable—requests for posts, bills, petitions, charity appeals—but others provided proof of treason. The
minority Jacobin faction in the Convention, which had been calling for the King's death, was triumphant. The guards at the Temple drew a crude sketch of a guillotine and its victim on the wall
where the King could see it, and wrote underneath, "Louis spit-
ting in the sack." "The guillotine is permanent," read another of
their graffiti, "it awaits the tyrant Louis XVI."

On December 11 the captives in the Temple were awakened
before dawn by the noise of drums throughout the city calling the
National Guard to arms. Into the Temple garden rode a troupe of
cavalry escorting artillery. Nothing more happened for several
hours, and Louis and his family ate their breakfast as usual.
Toward noon, while the King was sitting with the dauphin going
over his lesson, two municipal officials entered the room and announced that they were to take the boy to his mother, on orders of
the Commune. The King questioned them, but they would tell
him nothing more. Reluctantly, and with resignation, he kissed
his son tenderly and sent him with the men. When the dauphin
had left the room Louis was further informed that the Mayor of
Paris wanted to speak with him.

After several long hours the Mayor appeared, flanked by the
Procurer of the Commune, the Secretary, Santerre, Commander
of the National Guard, and several other officials.

"Louis Capet is to be brought to the bar of the National Convention," the Mayor said.

"Capet is not my name," the King remarked mildly, "it is the
name of one of my ancestors. I would have liked, Monsieur, for
the commissaires to have left my son here during the two hours I
have passed in waiting for you."

None of the officials made any answer to this. The King
went on.

"I will follow you, not because I am obeying the Convention,
but because my enemies have the upper hand."[8]

With dignity Louis asked his valet to bring him his riding coat
and hat, and put them on. Then without another word he followed the Mayor and the others out the thick oaken door of the
Temple and into a waiting carriage to be driven to face his accusers.

❧ 30 ❧

ISTY rain fell on the Place de la Revolution, and the hundred drummers had to blow into their hands to keep their fingers from freezing. For the moment, the drums were silent, and the huge crowd that had gathered in the square was silent as well, waiting uncomfortably for the morning's solemnities to begin.

It was the twenty-first of January 1793, the day the King was to die.

For weeks people had been denouncing Louis, telling one another that he was a traitor and a liar, that he had been conspiring with the Austrians and Prussians and had masterminded a plot to massacre the citizens of Paris. On Epiphany they had refused to eat the traditional *gâteau des rois*, or "Kings' cake" and had rechristened the pastry "gâteau Marat." Educated Parisians had bought accounts of the trial of the English King Charles I, executed on another raw January day one hundred and forty-four years earlier, from the booksellers outside the Convention hall. It was unpatriotic to think anything but ill of Louis Capet. The Convention had condemned him to death—admittedly by the narrowest of margins, and after thirty hours of ferocious debate—and logic demanded that he be removed from the scene, for the good of the revolution.[1]

Yet the stillness in the streets, the quiet of the crowd was in part the hush of awe. The King was sacred, an anointed icon, a once beloved father. A creature apart. And now that sacred being was to be destroyed. Who could say what dreadful misfortunes his destruction might unleash?

325

Dressed in a brown overcoat and a tricorn hat with the revolutionary cockade of red, white and blue, Louis left the Temple in a coach lent for the occasion by the Finance Minister Clavière. It had been difficult to find a coach; at first no one in the government had been willing to lend his vehicle for the distasteful purpose of carrying the deposed King to his execution. Yet Louis faced his last hours with remarkable serenity. He had made peace with his fate. He had avoided saying a final good-bye to his family, he asked his valet Cléry to apologize to Antoinette for that, to explain to her that he "wanted to spare her the pain of so cruel a separation." He gave Cléry his wedding ring to return to her. "I part from it in grief," he said, then handed the valet another keepsake, a packet containing locks of hair from all his relatives. This too was for Antoinette. "Tell them farewell for me."

He got into the coach, and was relieved to see there, sitting opposite him, the Irish priest Henry Edgeworth. Louis had secretly sent a message to the nonjuring Edgeworth—who had been confessor to his sister Elisabeth, and who continued to offer spiritual comfort to his parishioners despite the danger he ran—asking him, "as a pledge of attachment, and as a favor" to attend him in his last hours. But he had not been certain that Edgeworth would come, or that he would not be arrested if he did come. But the guards and prison officials had been lenient, they had allowed Citizen Capet his final request, to take a priest with him to the scaffold.

There were gendarmes in the carriage, and their presence prohibited Louis from speaking freely, or making his confession. But when Edgeworth handed Louis his breviary, he seemed pleased, and he and the priest read it together, reciting aloud the prayers for the dying and the penitential psalms.

While the gendarmes looked on, amazed at Louis's calm and piety, the carriage began to move. It was in the middle of a long procession, led by National Guards and Federates, pike-bearing citizens of the faubourgs, and two artillery brigades. After the royal carriage came more guardsmen and army troops in marching order. The solemn parade crept slowly through the wet, still streets, between ranks of guards standing four deep who watched it impassively. The cold was penetrating, from time to time a light rain fell from the dark skies. Louis, absorbed in his psalms, paid no attention to the rain or to the thousands of his subjects who had come to watch him die. He was not aware of the few scattered shouts and cries rising from the onlookers: a plea for the King's blessing, a scream of anguish from a young woman near the St.-Martin gate, a muffled shout as a royalist tried to push his way to the royal coach and was cut down in the street by one of the guardsmen. Louis was oblivious to the sudden disturbance caused by a shouting, sword-waving monarchist named Batz who with four companions tried in vain to lead a charge against the National Guard and rescue him. No one in the crowd joined Batz—though many might have liked to—and he slipped away before he could be apprehended, leaving his companions to be harried by the soldiers.

After nearly two hours the carriage finally reached the Place de la Revolution (formerly known as the Place Louis XV) and lurched to a halt in the center of a large open space surrounding the scaffold.

Louis closed the breviary and handed it back to Edgeworth.

"We are arrived, if I mistake not," he whispered to the priest. One of the guards opened the carriage door, and the gendarmes were about to get out when Louis stopped them.

"Gentlemen," he said to them, resting his arm protectively on Edgeworth's knee, "I recommend to you this good man. Take care that after my death no insult be offered to him. I charge you to prevent it."

He got out, and barely had time to take in the impressive scene—the ring of cannon surrounding the scaffold, the thousands of blue-jacketed guardsmen standing at attention rank on rank, the cavalry and the spectators, stretching away on all sides as far as could be seen, the inhuman quiet—before three guardsmen seized him and tried to take off his coat. According to Edgeworth, Louis "repulsed them with haughtiness," and proceeded to undress himself, laying his coat aside, untying his white neckcloth, removing his collar and opening the neck of his linen shirt. His tricorn hat was handed to one of the guards who, having been for the moment disconcerted by Louis's imperious manner, now attempted to seize his hands.

"What are you trying to do?" Louis demanded, snatching his hands back.

"To bind you."

"To bind *me*!" Louis answered indignantly. "No! I shall never consent to that. Do what you have been ordered to do, but you shall never bind me."

Edgeworth steadied Louis, who leaned on his arm, as together they climbed the rough wooden steps leading upward to the platform where the guillotine awaited. Beside the machine stood the public executioner, Charles-Henri Sanson, who stood ready to perform his task; he had executed many a nobleman, and not a few clerics, but never a king.

The drums were beating thunderously, trumpeters blew a fanfare. Louis seemed to climb the steps haltingly, Edgeworth worried that his courage might be failing him. But when they reached the top step, Louis let go of the priest's arm and crossed the breadth of the scaffold "with a firm foot," his face "very flushed."

Sanson moved toward him with a knife to cut his hair, but Louis tried to wave him away. "It is not necessary," he said gravely, but the executioner paid no attention, and cut off his queue. Then he took his hands and began binding them behind his back.

Louis shouted to the drummers. "Stop!" Briefly they halted the drumroll, and into the silence the former King's last words rang out.

"I die innocent of all the crimes laid to my charge! I pardon those who have occasioned my death, and I pray to God that the bloo—"

Unwilling to let Louis go on any longer, General Berruyer, in charge of the detachment of troops, gave the order for the drum-roll to resume. The final words were lost. Swiftly the gendarmes seized Louis and violently flung him face down under the suspended knife-blade of the guillotine. They "were in such haste," eyewitnesses said afterwards, "as to let fall the axe before his neck was properly placed in so that he was mangled." An agonized cry came from the victim, a cry to chill the blood.

"All this passed in a moment," Edgeworth recalled. "The youngest of the guards, who seemed about eighteen, immediately seized the head, and showed it to the people as he walked around the scaffold, and he accompanied this monstrous ceremony with the most atrocious and indecent gestures."

This broke the solemnity. After two hours and more of standing silently in the rain and cold, dreading the moment of horror, the Parisians were ready to burst into macabre joy. "*Vive la ré-*

publique!" someone shouted, and echoing shouts filled the square. Hats were thrown into the air, songs were sung, people ran up to catch drops of the blood that gushed from the headless corpse. In the frenzied chaos, the Marseillaise was heard, and some of the spectators formed themselves into a chain and danced around the scaffold.

Sanson, the hero of the hour, was auctioning off the dead man's hat and selling locks of his hair and his hair ribbon. The plain brown coat was cut into pieces and given out to whoever wanted it, and people fought for scraps of the cloth.

Edgeworth, unmolested, moved off into the crowd, no doubt saying his prayers. The gendarmes put the dead body and head into a wicker basket, loaded the basket into a waiting cart and drove off to the Madeleine Cemetery where a deep pit had been dug to receive the remains of "Louis the Shortened." The remains were transferred to an uncovered wooden coffin and lowered into the earth. There was no ceremony, no words were pronounced over the grave. A thick layer of quicklime was shoveled in. Louis XVI was no more.

In the Temple, his widow languished. She was thinner than ever, weak and somewhat frail. Her clothes hung loosely on her, and had to be taken in, and the officials charged with looking after her authorized a "medicinal soup" to be fed to her every day. She was in mourning, her appearance that of a respectable widow, "aged and in decrepitude," dressed in mourning black. Her husband's death made her moody and depressed, and for weeks she stayed in her room, knitting and brooding, her little terrier at her side. Her room in the Great Tower—into which she had moved several months earlier—was not without its comforts. She had upholstered furniture and linen sheets, a clavichord and even a bath, expressly installed for her by the Commune. She was only the Widow Capet, no longer Queen of France, but her surroundings were clean and decent, and she was often cold but not miserably so.

And she was not without hope. One of her guards, Toulon, became her champion at this time, just after Louis's execution. Formerly the most committed of revolutionaries, he reversed his loyalties and began conspiring to effect the escape of Antoinette,

Elisabeth and the two children. To prove that the prison was not impenetrable by outsiders Toulon smuggled in the monarchist General de Jarjayes, who had helped Antoinette earlier in her secret correspondence with Barnave. Jarjayes entered the Temple dressed in the clothes of the lamplighter who came every day to look after the lights, and none of the gendarmes took any particular notice of him.

Having demonstrated what he could do, Toulan told Antoinette his plan. He and another man, a venal municipal officer named Lepitre, would arrange to be on guard on the night of the escape. Lepitre, a classics teacher who had become head of the passport committee of the Commune, would forge passports and identity cards for all four of the royals—for a large fee—which would enable them, once out of the Temple, to escape to the Normandy coast and from there by boat to England. The two warders, Citizen and Citizeness Tison, would be given drugged snuff.

As in 1791, the family would rely on disguise to make their escape from the Temple. Antoinette and Elisabeth would be dressed in the trousers, jackets and hats of municipal officers; the sentries would not question them, Toulon felt sure, and would not even bother to examine their papers. They could merely walk out and get into one of the waiting cabriolets. Then Thérèse would go out, dressed in rags, her face blackened with soot, looking exactly like one of the lamplighter's assistants. Last of all would come the dauphin, concealed in a basket of dirty linen carried by a trusted servant.

Every detail was calculated. The conspirators felt certain that they would not be missed for four or five hours, and that even then it would take another hour or more to search the prison, inform the Commune, and send for the Mayor. Ample funds were at hand to pay for the cabriolets and to pay Lepitre's high fee. But weeks went by and still the passports were not ready. The war was widening, and once again going badly for the French. In February the revolutionary government had declared war on Britain—provoked into the declaration by the British Prime Minister William Pitt—and Pitt was galvanizing the continental powers into a firm coalition against the regicide French. (Pitt called the killing of Louis XVI "the foulest and most atrocious deed which the history of the world has yet had occasion to attest.") At the same time, a serious counter-revolutionary rebellion broke out in

Western France, in the Vendée region, where the malnourished and overtaxed peasants rose in protest against the Convention's decree conscripting three hundred thousand men into the army. Besieged on all sides by powerful enemies, and menaced from within by the Western rebellion, the Commune took protective measures. No more passports were to be issued by the Passport Committee. Without the forged passports, the fleeing royals would have a slim chance of avoiding capture as they passed through the string of towns and villages on the way to the coast, even if they succeeded in leaving the Temple. The plan was abandoned.

Or almost abandoned. There was still a chance that Antoinette could get away on her own, Jarjayes thought. But Antoinette refused to leave without her children. Nothing, not even freedom, could compensate for the guilt she would feel if she abandoned them, she told the General. Escape was only a lovely dream, a chimera that faded in the harsh light of day. She would never get free now. She told Jarjayes to emigrate while he still could, and gave him Louis' watch seal and wedding ring to take to Provence at Coblentz. She also gave him a memento for Fersen, a wax impression of her own seal which bore Fersen's crest—a homing pigeon with the words *"Tutto a te mi guida."* "Everything guides me to thee." It was Fersen that she mourned, not Louis; in her darker hours she dreaded that she might never see him again. She told Jarjayes to assure Fersen that the inscription on the seal "has never been more true."

But her stubborn will to survive did not desert her. She did her best to monitor the course of the war, relying on the few loyal servants who brought her news and conveyed it by secret hand signals. She counted the days until the allied armies could be expected to reach Paris, hoping that the Convention would let her and her children live, perhaps as hostages they could trade to the Austrians. As always, she worried less about herself than about her children, chiefly the dauphin, whom she now regarded as Louis XVII. He was chronically ill with pains in his side, high fevers and headaches. At times he could not lie down because if he did he began to choke. Having lost his beloved father to the guillotine, surrounded by frightened women, teased and taunted by the guardsmen who resented Antoinette's respectful treatment of her son as King of France, the little boy's constitution suffered.

His fourteen-year-old sister Thérèse moved her bed into her mother's room in order to be at hand in case either her brother or her mother became ill during the night.[2]

The revolutionary government was evolving to meet the challenge of a Europe-wide war. Committees of Vigilance in each of the Paris sections rooted out "enemies of the revolution" and turned them over to the Commune to be imprisoned. A Revolutionary Tribunal was established, consisting of a jury of twelve and a public prosecutor—the soon to be notorious Fouquier-Tinville—to try the imprisoned suspects. And a Committee of Public Safety was instituted to oversee the war effort. Day after day the Revolutionary Tribunal went about its grim work, under pressure from the Committee of Public Safety to dispense justice at top speed. Suspects were tried, convicted and summarily dispatched. The blade of the guillotine fell with chilling regularity, sometimes four times a day, sometimes six or eight or a dozen times, cutting short the lives of aristocrats, wig-makers, barbers and servants—a mélange of unfortunates whose most outstanding common characteristic was that they had belonged to the old social order or had served those who did.[3]

Even so the most hotheaded of the popular orators were unsatisfied. They denounced the Tribunal's judges for taking too long with their deliberations, and for acquitting too many suspects.[4] The wheels of public vengeance ground too slowly, they insisted; there ought to be a daily quota of executions. More guillotines were constructed, and sent out into the provinces on "patriotic tours" to purge the countryside of traitors and suspected traitors. Men, women, even children of fourteen and fifteen fell beneath their heavy blades. Anyone who spoke against the local Revolutionary Tribunal, or who wore a white cockade, or who harbored a nonjuring priest or opposed conscription was liable to be imprisoned and killed. And as the massive revolt in the Vendée spread, and smaller rebellions broke out in Bordeaux, Lyon and Marseille, thousands of people were engulfed in the tide of bloodshed.[5] Executioners were censured for inefficiency, for allowing the razor-sharp edges of their guillotines to become dulled or their mechanisms rusty. Crowds of provincial spectators grew restive if heads were not severed neatly, on the first try; at times, when the executioner was unfit or lazy, it took three or four attempts to slice the blade through bone, cartilage and flesh.

In the waking nightmare that was Paris, among a population habituated to gore, the guillotine became an object of fascination. Women wore jeweled miniature guillotines in their ears or around their necks. Men wore their hair short and shaved their necks, "*à la victime*," and women tied thin red ribbons around their throats as unsubtle reminders of what they might soon suffer. Songs were sung to Madame la Guillotine, or Saint Guillotine, or to the executioner Sanson. Children constructed little engines of decapitation out of twigs, bits of string and pocketknives and used them to cut the heads off birds and mice.

Like a ghoulish plague the killing madness raged, through the summer of 1793, as the armies of the European powers and the British navy closed in on renegade France. On August 2, at two o'clock in the morning, four officers of the Paris police came to the Temple to arrest the Widow Capet. She was suspected of being an enemy of the revolution. She was to face the Revolutionary Tribunal, and to be housed, until her trial began, at the prison of the Conciergerie.

❧ 31 ❧

HE tall, gaunt woman who was led by torchlight along the dark corridors of the prison on the Ile de la Cité wore a torn black dress and walked with the stiff gait of the elderly. She looked, one of the prison servants thought, like a magpie; another man called her "a deformed specter." But the skin of her sunken cheeks was still dazzlingly white, and she wore her one shabby dress with the indefinable but unmistakable air of a gentlewoman.

She was Marie Antoinette de Lorraine d'Autriche, also known as the Widow Capet, prisoner number 280, accused of having conspired against France.

She was shown into her cell, an airless dark room twelve feet square, with an uneven brick floor, a single low barred window and a few miserable pieces of furniture. The prisoner looked around at the narrow cot and cheap straw mattress, the stained screen, the cane chairs and old oaken table. She took in the rotting wallpaper falling off its wooden frames, and the ancient stone walls behind it, she smelled the mold that gathered on the stones and the musty odor of age and decay.

"Her eyes contemplated with astonishment the dreadful starkness of the room," wrote the maid Rosalie Lamorlière, who saw Antoinette for the first time when she entered her cell that night. She seemed more concerned with her surroundings than with Rosalie or the prison concierge, who was seated at the small table entering her name in his register. He took from Antoinette the small bundle of her belongings, later to be itemized: packets containing locks of hair from her dead and living children and from her late husband, an arithmetical table she had used during Louis-Charles's lessons, a sewing purse with scissors, needles and thread, a mirror, a gold ring with a lock of hair, miniature portraits of the Princesse de Lamballe and of two Austrian women, Mesdames Mecklembourg and Hesse, who had been her childhood companions, a scapular, and a sheet of paper with prayers to the Sacred Heart of Jesus and to the Immaculate Conception. These things, and the clothes she had on, were all she had left, except for the three rings she wore and the gold watch she took out and hung from a nail in the wall, standing on a low stool to reach it.

When the concierge, Richard, completed his entry and left, taking her things with him, Antoinette began to take off her dress. Rosalie tried to help her.

"Thank you, my girl, but since I have had no one to help me, I take care of myself." The voice was sweet and warm, "without any ill humor or pride."

She laid the black dress aside and lay down on the cot, which earlier Rosalie had made up with fine linen sheets and a bolster.[1]

She was numb with weariness, worn down by grief and sorrow and frustration and the daily struggle to endure. She was determined to remain self-possessed and polite, no matter what insults were directed at her, no matter how degrading her circumstances. This was her protection, this well bred persona behind which the angry, proud, wounded former Queen took refuge. No matter how she was treated, she was determined not to lower herself to the brutal level of those who victimized her. But maintaining the persona took enormous self-control and energy, and though her will remained strong her energy was failing. Her body suffered under the strain, her nerves, never strong, had given way; she bled profusely and often, and had to beg linen rags from Rosalie to staunch the excessive flow.[2] For years she had had what Madame Campan called "hysterical disorders"—a euphemism for menstrual irregularities and accompanying irritability and mood swings. Now this syndrome became more pronounced, and often it prostrated her.

The illness and weakness were made worse by anguish. A month before she was removed from the Temple to the Conciergerie Antoinette had been forcibly separated from her son.

Four guards officers came to take him away, on instructions from the Committee of Public Safety, in order to place him in a more democratic environment. Horrified, Antoinette had defended him for an hour or more, refusing to let the officers come near him, enduring their insults and threats and reduced, in the end, to pleading with the men not to take away what was dearest to her in the world. She knew that once Louis-Charles was gone his captors would never let him see his mother again, for their entire purpose in taking him away was to sever him from his past life of privilege. She could not bear to part from him, she wept and prayed and defended his bed until the officers lost patience with her and told her bluntly that they would kill both her children unless she let the boy go. This defeated her. She and Elisabeth dressed Louis-Charles, kissed him, and told him he had to do as the men asked, though he too wept piteously and clung to his mother.

The sequel to this heart-wrenching scene was even worse. Louis-Charles was given into the care of one of the Temple commissioners, Antoine Simon, an elderly cobbler whose vulgarity and crude oaths had been offensive to Antoinette from the start of her confinement in the Temple. The child's screams and cries went on for several days, and his mother, imagining the worst, must have thought that Simon was beating him into submission. Eventually she found a scrap of consolation in being able to watch the cobbler and his charge pass by a certain window on their way to walk in the Tower garden. Antoinette stood at the window for hours, waiting to catch a glimpse of her son, to reassure herself that he was well, if not happy. She blanched, though, when she heard him singing the revolutionary songs Simon taught him—the Marseillaise, the Carmagnole—and listened to him "blaspheme God and curse his family and the aristocrats" at the top of his lungs.

Now, in the Conciergerie, even the occasional glimpse of Louis-Charles was denied her. She languished in a "state of extreme weakness," crying whenever she thought of her children, clutching the pitiful relics of her son that she wore under her dress—a miniature portrait, a lock of hair and a small yellow glove—and trembling with fear. The prison apothecary prescribed a potion of lime-flower water, orange-flower water, maidenhair syrup and Hofman's liquor, and told Richard to have more medicinal soup made up for the prisoner, to include lean veal, chicken and herbs.

The dark, musty cell with its wretched furniture was part of Antoinette's punishment, intended to dampen her hauteur and to teach her about the sufferings of the poor who were now her equals. Like the poorest of the Parisians she lacked light, space, privacy; the two guards who slept on cots in her cell and watched her every move during the day did not even allow her to relieve herself unwatched. She squatted behind a half-curtain on a chamber pot, relying on Rosalie to freshen the air by burning juniper berries whenever a ruffian named Barassin came in to empty it. Rosalie thought that Antoinette was "of an excessive propriety, an excessive delicacy" when it came to modesty and cleanliness. Clearly she hated having her every act, even the intimate process of changing her bloodstained linen, exposed to view.

After a day or two in the tiny cell she longed for a bath, fresh air, a change of underwear. She asked Madame Richard, the concierge's wife, to supply her with clean linen but the woman, though kindhearted, did not dare to help the august prisoner out of fear of the Convention. After ten days one of the jailors went to the Temple to get some of Antoinette's things and came back with a large package. Antoinette opened it eagerly, no doubt hoping that it might contain a secret message. It did contain some delicate batiste chemises, lace-trimmed handkerchiefs, two pairs of black silk stockings and a white wrapper or morning gown, along with several nightcaps, some lengths of ribbon, fichus to cover the neck and a lawn headdress and black crepe sash.

"I see the hand of my poor sister Elisabeth in all this, her careful attention to things," Antoinette said as she went through the clothes. There was even a swansdown powder puff and a small tin box which held pomade for her hair. The cell contained no wardrobe, but eventually Antoinette was provided with a flimsy cardboard box to hold her things. Every day she dressed in either the black gown or the white wrapper, arranging her long white-gray hair in a plain chignon with pomade at her forehead and temples to hold back the wisps. Each morning the cook brushed the dirt of the cell floor off Antoinette's shoes—they were as dirty, the woman said, as if the prisoner had been walking in the rue St.-Honoré. Prisoners from other wings of the Conciergerie, most of them royalists, made a point of stopping by the kitchen during their morning exercise to kiss the Queen's shoes.[3]

The Conciergerie was a noisy center of constant activity. Its three hundred prisoners came and went throughout the day and half the night, leaving to attend their trials, returning under sentence of death, going to their executions. Visitors were received, caterers brought in food, peddlers supplied necessities. Priests who served the revolutionary government heard the prisoners' confessions and gave the last rites to those who were about to die. Lawyers and police came to question the prisoners and confer with them, and officers of the court brought in new prisoners to take the place of those who had been eliminated. Nearly every night there were macabre last suppers given by those condemned to die the following day; the jailers were indulgent, they allowed condemned men and women to entertain their friends, to stuff themselves with rich food and to get drunk on fine wine on the final night of their lives.

All this went on around Antoinette, yet she took part in none of it. She could not see out into the courtyard of the women's wing, to watch her fellow prisoners. There was no one to talk to, except for Rosalie and the soldiers who guarded her, and they were discouraged from making conversation with the former Queen. She was not allowed to do needlework, or to knit; her idle hands were restless, and Rosalie watched her sitting alone hour after hour, turning her rings around and around on her fingers, fretting and brooding. From time to time one of the jailers would bring in a sightseer to stare at her, having paid well for the privilege of seeing at close range the once glamorous inhabitant of Versailles and the Petit Trianon who had come to such a sorry end. But for the most part Antoinette was bereft both of congenial company and occupation, and she read the few books allowed her (*A History of Famous Shipwrecks* was her favorite, and she also liked *A Voyage to Venice*, which mentioned the names of people she had known as a child at her mother's court) many times. When her boredom was at its worst she tried to make the time pass by picking at the wallpaper, separating out some threads and using them to make very simple lace, using pins in place of needles.

For the first month of her confinement at the Conciergerie, Antoinette continued to believe that her relatives would find a way to rescue her—and presumably her children—from the revolutionaries. The coalition against France had widened during the summer to include virtually all the continental powers. In command of the Austrian troops was the Prince of Coburg, a more able and more aggressive general than Brunswick, who was advancing on the north and retaking the Belgian Netherlands. Though she was no longer able to follow the war news, as she had in the Temple, Antoinette knew that the revolutionary armies were outmanned. Only a miracle could turn back the allied forces, provided they pursued the war vigorously. And the Convention could not be so foolish as to subject her to trial—not while she could be used as a valuable hostage.

So she reasoned. But she was wrong.

True enough, the allied armies were advancing, the British navy was welcomed in Toulon and in the Vendée, peasant armies were on the march. The Committee of Public Safety, quite aware of Antoinette's potential value, was engaged in negotiations with the Austrian and Prussian courts over her fate, with some members hoping to win a general amnesty in exchange for her freedom in the event the allied armies besieged Paris. Yet the Parisians were clamoring for her death. They harangued the Revolutionary Tribunal, insisting that the Austrian bitch be guillotined. The newspapers joined the general cry for her blood, demagogues on the left shouted for vengeance. At one point the Tribunal's judges were all for having the former Queen poisoned in her cell, in order to rid themselves of the burden of dealing with her.

She was a much hated nuisance, yet the more sensible members of the Committee of Public Safety knew that they could not afford to dispatch her—that is, not until she once again proved how treacherous she could be. A group of conspirators, supplied with plenty of funds to bribe the prison concierge, several municipal officials and the gendarmes, arranged for Antoinette to escape on the night of September 2. One of the jailers, who was in on the plot, was to take the prisoner out of her cell, saying that he had orders from the Commune to return her to the Temple. Once she was outside, she would be spirited away in the darkness, and conveyed by swift posts to the Belgian border. The evening of September 2 came, the prisoner was brought out through the various doors and gates, almost to the main gate of the prison. But at the last minute one of the bribed gendarmes announced flatly that he could not look the other way and let the former Queen escape. He threatened to summon the guard if she was not returned to her cell. Realizing that the man's silence was essential to the success of the plot, the jailer took Antoinette back. The next day the gendarme denounced his colleagues and several of them were arrested.

After this there could be no question of permitting Antoinette to escape retribution, and she sensed it. She became much more uneasy, the maid Rosalie said, "much more alarmed." She paced up and down in her cell, sighing anxiously, her expression grave. She was moved to a smaller and more secure cell with two thick, nail-studded doors, each with several bolts and locks. The tiny room's three windows were completely blocked off, no light was permitted to enter from any source. A trusted gendarme stood at attention in the corridor, guarding the doors, and another was stationed in the courtyard to ensure that no one tried to reach the prisoner through one of the barred windows. Eventually a third man, an officer of the gendarmerie, was placed in the cell with her.

Meanwhile the most vocal of Antoinette's enemies redoubled their calls for her death. The "Austrian tigress" ought to be "chopped up like mincemeat," cried the journalist Hébert in his earthy, obscene paper *Le Père Duchesne*. The Convention and the Tribunal were deluged with letters and petitions from Paris and many of the provinces asking why "the shameless and despotic woman" had not yet been made to suffer for her crimes. Members of the Convention decided it was high time "the woman Capet" was punished, and demanded that the Revolutionary Tribunal accuse her formally. Fouquier-Tinville was provided with access to any papers he might need by the Committee of Public Safety, which had at last come to a decision concerning Antoinette. With the war news improving—the revolutionary army had turned back Coburg at Hondschoote, and by the first week of October the allies had won no further victories—it was determined that she was expendable. The vengeance of the people could at last be carried out.

It was a cold, rainy October and water trickled in rivulets down the worn stone walls of Antoinette's dark cell. Puddles formed on the brick floor, her shoes were constantly wet and covered in mildew. She had no warm clothing, only the one black dress, shiny at the elbows, patched once by a kindly elderly servant but badly in need of patching once again. There was no fireplace in the cell, and on frosty nights she suffered. The new concierge hung an old carpet around her bed, hoping to give her some shred of comfort, and Rosalie warmed Antoinette's nightgown in front of her own fire each night before taking it to her. But the orders of the Committee of Public Safety were stern. The Widow Capet was not to be allowed any indulgences, not even a cotton coverlet or a candle to light her cell at night.

Broken and fragile, her pains and hemorrhages leaving her exhausted, Antoinette was in a "state of extreme weakness" and "complained sweetly" to her captors. Though often in tears, the compassionate Rosalie was powerless to alleviate the misery of prisoner number 280, the former Queen of France. And the jailers and gendarmes did not dare to risk their own lives by trying to soften the rigors of Antoinette's confinement. During the long, cold nights she tossed on her narrow cot, weeping for her children, cursing her deprivation, her mind no doubt casting up a jumble of images and memories—of Fersen, of her stolid, pockmarked husband, of her mother and father, her sunlit childhood at Schönbrunn, her happy afternoons at the miniature village in the gardens of Versailles. And there must have been images of horror as well: of the screaming, cursing crowds outside the Tuileries, of bloody heads carried on pikes, of ugly, grinning faces and dirty hands reaching through carriage windows to snatch at her.

The cavernous room that had once housed the Paris Parlement and now held the Revolutionary Tribunal was in shadows when Antoinette was brought in on the night of October 12 for her interrogation. The marble walls were dark, the prisoner could barely make out the faces of the spectators or those of the judges sitting behind a long table covered with a green cloth. Two candles burning before the court clerk flickered as his quill pen scratched over the sheet in front of him, recording the accusations made by the examining magistrate.

"Before the Revolution you held a political dialogue with the King of Bohemia and Hungary, a dialogue injurious to the well-being of France, whose benefits you enjoyed.

"Since the Revolution you have continued your intrigues with foreign powers and your plots against liberty.

"You were the principal instigator of Louis Capet's treachery. It was on your advice, and perhaps because of your goading, that he desired to leave France, and to make himself leader of those madmen who wanted to destroy their country."

"My husband never desired to leave France. I followed him

everywhere, but if he had wanted to leave his fatherland, I would have tried to persuade him not to. But he never wanted to leave."

"You have never ceased to desire the destruction of liberty. You wished to reign no matter what the cost, to regain the throne by climbing over the corpses of patriots."

"We did not need to regain the throne. We had never lost it. We never wanted anything but that France should be happy. We were content so long as France was content."

Antoinette's answers were simple and unarguable, her tone reasonable and frank. Her apparent lack of guile was disconcerting, as was the fact that the judges had no actual proof of her alleged crimes, no secret cache of incriminating documents. And despite her evident poor health and pallor, she was alert and clever.

"Do you believe that Kings are necessary for a people's happiness?"

"An individual cannot make such a decision."

"No doubt you regret your son's loss of the throne which the people, finally aware of their rights, have destroyed?"

"I shall regret nothing for my son when his country is happy."

The interrogation went on through the small hours of the night, the questions ranging over a wide field from Antoinette's extravagance as dauphine through her opposition to the revolution to her involvement in the flight to Varennes and in the escape attempts at the Temple and the Conciergerie. At last the magistrate reached the end of his notes.

"Have you any counsel?"

"No. I know no one."

"Would you like the Tribunal to appoint one for you?"

"Willingly."

Two men were named, and then the prisoner was escorted back to her cell, where she paced the wet floor in great agitation. Two days later the trial began. Antoinette's lawyers had hardly been given time to prepare her defense against an indictment that accused her of bankrupting the country, starving its people, betraying its security and plotting, through her mythical "Austrian Cabinet" to massacre the Parisians. They did their best, and Antoinette herself, facing her accusers in her mourning gown and widow's cap, maintained an "imposing dignity" and calm throughout her ordeal.

"One saw sadness in the faces of the honest spectators," wrote an eyewitness sympathetic to the former Queen, "and madness in the eyes of a crowd of men and women placed in the room by design—madness which, more than once, gave way to emotions of pity and admiration. The accusers and judges did not succeed in hiding their anger, or the involuntary confusion they felt at the Queen's noble firmness."[4]

Antoinette won over the hostile crowd when she showed herself "much moved" by the ugliest of the accusations. Hébert claimed that the boy Louis-Charles, or "little Capet," had confessed to "acts of the most licentious debauchery" with his mother and aunt, including "an act of incest between the mother and son." When forced to respond to this outrageous calumny Antoinette became indignant, and stood up.

"I appeal to the conscience and feelings of every mother present, to declare if there be one amongst you who does not shudder at the idea of such horrors."

A wave of electricity swept the vast room. Women cried out, the judges had to call for order. Even the bloodthirsty *tricoteuses*, the group of women who sat knitting through all the trials and executions, were brought to the point of applauding—but they held back, remembering all that they had heard over the years about the former Queen's vice-ridden life.

For two very long days the trial continued. Dozens of witnesses were brought forward to blacken Antoinette, accusing her of an array of crimes ranging from assassination plots to counterfeiting assignats to making treasonous revelations to France's enemies. In the end the president of the court concluded that "all the political events of the last five years testify against her."

The outcome of the trial had never been in doubt. The members of the jury—among them two carpenters, a musician, a hatter, a cafe-keeper, a wig-maker and a printer—were hardly inclined to show mercy. They condemned her, and her sentence of death was read.

She heard it "with a calm air," one of her lawyers wrote later. "She gave not the least sign, neither of fear, or indignation, or weakness. She was as if numbed by overwhelming surprise." Without a word or a gesture she crossed the room, holding her head proudly when she passed the spectators, and let one of the gendarmes lead her back to her cell.

It was by this time nearly five o'clock on the morning of October 16, and the death sentence was to be carried out at midday. She wrote a final letter to Elisabeth, full of tenderness and feeling, asking her to care for Louis-Charles and Thérèse as if they were her own children. In her prayer book she wrote, "My God have pity on me! My eyes have no more tears to shed for you, my poor children. Adieu, adieu!"

When Rosalie came in, red-eyed with weeping, at seven o'clock to ask Antoinette if she wanted any breakfast she found the prisoner stretched out on her cot, fully dressed. She was lost in thought, her head on her hand, her face toward the one window which let in a few inches of light.

"My girl, I don't need anything," Antoinette said, her voice choked with sobs. "It's all over for me."

When Rosalie brought her some bouillon she could eat only a few mouthfuls, though she was obviously in need of nourishment, having eaten almost nothing the day before. Her face was white, and she was bleeding so heavily that the maid thought there was no more blood in her. She needed to change her clothes, and brought out a clean chemise that someone had given her, asking Rosalie to stand in front of the bed to block the gendarme's view while she undressed. But the guard was stubborn. He had his orders, and dared not take his eyes off the prisoner.

"The gendarme came up to us at once," Rosalie recalled, "and, standing by the headrest, watched her change. She put her fichu up to cover her shoulders, and 'with great sweetness,' said to the young man, 'In the name of decency, monsieur, let me change my linen in private.'"

"I cannot permit it," he said brusquely. "My orders are that I am to watch all your movements."

Sighing, Antoinette took off her stained petticoat with as much modesty as she could manage, and put on the clean chemise and over it the white wrapper, adding the muslin fichu at the neck. Rosalie noticed that she carefully rolled up the bloody petticoat and stuffed it into a chink in the wall. With the addition of her plain linen bonnet, her black stockings and worn but sturdy shoes, she was ready for her final appearance before the people of Paris.

When the judges entered her cell some time later they found her on her knees, praying. They read her her sentence, then stood aside while the executioner, the tall Henri Sanson—son of the man who had killed Louis XVI—came in to tie her hands and cut her hair. She had hoped to escape the humiliation of having her hands bound, and had hoped too to be carried to the Place de la Revolution in a coach. But as soon as she left the prison she saw that it was not a coach that awaited her, but a cart such as criminals rode in. She felt her bowels loosen, and asked Sanson to untie her hands so that she could relieve herself by the prison wall.

It was her worst moment. From then on, her hands bound once again, riding backwards in the cart as it rolled along between the lines of shouting, jeering Parisians, she did not weaken or give in to panic or tears.

"Vive la république! Vive la nation!"

There were monarchists in the crowd, and even a few pathetic conspirators who had hoped to cause a disturbance and rescue the former Queen. Aristocrats, their discomfiture evident in their faces, watched the cart pass in silence. In the square where the guillotine stood, peddlers sold wine and fruit to the eager onlookers, who pressed around the scaffold to get a good view. They saw the cart approach, come to a halt, and give up its victim, an old woman in a white dress whose lined face wore a sour expression. She mounted the steps rapidly, and, without pausing to attempt to speak, put herself into the hands of Sanson and his assistants. In her haste she stepped on Sanson's foot.

"Pardon, monsieur. I did not mean to do it."

They tied her down and snapped the wooden collar in place around her neck. The drums thundered, the blade fell. A soldier held up the dripping head by the lank white hair, and applause filled the square.

In the cemetery of the Madeleine, gravediggers cursed the cold and prepared a hole in the earth to receive the frail remains of another prisoner, as a harsh autumn wind blew up around the gravestones and bent the branches of the leafless trees.

❧ Notes ❧

Chapter 1

1 *Aus der Zeit Maria Theresias. Tagebuch des Fürsten Johann Josef Khevenhüller-Metsch, 1742–1776*, ed. Rudolf Graf Khevenhüller-Metsch und Hanns Schlitter (Vienna and Leipzig, 1911), III, 170ff.

2 Constance Lily Morris, *Maria Theresa: The Last Conservative* (New York and London, 1939), pp. 164–5.

3 *Ibid.*, 164.

4 *Aus der Zeit Maria Theresias*, ed. Khevenhüller-Metsch, V, 131.

5 *Ibid.*, 237.

Chapter 2

1 Nicholas Wraxall, cited in Mary Maxwell Moffat, *Maria Theresa* (London, 1911), p. 200.

2 Moffat, pp. 198–9.

3 Morris, pp. 87, 85.

4 J. Alexander Mahan, *Maria Theresa of Austria* (New York, 1932), p. 262.

5 *Ibid.*, 240.

6 *Ibid.*, 242.

Chapter 3

1 Morris, p. 196.

2 Mahan, p. 287.

3 *Ibid.*, 284–5. Maria Theresa's arithmetic was shaky, but her affection was pure.

4 Morris, pp. 284, 286–7.

5 The Marquise de La Tour du Pin, who was a member of Antoinette's court in France, recalled in her memoirs the stiff "grand corps" she had to wear at Versailles, "a specially made bodice, without shoulders, laced in the back, but so narrow that the lacing, about four inches wide at the bottom, showed a chemise of the finest batiste through which one could easily have noticed an insufficiently white skin. The chemise had sleeves that were only three inches high, without a shoulder, to leave the neckline bare. The top of the arm was covered with three or four rows of lace, which fell to the elbow. The chest was entirely exposed." *The Eighteenth-Century Woman.* An exhibition at the Costume Institute, The Metropolitan Museum of Art (New York, 1981), p. 25.

6 Helen Augusta, Lady Younghusband, *Marie Antoinette: Her Early Youth (1770–1774)* (London, 1912), p. 100.

7 *Ibid.*, 126.

8 *Ibid.*, 132.

Chapter 4

1 Saul K. Padover, *The Life and Death of Louis XVI* (New York and London, 1939), p. 28. In fairness to Louis Auguste, it should be pointed out that he inherited many of his more undesirable traits from his father. Had the elder Louis lived, he would most likely have been a mediocre, if well-intentioned, king. The memoirist D'Argenson, minister to Louis XV and an acute judge of men, wrote that the King's son was "an enemy of all movement and exercise, without passion, even without taste; everything stifles him, nothing stimulates him. If there is still some spark in him, it is a dying one, extinguished by fat and bigotry." Padover, p. 6.

As might have been predicted, Louis XV's son was puritannical where his father was sexually profligate, and became an advocate of limited monarchy out of reaction against his father's unenlightened absolutism. But there was an appealing humanity in the doomed dauphin, and he passed this on to his eldest son as well. He loved his children, and the people he would have ruled, had he lived. He once gave up plans for a trip throughout France because, he said, "my whole person is not worth what it could cost the poor people in taxes."

2 "The style of her handwriting is not particularly good," Vermond wrote in October of 1769. "What is most vexing is that partly through

idleness and inattention, partly also, as it is thought, owing to faults of her writing-masters, she has acquired the habit of writing inconceivably slow. . . . I often help her with her writing, but I confess that on this point I have made the least progress." Younghusband, p. 131.

3 Younghusband, pp. 129–31.

4 *The Guardian of Marie Antoinette: Letters from the Comte de Mercy-Argenteau, Austrian Ambassador to the Court of Versailles, to Marie Thérèse, Empress of Austria, 1770–1780*, ed. Lillian C. Smythe (London, 1902), I, 14.

5 Olivier Bernier, *The Secrets of Marie Antoinette* (New York, 1985), pp. 31–4.

6 Maxime de la Rocheterie, *The Life of Marie Antoinette*, trans. Cora Hamipton Bell (New York, 1906), I, 5–7.

7 *Ibid.*

Chapter 5

1 The young Goethe, then a law student at the University of Strasbourg, was outraged when he went to see the *salle de remise* and observed the tapestries. "Such subjects," he wrote, "appeared to me to be so little in harmony with the circumstances that I could not help exclaiming out loud, 'What! At the moment when the young princess is about to step on to the soil of her future husband's country, there is placed before her eyes a picture of the most horrible marriage that can be imagined! Might one not say that the most awful specter has been summoned to meet the most beautiful and happy betrothed?'" Cited in André Castelot, *Queen of France: A Biography of Marie Antoinette*, trans. Denise Folliot (New York, 1957), p. 18.

2 Younghusband, p. 65.

3 *Ibid.*

4 John Lough, *France on the Eve of Revolution: British Travellers' Observations 1763–1788* (Chicago, 1987), p. 235.

5 Mercy wrote to Maria Theresa on this point: "Your Majesty commands me to say whether the King has taken to drink. The report is not well founded, and arises from the fact that one may often observe in this monarch attacks of vacuity [*absences d'esprit*] which resemble the effect of drunkenness. It is obvious that the mind of the King weakens daily, and to the failing is added the apathy caused by the universal disorder that surrounds him." Mercy, I, 97.

6 Lough, p. 263.

7 Mercy, I, 96. He was writing in April, 1771, but his characterization applies equally well to the spring of 1770.

8 Padover, p. 28.

9 The couriers rode from Paris to Vienna and back again in a little under a month, allowing time for a day's halt at Brussels each way and pausing in both Paris and Vienna to give the correspondents time to digest their letters and reports and compose replies. Younghusband, p. 224.

10 Younghusband, pp. 176, 178.

11 Bernier, *Secrets*, p. 38.

12 *Ibid.*, 43.

13 Mercy, I, 24.

14 Bernier, *Secrets*, p. 45.

Chapter 6

1 Lough, p. 240.

2 *Lettres de Marie Antoinette*, ed. Maxime de la Rocheterie and the Marquis de Beaucourt (Paris, 1895–6), I, 5.

3 Mercy, I, 25–6.

4 Jeanne Louise Henriette Campan, *Memoirs of the Private Life of Marie Antoinette* (New York, 1917), I, 16–9.

5 This summary of Antoinette's day is taken from *Lettres de Marie Antoinette*, I, 9–11.

6 Campan, *Memoirs*, I, 28.

7 Bernier, *Secrets*, p. 71.

8 *Lettres de Marie Antoinette*, I, 8.

Chapter 7

1 Mercy, I, 40–1.

2 *Ibid.*, 41–2.

3 Bernier, *Secrets*, pp. 49–50.

4 *Ibid.*, 50.

5 Campan, *Memoirs*, I, xcix–c, 46.

6 *Ibid.*, I, 46 and 47 note.

7 Bernier, *Secrets*, pp. 36–7.

8 Mercy, I, 116–17.

9 *Ibid.*, I, 110–11. *Lettres de Marie Antoinette*, I, 19.

10 Mercy, II, 378–9. Mercy added of the Princesse de Lamballe, "She was that rarity—a Piedmontese without intrigue."

11 Mercy, I, 197–8.

12 Bernier, *Secrets*, p. 64.

13 Mercy, I, 130.

14 Edward Crankshaw, *Maria Theresa* (London, 1969), pp. 299–300.

15 Maria Theresa wrote to Antoinette that "You know how fond I am of your sister Caroline. I must do her the justice to say that, next to you, she has always shown the most genuine attachment to me and the greatest readiness to follow my advice." Moffat, p. 320. Antoinette's avowal to Mercy that she believed herself unloved is in Mercy, I, 197–8.

16 Mercy, I, 183.

17 *Ibid.*, I, 182.

18 Bernier, *Secrets*, p. 84; *Lettres de Marie Antoinette*, I, 22.

19 Antoinette missed four periods during her first eight months in France, probably because of emotional stress. Bernier, *Secrets*, pp. 39, 61.

20 Mercy, I, 204–5.

Chapter 8

1 Younghusband, p. 546.

2 Mercy, I, 243–4.

3 *Ibid.*, I, 225, 212. It seems that Provence was no more virile than his elder brother in the early days of his marriage. Several months after the wedding Josephine confided to Antoinette that she too was still a virgin.

4 *Lettres de Marie Antoinette*, I, 53; Bernier, *Secrets*, p. 108.

5 Mercy, I, 257–8.

6 *Ibid.*, I, 198, 252. Mercy was convinced that "the dauphin, with good sense and excellent ingredients in his character, will probably never have the strength or will power to permit him to reign by himself. If the Archduchess does not govern him he will be ruled by others." Younghusband, p. 547.

7 Mercy, I, 207–8.

8 *Ibid.*, I, 200.

9 *Ibid.*, I, 207. Antoinette's tongue-lashings were severe enough for Mercy to caution her about being overly vehement. Her language at times upset Louis so much that he burst into tears. Bernier, *Secrets*, p. 71.

10 Younghusband, p. 550; Castelot, p. 69; Mercy, I, 207–8. Mercy had more faith in Antoinette's abilities than her mother did. In August of 1773 Maria Theresa wrote to the ambassador, "I own to you frankly that I do not desire to see my daughter gain preponderating influence in affairs. I have only too thoroughly learned by my own experience what an overwhelming burden is the government of a vast monarchy. More-

over, I know her youth and levity, joined to her distaste for application (also that she knows nothing), which would make me all the more fearful for her success in a government so gone to pieces as is the French one at present. If my daughter could effect no improvement, or if the state of things grew worse, I should prefer that a Minister rather than my daughter should bear the blame." Younghusband, pp. 547–8.

Was Maria Theresa overly jaundiced in her view of Antoinette, measuring her too severely against her own austere standard, or did she simply know her daughter better than the ambassador knew her?

11 *Lettres de Marie Antoinette*, I, 51.

12 L. S. Mercier, *The Waiting City: Paris 1782–88*, trans. Helen Simpson (London, 1933), p. 44.

Chapter 9

1 Campan, *Memoirs*, II, 278–9.

2 Padover, p. 48.

3 *Ibid.*, 51.

4 Mercier, pp. 163–4.

Chapter 10

1 Campan, *Memoirs*, I, 249.

2 What follows is taken from *Souvenirs d'un Page de la Cour de Louis XVI, par Felix, Comte de France d'Hézècques, Baron de Mailly* (Paris, 1895), *passim*.

3 Somewhere within the large household were Mercy's spies who, he said, gave him "an exact account" of everything that went on in Antoinette's private apartments. In 1770 his informants were one of the bedchamber women and two pages of the chamber. Mercy, I, 61.

4 *Memoirs of Madame La Tour du Pin*, ed. and trans. Felice Harcourt (New York, 1971), pp. 89–90. Madame La Tour du Pin's husband was created a peer of France in 1815, and in 1820 was created Marquis de La Tour du Pin. Before that time he was the Marquis de Gouvernet.

5 La Tour du Pin, *Memoirs*, pp. 68–9.

6 *Ibid.*, 70–75.

7 *Ibid.*, 17.

Chapter 11

1 Castelot, p. 83. In an often quoted passage, the nineteenth-century architect Viollet-le-Duc told of visiting Versailles with an elderly noblewoman who had lived at Louis XVI's court. She seemed disoriented

in the vast palace, then unfurnished, until she and the architect came to a place where "a waste plug, which had burst owing to the frost, had covered the floor with filth." The stench was appalling, and it suddenly brought the old woman to life. "Ah! I know where I am now," she cried joyously. "That was Versailles in my day. . . . It was like that everywhere!"

2 Constantia Maxwell, *The English Traveler in France 1698–1815* (London, 1932), p. 109. Mercy, I, 253.

3 Mercy, I, 253.

4 Ian Dunlop, *Royal Palaces of France* (New York and London, 1985), p. 60.

5 Mercy, II, 588. The Duc de Lauzun commented that Madame de Guéménée was "a very singular person, with much esprit, which she used to plunge into the most mad follies." Castelot, p. 108.

6 Mercy, I, 321.

7 Hézècques, pp. 174–5.

8 Campan, *Memoirs*, I, 229–30.

9 Mercy, I, 63–4.

10 F. Funck-Brentano, *The Old Regime in France*, trans. Herbert Wilson (London, 1929), pp. 173–4.

11 La Tour du Pin, *Memoirs*, p. 75.

12 Campan, *Memoirs*, II, 339–42.

13 This account of Cahouette de Villers's adventures comes from Campan, *Memoirs*, I, 122–4.

14 Jacques Levron, *La Vie Quotidienne à la Cour de Versailles aux XVIIe et XVIIIe siècles* (Paris, 1965), pp. 232–4. The Countess of Walburg-Frohberg, who married Stanislas du Pont de la Motte, is not to be confused with the other Comtesse de la Motte-Valois who was a much better known villainess.

Chapter 12

1 Mercy wrote of Theresa that she was "very small, of very commonplace figure, although one cannot justly say that its defects are shocking; her skin is white enough, the face thin, the nose much too long and badly finished, and eyes not well shaped, a big mouth—altogether an irregular physiognomy, unattractive and most vulgar." Madame Campan, however, thought that Theresa had a very interesting face and an enviably white complexion, though she acknowledged that the Countess's unfortunate nose drew all the attention away from her fair skin.

Mercy, who was always eager to criticize the women around Antoinette in order to make her charm and attractiveness stand out the more, positively gloated when Theresa arrived at Versailles. She was, he said, "ungraceful in bearing, timid and awkward, cannot speak a word, no matter what pains her lady-in-waiting takes to prompt her, dances badly, and, in fact, there is nothing in her that does not point either to faults in her disposition or to an excessively neglected education." Mercy, I, 317–18.

2 An anonymous pamphlet circulated at court described how in the summer of 1774 Antoinette had held an orgy at Marly; this was a fictitious embroidery based on an innocent incident in which Antoinette, on a warm summer night, decided that she wanted to stay up to watch the sunrise and did so, in the company of her women and many others—all of whom knew the truth about what happened that night.

3 *Journal de Papillon de la Ferté, Intendant et contrôleur de l'argenterie, menus-plaisirs et affaires de la chambre du roi, 1756–80*, ed. Ernest Boysse (Paris, 1887), p. 378.

4 *Ibid.*

5 Eyewitnesses to the bread riots reported that the protesters did not scruple to cut open loaves and dye them green and black to make them look moldy, then wave them in the faces of the police and other officials. *Journal de l'Abbé de Véri*, ed. Baron Jehan de Witte (Paris, 1928–9), I, 290.

6 This account of the *guerre des farines* is taken from Padover, pp. 75–7 and Bernard Fay, *Louis XVI ou la Fin d'un monde* (Paris, 1955), pp. 154–7.

7 Rocheterie, I, 119.

8 Maxwell, p. 123.

9 Rocheterie, I, 117.

10 It was strongly suggested to Louis that he break with tradition and move the coronation to Paris, which would save costs in that the entire court would not have to be transported to Rheims and would also benefit the Paris artisans and merchants—a prudent gesture at a time when Paris had been disrupted by the grain riots. But Louis wanted to be crowned where his ancestors had been crowned, and the suggestion was withdrawn. As to the issue of whether or not to crown Antoinette Queen as part of the ceremony, it was decided that, to save money, only Louis would undergo the rite of coronation. No Queen of France had been crowned for two hundred years.

11 Campan, *Memoirs*, I, 288–94. Papillon de la Ferté, *Journal*, pp. 385–6.

12 *Véri Journal*, I, 304.

13 Mercy, II, 418.

14 Bernier, *Secrets*, p. 173.
15 Campan, *Memoirs*, I, 107.

Chapter 13

1 Mercy, II, 490.
2 Bernier, *Secrets*, p. 218.
3 Campan, *Memoirs*, I, 163.
4 *Ibid.*, I, 161–2.
5 Mercy, II, 496.
6 Bernier, *Secrets*, p. 217.
7 *Ibid.*, 215–16.
8 Because he was a Protestant, Necker was not permitted to hold the office of Controller-General, but he exercised its functions while titularly lower in authority. In every important respect, Necker was Controller-General.
9 Bernier, *Secrets*, pp. 223–4.
10 *Ibid.*, 227.
11 Mercy, II, 591–2.
12 *Ibid.*, 590.
13 *Ibid.*, 592–3.
14 Benjamin Franklin was taken up by the fashionable world and, like Antoinette's brother Joseph, much admired for his austere personal habits. Madame Campan recalled in her memoirs that Franklin appeared at Versailles in the dress of an American farmer, with his sparse gray-white hair worn straight and unpowdered. No trace of vanity or artifice was detectable in his appearance. His plain suit of brown cloth, his fur cap, his spectacles were a refreshing contrast to the laced and embroidered coats and the curled and powdered heads of the Versailles courtiers. He was unadorned, but perfectly groomed, Madame Campan wrote; his "air of cleanliness," his snow-white shirt and collar were always immaculate. (This was more than could be said of the unwashed courtiers with their soiled linen and yellowing lace. Down-at-heels noblemen, it was said, touched up their lace with powder to conceal its age and deterioration.) Franklin carried a stick, his only weapon, and wore a round hat with no feathers or jewels.

"Elegant entertainments were given to Dr. Franklin," Campan wrote, "who to the reputation of a most skilful natural philosopher added the patriotic virtues which had invested him with the noble character of an apostle of liberty. I was present at one of these entertainments, when the most beautiful woman out of three hundred was selected to place a crown of laurels upon the white head of the American philosopher, and two kisses upon his cheeks."

When the news of Franklin's death reached Paris in 1790, Mirabeau made a funeral oration in his honor, and the municipality of Paris held a ceremony in the rotunda of the corn market, which was draped in black for the occasion. Campan, *Memoirs*, I, 210, 306–7.

15 Mercy, II, 595.

Chapter 14

1 Campan, *Memoirs*, I, 182.

2 Padover, p. 103 note.

3 Mercy, II, 614.

4 According to Madame Campan, Antoinette "often testified the regret she felt in thinking that the numerous duties of her august mother had prevented her from watching in person over the education of her daughters; and modestly said, that she herself should have been more worthy if she had had the good fortune to receive lessons directly from a sovereign so enlightened, and so deserving of admiration." This tribute sounds like a backhanded criticism. No doubt Antoinette's deepest feelings about her mother were ambivalent. Campan, *Memoirs*, I, 191.

5 Campan, *Memoirs*, I, 192.

6 Castelot, p. 160.

7 Viewed for years as the man who singlehandedly brought about the cataclysm of 1789 by his misguided policies, Necker has been partially rehabilitated by recent studies. J. F. Bosher, *French Finances 1770–1795: From Business to Bureaucracy* (Cambridge, 1970), J. Egret, *Necker, ministre de Louis XVI* (Paris, 1975), R. D. Harris, *Necker, Reform Statesman of the Ancien Regime* (Berkeley, 1979) and the latter's *Necker and the Revolution of 1789* (Lanham, 1986) all moderate the traditional criticisms lodged against Necker by historians. Harris, in particular, argues that Necker's *Compte rendu au roi* was not a falsification of the state of French finances and presents a revised view of Necker's loans.

Chapter 15

1 What follows summarizes André Castelot's survey of the evidence for this, which when coupled with what we know of the personalities involved seems to me convincing. Fersen referred to Antoinette as "Josephine" in his private diary and kept up a secret correspondence with her. In 1878 some sixty letters from Antoinette to Fersen were published, full of suspicious *lacunae;* the editor of the letters, Fersen's grand-nephew Baron Klinckowström, subsequently burned them. The one letter that escaped the Baron's fire reads, "I can tell you that I love you and indeed

that is all I have time for. . . . Let me know to whom I should address the news I may write to you, for I cannot live without that. Farewell, most loved and loving of men. I kiss you with all my heart."

Alma Söderjhelm uncovered more material that argues that Fersen and Antoinette had a long love affair. Fersen at one point referred to "the parallel" that existed between his relationship to Antoinette and the Swedish Count Gyllenstierna's relationship with Queen Hedvig Eleanora, and the latter pair were lovers. Castelot, pp. 179–184. In 1787 Antoinette made alterations to her interior apartments at Versailles which correspond to those noted in Fersen's correspondence book. In that book he referred to "lodging upstairs" and "me living upstairs." Philippe Huisman and Marguerite Jallut, *Marie Antoinette* (New York, 1971), p. 157. While none of the above constitutes proof of a liaison, it is very strong evidence.

Historians and biographers have had to tread warily on the question of whether or not Fersen and Antoinette were lovers for a variety of reasons. Some have been so eager to idolize Antoinette, or to portray her as a tragic victim of her violent times, that they have been unwilling to besmirch her image by admitting that she might have been unfaithful to Louis with Fersen. After all, to admit the strong probability of one infidelity would open the door to the possibility of more than one, and to lend credence to the many accusations made against her of illicit love affairs and orgies and dissolute living on a grand scale. It would also, at least in theory, open the question of the Duc de Normandie's paternity.

What seems closest to the truth (which, barring the discovery of further documentary evidence, will never be known) is that her liaison with Fersen was Antoinette's one and only indiscretion, and that he was the only man she ever loved, deeply fond though she was of her husband.

2 Castelot, p. 177.

3 Mercy, II, 441–2.

4 Campan, *Memoirs*, I, 125, 128.

5 An unappealing character, Vaudreuil was highly cultivated. Madame Campan called him "a friend and protector of the fine arts" and described how he gave a dinner party every week to which writers and artists were invited. "The evening was spent in a saloon [sic]," she said, "furnished with musical instruments, pencils, colors, brushes and pens. Everyone composed or painted or wrote." Campan, *Memoirs*, I, 131–2 note.

6 Guy Chaussinand-Nogaret, *The French Nobility in the Eighteenth Century: From Feudalism to Enlightenment*, trans. William Doyle (Cambridge, 1985), pp. 53, 55.

7 Castelot, pp. 111–12.

8 Mercy, I, 118 and *passim*.

9 Cagliostro ended his life in Rome, charged by the Inquisition with heresy and sorcery and condemned to imprisonment in a dungeon for life.

Chapter 16

1 *Lettres de Marie Antoinette*, II, 92.

2 *Ibid.*, II, 112.

3 In fact, in 1786 Antoinette did spend some 272,000 livres on dress, which was nearly twice what her budget permitted. Castelot, p. 220.

4 Mercier, pp. 241, 240, 88; *Souvenirs du Baron de Frénilly pair de France, 1768–1828* (Paris, 1908), pp. 79–80; La Tour du Pin, *Memoirs*, p. 98.

5 *Lettres de Marie Antoinette*, II, 97, 99, 106.

6 Frénilly, *Memoirs*, p. 81.

7 Campan, *Memoirs*, I, 36.

8 Rocheterie, I, 322–3.

9 William Doyle, *Origins of the French Revolution* (Oxford, 1988), pp. 43–52.

10 Lough, p. 267; La Tour du Pin, *Memoirs*, pp. 71–2. The editor of Mercy's dispatches, Lillian Smythe, savagely described Louis as a "waddling, blinking, corpulent, bungling, incapable imbecile, defective in body, deficient in mind, with the low receding forehead of an idiot, and a monstrous double chin that measured the third of his face." Mercy, I, 229.

11 Hézèques, p. 217; Campan, *Memoirs*, I, 112, 297.

12 Campan, *Memoirs*, I, 294–7. Campan's source is the generally unreliable Soulavie, *Historical and Political Memoirs of the Reign of Louis XVI*, but on the design and contents of the King's rooms Soulavie's recollections are presumably trustworthy.

Chapter 17

1 *Diary and Correspondence of Count Axel Fersen* (New York, 1899), p. 68.

2 Huisman, p. 157.

3 Castelot, p. 224.

4 *Ibid.*

5 Campan, *Memoirs*, II, 43.

6 *Ibid.*, I, 36.

7 *Ibid.*, I, 102 note. Madame Campan wrote that Antoinette "affected to say that she had lost the German," though this is hard to credit. She spoke French very fluently, though she did not write it correctly. According to Campan, Antoinette also spoke Italian "with grace and ease, and translated the most difficult poets." Campan, *Memoirs*, I, 36.

8 Lough, p. 177.

9 Padover, p. 142.

10 Peter Robert Campbell, *The Ancient Regime in France* (Oxford, 1988), p. 78.

11 Historians now believe that, had Louis allowed a vote to be taken at the Royal Session, the result would have been favorable to the King. Doyle, p. 109.

Chapter 18

1 This was largely an illusion. As Doyle writes, the actual power of the parlements has been "much exaggerated, as has the degree of unity within them and between them. In particular, the conflicts between the nobles and the magistrates of the parlements have been emphasized by historians." Doyle, p. 122.

2 Napoleon believed that the French Revolution was a result of three factors: the diamond necklace scandal, the French defeat at the hands of the Prussians at Rossbach during the Seven Years' War, and the inability of the French to intervene in the Dutch Netherlands in 1787. Campan, *Memoirs*, I, xlix.

3 Padover, p. 146.

4 *Ibid.*, 146–7.

5 The King's right to order any subject arrested and indefinitely detained, by issuing a *lettre de cachet*, came to symbolize all arbitrary monarchical power at this time. Although Louis XVI used *lettres de cachet* against his opponents, both in the parlement and outside of it, in fact the use of these royal warrants was in decline during his reign. They were in any case used less often against political figures than against wayward members of aristocratic families—at the request of the families themselves. Richard Cobb, *Voices of the French Revolution* (Topsfield, Mass., 1988), pp. 9, 69.

6 *Lettres de Marie Antoinette*, II, 119, 116, 112–13.

7 *Ibid.*, 112, 115–16, 119.

8 Lough, pp. 212–14, 216.

9 *Lettres de Marie Antoinette*, II, 128.

10 Lough, p. 297.

11 *Ibid.*, 298–9.

12 *Ibid.*, 125. The Hôtel-Dieu had some four thousand patients, crowded into fourteen hundred beds. A traveler found it to be "a place of vermin, filth and horror," the "corrupt air and effluvia . . . loathsome and abominable." Patients in all stages of disease were crammed together six or seven to a bed; the beds were checked periodically and the corpses removed. Jacques Necker's wife became a public benefactress when she

founded a hospital in 1778 where every patient had a bed to himself, and good care.

13 Fersen, *Diary and Correspondence*, p. 70.

14 Olivier Bernier, *Words of Fire, Deeds of Blood* (Boston, 1989), p. 228.

15 *Lettres de Marie Antoinette*, II, 121.

Chapter 19

1 Madame Campan recalled in her life of Antoinette how, when the deputies came to the Petit Trianon, they could not believe what their eyes told them, having heard for so many years the tales of the Queen's extravagance and dissipation. "As the extreme simplicity of this pleasure-house did not correspond with their ideas, they insisted on being shown even the smallest closets, saying that richly furnished apartments were being concealed from them. Finally they designated one, which according to their account was ornamented with diamonds, and twisted columns studded with sapphires and rubies." Campan, *Memoirs*, II, 49.

2 Fersen, *Dairy and Correspondence*, p. 69.

3 Cobb, *Voices*, p. 38.

4 *Ibid.*, 30.

5 Bernier, *Words of Fire*, p. 235.

6 Castelot, p. 226. Madame Campan noted that the King "frequently kept from [Antoinette] particulars which it was proper she should know." Campan, *Memoirs*, II, 42–3.

7 Campan, *Memoirs*, II, 42–3.

8 Bernier, *Words of Fire*, p. 243.

9 Campan, *Memoirs*, II, 47.

10 Bernier, *Words of Fire*, p. 241, citing the deputy Duquesnoy.

11 Cobb, *Voices*, p. 48.

12 La Tour du Pin, *Memoirs*, pp. 105–6.

Chapter 20

1 Campan, *Memoirs*, II, 51–3; J. M. Thompson, *English Witnesses of the French Revolution* (Oxford, 1938), pp. 32–3. Madame Campan includes the pitiful detail that when Antoinette tried to bring candy to her dying son, his governors and valets turned her away.

2 Only ten months earlier, in August of 1788, the Ecole Militaire in Paris had been closed because of the new bankruptcy of the state treasury. All the furniture was sold at public auction. Lough, p. 295.

3 Cobb, *Voices*, p. 64.

4 Padover, p. 179.

5 As early as 1782 Mercier, the chronicler of Paris, wrote that "there was some talk of pulling down the execrable Bastille." Louis had in fact approved its demolition—though the treasury lacked the funds to carry it out, and the project had a low priority.

6 Authorities differ on the number of persons held in the Bastille, but the consensus is that there were seven. The British ambassador Lord Dorset, who recorded that "only four or five prisoners were found in the Bastille," described Major White with his yard-long beard. Another witness, a Norwich physician, recalled seeing some of the Bastille prisoners who had just been liberated, among them one old man who must have been Major White. Deeply affected by the sight of the prisoners, the physician burst into tears. Maxwell, p. 157.

Chapter 21

1 Campan, *Memoirs*, II, 55–7.

2 The well known entry in the King's diary for July 14, 1789, *"Rien,"* or "Nothing," has often been cited as an example of his rather fatuous indifference to the political crisis erupting around him. But it must be recalled that this was a hunting diary, not a record of daily events. Louis went hunting on July 14, killed no game, and so entered *"Rien"* in his journal. After the hunt he returned to the palace and went to sleep. But when the news of the siege of the Bastille was brought to him, he lost no time in addressing the National Assembly and going in person to Paris. He was conscientious, if ineffectual, in confronting his responsibilities.

3 Nearly three years later, in February of 1792, Louis confided to Fersen that he regretted having taken the safe but ultimately short-sighted advice of the men around him instead of following his wife's counsel. "I missed the moment," he told Fersen. "I should have left and wanted to, but what could I do?" Bernier, *Words of Fire*, pp. 31–2.

4 Campan, *Memoirs*, II, 63.

5 *Lettres de Marie Antoinette*, II, 134–6.

6 Campan, *Memoirs*, II, 64.

7 La Tour du Pin, *Memoirs*, pp. 112–14. Madame La Tour du Pin was convinced that the Great Fear was the result of a deliberate conspiracy on the part of the revolutionaries. She had a narrow escape at Gaillefontaine, where she was mistaken for Antoinette and mobbed. Fortunately, a man who had recently seen the genuine Antoinette persuaded the others that the real Queen was "at least twice as old and twice as large" as the slim young noblewoman, and so she was released. Meanwhile, the people of Forges-les-Eaux had armed themselves "with

anything they had been able to lay hands on" and were prepared for an assault by the mythical marauders.

8 Fersen, *Diary and Correspondence*, p. 72.

9 Tourzel, *Memoirs*, I, 24.

10 *Lettres de Marie Antoinette*, II, 144, 141–2.

11 The following account of the interview of August 25 is taken from La Tour du Pin, *Memoirs*, pp. 121–2.

12 Younghusband, pp. 21–2 described how, in 1751, more than twenty years before Antoinette came to France, Louis XV's daughter Sophie was credited with remarking, "If only those poor people could bring themselves to eat pastry!" when she heard that the Parisians were crying for bread. Louis XVI's brother Provence attributed the identical remark to his great-great-grandmother Queen Maria Theresa, wife of Louis XIV.

Chapter 22

1 Tourzel, *Memoirs*, I, 24.

2 Padover, p. 185.

3 Campan, *Memoirs*, II, 83ff.

4 *Ibid.*, II, 89.

5 *Ibid.*, II, 325.

Chapter 23

1 Hézècques, p. 318.

2 Thompson, pp. 71–2; Hézècques, p. 210.

3 Gouverneur Morris, *A Diary of the French Revolution*, ed. Beatrix Cary Davenport (Boston, 1939), I, 271. Morris, who met Fersen for the first time on October 25, 1789, remarked that Fersen's "merit consists in being the Queen's lover." He added that the Swede "had the air of a man exhausted."

4 *Lettres de Marie Antoinette*, II, 149.

5 Campan, *Memoirs*, II, 90.

6 Gouverneur Morris, I, 219.

7 Hézècques, p. 323.

8 *Ibid.*, 322.

9 Campan, *Memoirs*, II, 91.

10 Padover, p. 186 note.

11 Gouverneur Morris, I, 328.

12 Gouverneur Morris thought Necker "a very poor financier."

Gouverneur Morris, I, 385. Lafayette told Morris privately that Necker ought to be kept in office, but only "for the sake of his name."

13 Gouverneur Morris, I, 324.

14 *Ibid.*, I, 296.

15 Thompson, p. 113 cites the Englishman W.A. Miles's views of Mirabeau. The page Hézècques had quite a different view of "the brave vicomte de Mirabeau, the last of the French knights." Hézècques, p. 336.

16 Gouverneur Morris, I, 381.

17 Campan, *Memoirs*, II, 110.

18 *Lettres de Marie Antoinette*, II, 158.

19 *Ibid.*

20 Thompson, p. 77.

21 Campan, *Memoirs*, I, 6. Unfortunately, the Queen burned most of this collection in 1792, fearful of the consequences if her papers fell into the wrong hands.

22 Rocheterie, II, 106.

Chapter 24

1 Fersen, *Diary and Correspondence*, p. 79. Fersen kept journals that included, he believed, a good deal of valuable information about the King and Queen. In 1791 he entrusted them to a friend, who judged it prudent to burn them—an incalculable loss for historians.

2 Gouverneur Morris, I, 266.

3 Madame La Tour du Pin, among many others, lamented the amorality of the Old Regime and saw in it a breeding ground for lack of restraint among the revolutionaries. "When society is so corrupt that corruption itself seems natural," she wrote, "and when no one is shocked at anything, why should anyone be astonished at excesses among the lower classes, who have been set such a bad example?" La Tour du Pin, *Memoirs*, p. 83.

4 Fersen, *Diary and Correspondence*, pp. 81–2.

5 Padover, p. 205 note.

6 Tourzel, *Memoirs*, I, 53.

7 "Ça ira" was said to be Benjamin Franklin's favorite expression. According to Hézècques, the best known version of "Ça ira" was first sung by the prostitutes of the Palais-Royal. Hézècques, pp. 332–3.

8 Padover, p. 201.

Chapter 25

1 Campan, *Memoirs*, II, 119–20.

2 *Ibid.*, II, 111.

3 *Ibid.*, II, 108.

4 *Lettres de Marie Antoinette*, II, 177–8, 186, 183.

5 Campan, *Memoirs*, II, 115–16. It is clear that throughout 1790 there were escape plans aplenty. In March a nobleman, the Comte d'Inisdal, came to Madame Campan and told her the King would be carried away from the Tuileries that night. An entire section of the National Guard was won over, horses had been furnished by "some good royalists," a party of nobles were booted and spurred to serve as a protective escort. Louis had been told about the arrangements but had not actually consented to being carried off. Madame Campan went to Antoinette's apartments, where Louis and Antoinette were playing whist with Elisabeth, Provence and his wife. She interrupted them. Louis listened unemotionally to the message that his rescuers awaited him, and went on with his card game. "Tell Monsieur d'Inisdal that I cannot consent to be carried off!" was his only response. Antoinette, no doubt hoping to persuade him to change his mind, packed her traveling cases and told Madame Campan not to go to bed, she might be needed. But in the end nothing happened. Campan, *Memoirs*, II, 106–8.

6 Padover, p. 206.

7 Campan, *Memoirs*, II, 375ff.

8 Despite the efforts of some historians to minimize the handicap of the berlin, which was, after all, the usual conveyance for the aristocracy and as such was not conspicuous as a royal carriage, its slow speed was of the greatest importance in determining the outcome of the emigration attempt in June 1791. And this was not just any berlin, but one of exceptional size, according to Hézècques, who claimed that its hugeness alone awakened suspicion. Hézècques, p. 352. On the size and ingenious fittings of the vehicle, see Dunlop, p. 217. At a time when any and all aristocrats were being stopped as they passed through provincial towns, and their documents subjected to scrutiny, the use of such a vehicle was clearly unwise, and very likely objections to it were raised—and Antoinette very likely ignored them.

9 Before Joseph's death he wrote Antoinette a loving letter telling her how much he regretted having to leave her in such a cruelly difficult situation. The court put on mourning dress permanently, to save money—but according to Madame Campan, Antoinette's grief at his death "was not excessive." "She reproached him sometimes, though with great moderation, for having adopted several of the principles of the new philosophy." Joseph was a creature of the Enlightenment, a Voltairean liberal, with an impudent anticlerical streak. He once sent the very Catholic Antoinette an engraving "which represented unfrocked nuns and monks. The first were trying on fashionable dresses; the latter were getting their hair dressed. The engraving was always left in a closet, and

never hung up. The Queen told me to have it taken away . . ." Campan, *Memoirs*, II, 114 and note. *Lettres de Marie Antoinette*, II, 163.

10 Thompson, p. 96.

11 Tourzel, *Memoirs*, I, 261.

12 Fersen, *Diary and Correspondence*, pp. 94–5; *Lettres de Marie Antoinette*, II, 234 note; Padover, p. 213.

Chapter 26

1 Campan, *Memoirs*, II, 382 adds that there were two other servants in the cabriolet, the usher Diet and the *garçon de toilette* Camot. After the royals were returned to Paris Diet and Camot, along with Brunier and de Neuville, were imprisoned for several weeks and then released. Madame Campan's account of the escape attempt in June 1791 was based on what Antoinette told her about it, not on firsthand knowledge; Campan herself was away from court on leave at the time of the journey.

2 Tourzel, *Memoirs*, I, 329–30.

3 Hézècques, p. 354 asserts that Louis was recognized several times on his journey, though he was only stopped at Varennes. The post master at Châlons, "an honest man," kept his realization to himself.

4 Cobb, *Voices*, p. 120. Madame Campan, whose account was based on Antoinette's fresh recollection of the journey, gives a slightly different version of what happened. According to her, Louis looked out of the berlin and asked several questions about the road, at which point the post master, struck by the questioner's resemblance to the royal head on the assignats, approached the carriage and made the identification. Campan, *Memoirs*, II, 385–6.

5 Tourzel, *Memoirs*, I, 336–7.

6 Hézècques, p. 355.

7 Campan, *Memoirs*, II, 386–7.

8 Tourzel, *Memoirs*, I, 337, notes that the peasants of the Varennes district were afraid of Bouillé and "begged the King to protect them." According to her they "hesitated as to allowing him to continue his journey." But other witnesses stressed the savage anger of the citizenry.

Chapter 27

1 Madame Campan recounts this scene in two sightly different versions. Campan, *Memoirs*, II, 161–2 and note.

2 *Ibid.*, II, 160.

3 *Lettres de Marie Antoinette*, II, 307.

4 Fersen, *Diary and Correspondence*, p. 123.

5 Campan, *Memoirs*, II, 170–2. Campan's ignorance of the meaning of the ciphered messages is confirmed in *Lettres de Marie Antoinette*, II, 239.

6 Campan, *Memoirs*, II, 170–2.

7 *Ibid.*, II, 153 note. According to Madame Campan, Antoinette blamed an officer named Goguelas, whom Bouillé had seconded to assist Choiseul, for not taking bold action at Varennes to rescue the royal party despite the King's objections.

8 Campan, *Memoirs*, II, 179–80.

9 Fersen, *Diary and Correspondence*, p. 244.

10 This account of what passed between Fersen, Louis and Antoinette is based on Fersen, *Diary and Correspondence*, pp. 245–9.

Chapter 28

1 Cobb, *Voices*, pp. 96–7.

2 According to Padover, the first "Guillotine" was constructed by a German mechanic named Schmidt, a harpsichord maker. Padover, p. 290 note.

3 Anonymous account of the events of June 20 in Cobb, *Voices*, p. 145.

4 Tourzel, *Memoirs*, II, 134–50.

5 *Lettres de Marie Antoinette*, II, 406.

6 One escape plan Louis agreed to but at the very last minute—on the morning he was to leave, in late July—he backed out. Gouverneur Morris, II, 476.

7 Tourzel, *Memoirs*, II, 384.

8 *Lettres de Marie Antoinette*, II, 421, 409.

9 Tourzel, *Memoirs*, II, 204.

Chapter 29

1 Thompson, p. 173. Many years later Napoleon, who had watched the massacre from a safe vantage point in a shop window, recalled it with dread. Not in all his subsequent years in battle, he wrote, did he ever see such slaughter.

2 Campan, *Memoirs*, II, 233–4.

3 Tourzel, *Memoirs*, II, 217.

4 Maxwell, p. 170.

5 Madame de Tourzel's experience was a grotesque mixture of bru-

tality and humanity. In the clerk's office of the prison a court was set up, the prisoners were assembled in the courtyard, with "a great crowd of men of blood," badly clothed, half drunk and menacing. But there were among them some "honest men," one of whom told the noblewoman that he had seen to it that her daughter, who was in prison with her, would be spared. As Madame de Tourzel watched in horror, all the prisoners who were convicted were "massacred without mercy," going to their deaths with terror-stricken faces, sobbing and imploring their executioners for mercy.

After four hours of mortal agony, she presented herself before the Tribunal, which was impressed by her calm and by her fearless retorts to their questions. The court voted to liberate her, whereupon the same men who had been ready to kill her, she wrote, "threw themselves upon me to embrace me and congratulate me on having escaped the impending danger." They escorted her to a safe house in Paris, and even returned on the following day to assure themselves that she was well, and to warn her to leave the city lest the advance of the allied armies put her in renewed jeopardy. Tourzel, *Memoirs*, II, 260–9.

6 Campan, *Memoirs*, II, 217.

7 M. Cléry, *Journal de ce qui s'est passé à la Tour du Temple pendant la captivité de Louis XVI roi de France* (London, 1798), pp. 92–3.

8 *Ibid.*, 139–44.

Chapter 30

1 There are many accounts of Louis XVI's execution, and they do not agree in details. Contemporary prints and drawings also differ from one another. Monarchist or revolutionary bias creates distortions in the accounts of eyewitnesses, who were eager to ennoble or humiliate the royal victim. I have tried to reconcile the disparate narratives, relying in particular on the recollections of Edgeworth, the story as Gouverneur Morris heard it from others, the narratives of various English and French eyewitnesses and David P. Jordan, *The King's Trial: Louis XVI vs. the French Revolution* (Berkeley, 1981), pp. 217–21.

2 One of the sadder stories of Antoinette's later life was her relative neglect of her daughter. Madame Campan wrote that Antoinette began to treat Thérèse as her own mother had treated her. Their temperaments were very different. As a young child, Thérèse had been called "Mousseline la Sérieuse," and her natural gravity and, one suspects, sensitivity, must have contrasted with her mother's vivacious, outgoing and rather coarse-fibered personality. It was understandable that as heir to the throne the dauphin should receive more attention than his sister, but

Thérèse seems to have been put into the role of a background figure to a greater extent than was consistent with her position as Madame Royale. Now in the late spring of 1793 she voluntarily became something of a night nurse to her often hysterical mother and troubled brother, even though she herself was in pain from a bad leg. Tourzel, *Memoirs*, II, 300; Thompson, p. 227.

Antoinette told Madame de Tourzel—though she apparently said nothing to her daughter—that she and Louis wanted the Princess to marry Artois's son, the Duc d'Angoulême, "in spite of her extreme youth." In her imagination Antoinette had done a good deal of planning about the wedding, even down to the "minor arrangements." Years later, of course, Thérèse did marry the Duke, fulfilling her parents' wishes. Tourzel, *Memoirs*, II, 316–17.

3 Richard Cobb, "The Revolutionary Mentality in France 1793–4," *History*, XLII (1957), 182–3, citing Donald Greer, *The Incidence of the Terror During the French Revolution*. Greer has shown that a high percentage of the twenty-seven or twenty-eight hundred victims of the Terror were former servants and skilled artisans in the luxury trades—barbers, engravers, fan-makers and so on. Among the guillotine's victims was a refugee named Michel living in Bercy—Antoinette's former coachman.

4 By one estimate, some 2,250 were acquitted in Paris. Cobb, *Voices*, p. 179.

5 Under the law of March 29, 1793, armed rebels were shot, not guillotined. In all, some 35,000–40,000 people were executed in the French provinces during 1793 and 1794, far more than lost their lives in Paris during the Terror.

Chapter 31

1 G. Lenotre, *La captivité et la Mort de Marie-Antoinette* (Paris, 1910), pp. 230–1.

2 "The grief, the bad air, the lack of exercise altered the health of the Queen," Rosalie Lamorlière wrote. "Her blood warmed, she experienced great hemorrhages. I used to be aware of this; she secretly asked me for linen rags, and often I cut up my chemises and put the rags under her bolster." Lenotre, pp. 245–6.

3 Lenotre, p. 257.

4 *Ibid.*, 198.

❧ INDEX ❧